Palgrave Studies in Accounting and Finance Practice

More information about this series at
http://www.palgrave.com/gp/series/16220

Jonas Abraham Akuffo

Corporate Governance and Accountability of Financial Institutions

The Power and Illusion of Quality Corporate Disclosure

palgrave
macmillan

Jonas Abraham Akuffo
Monitor – NHS Improvement
London, UK

ISSN 2524-8251 ISSN 2524-826X (electronic)
Palgrave Studies in Accounting and Finance Practice
ISBN 978-3-030-64045-3 ISBN 978-3-030-64046-0 (eBook)
https://doi.org/10.1007/978-3-030-64046-0

This Palgrave Macmillan imprint is published by the registered company Springer Nature Switzerland AG
The registered company address is: Gewerbestrasse 11, 6330 Cham, Switzerland

Series Editors' Foreword

This book is the first of the series. It perfectly reflects the initial intention we had. Between the large galaxy of academic publications and practitioners' testimonials, we wanted to find a path in the middle. So, the series pursues two aims: first to create a forum for the practitioners struggling to gain access to a publication avenue and second to encourage these practitioners to ground their findings in rigorous academic debates.

This book nicely meets these aims. Jonas Akuffo has a wealth of experience in investigating accountability and compliance issues in British banks and other financial institutions. He has drawn on this experience in terms of first-hand data and demonstrated his exposure to governance and accountability issues in this sector. The completion of the author's DBA has led him to produce a comprehensive analysis combining a practitioners' point of views with relevant concepts. This is an uncovering of a blind spot in academic research—the interface between academic concepts and practitioners' views regarding accountability and governance issues. This has been materialised by focusing on the issues in financial institutions which is commendable as accounting and finance researchers have little studies on these. It is fascinating to see that mundane practices of governance, accountability and compliance scenarios shed some light beyond mere principles, codes of conduct or structures.

The book brings together management practices and actors who mobilise those practices. It shows that the bank which is the site of the analysis has not merely been considered a homogeneous terrain of action. Rather, it illustrates how a bank incorporates different actors, and how managerial practices and corporate governance mechanisms operate together making the book theoretically interesting while empirically rich. This is evidenced as the book covers the case of UK Financial institutions discussing two related areas. First is the broader structure of the UK's financial sector and its regulatory environment. Second are its corporate governance and accountability mechanisms.

So, the book's main contribution is the analysis of corporate governance and accountability mechanisms together. Usually, corporate governance aspects are analysed by financial scholars and accountabilities aspects are by accounting scholars. This book shows that corporate governance and accountability aspects are mutually facilitative and interdependent.

Hence, the publication of this book is timely. Its analysis is grounded in the pre-Brexit British financial industry. The issues discussed are related to only one industry, but they can be used to extrapolate other institutions in other countries. Thence, lessons can be learnt for post-Brexit scenarios, especially for compliance managers in financial institutions in countries with a strong and attractive financial industry.

Le Blanc, France — Vassili Joannidès de Lautour
Glasgow, UK — Danture Wickramasinghe
Antibes, France — Aude Deville

Preface

Corporate governance is concerned with structures and the allocation of responsibilities within companies. It deals with the decision-making at the level of the board of directors and is therefore to be distinguished from the day-to-day operational management of the company by the senior management. Thus, the presence of sound corporate governance in a financial institution within an economy and across the financial market is important in maintaining the confidence of the market and the public. The financial industry, especially the banking sector in a number of countries has been criticised for its role in the 2007/2008 global financial crisis. In fact, ineffective corporate governance of banks was often quoted as the main contributing factor in causing the financial crisis. Much of this concern about viability of banks comes from major stakeholders, namely regulators, society at large and government bodies that were interested in identifying, and in fact examining any potential gaps in the management of banks that may lead them to collapse. For example, in the United Kingdom, Sir David Walker was commissioned to recommend measures to improve board-level governance of banks to the government (Walker 2009). The commission's recommendations served as the basis for the 2010 UK Corporate Governance Code. The underlying pertinent concerns include an aim to prevent the dispersion of systemic risk from other sources, improving financial market capabilities, and the maintenance of the general principles of an efficient market.

There has been a great deal of interest worldwide in the subject of corporate governance in private and public sectors over the last thirty years. Much of this interest and the subject of debates has come from the accounting and finance practitioners, depositors, regulators, executives, investors and academic communities. Furthermore, it has become the sole focus of increasing numbers of business-related and accounting degree modules in universities across the United Kingdom/European Union and the United States with the topic fast becoming a standalone subject matter. Since the crisis and the reflections on the importance of governance in maintaining banking standards, there is more need than ever for more specialist practitioners in this area. This has resulted in extensive research into the contribution of accounting, in its broadest sense, and what it can make towards enhancing governance and accountability. However, relatively little empirical research has been carried out in this area in banking and other financial organisations regarding understanding the role of accountability in improving the quality of corporate governance disclosures to its stakeholders.

Given the above background information, this book has several objectives. Firstly, it aims to methodically assess the quality of corporate governance mechanism disclosures to various stakeholders. It is further intended to provide fresh insights into some specific corporate governance recommendations to help improve good governance in financial institutions, particularly in the United Kingdom and the EU but will also be applicable to other major economies. The motivational rationale underpinning this investigation of corporate governance disclosures can be attributed to the governance failures and weaknesses in the mechanisms of accountability observed in the global financial crisis in 2007–2008.

Secondly, it aims to explore what, when and how corporate governance has changed the financial institution functions and corporate executive behaviour by critically reviewing the pre- and post-financial crisis theoretical and empirical literature. A key distinctive feature of the book here is bringing the growing post-crisis empirical evidence to a bigger audience by critically evaluating the recent evidence in comparison to the pre-crisis debates and arguments.

Thirdly, the book specifically aims to investigate the interrelationship of corporate governance and accountability practices in financial institutions, and to suggest opportunities for future research in this field. One key motivation in this book is the overriding importance of improving corporate governance and its mechanisms of accountability disclosures in banking and other financial institutions. Increasingly driven by the nature of complications, complexities and opacity in the operations of financial systems, corporate governance reporting thus plays an important role in the banking sector. Additionally, the findings from this book would provide greater insights into corporate governance disclosures in the financial sector over a long-term basis. This book should be a valuable asset to support the research of practitioners, students and all academics due to its stimulating and reflective insights into this fascinating topic.

London, UK Jonas Abraham Akuffo

Acknowledgements

I wish to recognise and acknowledge the contribution of all those who made it possible for me to finish this book.

I would like to begin by giving a huge recognition and appreciation to my friend, Dr. Vassili Joannides, Associate Professor, Grenoble Ecole De Management (France) and Queensland University of Technology (Australia), for his unwavering support and insightful advice over the research period. Also, I would also like to thank the faculty and staff of the Doctoral Schools both Grenoble Ecole De Management and Newcastle University for their help in completing the empirical research part of this book.

A note of special gratitude goes to my friends and family for their uplifting guidance, infinite care and love and help. A special message of appreciation goes to my wife Lianne, parents-in-law Ken and Sandra Pearce and my family in Ghana. Without their constant encouragement, I would not have finished this book.

Contents

Abbreviations

ACCA	Association of Chartered Certified Accountant
ASB	Accounting Standards Board
BCBS	Basel Committee on Banking Supervision
BOE	Bank of England
FASB	Financial Accounting Standards Board
FCA	Financial Conduct Authority
FRC	Financial Reporting Council
FRS	Financial Reporting Standard
FSA	Financial Services Authority
FTSE	Financial Time Stock Exchange
HBOS	Halifax Bank of Scotland
HSBC	The Hong Kong and Shanghai Banking Corporation
IAS	International Accounting Standard
IASB	International Accounting Standards Board
IFRS	International Financial Reporting Standard
IMF	International Monetary Fund
OECD	Organisation for Economic and Co-operation and Development
PRA	Prudential Regulation Authority
RBS	Royal Bank of Scotland
SCB	Standard Chartered Bank
SEC	Securities and Exchange Commission
UNCTAD	United Nations Conference on Trade And Development

List of Figures

List of Tables

CHAPTER 1

Introduction

It seems that corporations are entering a new stage in their history in which integrated responsibilities for *people* (employment, health, education, and human rights), *profit* (economic and financial continuity) and *planet* (clean environment and preservation of resource stocks) are emerging as prerequisites for sustainable entrepreneurship. The recent rise to eminence of this phenomenon—also known as *triple bottom line management*—is the most visible sign that governance and ethics are gaining ground on the business agenda. A paradigmatic shift from shareholder value maximisation towards stakeholder value maximisation is becoming apparent and even seems to have achieved something close to a consensus in the corporate governance arena. Corporate governance is concerned with structures and the allocation of responsibilities within companies. It deals with the decision-making at the level of the board of directors and is therefore to be distinguished from the day-to-day operational management of the company by the senior management. Thus, the presence of sound corporate governance in a financial institution and across the United Kingdom, the US and the EU financial market systems and banking industry specifically, is important in maintaining the confidence of the market and the public trust in these institutions.

The financial sector particularly the banking industry in a number of countries has been criticised for its role in the 2007/2008 global financial

J. A. Akuffo, *Corporate Governance and Accountability of Financial Institutions*, Palgrave Studies in Accounting and Finance Practice, https://doi.org/10.1007/978-3-030-64046-0_1

crisis. In fact, ineffective corporate governance of banks was often quoted as the main contributing factor in causing the financial crisis (Holland 2010; Kirkpatrick 2009; FSA 2011; Tomasic 2011). Also, much of this concern about viability of banks comes from major stakeholders, namely regulators, society at large and government bodies that were interested in identifying, and in fact examining any potential gaps in the management of banks that may lead them to collapse. For example, "*in the UK, Sir David Walker was commissioned to recommend measures to improve board-level governance of banks to the government* (Walker 2009). *The commission's recommendations served as the basis for the 2010 UK Corporate Governance Code*" (Haan and Vlahu 2013, p. 2). The underlying pertinent concerns include an aim to prevent the dispersion of systemic risk from other sources, improving financial market capabilities, and the maintenance of the general principles of an efficient market.

Corporate governance is defined as the "exercise of power over" a commercial body or an organisation. It has therefore become one of the central issues in the running and the regulating of modern enterprise today (Akuffo 2018; Mallin 2010; Tricker 2009). However, the fundamental beliefs and thoughts behind corporate governance have been remarkably gradual in the finance and accounting literature. According to Tricker (2009, p. 7) "*the underlying ideas and concepts of corporate governance have been surprisingly slow to evolve. The basic underpinning framework still owe more to mid-19th century thinking than they do to the realities of complex modern business*". In 1992, the Cadbury Report in the United Kingdom describes the subject of corporate governance as "the system by which companies are directed and controlled". Contemporary corporate governance is often reflected to have originated with the innovative, voluntary approach outlined in the code of best practice that formed part of the report and that is still commonly called the Cadbury Code. Subsequently copied around the world, the code has also been extended, but many enhancements have often had the effect of reducing governance to box-ticking compliance exercises (ACCA 2014).

According to Tricker (2009), the definition of corporate governance cannot be attributed particularly to one accepted definition within the existing academic literature. There are major variations in the definition depending on the viewpoint of the subject—and the country involved is taken into account. However, even within the confines of one country's system such as the United Kingdom, arriving at "a" definition of corporate governance is no easy task. The concept of corporate governance as a stand-alone subject has been considered a recent phenomenon and may be viewed in a restrictive ("narrow") or a wider perspective based on the viewpoint of the research investigator. The current definitions of corporate governance may be classified in terms of a narrow view at one end and more inclusive "broad" views placed at the other. The narrow view of corporate governance seems to restrict it as the relationship between a company and its shareholders. This is the traditional finance paradigm expressed in agency theory (Fama 1980; Fama and Jensen 1983; Shleifer and Vishny 1997). At the other end of the spectrum, corporate governance may be seen as a web of relationships between a company and its owners and other key stakeholders (Donaldson and Preston 1995; Freeman et al. 2004). This broader perspective is thus gradually attracting greater attention by research practitioners in the United Kingdom, United States and other parts of the world.

The first chapter of this book will introduce the corporate governance industry and the concept of accountability to the reader. Chapter 2 looks at the history of the key developments over the past three decades. It focuses on the United Kingdom as a key starting premise on the basis that it has led the way towards good corporate governance guides for listed firms since the 1990s, but it goes on to explore wider influences across the globe. It will also discuss developments such as The Cadbury Code 1992, The Greenbury Report 1995, the Stewardship Code 2010, other major developments since the financial crisis and key developments in the European Union, United States and elsewhere. Chapter 3 will look at theories of Corporate Governance of Financial Institutions. It will review the relevant prior literature in the field of corporate governance, mechanisms of accountability and disclosure research. The chapter also review specific and relevant studies regarding bank and other financial institutions corporate governance frameworks. Chapter 4 will outline corporate governance, accountability mechanisms and disclosure Literature and discuss a number of growing studies and debates within the academics, practitioners and developed communities about the different accountability typologies and its impact on corporate governance. Chapter 5 explores and examines the implication of ineffective corporate governance and the various mechanisms of accountability, which contributed to the collapse of a variety of banking and other financial institutions, specifically linked to the financial crash of 2007–2008. Chapter 6 will outline and discuss the structure of the UK financial sector and its regulatory framework for corporate governance. Chapter 7 will focus on the evaluation of corporate governance and accountability mechanisms in Financial Institutions in the United Kingdom. Financial institutions corporate governance has been recognised as multidimensional, very complex in character and can be embodied in a variety of systems. Chapter 8 also focuses on the role of disclosure and the quality of corporate governance reporting as discovered from the empirical study conducted. Chapter 9 looks at a stakeholder's perspective on financial institution corporate governance and examines corporate governance issues in other financial institutions. The issue of corporate governance does not just exclusively effect banking organisations, but is a wider reaching challenge faced by multiple institutions across the wider financial market. Chapter 10 looks forward to the future of corporate governance, addressing what practitioners need as well as the need for broader research to increase the scope of stakeholder accountability. All chapter's summary and discussions of the book are presented in Chapter 11 of the book.

References

Akuffo, J. A. (2018). *Corporate governance and bank accountability: The role of accountability in improving the quality of corporate governance disclosures in bank annual report, A UK perspective*. DBA Thesis, Grenoble Ecole De Management.

Association of Chartered Certified Accountant (ACCA). (2014, December). *Culture vs regulation: What is needed to improve ethics in finance*.

Donaldson, T., & Preston, L. E. (1995). The stakeholder theory of the corporation: Concepts, evidence, and implications. *Academy of Management Review, 20*(1), 65–91.

Fama, E. F. (1980). Agency problems and the theory of the firm. *Journal of Political Economy, 88*(2), 288–307.

Fama, E. F., & Jensen, M. C. (1983). Separation of ownership and control. *Journal of Law and Economics, 26*(2), 301–325.

Financial Services Authority (FSA). (2011, December). *The failure of the Royal Bank of Scotland*. Financial Services Authority Board Report.

Freeman, R. E., Wicks, A. C., & Parmar, B. (2004). Stakeholder theory and "the corporate objective revisited". *Organization Science, 15*(3), 364–369.

Haan, J. D., & Vlahu, R. (2013). Corporate governance of banks: A survey (DNB Working Paper). Netherland.

Holland, J. (2010). Banks, knowledge and crisis: A case of knowledge and learning failure. *Journal of Financial Regulation and Compliance, 18*(2), 87–105.

Kirkpatrick, G. (2009). The corporate governance lessons from the financial crisis. *Financial Markets Trends, OECD: Financial Regulation and Compliance, 16*(1), 8–18.

Mallin, C. (2010). *Corporate governance* (3rd ed.). Oxford: Oxford University Press.

Shleifer, A., & Vishny, R. W. (1997). A survey of corporate governance. *Journal of Finance, 52*(2), 735–782.

Tomasic, R. (2011). The financial crisis and the haphazard pursuit of financial crime. *Journal of Financial Crime, 18*(1), 7–31.

Tricker, B. (2009). *Corporate governance: Principles, policies and practices* (1st ed.). New York: Oxford University Press Inc.

Walker, S. D. (2009). *A review of corporate governance in UK banks and other financial industry entities*. Final recommendations.

CHAPTER 2

Corporate Governance Development: A Reaction or Deliberate Policy Thought?

2.1 Introduction

The concerns around corporate governance for many years have attracted a considerable attention, deliberations and investigations internationally as well as nationally for many decades. The subject of corporate governance is not a modern historical development in the field of economics and finance. Although the concept is frequently presented as a fresh improvement, its various mechanisms of accountability for monitoring director's actions have lived since the start of the concept of corporate entity. It is now firmly acknowledged that there is no one model of corporate governance that works in all countries and in all companies (Tricker 2009). Many difference models or codes of "best practice" exist that may take different legislation, board structures, processes and business practices within individual companies. Despite this, there are standards that can apply across a broad range of legal, political and economic environments. However, the topic of corporate governance is a vast subject and it incorporate managerial accountability, board structure and shareholder rights. The issue of balance of power and decision-making between board of directors, senior executives and shareholders has been evolving for centuries. This in effect has been a hot topic among academic scholars, executives, investors and regulatory bodies in particular, are insisting

J. A. Akuffo, *Corporate Governance and Accountability of Financial Institutions*, Palgrave Studies in Accounting and Finance Practice, https://doi.org/10.1007/978-3-030-64046-0_2

on implementation of adequate corporate governance practices by the companies.

Several attempts to get better corporate governance in different countries have resulted in numerous statutory instruments and mandatory and voluntary best practice codes of conduct. This chapter looks at the history of the key developments over the past three and half decades. It focuses on the United Kingdom as a key starting premise on the basis that it has led the way towards good corporate governance guides for listed firms since the 1990s, but it goes on to explore wider influences across the globe in advancing the nature of corporate governance and its mechanisms of accountability.

2.2 Defining Financial Institution Corporate Governance?

A key generic concept of defining the term "Corporate governance" is referring to it as "the set of rules and incentives by which the management of a company is directed and controlled". According to an extract from the World Bank report *"corporate governance frames the distribution of rights and responsibilities among the main corporate bodies and provides the structure through which company objectives are set, implemented and monitored. A firm committed to good corporate governance has an empowered board, a solid internal control environment, high levels of transparency and disclosure, and well-defined and protected shareholder rights"* (UNCTAD 2010, p. 80). For corporate governance at banking firms and other financial institutions, if this definition is implemented in a rigorous and reliable manner, then it becomes a key pillar for maintaining confidence in the institution particularly and the financial market in general. To date, there is no singular accepted way of defining corporate governance for financial institutions. For example, the legal status in the United States of several financial institutions as publicly listed firms implies that they are treated much like non-financial institutions in the eyes of corporate law (Mehran and Mollineaux 2012). Conceivably, it is not surprising that much of the studies on the financial institutions corporate governance has utilised governance and performance measurements based on value maximisation. The OECD[1] however defines corporate governance as "a

[1] OECD: Organisation for Economic Co-operation and Development.

series of relationships between the organisation's management, its board members, its employees and other individuals with interest in the activities of said organisation". Thus, we can construe that corporate governance of financial organisation being a set of standards and principles that seek to regulate the design, composition and functioning of the governing bodies of the organisation. In addition, the Corporate Governance Principles, that has been established by the Bank for International Settlement (BIS) in its publication document "Enhancing Corporate Governance for Bank Organisations" have been widely used for basis of defining financial institutions corporate governance.

Financial organisations and particularly banks have some specific corporate governance issues that make them different from non-financial firms. In fact, the key stakeholders of banks diverge more broadly than other firms, this include not only the stockholders but also, and more importantly, bank customers, regulators, the government and individual citizens at large. According to the UNCTAD report published after the financial crash, "banks deliberately take and position financial risk as the primary function through which to generate revenue and serve their clientele, leading to an asymmetry of information, less transparency and a greater ability to obscure existing and developing problems. They can also quickly change their risk profile, so weak internal controls can rapidly cause instability. As a result, sound internal governance for banks is essential, requiring boards to focus even more on risk assessment, management, and mitigation" (UNCTAD 2010, p. 80).

However, the report further maintains that "*good governance also complements financial supervision and is an integral factor to implementing effective risk-based financial oversight*" (UNCTAD 2010). The Basel Committee established a number of key frameworks that would enable effective implementation of good financial firm corporate governance systems. Financial institutions, especially banks, are mandated to maintain strong internal governance processes and procedures via the Basel II Framework. Specifically, "Pillar II (supervisory review) requires that banks maintain well-functioning systems of internal controls and risk measurement, management and mitigation—and adequate review processes by management and directors. Pillar III (market discipline) mandates additional risk disclosures to provide transparency and allow the market to provide discipline on poorly functioning banks that lack the risk systems to handle the institution's risk profiles" (UNCTAD 2010).

2.3 The Importance of Sound Financial Institution Corporate Governance

It is difficult to predict the impact that the governance initiatives of the past decade will have. Clearly, there is now the expectation that a company should act ethically towards its stakeholders especially financial institutions. At the same time, the sanctions against companies which violate existing codes, remains uncertain. By contrast to the United States, the United Kingdom and EU have a relatively weak market for corporate control which hinders shareholders from identifying and curbing corporate misconduct. Calls for better governance and risk management frameworks are usually directly linked to scandals and/or disasters (HM Treasury 2009a, b; FSA 2009). One would wonder why government's concerns regarding the difficulties in the financial sector tend to manifest frequently in relation to other sectors. In fact, there are numerous motives for this high scrutiny and supervision within the banking industry and other financial market participants by regulators and Government agencies. This includes:

- Instability in banks and other financial firms will lead to contagion effect (systemic risk), which would affect a class of banks or the entire financial system.
- Bank assets and some liabilities are usually opaque and lacking in transparency and liquidity.
- Bank depositors cannot protect effectively their interest or themselves because they do not have adequate information and influence.
- The impact of Bank failure has huge effects on the economy.

Despite the importance of banks (and other financial intermediaries) and the apparent availability of disclosure data, there is little research so far investigated on the quality bank and other financial institutions corporate governance disclosures. Many of the prior studies are on effects of law and regulations for corporations, firm performance and governance in general but relatively limited or few on insurance firms, hedge funds and banks, especially disclosure studies in the financial and banking sector. In fact, the causes of corporate failure are numerous, but are quite often due to ineffective control over directors, resulting in mismanagement, fraudulent behaviour and excessive remuneration packages. Many countries are now establishing legal and non-legal controls over directors and the way companies are run in an attempt to prevent future disasters. Why has corporate governance become such a major topic/issue in the past two decades and so prominent in the United States, United Kingdom and Europe? In general, the main but not the only, drivers associated with the demand for the development of effective governance were:

- The numerous takeovers or mergers and acquisitions wave of the 1980s.
- Increasing internationalisation and globalisation meant that investors and institutional investors in particular, began to invest outside their home countries.
- Deregulation and the integration of capital markets
- Pension fund reforms and the growth of private savings
- Issues concerning financial reporting were raised by many investors and were the focus of much debate and legal action. In many cases, confidence in the management and reporting of companies was eroded. The introduction of codes of conduct was seen as a necessity to rebuild it.
- An increasing number of high-profile corporate scandals and collapses prompted the development of governance codes in the early 1990s and 2000s.

In any sector of the economy, reciprocal trust between the various economic participants is crucial for effective and smooth running of their undertakings. Economic transactions are thus based on the compliance with recognised rules, procedures and the conditions of contract agreements. This is very important for financial institutions' operations. For example, given the nature of financial intermediaries such as banking business activity, where there is a mismatch between credits and deposits and where balances depend on the different decisions by the economic agents that are involved, maintaining trust becomes even more essential than in any other sector of the economy. Hence, a pre-eminent reason in constructing and retaining mutual trust is for financial and banking firms to have in place a correct corporate governance structure within their institutions. Corporate governance has become an increasingly critical issue after the corporate scandals which occurred all over the world and its specific role in the stability of financial intermediaries was highlighted by the severe crisis which hit the financial markets from the summer of 2007. On numerous occasions, corporate governance disasters have driven several large institutions into bankruptcy, triggering major "fiscal expenses owing to the impact of bailout and deposit insurance schemes on the public budget" (ASBA 2009). In fact, for financial intermediaries the governance system is all the more important not only because intermediaries are basically in the business of risk acceptance but also due to their special role within the economy in the aggregation and transfer of financial resources. Regulation may impact on financial risk-taking by financial intermediaries by way of the decision-making process envisaged in the various possible legal structures set forth by the law. We can reasonably conclude, that the global financial crisis serves as a strong notice that financial institutions are distinctive and perhaps mandate both an alternative concept for assessment and different technique for measuring their corporate governance and ensuing performance. One such probable methodology as suggested by Mehran and Mollineaux (2012) is to evaluate corporate governance of financial institutions through potentially conflicting demands: safety and soundness against innovation and improvement.

2.4 United Kingdom Corporate Governance Development

The advancement of corporate governance studies around the world has benefited greatly from the contribution of the United Kingdom. For over two and half decades after the Cadbury Report, one may wonder if corporate governance should have come of age. Within the confines of the United Kingdom, in the aftermath a number of high-profile corporate demise and scandals such as Barings, BCCI, Polly Peck, BA, etc., the UK government introduced the Cadbury Code of Conduct (ACCA 2014; Kay Review 2012). The development of corporate governance is not a recent historical event. A number of scholars have suggested that the origin of the subject of corporate governance can be traced back to the creation of the registration of the company under the 1844 Joint Stock Company Act in the United Kingdom[2]. However, according to Parker et al. (2002) the mechanisms of corporate governance started

[2] "the Joint Stock Companies Acts" means the Joint Stock Companies Act 1856 (c. 47), the Joint Stock Companies Acts 1856, 1857 (20 & 21 Vict. c. 14), the Joint Stock Banking Companies Act 1857 (c. 49), and the Act to enable Joint Stock Banking

its actual development to protect companies from the action of professional managers with the passage of the 1855 UK Limited Liability Act in order to protect shareholders. Nonetheless, the issue of governance really gained impetus in the 1980s as a result of stock market crashes an increasing number of high-profile corporate scandals and collapses prompted the development of governance codes in the early 1990s and 2000s because of the then existing corporate governance framework not being able to prevent these corporate failures. Figure 2.1 summarises the key development timeline and influences of corporate governance code of best practice and policy proposals in the United Kingdom.

The development of corporate governance code of ethics and best practice guidance over the years have mirrored the need to ensure accountability for the various stakeholders that are being affected by the company's core decisions. This development has largely been driven as a reaction to corporate catastrophe by the governments, financial regulators and supervisors around the world of which the United Kingdom is no exception. It must be emphasised that the United Kingdom originated the process of any major governance committee that started to address corporate governance issues seriously[3]. The approach adopted by the United Kingdom for the development of corporate governance policy reforms and disclosure requirement is now recognised and earned the United Kingdom a place as a world leader in corporate governance development. We can attribute this acknowledgement not necessarily to a well thought strategic vision planning but due to a reactionary approach to specific emerging corporate governance concerns over time within the UK company boardroom behaviours, the Government and concerns from the institutional investment community. The UK corporate governance policy process commences with a clear acknowledgement of the issue, creating a committee with term of reference, discussion and public consultation of the committee with stakeholders including debates, drawing together final report, presentation and publication and implementation (Solomon 2013).

The UK government commissioned three committees namely Cadbury, Greenbury and Hampel during the 1990s in response to the

Companies to be formed on the principle of limited liability (1858 c. 91) but does not include the Joint Stock Companies Act 1844 (c. 110).

[3] See UK literature discussion by Jones and Pollitt 2002 & 2004 work.

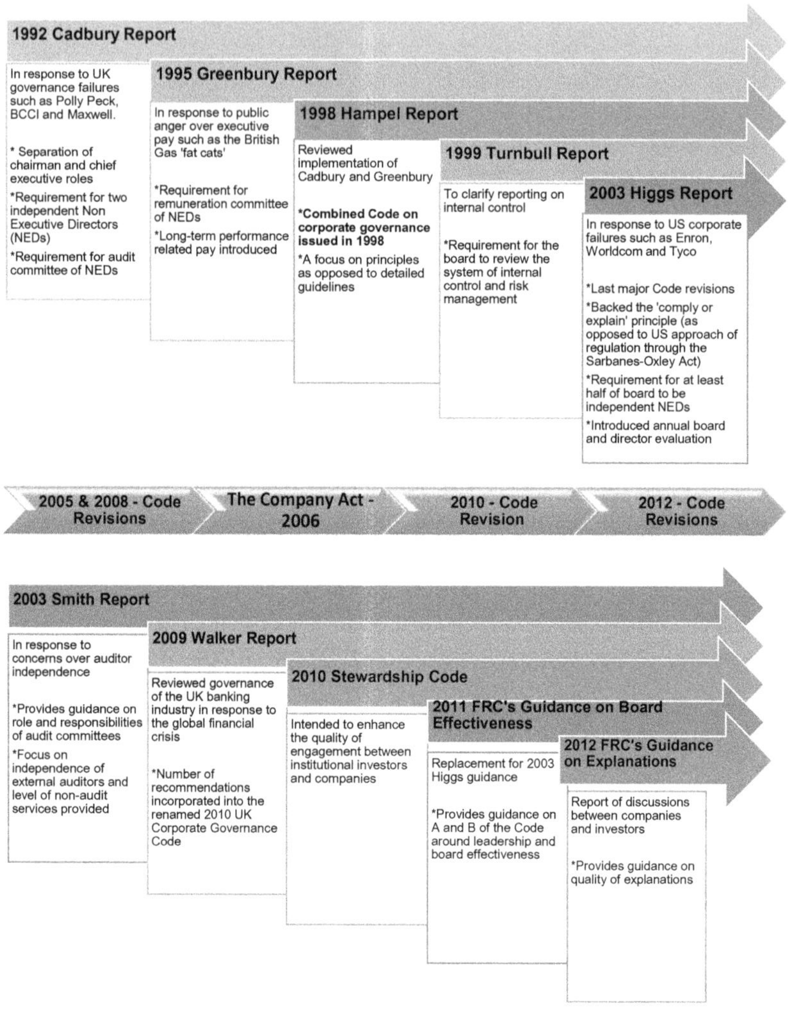

Fig. 2.1 Historical Development of UK Code on Corporate Governance Disclosure Reporting Timeline (*Source* Compiled by the author)

increased need for good corporate governance due to various corporate scandals. Looking at the journey of corporate governance in Fig. 2.1 from 1992 through to 2012, various incidents year-on-year, have led to repeated needs to create new reforms or laws, update or improve governance codes with the aim of addressing either new or resurfaced issues. Surprisingly, many of these corporate governance reforms have stemmed from issues with similar themes reoccurring over time. The repetition of challenges shows that learning has not been fully embedded when reissuing plans for the following years. Although some improvement can be seen in each recommendation issued, lack of accountability and enforcement of the enacted reforms can also be attributed to the emerging governance issues that continue to resurface.

In the United Kingdom, the 1992 Cadbury Report is a good example of a direct reaction to UK governance failures in companies such as Polly Peck, BCCI and Maxwell. An original investigation into corporate governance promotions came into being in the later part of the 1980s and early on in the 1990s as a result of corporate scandals. The number of irregularities found in Financial reporting led to the establishment of the "Financial Aspects of Corporate Governance Committee" led by Sir Adrian Cadbury. The Committee in producing its reports investigated accountability of the Board of Directors to shareholders and society. The resultant outputs led to an introduction of codes of compliance and disclosures such as the separation of chairman and chief executive roles, the requirement for two independent Non-Executive Directors (NEDs) and finally the requirement for an audit committee of NEDs with a clear aim of improving financial reporting, accountability and directors of board oversight as well as the need for good internal controls. The Cadbury Report included a set of principles of good corporate governance Code of Best Practice recommendations which were incorporated into the Listing Rules of the London Stock Exchange. It is important to stress that The Cadbury Code was not legally mandated or binding on boards of directors. However, the implication of incorporating the Code into the Listing Rules means that all firms publicly listed on the Stock Exchange would have to state in the annual financial reports on whether they had implemented the Code on all aspects. It also introduced the principle of "comply or explain". Where a firm "had not complied with the entire Code, they were then compelled to make a clear statement of the reason why, detailing and explaining the points of non-compliance" (Solomon

2013; Mallin and Jelic 2000). This in effect becomes the central foundation for the "comply or explain" approach to UK corporate governance framework and subsequently influences the development of code of best practices corporate governance around the world (Jones and Pollitt 2002, 2004).

Also, the impact of the Cadbury Report from the United Kingdom in shaping the philosophical definition of corporate governance is very significant. It is now virtually impossible to read any scholarly work around corporate governance definition without reference to it. For example, "The Cadbury Committee (1992) defines corporate governance as 'the system by which companies are directed and controlled' is one of the most cited in the finance and economics literature. As mention above already, 'modern corporate governance is often considered to have originated with the innovative, voluntary approach outlined in the code of best practice that formed part of the report and that is still commonly called the Cadbury Code. Subsequently copied around the world, the code has also been extended, but many enhancements have often had the effect of reducing governance to box-ticking compliance exercises" (ACCA 2014).

The development of the Greenbury Report came shortly after Cadbury in 1995, following key stakeholders' (from shareholders and public complaints) disquiets about directors' compensation and share options. The Report suggested an extensive recommendation for disclosure in companies' annual reports of UK companies on remuneration and thus recommended the establishment of a board remuneration committee comprised of NEDs to determine senior directors pay in order to avoid potential conflict of interest with management. It also made recommendation that shareholders' approval should be sought if long-term incentives are given to directors. The bulk of the recommendations once more were endorsed by the Stock Exchange and incorporated into the Listing Rules. The pivotal driving force to the Greenbury Report policy proposals was to enhance the performance of directors and strengthening accountability. It is now established since 1995 that disclosure of directors' remuneration has become high-volume in firm accounts in the United Kingdom.

In 1998, The Hampel Committee was created to review the extent to which the objectives of the Cadbury and Greenbury Reports were being achieved. The 1998 Hampel Report established much of the underlying work of Cadbury and Greenbury and headed to The Combined Code on Corporate Governance (the Combined Code) in 1998 applicable to all listed firms. However, it added that—the Chair of the board should be seen as the "leader" of the non-executive directors; institutional investors should consider voting the shares they held at meetings, though rejected compulsory voting; and all kinds of remuneration including pensions should be disclosed. For UK-listed firms, compliance of the Code is a Stock Exchange requirement. Interestingly, the Hampel Report affirmed the important role of the need for consideration of various stakeholder interests by boards of directors of a company. It specifically stated that "the directors as board are responsible for relations with stakeholders; but they are accountable to the shareholders". However, as Mallin alluded to "the report does also state that 'directors can meet their legal duties to shareholders and can pursue the objective of long-term shareholders value successfully, only by developing and sustaining these stakeholder relationships" (Mallin 2010). To further improve the corporate governance disclosure reporting, the Turnbull Committee was established in 1999 to offer some direction on the internal control requirements of the Combined Code, including how to carry out risk management. The report led to guidance that helps board of directors meet the Code's requirements that they should maintain a sound system of internal control, conduct a review of the effectiveness of that system at least annually, and report to shareholders that they have done so.

Another key development would be the 2003 Higgs Report in the United Kingdom which resulted from US corporate failures from companies such as Enron, WorldCom, Adelphi and Tyco due to the malfunction of corporate governance systems. It was established in the United States that within each of these firms, members of board of directors and senior executives "did not live up to the legal standard of duty of care that obligates top corporate officials to act carefully in fulfilling the important tasks of monitoring and directing the activities of corporate management" (Mintz 2006). These led to introductions of new laws and major code of compliance changes and revisions in the United Kingdom, United States and other jurisdictions. Examples of these changes included a requirement for half of the board at a minimum to be independent NED's, that a senior independent director be nominated and made available for shareholders to express any concerns to, and the introduction of annual board and director evaluations. The Higgs Report recognised the necessity for non-executive director of boards to play an increasingly significant role in the running of a firm. Also, the development of corporate governance in the United Kingdom has significantly been influenced by the European Union. For example, the 2003 European Commission's "Corporate

Governance and Company Law Action Plan" recommended a mixture of regulatory and legislative measures which would affect all member States relating to: disclosure requirements; exercise of voting rights; cross-border voting; disclosure by institutional investors and responsibilities of board members. The Combined Code version was revised in June 2008 and applied to financial years beginning on or after 29 June 2008. This revision was necessitated to reflect changes in new EU requirements relating to Audit Committees and corporate governance statements.

A final example that I would highlight from Fig. 2.1 would be the resultant output of both the 2009 Walker Report and the 2010 Stewardship Code to improve several key stakeholders' accountability with regard to corporate governance. Both these changes resulted from collapses of major financial institutions due to the financial crisis of 2008. In fact, the crisis occurred seven years since corporate giant—Enron placed corporate governance under the spotlight. Not surprisingly, insufficiencies and failures in corporate governance led to the crisis that commenced with the collapse of the US investment bank—Lehman Brothers in September 2008 followed by several UK and European Banking Groups. Again, boards practices and behaviours and questions around remuneration packages for senior directions were identified as issues at fault. These events have confirmed that the 'soaring pay packages for top bank executives were driven by extraordinary risk-taking rather than real sustainable profits. The Walker (2009) review examines corporate governance in the UK banking and other financial industry entities and makes 39 key recommendations with regard to: the effectiveness of risk management at board level, including the incentives in remuneration policy to manage risk effectively; the balance of skills, experience and independence required on the boards of UK banking institutions; the effectiveness of board practices and the performance of audit, risk, remuneration and nomination committees; the role of institutional shareholders in engaging effectively with companies and monitoring boards and whether the UK approach is consistent with international practice and how national and international best practice can be promoted. Following the review, a number of recommendations were enacted during this time and the newly titled 2010 UK Corporate Governance Code for institutional investors was launched. The Combined Code on Corporate Governance sets out standards of good practice in relation to specific issues and provisions such as board composition and development, remuneration, accountability and audit and relations with shareholders. The revised version of the Code changes included a format to give clearer advice on board composition; that all FTSE 350 directors be put forward for re-election every year; and improved risk management reporting provisions.

The 2010 Stewardship Code was then updated in 2012 and intended to improve the level of engagement between institutional investors and companies. The Code's main aims were to enhance the quality of engagement between institutional investors and companies to help improve the long-term shareholders' returns and the efficient exercise of setting good governance accountability best practices on investors engagement. The specific corporate governance improvement included better reporting by Audit Committees; confirmation by Boards that the annual report and accounts taken as whole are fair, balanced and understandable and that companies explain and report on progress with their policies on boardroom diversity. Since 2012 to date, there has been year-on-year update on the Codes. For example, in 2014, new governance disclosure enhancement via the implementation of the Code was revised to enhance the quality of information received by investors about the long-term health and strategy of listed companies. It also updated the remuneration section to ensure executive remuneration is designed to promote the long-term success of the company and to demonstrate how this is being achieved more clearly to shareholders. Furthermore, in 2016, The United Kingdom made another improvement to reflect the changes needed to implement the EU Audit Regulation and Directive (FRC 2015, 2018).

2.5 Corporate Governance Development in the European Union

Like the United Kingdom, the corporate failure of an Italian firm, Parmalat, led the European Union to start a series of proposals with requirements aimed at reforming and modernising corporate governance structures applicable to corporations and entities among its member states to act. To date, there has been no concerted effort made within the European Union[4] to develop an all-encompassing corporate governance set

[4] EU legal standardisation—it is important to note that although the 28 member states have different legal systems, the EU is founded on treaties that have been voluntarily and democratically agreed to by all member states. These binding agreements set out legal principles that all EU governments are required to apply.

of rules and codes of best practice for its member state. The advancement of corporate governance matters and rules have been viewed by the European Commission[5] as a subject that should remain for individual member states to resolve. The Commission did acknowledge that a collective approach was essential for a number of vital corporate governance concerns and hence it established a series of necessary directives as a basis for all member states to abide by.

However, the European Commission over the past two decades has been effective in the development of action plans, recommendations and policy directives related to corporate governance. Nonetheless, differences exist that in fact may hinder efforts to converge corporate governance structures and enable free flowing of international capital investment (Solomon 2013). The underlying debates and policy deliberation within the Commission over the last several years seems to focus on methods and ways in which it could offer guidance to its member states on corporate governance and disclosures. According to IFC (2015), "within Europe's public, private, and not-for-profit sectors there exists a wide variety of legal forms of organization. Each sector faces different governance challenges, and specific codes have been developed to identify best-practice principles for each of the sectors". In providing guidance to the member states within the EU, the IFC indicate that companies "adopting corporate governance best practices improves competitiveness and can lead to improved access to external financing, a lower cost of capital, improved operational performance, increased company valuation and improved share performance, improved company reputation, and reduced risk of corporate crises and scandals".

In this subsection, I will briefly touch on the history of corporate governance in the EU intervention and seek to identify up-to-date key initiatives. A comprehensive chronology of EU initiatives and directives is listed in Fig. 2.2. Since the early 2000s, the European Union measures on corporate governance and its various accountability instruments have generally concentrated on constructing a structure whereby 'effective and accountable companies report to responsible shareholders. It has, therefore, tended to promote shareholder rights and responsibilities. According

[5] Under the EU Treaty, the Commission is responsible for planning, preparing and proposing legislation; for managing EU policies, including the monitoring of implementation of EU legislation and ensuring its enforcement and allocating EU funding; and for representing the EU internationally.

Year	Name of Policy Directive Action	Description
1999	Financial Services Action Plan (FSAP)	Established policy action areas to improve financial market initiatives that focusses on financial integration and harmonisation; limited direct emphasis on corporate governance and accountability.
2002	High Level Group of Company Law Experts Report (Winter Report)	Establishes a framework for modernising European law and corporate governance on issues that include improved corporate disclosures, shareholder rights and voting, board effectiveness, remuneration, audit quality, and the responsibilities of institutional investors.
2003	Corporate Governance Action Plan	Avoids the adoption of a Europe-wide code; focus on corporate governance disclosure, strengthening shareholders' rights, and modernising the board of directors.
2003	Prospectus Directive	Set up rules about the prospectus that European Union firms are required to publish when they issue securities. There was a growing emphasis on financial market infrastructure and SMEs and a limited focus on corporate governance.
2004	Directive on Transparency Requirements for Listed Issuers	Set up policy directive aimed at harmonises transparency requirements in relation to information about issuers whose securities are admitted to trading on a regulated market.
2004	Markets in Financial Instruments Directive (MiFID)	Focusses on harmonising consumer protections, particularly regarding financial and investment services provided by investment firms and banks.
2004	Recommendation on Remuneration	Placed attention on long-term, performance-based pay; public disclosure; remuneration committee; and shareholders' roles.
2004	Directive on Takeover Bids	Attention on minimum standards for takeover bids and protecting minority shareholders and employees.
2005	Recommendation on Boards	Seek emphasis on board independence and committees.
2005	10th Company Law Directive on Cross-Border Mergers	Focus on facilitating cross-border mergers of limited liability companies in the EU.
2005	Amendments on 4th and 7th Company Law Directives	Policy objective to provides updated guidance for annual corporate governance statements, disclosure on risk management, and material RPTs.
2006	Directive on Statutory Audit of Annual and Consolidated Accounts	This EU directives focus on auditor quality and the audit process, including auditor appointment and audit committees.
2007	Shareholder Rights Directive	Emphasis on access to annual general meeting information and proxy voting.
2009	Recommendation on Remuneration	Develops from the 2005 Recommendations and provides greater guidance on the balance between long-term and short-term criteria, deferred pay, minimum vesting periods, and executive share retention, as well as the governance of remuneration.
2009	Solvency II Framework Directive	Focusses on risk-based prudential and solvency rules for insurers.
2010	Green Paper on Audit Policy: Lessons from the Crisis	Focus on the role and scope of auditors, including appointment, remuneration, and mandatory rotation.
2010	Green Paper on Corporate Governance in Financial Institutions	Focus on systemic risk, board effectiveness, risk management, effectiveness of comply or explain, shareholders' roles, and remuneration.
2011	Directive on Alternative Investment Fund Managers	Focusses on such issues as liquidity, leverage, reporting, risk management, and conflicts of interest for alternative funds, including hedge funds.

Fig. 2.2 Key European Union Corporate Governance Policy & Regulatory Timeline (*Source* Adapted by the Author from various source such as EU, CFA, Mallin 2010 and Solomon 2013)

2011	Green Paper on Corporate Governance in Listed Companies	Focus on board effectiveness (composition, diversity, commitment, and board evaluations), remuneration, shareholder rights and responsibilities, short-termism in the capital market, how to make comply-or-explain work, and employee ownership.
2012	Corporate Governance Action Plan	A 14-point plan focussing on bolstering corporate transparency, engaging shareholders, and law harmonisation.
2012	Proposed Directive on Improving Gender Balance on Boards	Sets an objective of a 40% presence of the under-represented gender on boards.
2012	Communication on Banking Union	Focusses on a "single rulebook," including stronger prudential requirements for banks, improved depositor protection, and rules for managing failing banks.
2013	Capital Requirements Directive (CRD IV)	Prescriptive governance measures focussing on remuneration, including pay caps, for financial institutions.
2013	Transparency Directive	Reduces reporting burden for SMEs, abolishes quarterly reporting, and requires disclosure of major holdings.
2013	Accounting Directive	Covers governance-related provisions, including the requirement for a corporate governance statement that includes comply-or-explain relative to a given code, prudential reporting, audit reporting, and country-by-country reporting (extractive companies).
2014	Proposed Revisions to the Shareholder Rights Directive	Multifaceted review seeking to address the lack of adequate corporate transparency and insufficient engagement of shareholders. Key proposed provisions relate to shareholder identification, facilitation of voting rights, investor transparency regarding voting and engagement, proxy adviser transparency, say-on-pay vote, and shareholder vote on RPTs.
2014	Accounting Directive Amendment on Disclosures	Focus on nonfinancial statement disclosures, including information relating to ESG issues, sustainability, and disclosure of diversity policies.
2014	Proposed Revisions to Shareholder Rights Directive	Key proposed provisions relate to shareholder identification, facilitation of voting rights, investor transparency regarding voting and engagement, proxy adviser transparency, say-on-pay vote, shareholder vote on RPTs, and country-by-country reporting.
2014	Statutory Audit of Public-Interest Entities (Regulation 537)	Addresses non-audit fees, audit reporting, auditor independence, and a 10–20-year mandatory rotation.
2014	Long-Term Financing Communication	Focusses on funding for long-term infrastructure initiatives and providing additional sources of financing for companies, particularly for SMEs. Consultation on investor use of ESG information linked to long-term investment (2015).
2015	Capital Markets Union Action Plan	Focusses on broader financing alternatives to fund SMEs, including the use of bonds and other fixed-income instruments to provide financing to corporations and green infrastructure, as well as to reinvigorate the practice of securitisation more generally.
2015	Review of the Prospectus Directive	Focusses on simplifying and limiting prospectus requirements, especially for SMEs, and on simplifying risk disclosure for retail investors.

Fig. 2.2 (continued)

to CFA—"the process has been slow and predictable, as befits a European corporate landscape that is heterogeneous legally and politically, that includes different philosophical approaches to governance, and that has markedly different ownership structures. Rather than establish a uniform code or set of rules for corporate governance, the EU has adopted a principles-based comply-or-explain regime for member state–based corporate governance codes". This implies that the approach adopted by the European Union is therefore consistent with the evidence emanating from political debates that shareholder intervention improves corporate and economic performance. For example, there is often an assumption by national governments and politicians that shareholder interventions are short-term in nature and thus granting further powers to shareholders may not be good public policy. This viewpoint is not substantiated by empirical studies (Bebchuk et al. 2015).

The advancement of corporate governance within the European Union seems to be somehow different to that of the United States and to a large extent the United Kingdom. The anticipated and judiciously crystal-clear method to the European corporate gov-ernance policy-decision making process from the early 2000s stem from what tends to be very deliberate and a gradual move toward policymaking. Predictably, the decision process starts with the commissioning of reports; then these reports become consultative "Green Papers", which then are turned into "Action Plans", and then into specific Laws, EU Directives, or Recommendations in a process that tend to last for several years. A few scholars and institutional researchers have sought to understand what is behind the EU approach and viewpoint in advancing corporate governance for its member states. For example, the CFA has suggested that the objectives and the progression in the "thinking of corporate governance reform in Europe can best be observed in three Green Papers published in 2003, 2010, and 2011, which articulate the Commission's thinking at the time with regard to its broad philosophical approach and set the stage for further regulatory initiatives". It is important to emphasise that much of the EU corporate governance supervisory and regulatory structure lay emphasis on disclosure and a comply or explain approach over what is hard law. Several of the policies and directives that the European Union has provided seek to address very specific issues, including item such as (a) enhancing board effectiveness; (b) shareholder protection rights; (c) enhancing corporate transparency and disclosure and (d) building shareholder engagement and stewardship.

In 2002, a report was completed at the request of the European Commission, this was the High Level Group of Company Law Experts report. Stemming from the learnings in this account, the Green Paper that was issued in 2003 provided a detailed overview of resultant reviewed corporate governance and legal harmonisation outcomes. Both the 2004 Transparency Directive and 2007 Shareholder Rights Directive and also the European Commission Recommendations included certain regulations that were a direct result of this paper, in particular regarding boards and remuneration. Further issuance of Green Papers focusing on European corporate governance were also based in the intellectual foundations of this 2002 work (CFA Institute 2016). The European Commission approach from 2003 onwards has been vigorous in the areas of advancing action plans, recommendations and directives related to addressing corporate governance and its mechanisms of accountability to society. The EU Corporate Governance Forum was established in 2004 consisting of 15 members that represents various stakeholders across the European Union. The main purpose of the Forum is to coordinate corporate governance among all member states. In 2006, it recommended (Directive 2006/46/EC) that all firms that are listed on the stock exchanges are required to publish a corporate governance statement in their annual financial reports to their stockholders (European Parliament 2015).

A key corporate governance development that the EU has championed is in the area of transparency and disclosure. Companies in Europe are obliged to have high levels of transparency and disclosure. Transparent disclosure enables stakeholders to gain an informed and accurate view of the company and the way it is doing business. In 2004, the EU published the Directive on Transparency Requirements for Listed Issuers. It set up policy directive for its member states aimed at harmonising transparency requirements in relation to information about issuers whose securities are admitted to trading on a regulated market to enhance corporate governance and accountability among entities operating in individual members states. In Europe, firms should ensure that timely and accurate disclosure is made on all material matters regarding the company, including the financial situation, performance, ownership and governance of the company. Information should be prepared and disclosed in accordance with high-quality standards of accounting and financial and non-financial disclosure by applying International Financial Reporting Standards (IFRS). Additionally, in 2005, the EU issued the Amendments on 4th and 7th Company Law Directives for its member states to adopt. Its key policy objective was to provides updated guidance for annual corporate governance statements, disclosure on risk management and material Related Party Transactions (RPTs).

It has been argued by many that the 2007–08 financial crisis was inadvertently caused by failures in corporate governance and had a serious material negative effects on many European country's economy and financial markets. The impacts of the crisis forced greater scrutiny of systemic safety and resulted in both the principles and associated assumptions about corporate governance being reflected on further. One vital example of such reflection was on the role of shareholder's dominant view of corporate governance and accountability framework. A key figure who voiced his scepticism regarding the comply or explain systems and the reliance on voluntary codes to ensure good governance standards was Michel Barnier. In 2009, he held the role of commissioner for the Internal Market and Services Directorate General and asserted in 2010 that [*"I am clear that we will not be able to rely only on voluntary codes"* (Doyle 2014).] (CFA Institute 2016, p. 9). Following the financial crisis, there has been a series of initiative and policy recommendation from the EU on corporate governance and accountability mechanisms as outlined in Fig. 2.2. For example, two Green Papers were issued in 2010. The First was a Green Paper on Audit Policy: Lessons from the Crisis—where it exclusively places emphasis on improving governance on the role and scope of auditors, including appointment, remuneration and mandatory rotation. Second, a Green Paper on Corporate Governance in Financial Institutions—with a particular emphasis on systemic risk, board effectiveness, risk management, effectiveness of comply or explain, shareholders' roles and remuneration. Similar to the United Kingdom and the United States, many of the corporate governance developments in Europe have concentrated on listed firms, because they typically employ a large proportion of a country's working population and account for a significant percentage of Gross National Product.

The vital motivation for the development of corporate governance in the European Union can be categorised into three key areas. The first is regarding shareholders, they have been a core focus of the commission as an effective instrument in governance to place more accountability on the boards of directors. Another is the "one share one vote" approach which has been the subject of some controversy despite it being a central principle of corporate governance with the aim of treating shareholders on an equal basis (OECD 2004). The basic translation for this method is that for every singular share that the shareholder has, they are awarded one vote. The notion in reality is that shareholders are not treated equally, this is part of the illusion that all shareholders in governance are somehow receiving equal treatment in terms of accountability. The final matter is regarding board structure and performance in member states and the issue centres around the hiring of independent non-executive directors sitting on corporate boards across the EU. As such, most of the current EU directives on corporate governance are aiming at harmonisation and are encouraging each member state to follow practice that can be comparable and recognisable across each state.

2.6 Development in the United States

Corporate governance in the United Kingdom and United States historically focuses on large part the problem caused by the non-existence of effective corporate ownership. Corporate governance for many decades has been a passionate topic in the United States. What happens to corporate governance in the United States has a major or wide ramification and extends beyond the borders of America. In our recent memory, any discussion around corporate governance policy proposal seems to reference the issues and problems that were exhibited by Enron and WorldCom. Almost consistently, such issues and effort gain impetus in the wake of some major financial fraud and corporate failure, as these tend to underline the demand for tougher supervision over corporate actions. Corporate governance is fundamentally concerned with the overall manner by which organisations are managed, controlled and governed. The concept of corporate governance development in the United States primarily hinges on the notion of complete transparency, integrity and accountability of senior management, with an increasingly greater focus on investor protection and public interest. The United States with the most developed securities market has always been the pioneering country in making and applying regulations for corporate governance. Hence, investigating the progression of corporate governance in the United States is useful for understanding current practices.

The route meaning of corporate governance is all about the methods of controlling organisations and the process by which answerability is attributed to those who are ultimately in control. The top levels of companies (namely the boards and core executives) are focused on, making sure that they are inputting reasonable strategies to manage risk, increase competitiveness and are transparent and accountable to shareholders on a national and firm level. The first development notion of corporate governance was seen in 1962. It was brought into protect investors against management not making decisions in the interest of their investors especially as it relate to fair returns on investment and not misappropriate their capital (Arsalidou and Wang 2005). However, the subject gained foremost prominence in the United States during the 1970s. Prior to this period, many scholars and researchers believe that corporate governance was not a priority for policymakers and regulators in the United States amidst the post-WWII economic prosperity the US businesses and households were experiencing (Tricker 2009; Cheffins 2010, 2012; Monk and Minow 2001). According to Tricker (2009), three important events that transpired which started to influence the thinking of corporate governance reforms in the 1970s namely (1) "the significance of independent outside directors on boards was recognised and audit committees were introduced"; (2) the promotion of two-tier board of directors in Europe and (3) the emergence of a serious deliberations regarding board of directors duties towards other stakeholders on both sides of the Atlantic. Nonetheless the manner and practical deliberations around US corporate governance have been strongly shareholder focused. Arguably, board of directors of corporations stands out as the central corporate governance foremost institution in ensuring managerial accountability by shareholders. The literature in accounting and finance on corporate governance is large and overwhelmingly based on development in the United States.

Over the past two centuries there have been some key events that have triggered the large shifts in corporate governance changes in the United States. The presentation of the key landmark developments of corporate governance in the United States is represented in Fig. 2.3. It is important to stress that not only did these legislative acts and laws passed institute best practices, but they have also facilitated most important changes in accounting, auditing, disclosure information, stockholder investments, and business policies and processes in general. It can be observed that the most challenged and contentious driver of corporate governance exercises is that of shareholder rights. In the United States, there has been a general move over the last 15 years towards increasing shareholder rights, or accountable governance structures, that allow shareholders to take certain actions that are in their own best interests.

In 2002, Sarbanes–Oxley Act (SOX) legislation was passed in the United States with the key objective of restoring confidence in the markets after the failure of the dot.com stock market boom and corporate governance scandals by a number of large American corporations. The legal provisions set out in SOX barred corporate loans to senior directors, mandated CEO certification of financial statements and bolstered regulation of audits and audit committees. At the onset of its passage, the US President Bush stated that "The most far-reaching reforms of

Year	Name of Policy Directive Action	Description
1933	The Security Act	Enacted as a result of the stock market crash in 1929 to deal with the need to improve regulations regarding corporate governance procedures and security market supervisory entities. The act focuses on delivering improved transparency in financial statements and enacted laws against fraudulent misrepresentation activities.
1934	The Security Exchange Act	Focuses on listed companies regarding establishing laws to provide governance of security transactions on secondary markets. It also sought to regulate the stock exchanges and broker-dealers so that the public who were investing were better protected. The act enabled the creation of the Security Exchange Commission with regulatory and disclosure enforcement powers.
1938	The Maloney Act	Worked to broaden the regulatory jurisdiction of the Security Exchange Commission to include the Over-The-Counter market regulation and oversight regarding security firms.
1940	Investment Company Act	Legislation passed by the US congress that focusses on regulation and supervision of investment funds, trading in securities, reinvestment, and companies whose own securities are presented to the investing public to minimise conflict of interest.
1940	Investment Advisors Act	Authorisation by the Securities and Exchange Commission (SEC) in relation to monitoring and regulating individuals or companies who provide advice on investment matters or activities for a fee. Requirement set for advisors to register with SEC and adhere to regulations that work to protect investors.
1974	Employee Retirement Income Security Act (ERISA)	Set out federal laws regarding mandating the duties of loyalty and prudence for both managers and the trustees of private pension funds.
1977	Foreign Corrupt Practices Act (FCPA)	Anti-Bribery Provisions established the guidelines and provisions regarding ethical behaviours and the preventing the now illegal foreign influence of bribes and transactions for corporate public officials. It also served to improve public disclosures and transactions in corporate reporting.
1977	Foreign Corrupt Practices Act (FCPA)	Accounting and Record-Keeping Provisions set up internal control measures and a mandated requirement for listed companies regarding correct and accurate record keeping.
1977	Foreign Corrupt Practices Act (FCPA)	Enforcement and Penalties for violations of the FCPA focusses on specification of enforcement violations (either civil or criminal) and penalties for non-compliance in relation to the FCPA.
1988	FCPA Amendments	Congressional amendments made to the 1977 FCPA Act in relation to US corporations in relation to anti-bribery provisions.
1997	OECD Anti-Bribery Conventions	The US provided agreement for the ratification of the OECD conventions and provisions making it possible to enable its implementation.
2002	Sarbanes-Oxley Act	Law created as a result of major US corporate failures such as Enron, World-com, Tyco and Arthur Andersen due to accounting and fraudulent practices. The Act aims to improve external auditor roles and audit committees, improve financial disclosures, and eradicate corporate and accounting fraud. Launches a new regulatory body for all auditors of companies based in the US —

Fig. 2.3 Key United States of America Corporate Governance Policy & Regulatory Timeline (*Source* Compiled by the Author)

		the Public Company Accounting Oversight Board (PCAOB). Imposes new penalty requirement for not disclosing corporate governance requirements.
2003	New York Stock Exchange (NYSE) Corporate Governance Rules	Focussed on increasing standards for listed companies in the areas of board of directors' independence, disclosure requirements on websites/charters, CEO annual certification to NYSE regarding violations.
2008	Emergency Economic Stabilisation Act	The act mainly targeted financial institutions with corporate governance requirements regarding the taking of excessive risks by directors, restrictions on bonuses and remuneration packages based on incentives.
	National Association of Corporate Directors Agreed Principles	Established a set of principals based around good quality governance and disclosure requirements, moving away from a tick-box exercise in the areas of board accountability, leadership and responsibilities.
2010	Dodd-Frank Wall Street Reform Act	Law created following the financial crisis and large US financial institutions failures. Focused mainly on financial regulations by incorporating new corporate governance regulations to cover not just financial institutions but all major corporations. The key provisions cover areas such as mandatory "Say-on-Pay", proxy access, independence of compensation committees, disclosure on executive compensation etc.

Fig. 2.3 (continued)

American business practice since Franklin Delano Roosevelt". SOX aims to improve external auditor roles and improve financial disclosures and eradicate corporate and accounting fraud and launches a new regulatory body for all auditors of companies based in the United States—the Public Company Accounting Oversight Board (PCAOB) and imposes new penalty requirement for not disclosing corporate governance requirements.

Another significant development in reforming US corporate governance with the passage of Dodd–Frank Wall Street Reform Act 2010. The Act was created following the financial crisis that occurred and large US financial institutions failures. Focused mainly on financial regulations by incorporating new corporate governance regulations to cover not just financial institutions but all major corporations across the United States. The key provisions cover areas such as mandatory "Say-on-Pay", proxy access, independence of compensation committees, disclosure on executive compensation, etc. Some scholars have debated that the financial crisis of 2008 demonstrated that the US corporate governance and regulation system were flawed, and reforms were long overdue (Cheffins 2010; Monk and Minow 2008). A view that I also concur to especially in the area of financial institution corporate governance and accountability mechanisms especially where no real reforms toward enactment of stakeholder legal accountability regulations.

Corporate governance of financial institutions in the United States is comprised of multifaceted legal and institutional mechanisms that is designed to safeguard the interests of corporate shareholders and to reduce the agency costs that derive from the separation of ownership from control. Several mechanisms seek to increase the nature of information available to shareholders so that they can monitor corporate managers and enhance market discipline. Other mechanisms seek to protect shareholders by imposing liability on directors and managers and penalising them for engaging in activities counter to the interest of shareholders. Like the United Kingdom and many major advanced countries, the development of corporate governance in the United States has been enacted based on key adverse economic crisis or major corporate scandals and failures with consequential effects on both public and market confidence directly. To date, corporate governance in the United States is viewed is as a set of fiduciary and managerial responsibilities that bind a company's management, shareholders and the board within a larger societal context that is defined by legal, regulatory, competitive, economic, democratic, ethical and other societal forces. Governance in the United States has evolved as a medley of federal law—including not only corporation law but also tax and labour law, among others—state law, and a series of codes of various self-regulating authorities ranging from the New York Stock Exchange (NYSE) to the accounting industry. It should be noted that state law has traditionally been the ultimate arbiter of governance issues. In contrast, in the United Kingdom, corporate reform can be affected simply through an Act of Parliament.

2.7 Conclusion

This chapter discussed the history of key corporate governance development focusing on the United Kingdom, United States and the EU. Corporate governance structures worldwide continue to evolve and most of its development has significantly affected major events. Corporate governance is concerned with structures and the allocation of responsibilities within companies. It deals with the decision-making at the level of the board of directors and is therefore to be distinguished from the day-to-day operational management of the company by the senior management.

The philosophical viewpoint that seems to drive the development have been affected by several disciplines including law, economics, finance, accounting, organisation and management. The presence of sound corporate governance within an economy and across the financial market is important in maintaining the confidence of the market and the public. There has been a great deal of interest worldwide in the subject of corporate governance in private and public sectors over the last thirty years. Much of this interest and the subject of debates have come from the accounting and finance practitioners, depositors, regulators, executives, investors and academic communities. Hence, government, private parties, markets and its participants seek to strengthen their firms and economies. Over the last three decades or so, the development of corporate governance and accountability disclosure requirements indicate that each year there is an introduction of a new report leading to a new law, a new corporate governance code or a revision of a code in the United Kingdom, United States and the European Union.

The financial industry, especially the banking sector in a number of countries has been criticised for its role in the 2007/2008 global financial crisis. In fact, ineffective corporate governance of banks was often quoted as the main contributing factor in causing the financial crisis. Much of this concern about viability of banks comes from major stakeholders, namely regulators, society at large and government bodies that were interested in identifying, and in fact examining any potential gaps in the management of banks that may lead them to collapse. For example, in the United Kingdom, Sir David Walker was commissioned to recommend measures to improve board-level governance of banks to the government (Walker 2009). The commission's recommendations served as the basis for the 2010 UK Corporate Governance Code. The underlying pertinent concerns include an aim to prevent the dispersion of systemic risk from other sources, improving financial market capabilities, and the maintenance of the general principles of an efficient market. Since the crisis and the reflections on the importance of governance in maintaining banking standards, there is more need than ever for more specialist practitioners in this area. This has resulted in extensive research into the contribution of accounting, in its broadest sense, and what it can make towards enhancing governance and accountability.

In a nutshell, the key reasons compelling the development of best practice Codes and governance centres around the belief that it should minimise instances of fraud and corruption with the aim of improving shareholder perception and market confidence. There is a significant amount of evidence that poor corporate governance equates to poor performance. The evidence has shown that global investors were willing to pay a significant premium for companies that are well governed. The existence of good governance is a decision factor for institutional investors and other stakeholders. Even if it does not add value, it reduces risk and huge potential losses to shareholders. Nonetheless, I can say that the UK, EU and the US approach to the need to improve governance process is reactionary rather than a proactive approach based on a deliberate policy thought, responding to major failures in governance rather than setting the agenda. Some practitioners also believe that the impact of the Codes varies depending on the nature of the company and the global viewpoint. Many senior managers and executive directors complain that it restricts or even dilutes individual decision-making powers, adds red tape and bureaucracy in the use of committees and disclosure requirements and much adherence to governance requirements harms competitiveness and does not add value.

References

Arsalidou, D., & Wang, M. (2005). Difficulties with enforcing western standards of corporate governance in Asia. *European Business Law Review, 16*(2), 329–340.

Association of Chartered Certified Accountant (ACCA). (2014, February). *Creating value through governance—Towards a new accountability: A consultation*. London.

Association of Supervisors of Banks of the Americas (ASBA). (2009). *Corporate governance in banking institutions*. Mexico, D.F.

Bebchuk, L. A., Brav, A., & Jiang, W. (2015). The long-term effects of shareholder activism. *Columbia Law Review, 115*(5), 1085–1156.

Cadbury Committee. (1992). *The financial aspects of Corporate Governance*. London: Committee on the Financial Aspects of Corporate Governance.

Cheffins, B. (2010, October). "The History of Modern U.S. Corporate Governance"—Understanding risk lunchtime seminar series centre for risk studies/CJBS. In a seminar based on the introductory chapter for the history of modern US corporate governance, Edward Elgar, forthcoming.

Cheffins, B. (2012). *The history of Modern U.S Corporate Governance: Introduction*. Northampton, MA: Edward Elgar.

CFA Institute. (2016). *Corporate Governance policy in the European Union: Through an investors lens*.

Combined Code. (2003). *The combined code on Corporate Governance*. London: Financial Reporting Council.
Combined Code. (2006). *The combined code on Corporate Governance*. London: Financial Reporting Council.
Combined Code. (2008). *The combined code on Corporate Governance*. London: Financial Reporting Council.
Doyle, D. P. (2014). The EU Corporate Governance legislative environment. In Mark Cardale (Ed.), *A practical guide to Corporate Governance* (5th ed.). London: Sweet & Maxwell.
European Parliament. (2015). *Report on the proposal for a directive of the European Parliament and of the Council amending directive 2007/36/EC as regards the encouragement of long-term shareholder engagement and directive 2013/14/EU as regards certain elements of the Corporate Governance statement.*
Financial Reporting Council. (2015). *Developments in Corporate Governance and stewardship 2014*. London: Financial Reporting Council.
Financial Reporting Council (FRC). (2000, December). *FRC launches proposed reforms to the UK Corporate Governance code*. London: Financial Reporting Council.
Financial Reporting Council (FRC). (2009, March). *Review of the effectiveness of the combined code-call for evidence*. London: Financial Reporting Council.
Financial Reporting Council (FRC). (2010). *The UK corporate governance code*. London: Financial Reporting Council.
Financial Reporting Council (FRC). (2012). *The UK corporate governance code*. London: Financial Reporting Council.
Financial Reporting Council (FRC). (2018, July). *The UK corporate governance code*. London.
Financial Service Authority (FSA). (2009, September). *Reforming remuneration practices in the financial services, Consultation Paper*. London: Financial Service Authority.
High Level Group of Company Law Experts. (2002). *Report of the high level group of company law experts on a modern regulatory framework for company law in Europe*.
HM Treasury. (2009a, November). *A review of corporate governance in UK banks and other financial industry entities: Final recommendations*. London.
HM Treasury. (2009b, November). *Government introduces financial services bill, press release*. London.
Jones, I., & Pollitt, M. (2002). Who influences debates in business ethics? An investigation into the development of corporate governance in the UK since 1990. In I. W. Jones, & M. G. Pollitt (Eds.), *Understanding how issues in business ethics develop*. Basingstoke: Palgrave.

Jones, I., & Pollitt, M. (2004). Understanding how issues in corporate governance develop: Cadbury report to Higgs review. *Corporate Governance: An International Review, 12*(2), 162–170.

International Finance Corporation (IFC). (2015). *A guide to corporate governance practices in the European Union*. Washington, D.C.: World Bank Group.

Kay Review. (2012, July). *The Kay Review of UK equity markets and the long-term decision making, final report*.

Mallin, C. (2010). *Corporate Governance* (3rd ed.). Oxford: Oxford University Press.

Mallin, C., & Jelic, R. (2000). Developments in Corporate Governance in Central and Eastern Europe. *Corporate Governance: An International Review, 8*(1), 43–51.

Mehran, H., & Mollineaux, L. (2012). *Corporate governance of financial institutions* (Staff Report No. 539). Federal Reserve Bank of New York.

Mintz, S. M. (2006). A comparison of corporate governance systems in the US, UK and Germany. *Corporate Ownership & Control, 3*(4), 24–34.

Monk, R. A. G., & Minow, N. (2001). *Corporate governance* (2nd ed.). Chichester: Wiley.

Monk, R. A. G., & Minow, N. (2008). *Corporate governance* (4th ed.). Chichester: Wiley.

OECD. (2004). *OECD principles of corporate governance*. France: Organisation for Economic Co-operation and Development.

Parker, S., Peters, G. H., & Turetsky, H. F. (2002). Corporate governance and corporate failure: A survival analysis. *Corporate Governance: The International Journal of Business in Society, 2*(2), 4–12.

Solomon, J. (2013). *Corporate governance and accountability* (4th ed.). John Wiley and Sons Ltd.

Tricker, B. (2009). *Corporate governance: Principles, policies and practices* (1st ed.). New York: Oxford University Press.

United Nations Conference on Trade and Development (UNCTAD). (2010, October). *Corporate governance in the wake of the financial crisis, selected international reviews*. New York and Geneva: United Nations.

Walker, S. D. (2009). *A review of corporate governance in UK banks and other financial industry entities*. Final recommendations.

CHAPTER 3

Rethinking of Corporate Governance in Financial Institutions: Do we Need a New Theory?

3.1 Introduction

Financial institutions are businesses that deliver financial services to customers. They carry out the following main functions: transformation of financial assets; broker-dealer services; asset management. This can be identified and grouped into four types of financial firms: financial intermediaries; investment firms; asset managers and financial market infrastructures as a special type of financial institution, whose relevance is on the rise in today's financial markets. Financial intermediaries transform financial assets acquired through the market and constitute them into a different type of asset, more widely preferable, which becomes their liability. Financial intermediaries include banks of all types and credit unions; insurance companies; pension funds; investment funds and finance companies. Their transformation function involves at least one of the following: "(a) providing maturity intermediation; (b) reducing risk via diversification; (c) reducing the costs of contracting and information processing; and (d) providing a payments mechanism". Banking firms in general tend to offer all of these functions. Insurers tend to offer the first three, while pension funds and investment funds provide risk diversification and transaction costs' reduction.

Specialised institutions offer payment services in addition to banking firms. Investment firms provide broker-dealer functions, such as

J. A. Akuffo, *Corporate Governance and Accountability of Financial Institutions*, Palgrave Studies in Accounting and Finance Practice, https://doi.org/10.1007/978-3-030-64046-0_3

exchanging financial assets on behalf of customers and/or for their own account, and/or underwriting functions (i.e. they assist their clients in the creation of financial assets, which they then offer to market participants). Asset managers provide investment advice to other market participants (including financial intermediaries) and/or manage their assets. Financial market infrastructures are established as multilateral systems among participating institutions, including the operator of the system, for the purposes of clearing, settling or recording payments, securities, derivatives or other financial transactions. They foresee a set of common rules and procedures for all participants, a technical infrastructure, and a specialised risk management framework. Through the centralisation of specific activities, they allow participants to manage their risks more efficiently and, in some instances, eliminate certain risks. Hence, the nature of the types of business operations for financial organisations makes them unique and very complex.

Corporate governance is concerned with structures and the allocation of responsibilities within companies. It deals with the decision-making at the level of the board of directors and is therefore to be distinguished from the day-to-day operational management of the company by the senior management. It has now been established that the way and the manner corporate governance of banks and other financial institutions operate varies significantly from conventional corporate governance. The presence of sound corporate governance across an economic financial industry is important in maintaining the confidence of the market and the public in these institutions. For financial institutions the scale of corporate governance and its mechanisms of accountability goes far beyond the traditional shareholder model of governance that has dominated the finance and accounting literature over the past four decades.

This chapter critically examines the nature of the mechanisms of accountability in corporate governance regarding financial institutions and market and its associated philosophies employed. It starts by stressing the need and relevance of financial institutions corporate governance and focuses on the key characteristics which makes these firms special (for example, highly leveraged, regulation and supervision, opacity and complex mechanism, etc.) compared to ordinary firms. Hence, corporate governance of financial organisations must be organised and regulated with a special focus on risk governance, a concept that emphasises the central role of risk management and board oversight on the relevant activities. The chapter also discusses the specific features of corporate governance differences between financial firms and ordinary institutions with regard to the various underlying theories.

3.2 Corporate Governance Framework in Financial Institutions Research

Corporate governance is concerned with structures and the allocation of responsibilities within companies. It deals with the decision-making at the level of the board of directors and is therefore to be distinguished from the day-to-day operational management of the company by the senior management. The presence of sound corporate governance in a financial organisation and across many OECD countries' financial industry is important in maintaining the confidence of the market and the public at large.

The financial sector governance has been the topic of much recent academic and policy discussion and has been criticised regarding the part it played in the 2007/2008 bank crash (Committee of European Banking Supervisors 2009; Holland 2010; Kirkpatrick 2009; FSA 2011; Senior Supervisors Group 2008, 2009; Pirson and Turnbull 2011; Tomasic 2011). However, as noted by Haan and Vlahu (2013) paper, the observed data research following the crisis indicated a contrary path: "For example, using a large sample of data on non-financial and financial firms for the period 1996-2007, Adams (2012) reports that governance of US financial firms is not obviously worse than non-financial firms. Comparing eight governance characteristics of financial and non-financial firms from the perspective of agency theoretical framework, it turns out that while financial firm governance is worse in some dimensions, it appears better in others. Similarly, Beltratti and Stulz (2012) and Erkens et al. (2012) find no evidence that better governance of financial firms led to better performance during the crisis" (Haan and Vlahu 2013, p. 2).

A large number of countries including the United Kingdom have introduced governance legislation regarding enforcing the banking code of ethics following the 2008 crisis. I note that because of the contemporaneous nature and complexity, there has been little connection between the academic approach and practical policy analysis using a sound theoretical approach. One key purpose of this book is to make such a connection and offer the policy debates on scientific evidence.

Between 1980 and 2009, over 150 countries, comprising three-fourths of the member countries of the International Monetary Fund (IMF) have experienced important problems with their banks (Lindgren et al. 1996; IMF 2009a, b). The fact that these crises occurred after implementation of far-reaching reforms of the financial system revived long-standing debates in economics and finance on the role of financial regulation and governance. The mutually exclusive relationship between financial regulation and corporate governance, particularly financial institutions, offers a paradigm shift in approach about accountable governance. Notably absent in the debate, however, is consideration of the corporate governance of banks and the role it might play in systemic crisis (Ciancanelli and Gonzalez 2000; IMF 2009a, b). Although a number of countless academic investigations have been conducted on corporate governance, there is virtually no research to date that addresses the specific conduct of bank directors and proprietors using a specific philosophical viewpoint. In addition, there is no clear theoretical path between governance as a microeconomic concept and regulation as a macroeconomic concept. There is, therefore, little guidance as to the conceptual framework that is suitable to understanding governance in financial institutions, particularly financial intermediation.

There has been previous research that showed a direct correlation between how for example, a bank can impact a reduced cost of equity capital to firms, improve capital formation, growth of productivity and economic development (Ciancanelli and Gonzalez 2000; Levine 2004). The prominence of internal supervisory structures (such as corporate governance) within banking was amplified by the deregulation of the banking sector by the legislation of diverse acts—for example, the Gramm–Leach–Bliley Act of 1999 in the United States. Despite the importance of corporate governance within banking, limited academic studies have been conducted to explore the systems of corporate governance in banks and the relationship with bank output. In addition, almost all of the current financial supervisions and regulations in relation to financial institutions corporate governance and its accountability measures such as rules, conducts, policies and expected practices use banking firms as standard.

The Basel Committee on Banking Supervision (BCBS) has called attention to the need to study, understand and improve the corporate governance of financial entities. The BCBS especially advocates a governance structure composed of a board of directors and senior management (Enhancing Corporate Governance for Banking Organizations, September 1999 and February 2006). The need for detailed study will greatly enhance our understanding regarding the concept of managerial accountability in financial institutions. The core of the BCBS message is the conviction that good corporate governance increases monitoring efficiency. Furthermore, the Committee believes that corporate governance is necessary to guarantee a sound financial system and, consequently, a country's economic development. This explicit belief which has been over the years codified into governance practices in financial entities challenges the foundations of both the agency and stakeholder theories (Akuffo 2018).

To date, there are many studies on corporate governance, yet only a few papers focus on financial institutions and in particular, banks' corporate governance (e.g. Akuffo 2018: Adams and Mehran 2005; Caprio et al. 2007; Levine 2004; Macey and O'Hara 2003), even though the key aspects of corporate governance can be applied to banks. There is even more limited research on other financial institutions corporate governance and its mechanisms of accountability. The problems of collective action faced by stakeholders who wish to ensure the efficient allocation of resources and the distribution of quasi rents, and the problems derived from different types of ownership and control, are clearly relevant to financial entities. Banking institutions information is largely omitted from the majority of the empirical investigations on corporate governance (Adams et al. 2010; Haan and Vlahu 2013). Still, in contrast to the assertion by Adams and Mehran (2012) there is some research on the governance of financial institutions. According to the Haan and Vlahu (2013) paper, "this research is scattered; papers have been published in diverse journal and cross-references are often lacking" (see Mulbert (2010) and Sauerzopf (2008) for overviews of recent reforms in the area of corporate governance of banks.

However, the relevance of financial institutions in the economic system and the nature of the banking business particularly make the problems involved in their corporate governance highly specific, as are the accountability mechanisms available to deal with such problems. The complexity of the banking, insurance, investment firms, hedge fund and asset managers businesses increase the asymmetry of information and diminishes stakeholders' capacity to monitor senior director's or managers' decisions. Financial intermediaries are a key element in the payment system and play a major role in the functioning of economic systems. They are also highly leveraged firms, due mainly to the deposits taken from customers. For all these reasons, financial intermediaries are subject to more intense regulation than other firms, as they are responsible for safeguarding depositors' rights, guaranteeing the stability of the payment system, and reducing systemic risk.

Regulation presents several challenges in the field of corporate governance and its underlying philosophies. Even though regulation can be considered an additional mechanism of corporate governance, in most situations it reduces the effectiveness of other mechanisms in coping with corporate governance problems. This is the case when regulation imposes financial organisation ownership restrictions, or when it reduces operations allowed to banks or other financial firms and applies coefficients that lessen competition in the industry, or when it designs a deposit insurance that restricts depositors' supervision. Moreover, the main aim of the regulator, which is to reduce systemic risk, might come into conflict with the main goal of shareholders, which is to increase share value. This makes the financial regulator or regulation a legitimate stakeholder that can hold managers accountable for their actions. The conflicting goals thus introduce a new agency problem.

The role of boards as a mechanism for corporate governance of financial institutions takes on special relevance in a framework of limited competition, intense regulation and higher informational asymmetries due to the complexity of the financial firm business. Thus, the board becomes a key mechanism to monitor managers' behaviour and to advise them on strategy identification and implementation. Senior directors' specific knowledge of the complexity of their business enables them to monitor and advise managers efficiently. To avoid any conflict of interest between the firm directors and the regulator, the board takes charge of links with the regulator. As in other firms, financial institution boards must also cope with legal responsibilities.

In the financial industry, corporate governance refers to the manner in which the business and strategy of the institution are governed by the firm's board and senior management. An accurate and succinct description of it is given by the BIS (BIS 1999), which describes the mechanics of bank corporate governance as (i) setting the bank's objectives, including target rate of return for shareholders; (ii) setting the control framework that oversees the daily operations of the bank; (iii) protecting customer deposits; (iv) setting strategy that accounts for the interests of all stakeholders, including shareholders, employees, customers and suppliers and (v) maintaining the bank as a going concern irrespective of economic conditions and throughout the business cycle. The BIS principles and framework are not only intended to cover banks but also apply to other financial institutions as well.

The banking crisis highlights the failure of bank corporate governance with dramatic effect. The financial crash and economic recession of 2007–2009 resulted in the demise of a number of banks, of varying size and systemic importance, in the United Kingdom, United States and Europe. The evidence from the crash is that corporate governance at many banks and other key financial firms failed completely, at least with respect to points (iv) and (v) above, and in many cases with respect to all five governance objectives. This was despite the fact that the banking sector is heavily regulated and subject to internationally agreed rules on capital buffers and accounting transparency. This has prompted the call for the re-examination and evaluation of the current prevailing theoretical assumptions that underscore the role and functions of financial institutions, accountable governance and the financial market infrastructure in the modern-day economy (Turner 2009).

Studies on financial intermediaries tend to focus on banks. These studies are considered relevant for the purposes of the present study since banks and insurance companies are: (i) active in the risk acceptance business, (ii) strongly regulated and capital constrained and (iii) over products which may be substitutes. There are numerous studies which support the idea that banks should be subject to particular governance provisions due to their greater regulation compared to other sectors (Levine 2003; Caprio and Levine 2002; Buster 2008), or their operating characteristics, namely the deposit guarantee fund, deposit insurance and the systemic risks deriving from the management of payment systems and the transmission of monetary policy (Macey and O'Hara 2003). Studies which in general show that governance is affected by industry also indirectly supports the idea that intermediaries are different (Black et al. (2006); Gillan and Starks 2003; Gillan et al. 2003). Until the financial crisis occurred in 2008/9, many other financial firms such as hedge funds, credit rating agencies, asset managers, derivatives market firms and their activities were largely unregulated.

3.3 Is There a Difference Between Financial Institutions and Generic Concept of Ordinary Firm?

The nature of financial intermediaries are different from non-financial organisations in general (e.g. A Manufacturing firm or Airline firm) for a variety of reasons that matter with respect to a corporate governance perspective. Banks, in particular are substantially different from a generic firm in a number of important respects. Unlike any generic firm, banks have a specific role in society. They are entrusted with safeguarding savings and deposits, reallocating financial resources into productive projects, have a specific capital structure and they are regulated very differently from the rest of profit-making businesses. Banking regulation according to Ciancanelli and Gonzalez (2000, p. 6) "is an intriguing element, for the existence of regulation can be considered as either an outcome of the distinct nature of banks or as an endogenous feature distinguishing banks from other public listed companies".

Awareness that commercial banks or investment banks are somehow different from other corporations may explain why there has been very little research—either empirical or theoreticalon their corporate governance for many years. I also concur with the view that previous research on corporate governance is limited mainly to empirical research using data on US financial firms and banks. These researches make the assumption that banking firms adhere to the agency view of firms. That is, it assumes that moral hazard in banks is the same as that identified for any company in which control and ownership are separated.

Despite the strong evidence from agency theory and empirical work (Larcker et al. 2007) about the link between effective corporate governance leading to improved firm performance, there have been a number of research pieces that have supported this assertion. The previous research tended to focus on a single element of corporate governance as well as a single element of accounting measure in their investigation.

Jensen and Meckling (1976) postulates that agency problems in the management decision-making process arise due to the "Separation of Ownership and Control" of the firm resulting in creating a "conflict of interest" between "decision managers and proprietors". According to the work of Tandelilin et al. (2007, p. 10) "this creates opportunities for managers to spend firm resources maximising their utilities rather than owners' utilities. Agency problem not only occurs in the conflict of interests between managers and owners, but also in broader conflict areas, such as shareholders through managers versus bondholders, and major (dominant) shareholders versus minor ones".

Furthermore, "agency theory suggests that there are several mechanisms to reduce the agency problem in the firm. For example, managerial incentive mechanism compensates managerial efforts to serve the owners' interests; dividend mechanism reduces managerial intention to make an over-investment decision which will be financed by internal free cash flow; bonding mechanism reduces managerial moral hazard which potentially occurs when they are not restricted by bond contract and bankruptcy risk. Other owners' efforts to reduce agency cost of equity, potentially created by moral hazard managers, include the intention of owners to choose reputable board of directors; direct intervention by shareholders, the threat of firing, and the threat of takeover" (Tandelilin et al. 2007, p. 10).

The manifestation of the agency problems in financial institutions, especially banks and insurance firms, presents an anomaly. The conflicts that arise in relation to either theoretical or practical application are not binary due to direct or indirect multiple legitimate claimants such as regulators, stockholders, investors, depositors, governance and the public interest (Tandelilin et al. 2007; Bhattacharya et al. 1998) of a financial institution.

However, from a theoretical perspective, previous research is even more limited. The application of "Agency Theory" to financial institutions assumes that they operate in the same type of competitive markets and are structured managerially by the same forces as all other firms. This assumption is completely at odds with that found in both the banking literature (Ciancanelli and Gonzalez 2000; Turner 2009) and supervisory and prudential practices in many OECD countries and elsewhere. Specialists in financial sector studies (whether economists, legal scholars or political scientists) regard banks in particular as different and distinct from "ordinary firms", either because that is the empirical state of affairs (e.g. they are highly regulated) or because their specific characteristics require regulation (Ogus 1994; Goodhart et al. 1998). In either case, the fact of (or need for) regulation and financial supervision makes it untenable to assume competitive markets in the normal sense. In many developed countries, financial institutions such as insurance firms, investment entities, along with others, are heavily regulated both at an entity level as well as the industry in which they operate.

In order to illustrate the lack of fit between standard agency models and the firm (a bank for example), it will be useful to review its assumptions and compare those to the characteristics of banks. According to Ciancanelli and Gonzalez (2000), "Agency Theory" makes at least three assumptions applicable to generic firms, namely "(a) Normal or competitive markets; (b) The nexus of information asymmetry is the principal-agent relationship between owners and managers and (c) Optimal capital structure requires limited gearing" (Ciancanelli and Gonzalez 2000, p. 5).

However, on the contrary, one finds that financial intermediaries (specifically banks) exhibit the following practical functions described below:

> Firstly, the liquidity producing function of banks based on a maturity mismatch between the two sides of a bank's balance sheet. That is, existence of banks depends crucially on uninterrupted continuous access to liquidity (BIS 2008, 2009a, b). A bank core business is to accept voluntarily a mismatch in terms of structure of its assets and its liabilities. Indeed, the importance of banks' access to liquidity was forcefully demonstrated in the financial 2007–2008 crisis when all possible sources of liquidity dried up at the same time for all banks in (most) Western countries and central banks had to intervene to prevent a collapse of the banking systems in the countries affected. Hence, for regulators, one of the important lessons of the crisis was to provide for more demanding prudential regulation pertaining to banks' liquidity risk and its management. From a corporate governance perspective, a key lesson has been called for reforms for strengthening accountability of the role of boards in enhancing risk disclosures and board leadership for financial institutions.
>
> Secondly, banks do substantial and/or even major parts of their business with other banks, i.e. banks are highly interconnected among themselves. In fact, important elements of the interbank business are, inter alia, activities on the interbank market, the OTC derivatives market, and the foreign exchange market. Hence, unlike the situation in other industries, from a bank's perspective, competitors are also important business partners and pose a major counterparty risk. Moreover, the banking system is prone to contagion, i.e. problems

at one bank will spread to other banks and system-wide at a very fast rate, hence banks are considered as systemic importance. Financial institutions, especially banking firm volatility, tends to cause "contagion effect", that could result in banking systemic shock (BOE 2010, 2011; IMF 2011; Mulbert 2010; Turner 2009 and Walker 2009).

Thirdly, Banks operate in regulated or administered markets. Because of their systemic importance on one hand and their vulnerability to run on the other hand, banks are heavily regulated and supervised entities, hence banking regulation[1]. Their failure may have more severe outcomes for the whole economy. According to Laeven (2012), the owners of banks do not internalise the risks that the failure of their bank will pose to the rest of the financial system, even though such systematic risk can pose significant threats to the broader economy. A number of empirical papers support the systemic effect argument posed by banks (Haan and Vlahu 2013).

Fourthly, the agency problem is more complex in the banking system. Most of the existing literature on bank corporate governance is grounded upon the principal–agent theory (either conventional or adapted). The principal–agent theory is directed at various principal–agent relationships, in which the principal delegates work to the agent, who undertakes that work (Clarke 2004, p. 97). There is a wide range of potential principal–agent relationships in banks, involving, inter alia, shareholders, management, directors, creditors (e.g. depositors and sophisticated debtholders), taxpayers, and bank regulators/supervisors.

The principal–agent theory uses the metaphor of contracts to refer to principal–agent relationships between the principal and the agent (Jensen and Meckling 1976, 306 at 208). The metaphor that the company is a nexus of contracts implies that no class of "claimants to the products and earnings" of the company has preference over any other. This means, as Macey and O'Hara argue, that in a

[1] Banking regulation focus on a number of areas such as (a) limits the amount of risk a bank may take, in particular, under Pillar 1 of the Revised Framework in Basel II by stipulating risk-adjusted minimum capital requirements, i.e. by linking the required regulatory capital for a bank's assets (loans, securities, and other assets) in a rather sophisticated approach to the adjusted risk-weight of the different assets, (b) limits a bank's exposure to a single creditor or group of creditors and (c) addresses the risk from disruptions in the access to sufficient liquidity by setting standards for liquidity management.

bank, shareholders have no preference over other types of stakeholders. In their roles as deposit insurers and lenders of last resort, the regulators have no preference over bank directors, management and shareholders. This implication is at odds with the "enlightened shareholder value" duty of directors under the UK Companies Act 2006 (c.46), Sect. 172 and the hierarchical principal–agent relationship between the FSA and bank directors and management since the FSA is entitled by the Financial Services and Markets Act (FSMA) 2000 (c.8) to have regulatory authority over them.

Fifthly, the role of leverage differs significantly across industries where in a non-financial firm leverage is considered a source of financing, whereas in the banking sector it is a factor of production. Hence, capital structure in banking is highly geared towards reflecting the bank's function as an intermediary. Owners rarely provide more than 10% of funds loaned; bond holders and depositors provide the rest. Banks are highly leveraged institutions[2]. Banks which consist of more than 90 per cent debt (as opposed to an average of 40 per cent for non-financial firms) have more key direct stakeholders[3] than non-financial firms. Beyond the shareholders, the stakeholders in a bank include government, debtholders (the majority of which are the depositors) and the holders of subordinated debt.

Sixth, banks balance sheets (assets and liabilities) are notoriously more opaque and complex than those of generic firms (Flannery et al. 2004). According to Levine (2004), "Banks can alter the risk

[2] Banks are compensated for accepting a maturity mismatch by a premium charged to creditors, i.e. a bank's creditors have to pay a higher interest rate than the bank pays for its refinancing. Hence, ceteris paribus, a bank's profit increases directly in proportion with the volume of lending to creditors. The upper bound for an increase in lending is derived from the marginal cost of a bank's refinancing, given that an increase of the bank's leverage will increase its probability of default, and depositors as well as other debtholders will demand a higher risk premium as compensation for the higher risk of insolvency, and from minimum capital requirements provided for by prudential regulation.

[3] Despite, the multitude of stakeholders, the board represents solely the views of shareholders, subject to regulatory constraints. Most researchers have argued that, shareholders' interest may diverge substantially from those of other stakeholders, especially on risk, where shareholders prefer volatility and short term perspective. On the other hand, debtholders and regulators prefer low volatility and long term view. See Bolton et al. (2011) for in depth analysis.

> composition of their assets more quickly than non-financial industries, and banks can readily hide problems by extending loans to clients that cannot service previous debt obligation". Moreover, the quality of bank loans is not readily observable where the quality of assets of industrial firms, in particular physical assets such as machinery, plants, etc., is much more easily discernible by third parties. The same holds true for other assets banks invest in, e.g. securities, such as Asset-Backed Securities (ABSs), Collateralized Debt Obligations (CDOs), and Credit-Default Swaps (CDSs). In fact, to a large extent, the financial turbulence in the autumn of 2008 was caused by these difficulties. After the collapse of Lehman Brothers, the interbank-market virtually crashed even for (very) short-term lending since, all of a sudden, an all-out distrust prevailed among banks about the quality of other banks' assets. In addition, the business of securitisation has in essence (a) speeded up the process of lending at the origination stage and in interbank markets and (b) increased opacity by merging large amounts of information and relying on credit ratings (Mehran et al. 2011). The process of financial assets securitisation and credit facilitation provided by other financial institutions further added to the complexity structure and information asymmetry problems in regard to balance sheet issues in the financial market.

Additionally, in terms of corporate governance and managerial accountability, the more complex agency problem is specifically significant for financial institutions. Ciancanelli and Gonzalez (2000) also identified in their research paper that further to information asymmetry that are created between owners and managers, "there are at least three additional loci of asymmetric information in banks' major stakeholders: (1) Between depositors, the bank and the regulator; (2) Between owner, managers and the regulator; and (3) Between borrowers, managers and the regulator)". They concluded in their study by "*stating that the importance of these additional loci of information asymmetry suggests that the nature of a bank is qualitatively different from the nature of the firm implied by Agency Theory*". .... "*even though we consider Agency Theory to be of limited use in the analysis of bank governance, the agency problem remains an important conceptual tool*" (Ciancanelli and Gonzalez 2000, p. 7) in addressing the issue of corporate governance. Additionally, opacity, scope and complexity play a role in governance in both the interaction between board and management and the relationship between the bank and its regulators. This in fact, raises the question of how well boards represent shareholders and depends on whether boards understand the inner workings of the banks. The notion that independent board members should have more financial experience has become an important issue in corporate governance of banks and other financial institutions in offering accountability to stakeholders.

Furthermore, insurance firms differ from non-financial organisations for reasons that are not entirely similar to those applicable to banks. The business of insurance covers risk for financial and corporate undertakings, and households. In fact, unlike what is traditionally considered as most financial products, it "is characterised by the reversal of the production cycle insofar as premiums are collected when the contract is entered into and claims arise only if a specified event occurred. Insurers intermediate risks directly, and they intend to manage these risks through diversification and risk pooling enhance by a range of techniques" (IAIS 2015). Also, insurance firms "bear risks, technical risks, which concern the liability side of their balance sheet and relate to the actuarial and/or statistical calculations used in estimating liabilities" (IAIS 2015). In addition, they encounter risks that emanate from their financial and investment activities, including those that arise from mismatching of assets and liabilities. A problem that has not really been properly addressed within the corporate governance literature.

In a nutshell, the discussions above demonstrate on one hand, the importance of underlying theory of corporate governance for financial institutions; and, on the other, the reflection of the uniqueness of banking firms and insurers' governance as a manifestation of their specialness. The characteristics of banking organisations and the sector as a whole as discussed make corporate governance effectiveness challenging. In fact, banking firms particularly, are fundamentally delicate given the nature of the liquidity of their deposits and the illiquid nature of their assets, which makes them more than ever susceptible to crisis. Other financial institutions such as asset managers, are less delicate, "to the extent that they undertake risks on behalf of investors, while their activities are more similar to other professional activities, including those of lawyers and accountants. The corporate governance of asset managers, albeit important, is less special than in the case of banks and is mainly focused on the quality of services offered to clients and on the prevention of conflicts of interest" (Ferrarini 2017). The nature of the issues discussed and its uniqueness calls for the necessity for financial institutions to have tougher and more robust corporate governance systems than other organisations. This will also undoubtedly require a clear assessment and re-evaluation of the prevailing theories and assumptions regarding the governance of financial organisations.

3.4 Research on Financial Intermediaries Internal Corporate Governance and Mechanisms of Accountability

The implementation of effective corporate governance in organisations can be done in a variety of means. "The institutions and the processes of corporate governance have evolved with the economic development of industry and organisations, with the adaptation of different governance structures to meet the emerging business opportunities and economic challenges" (Clarke 2004). The following sections present the literature on the type of mechanisms for implementing effective corporate governance in order to ensure that stakeholders' interests are aligned with firm objectives. The section draws on the philosophical viewpoint as postulated by the proponents of stakeholder theory of corporate governance.

3.4.1 The Role of Bank Boards of Directors in Corporate Governance

This review section addresses the question of what the role of directors is, and to whom they are accountable. It is intended to help understand how they can fulfil their tasks more effectively. It also draws attention and sheds light on the state of the underlying theoretical viewpoint to ensure managerial accountability. The board has been formally defined as "the link between the shareholders of the firm and the management entrusted with undertaking the day-to-day operation of the organization" (Stiles and Taylor 2001, p. 4). The board duties outlined in the OECD Principles (1999) also emphasise overseeing management, but more explicitly state the duties of "fulfilling its accountability obligations to the company and to the shareholders".

The board of directors is regarded as an integral part of the governance in any publicly held organisation because of its fiduciary duty to monitor the activities of management and provide strategic directions on behalf of shareholders (Cadbury Report 1992 in the United Kingdom).

A key driver for the reforms proposed by the Cadbury Report supports the agency theory in general and affirm the shareholder-centric approach to governance. A number of studies and publications support this view (BIS 1999; Tandelilin et al. 2007) on emphasising the need for boards to ensure management responsibility systems and supervision in maintaining effective governance.

An important stream of the literature in the financial economics and management field focuses on organisational outcomes of board compositions and structural characteristics. A number of studies have argued that boards are stakeholders' (for example, the dominant stakeholder—shareholders) first line of defence in corporate governance, focusing on factors that influence board effectiveness (see Hermalin and Weisbach 2003; Adams and Mehran 2003; Adams et al. 2010; and Adams 2010). In fact, the selection of boards gives bondholders or stockholders the structure to protect their concern and control senior management actions. According to Jakob de Haan and Razvan Vlahu (2013) "the two utmost vital tasks for boards are supervising and advising senior managers". However, other researchers have argued that these important tasks are less effective regarding efficient governance when it comes to banking firms due to the inadequacy of agency theory perspective on governance (Haan and Vlahu 2013, Mehran et al. 2011 and Adams and Mehran 2012).

Adams and Mehran (2003) provide empirical evidence to show that the Boards in banks play a relatively higher role than boards in manufacturing companies. The fiduciary duty of the board is a valuable devise in the banking context because of the nature of high-level information asymmetry in prevailing banks (Macey and O'Hara 2003). Accordingly, the boards in banks have more outside directors, more committees, and meet more frequently than the boards of manufacturing organisations. Furthermore, the Boards in a bank have a wider role to play, because in addition to the shareholders, other stakeholders such as regulators and depositors have a direct interest in the performance of the bank. Analyses which investigate the board characteristics for banks show that bank boards are larger and have a higher number of independent members, Adams R., Mehran H. (2003), that compare a sample of bank holding companies with a sample of US manufacturing companies and Schwizer et al. (2012) who found similar results for Italian companies and intermediaries which make up the S&P MIB 40 index. Also, I find no serious studies to date addressing the issues on other financial institutions such as insurance, hedge funds or fund managers with respect to board's role in governance.

3.4.1.1 *Board Size, Expertise and Independence*

According to Haan and Vlahu 2013 in quoting the Walker report in the United Kingdom, "boards of listed UK banks were larger than those of other listed companies and this is considered problematic because of a widely-held view that the overall effectiveness of the board, outside a quite narrow range, tends to vary inversely with its size (Walker 2009 p. 41). There is evidence that this might be correct for non-financial firms (Hermalin and Weisbach 2003), but does it also hold true for banks?" (Haan and Vlahu 2013, p. 12).

Multiple stances have been presented regarding the optimum size of a board of directors. At the alternate ends of the spectrum are Dalton et al. (1999) who, from a society viewpoint, claimed that the bigger the number of board members means greater access to experienced minds and resources available that a company can draw on; whereas Hermalin and Weisbach (2003), taking the viewpoint from an economists perspective, stated the opposing thought that as a board grows, the greater the negative impact on the organisations performance level. In support of Hermalin and Weisback's argument, Jensen (1993) suggested that the supervisory and monitoring function performed by boards is diminished as the size of the board grows, due to the inability to make efficient decisions on time. Adams and Mehran (2003) conducted a piece of empirical investigation into the banking industry that found contradicting evidence to show that banking firms have bigger boards than manufacturing organisations, as well as better performance when correlated with their board size. In a similar study, Belkhir (2009) evidenced that there is a direct positive relationship regarding the size of a board and performance using agency theory viewpoint. In providing an explanation for this assertion, Adams and Mehran (2003) "speculate that banks have larger boards due to their complex organisational structure and the requirement to have more committees (e.g., lending and credit risk committees) and thus require more members". Given the inconclusive findings on this matter, I am unable to make a definite hypothesis regarding the impact of the relationship between corporate governance and the size of a board of directors in financial institutions.

The emphasis on the impartiality of board directors is justified in the conventional philosophy of agency which addresses agency problems that arise in the management of a firm. It is argued that a board composed of independent directors is more likely to provide effective oversight of the company's CEO and other executive directors. Independent directors are generally believed to be more effective in protecting shareholder's interests, resulting in higher firm performance. A viewpoint that is mostly aligned with both agency and transaction theoretical framework. Furthermore, there is considerable literature regarding the effect of the composition of the board of directors (i.e. inside versus outside directors) on firm performance. Boards dominated by outsiders are arguably in a better position to monitor and control managers. Outside directors are independent of the firm's manager, and in addition bring a greater breadth of experience to the firm (Firstenberg and Malkiel 1980; Vance 1983).

A number of studies have linked the proportion of outside directors to financial performance and shareholder wealth (see Brickley et al. 1994; Byrd and Hickman 1992; Dalton et al. 1999; Subrahmanyam et al. 1997; Rosenstein and Wyatt 1990). These studies consistently find better stock returns and operating performance when outside directors hold a significant percentage of board seats. Consequently, if outside directors on the board enhance monitoring, they should also be associated with lower use of strong corporate governance and better corporate performance.

3.4.1.2 Board Meeting Frequency

An implicit assumption has been made by a number of scholars that suggests that the more often a company board of directors meet, although this may suggest more effective monitoring of activities (Conger et al. 1998), it can also point to a decline in performance (Vafeas 1999). Jensen (1993) went on to develop this by accusing board meetings of taking place mainly in response to a period of poor performance rather than actively completing their monitoring function. This was evident when looking at meeting frequencies in the time that led up to the financial crisis in 2007/08. A barrier to this desired frequency is the management of multiple members diaries to find suitable times to converge, and also due to the size of the banking firms and the plethora of committees that all need to meet. Adams and Mehran (2003) argued that this consideration made it even more important for boards to meet regularly to ensure a smooth running of all functions. As such, effective corporate governance is predicted to have a significant relationship with a higher occurrence of board meetings.

3.4.1.3 Role of Audit Committee

The evidence regarding the task of audit committees has been established within corporate governance through either a legislative requirement (for example, The Company Act of 2006 in the United Kingdom) or through voluntary guidance for admitted organisations (i.e. the listing requirements of the London Stock Exchange). In the United States in 2003, as a response to the requirement mandated by the Sarbanes–Oxley Act, the Security and Exchange Commission introduced a listing rule that public held companies must create audit committees in order to scrutinise the performance of external auditors. Additionally, the role of an internal audit committee is also to independently verify, audit and quality assure internal processes of every company. If the audit members are not independent in their function, there is likelihood that this will have a negative impact on the performance of the committee (Carcello and Neal 2000). The research from Klein (2002) and Vafeas (2005) suggested that "a greater percentage of affiliated or inside directors on the audit committee are associated with a decreased likelihood of an auditor issuing a going-concern report and a lower qualitfy of earnings in terms of more discretionary accruals".

Very few studies looking into roles played by audit committees within financial institutions' and especially banking, corporate governance have been conducted. The research done by Zhou and Chen (2009) found that "a more independent audit committee is an important factor in constraining earning management with respect to banks' loan loss reserves". It has also been argued within the literature that due to the need for discretion and levels of complexity within certain areas of banking and other financial firms' annual reports, the need for a completely independent audit has been deemed vital. Hence, the weaker the independence of internal audit committee members, the more ineffective the corporate governance, with regard to the work of scrutinising external auditors work.

The reasons stated above lead us to consider that bank boards should play a major role in controlling and advising managers. Therefore, examination of the characteristics that bank boards should display if they are to perform their dual role efficiently needs to be evaluated. The size, composition, and functioning of boards might show directors' motivation and their ability to adequately supervise and advise managers' decisions. In contrast to agency theory, such an assessment might provide a good analytic framework from stakeholder theory in financial institutions.

3.4.2 *Senior Management Compensation and Corporate Governance*

Another approach to guaranteeing the welfare of owners or investors by senior executives is to construct their reward properly (for example, linking senior executive reward to banks accomplishment). I have noticed that top executives in the financial industry demand very high salaries and rewards to reflect the work they undertake. The evidence seems to suggest that this is very complicated in banking as an effective corporate governance method contrary to other industries (Adams and Mehran 2003; Haan and Vlahu 2013; Walker 2009).

The large body of literature on executive management compensation in general suggests that it is an efficient corporate governance mechanism predominantly using agency theory approach. However, management compensation plans have been the subject of extensive discussion in recent years due to excessive levels of payments, especially to managers whose firms are in decline or have filed for bankruptcy. This situation has led to questions being raised about the effectiveness of compensation arrangements and contracts to align managers' and shareholders' interest (Turner 2009; Walker 2009) that are applicable to financial institutions.

However, banking and other financial organisation norms and customs regarding rewards drew significant attention following the global banking crisis in 2007/08. There was a strong key allegation that excessive reward to senior bank executives influences their risk-taking behaviours. Yet, DeYoung et al. (2013) research investigation found no conclusive evidence to support this assertion. A number of supervisory authorities have expressed the fundamental and practical viewpoint that the composition of senior banking manager's reward could influence how much risk they take and consequently jeopardise the viability of the banks especially where the rewards are linked to the banks stock price (See Bebchuck and Fried 2003, 2004, 2005, and 2009[4]; Bebchuck and Spamann 2010; Haan and Vlahu 2013).

[4] For detailed discussions on the key features of performance-based compensation schemes that incentivised firms' executives to take excessive risk.

Although most findings from the literature in relation to executive compensation in firms in general could be relevant to the banking sector, there are also bank-specific issues relating to compensation accountability. For example, John and Qian (2003) argued that, since depositors are the primary claimants in banks, the objective of corporate governance is not only to associate senior executive benefits closely with equity holders' interest as hypothesised by the proponents of agency theory, but also with those of debtholders. Thus, both equity and debt holders' interests need to be considered when designing managerial compensation packages in banking if such systems were to be used for corporate governance purposes. This view is particularly more relevant and broadly in line with stakeholder's philosophical viewpoint of corporate governance for financial industry given the legitimacy of various claimants. The scale and extent of corporate governance for financial institutions goes far beyond the shareholders to include insurance policy holders, debtholders, debt guarantors and other creditors.

Mehran and Winton (2001) in their research argued that because banks are highly leveraged compared to non-bank firms, cash compensation would be more appropriate than equity-based compensations. The implication is that if equity-based compensation is provided, managers are likely to have a strong incentive to undertake high-risk investments. Although, such behaviour could create worth for main shareholders, it could reduce the value of debt capital via shifting the risk from the shareholder to debt holder especially in the banking sector.

A function that was severely criticised for its work in the lead-into the financial crisis was the compensation committees' scrutiny of executive management pay and reward among financial institutions (UNCTAD 2010). It has long been established within the literature that the work of this committee is vital for good governance. Despite this, the empirical work seems to indicate a mixed result regarding its effectiveness as a corporate governance tool. For example, this is highlighted by the US ruling in 2004 that a committee must be made up of three independent non-executive directors as a minimum in order to perform its function objectively. However, the work of Klein (2002) seems to suggest that the appointment of a CEO to join the committee has a positive effect on firm performance (i.e. earnings management and corporate governance). On the other hand, it was also observed that a CEO sitting on a compensation committee could lead to weaker corporate governance in the form of the CEO receiving favours at the expense of stockholders. Nonetheless, at the time of writing this book, I found very limited or rarely any major academic research that has been conducted in this area for financial institutions using any sound theoretical foundation of corporate governance.

3.5 Research on Financial Intermediaries External Corporate Governance and Mechanisms of Accountability

In addition to internal corporate governance and controls as discussed in the previous section, there is control from outside—i.e. external corporate governance. For example, mandatory or non- mandatory disclosure to the market and control by the auditors, rating agencies, the market for corporate controls, and others to name a few. The following section presents the relevant academic work regarding the external methods and structure affecting good corporate governance in the financial industry with a particular emphasis on banking firms. Although, these forces are essentially the same for all firms, there are again considerable differences for banks and other financial institutions and how it affects the prevailing governance theories.

3.5.1 Role of Regulation, Supervision and Law and Corporate Governance

Bank regulation and supervision are designed to ensure that risks can be sufficiently managed such that the drive for profitability does not adversely threaten the stability of the bank and market confidence. Bank regulators may take either a prescriptive or a market-oriented approach to their task. A prescriptive approach usually limits the scope of activities of banks and often results in regulations for all risks known to the regulators. The danger of such an approach is that regulations quickly become outdated and cannot address the risks stemming from financial innovation (BIS 2009a at 286). This approach also has at times caused distortions in financial markets by providing negative incentives for the evasion of regulations, rather than encouraging the adequate management of financial risk. These regulatory shortcomings have led to a shift to a more market-oriented, risk-based approach to bank supervision. Bank regulators that subscribe to a more market-oriented regulatory approach believe that to aid compliance with the external regulatory framework, formal mechanisms of internal self-regulation should be employed. Such an approach has been adopted in the Basel II and the UK FSA's (now FCA) bank governance regulatory system.

The corporate governance framework suggested by the OECD (2004) recognises the rights of shareholders, equitable treatment of shareholders (including minority and foreign shareholders) and the rights of shareholders established by law or through mutual agreements. The legal framework is an important determinant of corporate structure and banking behaviour. Governments typically influence activities in the banking sector by various laws, rules and regulations. The stability of the financial sector in a country is largely dependent on the strength of financial institutions. These methods include prudential regulation, supervision, restrictions on bank ownership and competition, new entrants, guarantees and regular audits (Alexander 2004, 2006).

It is important to note that most national banking supervisors' concern over corporate governance is sometimes referred to as a financial stability perspective. The supervisor's interest in maintaining the financial stability of individual financial firms parallels the perspective of a bank's depositors and its other debtholders. Indeed, the banking supervisory authority is regarded as a mechanism of debt governance of banks (Adams and Mehran 2003)—a key source of moral hazard that is yet to be fully resolved by any financial management theory of governance. Even more to the point, the existence of such an authority is deemed necessary in order to compensate the negative impact of deposit insurance on depositors' and other debtholders' incentives to monitor a bank's risk-taking. Further, it is believed that effective oversight of a bank's business and affairs by its board and senior management contributes to the maintenance of an efficient and cost-effective supervisory system and, in addition, permits the supervisor to place more reliance on the bank's internal processes (BIS 2006a, b).

In most jurisdictions, depositors[5] depend on the state authority to safeguard their funds deposited in financial banking institutions from

[5] Under company law, the relationship between depositors and the bank is a contractual relationship, in the sense that banks only bear the obligation of "pay on demand" (Edward Thomas Foley v. Thomas Hill [1848] II HLC 1002 at 1005-6. Also see A. Campbell et al., 'A New Standard for Deposit Insurance and Government Guarantees After the Crisis', Journal of Financial Regulation and Compliance, 17/3 (2009), 210 at 212-13). Banks therefore owe no fiduciary obligation to depositors.

executive misuse or risk-taking. According to Tandelilin et al., this "*might encourage economic agents to deposit their funds into banks because a substantial part of the moral hazard cost is guaranteed by the government. In other words, even if the government may explicitly provide deposit insurance, bank managers probably still have an incentive to opportunistically increase their risk-taking, however it will bear the government's expense. This moral hazard problem can be restored through the use of economic regulations such as asset restrictions, interest rate ceilings, reserve requirements, and separation of commercial banking from insurance and investment banking*" (Tandelilin et al. 2007, p. 13). This statement in essence constitutes one of the main arguments that calls for the use of bank supervision to ensure effective corporate governance whereby both senior directors and proprietors are regulated in banking.

Researchers on banking and the financial sector governance have indicated that regulations in banks and most other external corporate governance mechanisms seem to be less effective than this mechanism. Regulation minimises information and transaction cost (Levine 2004; Laeven and Levine 2009) and it provides safety and soundness in the financial sector. Although regulatory supervision is often linked to the failure in the market, the academic research work on financial supervision highlights the avowed objective of supervision as preserving the integrity of the financial marketplace (Tandelilin et al. 2007, p. 13).

A significant tool for the regulator in ensuring that its regulatory standards are met is the use of administrative penalties and civil sanctions on banks or their directors and employees for taking actions in breach of regulation. Effective regulatory intervention requires that regulators have the resources and discretion to bring enforcement actions for alleged breaches. Such discretion could include fact-finding in administrative hearings which can only be reviewed on judicial review on the basis of abuse of discretion or based on substantial facts. This type of discretion, however, has been criticised on the grounds that it places too much power in the hands of the regulator to act in a way that some might view to be arbitrary and capricious. Thus, the existence of a banking supervisory authority in the financial industry constitutes an outside governance system (Ciancanelli and Gonzales 2000). The legitimacy of this imposition on financial institutions as an external governance structure, I may argue, would bolster the importance of using stakeholder theory for ensuring managerial accountability.

3.5.2 *Institutional Ownership and Corporate Governance*

The make ups of proprietorship affect the corporate governance policies and accountability in banking. Many locations around the world have adopted a combination of ownership structures within their financial institutions. Haan and Vlahu provided commentary on this in their 2013 work, reflecting on the options of public, private and mutual ownership structures and the huge resultant effect of this choice on their financial systems.

Shareholders monitoring in the banking sector is an important corporate governance function. Accountability in the form of external reporting, which contains both financial and non-financial information, helps to minimise information asymmetry between insiders of the firm (BOD and managers), and other interested parties (shareholders and other stakeholders). However, the opacity of banks restricts the monitoring role of shareholders (Levine 2004), and regulations can reduce their motivation to monitor banks effectively (Adams and Mehran 2003). The opacity of banks could also provide an opportunity for their managers to manipulate financial affairs of the banks (Levine 2004). Further, block holders are unlikely to exist in the banking sector due to the presence of special laws and regulations which prohibit or discourage such acquisitions, and thus reduce the ability of shareholders to monitor banks (Adams and Mehran 2003).

A key corporate governance instrument in directing senior managers is "concentrated" proprietorship in organisations. There are a number of studies[6] that either support or refute the effectiveness of "concentrated ownership" as a corporate governance tool in banking (Johnson et al. 2000; Adams and Mehran 2003; Cheng et al. 2012; Haan and Vlahu 2013). For example, Haan and Vlahu 2013 suggest that "in atomistic markets, individual shareholders do not have strong incentives to monitor management due to the lack of monitoring expertise, poor shareholder protection and the free-rider problem generated by costly monitoring. The problem of free-riding that occurs due to diffuse shareholders may be less acute in the case of large, concentrated ownership. Large shareholders are also more likely to be well informed and to make better use of their voting rights" (Haan and Vlahu 2013, pp. 28–31). However, "ownership

[6] For extensive literature review summary, see Jakob de Haan and Razvan Vlahu 2013 paper.

concentration" in banking differs significantly compared to other sectors due to regulatory requirements in different jurisdictions. Research suggest that "banks are not widely held" around the world (Adams and Mehran 2003; Caprio et al. 2007). Despite a large number of studies regarding corporate governance and the type of ownership structure, the results are mixed or inconclusive (Berger et al. 2012; Fahlenbrach and Stulz 2011; Cheng et al. 2012; Cebenoyan et al. 1999; Barry et al. 2011; Shleifer and Vishny 1997)[7]. Many of these studies have employed agency theory as their analytic framework for interpreting corporate governance outcomes.

However, we note that there is limited research that has investigated the relationship between bank performance and risk-taking and how this is significantly related to bank institutional stockholdings. Again, the findings from the studies are inconclusive. Large organisation shareholders, for example investment trusts, still possess a high percentage of investment or shares in publicly listed companies. There is a mixed result in the academic work so far regarding block holdings in public firms and effective corporate governance (Shleifer and Vishny 1997; Hartzell and Starks 2003; Larcker et al. 2007). For example, the work of Bushee (1998) seems to contradict Vishny and Shleifer's conclusion by indicating that short-term performance was being promoted by institutional shareholders to the detriment of long-term financial performance decisions. Furthermore, despite institutional shareholders being small in banking compared to manufacturing companies, the task they perform in bank corporate governance is regarded as essential in supervising and scrutinising the work of director of directors and senior management (Elyasiani and Jia 2008).

3.5.3 *Market for Corporate Control (Anti-Takeover) and Corporate Governance*

Another important external governance method in directing and monitoring the behaviour of senior managers is via the use of "market for corporate control" to ensure accountability and disclosures. This can take different forms, namely: "proxy contests, friendly mergers and takeovers, and hostile takeovers" (Haan and Vlahu 2013, pp. 9–10). Of these methods, the most vital one is probably the use of a "hostile takeover"

[7] Another possible explanation for the mixed evidence or inconclusive results can be attributed to the issue of "endogeneity of ownership structure".

where the interest of stockholders can coerce executive directors to behave in the expectation and wishes of shareholders. As noted in Haan and Vlahu studies (2013, p. 9), "*If a firm does not exploit all of its growth potential, some outsiders may consider the firm an attractive takeover target. Acquiring outsiders may decide to replace the incumbent management. This threat gives managers the right incentives to behave in the interest of current shareholders* (Jensen 1988)".

There are comprehensive prior academic studies on takeovers regarding the banking industry and other financial institutions. Despite these large research studies, there is no explicit focus on corporate governance and disclosure of accountability but rather focus on operational performance elements for the parties in the merger process using agency theory. In fact, Adams and Mehran (2003) argue that "*the market for corporate control is largely absent in the case of banks, notably due to the absence of the threat of hostile takeovers*". However, some researchers in banking have offered a number of possible reasons for this lack of "hostile acquisition in banks" (Adams and Mehran 2003; Laeven 2012; Hughes et al. 2003; DeYoung et al. 2013). For example, these studies suggest that the banking supervision laws and the structure of bank capital requirements in different economies prohibit banks' aggressive mergers and acquisitions.

There are a number of studies that have concluded that several types of mergers and acquisition strategies have responded negatively in the financial stock market (Ryngaert 1988; Akhigbe and Madura 1996; Larcker et al. 2007). The findings from these academic investigations often advocate the need to insert mergers and acquisition stipulation clauses to prevent hostile takeovers in the market. Larcker et al. (2007) research concluded that there is no association concerning firm performance outcome and putting a negative requirements clause into acquisition plans. Therefore, I do, on the basis of evidence from prior academic work, believe that the existence of negative or anti-acquisition mechanisms can be classified as an ineffective corporate governance tool in banking.

3.6 The Academic Data on the Link Between Corporate Governance Performance

Financial organisation and banking firms in particular are the critical infrastructure component in an economy. They provide financing for individuals and corporations and facilitate the transmission of funds across payment systems. The effective functioning of any economy depends on banks and other financial institutions ensuring the supply of credit and liquidity throughout the business cycle and in all market conditions. The importance of banks to human well-being and societal development is recognised by the fact that in every country banking is a regulated industry and protected by taxpayer-funded safety nets. The efficient mobilisation and allocation of funds is dependent on efficient corporate governance at banks. When they are able to undertake this, the cost of capital is lowered for all market participants. This in turn increases capital formation and raises productivity growth. Therefore, the management of banks has implications for corporate as well as national prosperity. This in turn highlights the importance, and central function, of bank governance. It is self-evident then, that bank corporate governance must be robust, effective, and adaptable to changing circumstances and fit for purpose.

There are a number of pieces of empirical research that investigated the effects of the relationship regarding better implementation of corporate governance and improvement in the credibility of the capital market in general (Tandelilin et al. 2007; Black et al. 2006). The studies that provide academic support that effective and good corporate governance improve financial performance includes Black et al. 2006; La Porta et al. 2002, La Porta et al. 2002, Klapper and Love 2004.

The empirical evidence from a number of studies has also pointed to the fact that the nature of bank proprietorships and the type of resemblances do affect bank performance. These studies argued that the performance and the policies of the bank can be influenced by the parties owning large proprietorship stakes (Jensen and Meckling 1976; Tandelilin et al. 2007; Arun and Turner 2003; Boot and Thakor 1993). In fact, according to Tandelilin et al. (2007, p. 17) “structure of bank ownership is more concerned about the shareholder proportion of control, whilst type of bank ownership concerns different organisational culture between the parties, such privately domestic-owned banks (private-owned banks), state owned banks, and foreign-owned banks. The three types of bank ownership may have different cultures, attitudes, and behaviours in nature to manage the banks which led the different level in risk-taking behaviour and bank performance”. Within the financial literature, the agency philosophical viewpoint has been used to explain the correlations between the nature of governance mechanism and better firm performance.

In common practice in most jurisdictions, risk management and control function is regarded as a key fundamental corporate governance tool for both insurance firms and in banking organisations as part of bank regulation (although there is currently specific insurance regulators in most countries). In providing support for this argument within the literature, Tandelilin et al. 2007 opined that although banking firms confront several different risks, "banks which better implement the risk management may have some advantages: (i) It is in line with obedience function toward the rule; (ii) It increases their reputation and opportunity to attract more widespread customers in building their portfolio of fund resources; (iii) It increases their efficiency and profitability" (Tandelilin et al. 2007, p. 20).

The bank's motivation for risk management comes from those risks which can lead to bank underperformance. Issues of risk management in the banking sector have greater impact not only on the bank, but also on the economic growth in general. Researchers have concluded that some empirical evidence indicates that the past return shocks emanating from the banking sector have significantly impacted not only on the volatilities of foreign exchange and aggregate stock markets, but also on their prices, suggesting that banks can be a major source of contagion during the crisis.

3.7 Conclusion

This chapter has also reviewed specific and relevant studies regarding financial institutions with a particular focus on bank corporate governance framework. There are a number of studies from the literature that indicate that financial institutions, specifically banks, are different from non-financial institutions regarding corporate governance and effectiveness of its mechanisms of accountability. The causes of these differences from the literature have largely been attributed to a number of key factors including the role of board of directors, regulation and supervision. This review supports the assertion that valuation metrics ought not to be the single guide in evaluating how banking firms are performing but that other metrics need to be taken into account in holding banks accountable for their actions. In addition, it was noted that the overwhelming amount of the academic studies reviewed largely focused on using agency viewpoint to assess bank corporate governance with mixed results that were contradictory to other findings on non-banking organisations.

References

Adams, R. B. (2010). Governance at banking institutions. In Baker, H. Kent, & Ronald Anderson (Eds.), *Corporate Governance*. Hoboken, NJ: Wiley & Sons.

Adams, R. B. (2012). Governance and the financial crisis. *International Review of Finance, 12*(1), 5–329.

Adams, R. B., Benjamin, E. H., & Weisbach, M. S. (2010). The role of boards of directors in corporate governance: A conceptual framework and survey. *Journal of Economic Literature, 48*(1), 56–103.

Adams, R. B., & Mehran, H. (2003). Is corporate governance different for bank holding companies? *Federal Reserve Bank of New York, Economic Policy Review, 9*(1), 127–141.

Adams, R. B., & Mehran, H. (2005). *Corporate performance, board structure and its determinants in the banking industry* (Working Paper), SSRN.

Adams, R. B., & Mehran, H. (2012). Bank board structure and performance: Evidence for large bank holding companies. *Journal of Financial Intermediation, 21,* 241–256.

Akhigbe, A., & Madura, J. (1996). Impact of anti-takeover amendments on corporate performance. *Applied Financial Economics, 6*, 519–529.

Akuffo, J. A. (2018). *Corporate Governance and Bank Accountability: The role of accountability in improving the quality of corporate governance disclosures in bank annual report, A UK perspective'*. DBA Thesis, Grenoble Ecole De Management.

Alexander, K. (2004). *Corporate governance and banking regulation* (Vol. 17, pp. 2–38) (Working Paper), CERF Research Programme in International Financial Regulation, Cambridge.

Alexander, K. (2006). Corporate governance and banks: The role of regulation in reducing the principal-agency problem. *Journal of Banking Regulation, 7*(1), 17–40.

Arun, T. G., & Turner, J. D. (2003). *Corporate governance of banks in developing economies-concepts and issues* (Policy Working Paper No. 2/2003). University of Manchester, School of Environment and Development.

Bank for International Settlements (BIS). (1999). *Enhancing corporate governance for banking organisations*. Basel: Basel Committee on Banking Supervision.

Bank for International Settlements (BIS). (2006a). *Enhancing corporate governance for banking organisations*. Basel: Basel Committee on Banking Supervision.

Bank for International Settlements (BIS). (2006b). *International convergence of capital measurement standards*. Basel: Basel Committee on Banking Supervision.

Bank for International Settlements (BIS). (2008). *Principles for sound liquidity risk management and supervision*. Basel: Basel Committee on Banking Supervision.

Bank for International Settlements (BIS). (2009a). *Enhancements to the Basel II framework*. Basel: Basel Committee on Banking Supervision.

Bank for International Settlements (BIS). (2009b). *History of the Basel committee on banking supervision*. Basel: Basel Committee on Banking Supervision.

Bank of England (BOE). (2010). *The financial stability report* (Issue No. 28). Bank of England.

Bank of England (BOE). (2011). *The financial stability report* (Issue No. 30). Bank of England.

Barry, T. A., Lepetit, L., & Tarazi, A. (2011). Ownership structure and risk in publicly held and privately owned banks. *Journal of Banking and Finance, 35*, 1327–1340.

Bebchuck, L. A., & Fried, J. (2003). Executive compensation as an agency problem. *Journal of Economic Perspectives, 17*(3), 71–92.

Bebchuck, L. A., & Fried, J. (2004). *Pay without performance: The unfulfilled promise of executive compensation*. Harvard University Press.

Bebchuck, L. A., & Fried, J. (2005). Pay without performance: Overview of the issues. *Journal of Applied Corporate Finance, 17*(4), 8–22.

Bebchuck, L. A., & Fried, J. (2009). Paying for long-term performance. *University of Pennsylvania Law Review, 158*, 1915–1959.

Bebchuck, L. A., & Spamann, H. (2010). Regulating bankers' pay. *Georgetown Law Journal, 98*(2), 247–287.

Belkhir, M. (2009). Board of directors' size and performance in banking industry. *International Journal of Managerial Finance, 5*(2), 201–221.

Beltratti, A., & Stulz, R. M. (2012). The credit crisis around the globe: Why did some banks perform better during the credit crisis? *Journal of Financial Economics, 105*(1), 1–12.

Berger, A. N., Kick, T., & Schaeck, K. (2012). *Executive board composition and bank risk taking*. Deutsche Bundesbank Working Paper No. 3.

Bhattacharya, S., Boot, A. W., & Thakor, A. V. (1998). The economics of bank regulation. *Journal of Money, Credit and Banking, 30*(4), 745–770.

Black, B. S., Jang, H., & Kim, W. (2006). Predicting firm's corporate governance choices, evidence from South Korea. *Journal of Corporate Finance, 12*, 660–691.

Boot, A. W. A., & Thakor, A. V. (1993). Self-interested bank regulation. *The American Economic Review*, 206–212.

Brickley, J., Coles, J., & Terry, R. (1994). Outside directors and the adoption of poison pills. *Journal of Financial Economics, 35*, 371–390.

Bushee, B. (1998). The influence of institutional investors on myopic R&D investment behavior. *Accounting Review, 73*, 305–333.

Buster, I. (2008). *Corporate governance in banking. A European study.* PhD series, Copenhagen Business School.
Byrd, J., & Hickman, K. (1992). Do outside directors monitor managers? Evidence from tender offer bids. *Journal of Financial Economics, 32*, 195–221.
Cadbury Report. (1992). *Report of the committee on the financial aspects of corporate governance.* London: Gee.
Caprio, G., & Levine, R. (2002). Governance in finance. Concepts and international observations. In R. E. Litan, M. Pomerleano, & V. Sundararajan (Eds.), *Financial sector governance: The role of the public and private sectors.* Washington, D.C.: The Brookings Institution.
Caprio, G., Laeven, L., & Levine, R. (2007). Governance and banks valuations. *Journal of Financial Intermediation, 16*, 584–617.
Carcello, J. V., & Neal, T. L. (2000). Audit committee composition and auditor reporting. *The Accounting Review, 75*, 453–467.
Cebenoyan, A. S., Cooperman, E. S., & Register, C. A. (1999). Ownership structure, charter value, and risk-taking behaviour for thrifts. *Financial Management, 28*(1), 43–60.
Cheng, I., Hong, R. H., & Scheinkman, J. A. (2012). *Yesterday's heroes: Compensation and creative risk-taking.* Mimeo.
Ciancanelli, P., & Gonzalez, J. A. (2000). 'Corporate Governance in Banking: A Conceptual Framework', *Social Science Research Network*, European Financial Management Association Conference, pp. 2–24.
Clarke, T. (2004). *Theories of corporate governance: The philosophical foundations of corporate governance.* Oxon, NY and Canada: Routledge.
Committee of European Banking Supervisors. (2009, April). *High-level principles for remuneration policies.*
Conger, J., Finegold, D., & Lawler III, E. (1998). Appraising boardroom performance. *Harvard Business Review, 76*(1998), 136–148.
Dalton, D. R., Daily, C. M., Johnson, J. L., & Ellstrand, A. E. (1999). Number of directors and financial performance: A meta-analysis. *Academy of Management Journal, 42*(6), 674–686.
DeYoung, R., Evanoff, D., & Molyneux, P. (2009). Mergers and acquisitions of financial institutions: A review of the post-2000 literature. *Journal of Financial Services Research, 36*, 87–110.
DeYoung, R., Peng, E., & Yang, M. (2013). Executive Compensation and Business Policy Choices at US Commercial Banks. *Journal of Financial and Quantitative Analysis, 48*(1), 165–196.
Elyasiani, E., & Jia, J. (2008). Distribution of institutional ownership and corporate firm performance. *Journal of Banking & Finance, 34*(2010), 606–620.

Erkens, D. H., Mingyi, H., & Pedro Matos, P. (2012). Corporate governance in the 2007–2008 financial crisis: Evidence from financial institutions worldwide. *Journal of Corporate Finance, 18*(2), 389–411.

Fahlenbrach, R., & Stulz, R. M. (2011). Bank CEO incentives and the cost of the credit crisis. *Journal of Financial Economics, 99*(1), 11–26.

Ferrarini, G. (2017). 'Understanding the role of corporate governance in financial institutions': *A Research Agenda*, ECGI Working Paper Series in Law.

Financial Services Authority (FSA). (2011, December). *The failure of the Royal Bank of Scotland*. Financial Services Authority Board Report.

Firstenberg, P., & Malkiel, B. (1980). Why corporate boards need independent directors. *Management Review, 69*, 26–38.

Flannery, M. J., Kwan, S. H., & Nimalendran, M. (2004). Market evidence on the opaqueness of banking firms' assets. *Journal of Financial Economics, 71*(3), 416–460.

Gillan, S. L., & Starks, L. T. (2003). *Corporate governance, corporate ownership, and the role of institutional investors: A global perspective*. Weinberg Center for Corporate Governance Working Paper No. 2003–01.

Gillan, S. L., Hartzell, J. C., & Starks, L. T. (2003, August). *Explaining corporate governance: Boards, bylaws, and charter provisions*. Weinberg Center for Corporate Governance Working Paper No. 2003–03.

Goodhart, C., Hartman, P., Llewllyn, D., Rojas-Suárez, L., & Weisbrod, S. (1998). *Financial regulation why how and where now?* London: Routledge.

Haan, J. D., & Vlahu, R. (2013). *Corporate Governance of Banks: A survey* (DNB Working Paper), Netherland.

Hartzell, J. C., & Starks, L. T. (2003). Institutional investors and executive compensation. *Journal of Finance, 58*(6), 2351–2374.

Healy, P. M., & Palepu, K. G. (2001). Information asymmetry, corporate disclosure, and the capital markets: A review of the empirical disclosure literature. *Journal of Accounting and Economics, 31*(1–3), 405–440.

Hermalin, B. E., & Weisbach, M. S. (2003). Board of directors as an endogenously determined institution: A survey of the economic literature. *Federal Reserve Bank of New York Economic Policy Review*, 7–26.

Holland, J. (2010). Banks, knowledge and crisis: A case of knowledge and learning failure. *Journal of Financial Regulation and Compliance, 18*(2), 87–105.

Hughes, J. P., Lang, W. W., Mester, L. J., Moon, C., & Pagano, M. S. (2003). Do bankers sacrifice value to build empires: Managerial incentives, industry consolidation, and financial performance. *Journal of Banking and Finance, 27*, 417–447.

International Association of Insurance Supervisors (IAIS). (2015, November). *Insurance core principles*. The International Association of Insurance Supervisors.

International Monetary Fund (IMF). (2009a). *Debt bias and other distortions: Crisis-related issues in tax policy*. Washington, D.C.: International Monetary Fund.

International Monetary Fund (IMF). (2009b). *Annual report. Fighting the global crisis*. Washington, D.C.: International Monetary Fund.

International Monetary Fund (IMF). (2011). *United Kingdom: Financial system stability assessment*. IMF Country Report No. 11/222. International Monetary Fund. Washington, D.C.

Jensen, M. C. (1988). Takeovers: Their causes and consequences. *Journal of Economic Perspectives, 2*, 21–48.

Jensen, M. C. (1993). The modern industrial revolution, exit, and the failure of internal control systems. *Journal of Finance, 48*(3), 831–880.

Jensen, M. C., & Meckling, W. H. (1976). Theory of the firm: Managerial behavior, agency costs and ownership structure. *Journal of Financial Economics, 3*(4), 305–360.

John, K., & Qian, Y. (2003). Incentives features in CEO compensation in the banking industry. *Federal Reserve Bank of New York Economic Policy Review, 9*, 109–121.

Johnson, S., La Porta, R., Lopez-de-Silanes, F., & Shleifer, A. (2000). Tunneling. *American Economic Review, 90*(2), 22–27.

Kirkpatrick, G., (2009). The corporate governance lessons from the financial crisis. *Financial Markets Trends, OECD: Financial Regulation and Compliance, 16*(1), 8–18.

Klein, A. (2002). Audit committee, board of director characteristics, and earnings management. *Journal of Accounting and Economics, 33*, 375–400.

La Porta, R., Lopez-de-Silanes, F., & Shleifer, A. (2002a). Government ownership of banks. *Journal of Finance, 57*(1), 265–301.

La Porta, R., Lopez-de-Silanes, F., Shleifer, A., & Vishny, R. (2002b). Investor protection and corporate valuation. *Journal of Finance, 57*, 1147–1170.

Laeven, L. (2012). Corporate governance: What's special about banks? Keynote lecture at the DNB-CGIC conference on corporate governance of financial institutions, Amsterdam.

Laeven, L., & Levine, R. (2009). Corporate governance, regulation, and bank risk taking. *Journal of Financial Economics, 93*(2), 259–275.

Larcker, D. F., Richardson, S. A., & Tuna, I. (2007). Corporate governance, accounting outcomes, and organizational performance. *The Accounting Review, 82*(4), 963–1008.

Levine, R. (2003). *The corporate governance of banks: A concise discussion of concepts and evidence*. World Bank Policy Research Working Paper No. 3404.

Levine, R. E. (2004, September). *The corporate governance of banks: A concise discussion of concepts and evidence.*

Lindgren, C.-J., García, G., & Saal, M. I. (1996). *Bank soundness and macroecoomic policy*. Washington: International Monetary Fund.
Macey, J. R., & O'Hara, M. (2003). The corporate governance of banks. *FRBNY Economic Policy Review, 9*, 91–107.
Mehran, H., & Winton, A. (2001). *Executive compensation, leverage and banks*. Theoretical Considerations, Unpublished Paper. Federal Reserve Bank of New York.
Mehran, H., Morrison, A. D., & Shapiro, J. D. (2011, June 1). *Corporate governance and banks: What have we learned from the financial crisis?* FRB of New York Staff Report No. 502.
Mulbert, P. (2010). *Corporate governance of banks after the financial crisis—theory, evidence and reforms*. ECGI Law Working Paper No. 130.
OECD. (1999). *OECD principles of corporate governance*. Paris: OECD Publishing.
OECD. (2004). *OECD principles of corporate governance*. France: Organisation for Economic Co-operation and Development.
Ogus, A. (1994). *Regulation: Legal forms and economic theory*. Hart Publishing.
Pirson, M., & Turnbull, S. (2011). Corporate governance, risk management, and the financial crisis: An information processing view. *Corporate Governance: An International Review, 19*(5), 459–470.
Rosenstein, S., & Wyatt, J. (1990). Outside directors, board independence, and shareholder wealth. *Journal of Financial Economics, 26*, 175–184.
Ryngaert, M. (1988). The effect of poison pill securities on shareholder wealth. *Journal of Financial Economics, 20*, 377–417.
Sauerzopf, B. (2008). *Corporate governance and credit institutions*. Financial Stability Report No. 16.
Schwizer, P., Soana, M. G., & Cucinelli, D. (2012). *The relationship between board diversity and firm performance: The Italian evidence*.
Senior Supervisors Group. (2008). *Observations on risk management practices during the recent market turbulence*.
Senior Supervisors Group. (2009). *Risk management lessons from the global banking crisis of 2008*.
Shleifer, A., & Vishny, R. W. (1997). A survey of Corporate Governance. *Journal of Finance, 52*(2), 735–782.
Solomon, J. (2007). Corporate Governance and Accountability: 3rd edition. Chichester, UK: Wiley.
Stiles, P., & Taylor, B. (2001). *Board at work*. Oxford: Oxford University Press.
Subrahmanyam, V., Ranjan, N., & Rosenstein S. (1997). The role of outside directors in bank acquisition. *Financial Management, 26*(1), 23–36.
Tandelilin, E., Kaaro, H., Mahadwartha, P. A., & Supriyatna. (2007). 'Corporate governance, risk management and bank performance: Does type of ownership

matter?' Final Report of an EADN Individual Research Grant Project, EADN Working Paper.
Tomasic, R. (2011). The financial crisis and the haphazard pursuit of financial crime. *Journal of Financial Crime, 18*(1), 7–31.
Tricker, B. (2009). *Corporate governance: Principles, policies and practices* (1st ed.). New York: Oxford University Press Inc.
Tse, T. (2011). Shareholder and stakeholder theory: After the financial crisis. *Qualitative Research in Financial Markets, 3*(1), 51–63.
Turner Review. (2009). *The Turner review: A regulatory response to the global banking crisis*. London: Financial Service Authority.
United Nations Conference on Trade And Development (UNCTAD). (2010, October). *Corporate governance in the wake of the financial crisis, selected international reviews*. New York and Geneva: United Nations.
Vafeas, N. (1999). Board meeting frequency and firm performance. *Journal of Financial Economics, 53*, 113–142.
Vafeas, N. (2005). Audit committee, boards, and the quality of reported earnings. *Contemporary Accounting Research, 22*(4), 1093–1122.
Vance, S. C. (1983). *Corporate leadership: Boards, directors, and strategy*. New York: McGraw-Hill.
Walker, S. D. (2009). *A review of corporate governance in UK banks and other financial industry entities'*. Final recommendations.
Williamson, O. E. (1984). Corporate governance. *Yale Law Journal, 93*(7), 1197–1230.
Yeoh, P. (2010). Causes of the global financial crisis: Learning from the competing insights. *International Journal of Disclosure and Governance, 7*, 42–69.
Zhou, J., & Chen, K. Y. (2007). Audit committee, board characteristics, and auditor switch decisions by andersen's clients. *Contemporary Accounting Research, 24*(4), 1085–1117.

CHAPTER 4

Walking a Fine Line: Governance, Accountability Mechanisms and Disclosure Literature

4.1 Introduction

Corporate governance is about promoting corporate fairness, transparency and accountability. Governance is a requisite for survival and a gauge of how predictable the system for doing business in any country is. International standards and guidelines on corporate governance have been established by many multilateral organisations including the OECD and the Basle Committee in an effort to ensure improved statutory, institutional and supervisory structures for enhancing corporate governance in institutions such as banks and financial markets. Specifically, the World Bank has proposed guidelines in the financial industry regarding better governance, because of its critical task as the main vehicle for robust economic growth and effective transmission of monetary policy.

This chapter discusses a number of growing studies and debates within the academics, practitioners and developed communities about the different accountability typologies and its impact on corporate governance. Two core areas that this chapter will explore fall into two research topics: (a) to understand and assess how the overall quality of corporate governance disclosure levels and its accountability categories have been provided by accounting and finance scholars in their annual reports on a long-term basis; (b) to identify the corporate governance accountability categories and subcategories which are most and least disclosed within a

J. A. Akuffo, *Corporate Governance and Accountability of Financial Institutions*, Palgrave Studies in Accounting and Finance Practice, https://doi.org/10.1007/978-3-030-64046-0_4

selection of the largest UK banking firms' annual reports. In order to fully understand and offer answers to the research questions raised above, this chapter will specifically review the related empirical literature regarding the relationship between corporate governance and the nature of accountability mechanisms within accounting and finance studies. Accountability is one of the cornerstones of good corporate governance; however, it can be difficult for scholars and practitioners alike to navigate the myriad of different types of accountability within the norms of corporate governance to various stakeholders. This chapter presents a critical literature review and it is aimed at reviewing the relevant prior empirical literature in the field of corporate governance, mechanisms of accountability and disclosure research.

4.2 How Is Corporate Governance Defined?

Corporate governance is about the exercise of power over corporate entity (Clarke 2004; Tricker 2009). The development of this power has meant that the subject of governance is now one of the underlying core factors for mechanisms of control and management in today's organisations. According to Tricker (2009, p. 7) "*the underlying ideas and concepts of corporate governance have been surprisingly slow to evolve. The basic underpinning framework still owe more to mid-19th century thinking than they do to the realities of complex modern business*". Hence, corporate governance has become an instrumental factor in managing and guiding many organisations in the present global and business environment. In order to understand corporate governance, it is imperative to highlight its definition. It is important to note that while it appears that there is no one particular established definition of corporate governance, the subject can be described as "a set of processes and structures" for controlling, managing and directing an organisation. It constitutes a set of rules, which governs the relationships between management, shareholders and stakeholders of a corporate enterprise. For the purposes of this book, corporate governance must be viewed as a combination of procedures, policies and structures that must govern the interrelationships among corporate management, stockholders and stakeholders to ensure effective accountability.

Corporate governance includes all types of firms and its definitions could extend to cover all of the economic and non-economic activities. Literature in corporate governance provides some form of meaning on governance but falls short in defining the precise meaning of governance. Such ambiguity emerges with many scholars using words like control, regulate, manage, govern and governance. Owing to such ambiguity, there are many interpretations. It may be important to consider the influences a firm has or is affected by in order to grasp a better understanding of governance. Owing to vast influential factors, proposed models of corporate governance can be flawed as each social scientist is forming their own scope and concerns.

The definition of corporate governance embodied in the OECD Principles of Corporate Governance takes a broader, more flexible view, while maintaining the emphasis on the relationship between shareholders and directors. The OECD in its preamble section of their reporting guidelines offered the following definition:

> *corporate governance involves a set of relationships between a company's management, its board, its shareholders and other stakeholders. Corporate governance also provides the structures through which the objectives of the company are set, and the means of attaining those objectives and monitoring performance are determined. Good corporate governance should provide proper incentives for the board and management to pursue objectives that are in the interest of the company and shareholders and should facilitate effective monitoring* (OECD 2004, p. 11)

Under this definition, the introduction of other stakeholders raises the question of where exactly the shareholders' interests rank in terms of directors' priorities, notwithstanding the emphasis subsequently placed on the primacy of shareholders' interests in what the OECD perceives as good corporate governance. The OECD to some extent answers this question in its remarks on the role of stakeholders: "*The corporate governance framework should recognize the rights of stakeholders as established by law and encourage active co operation between corporations and stakeholders in creating wealth, jobs, and the sustainability of financially sound enterprises*" (OECD 2004, p. 21). The corporate governance structure specifies the allocation of privileges and tasks among different participants in the corporation, such as the board, managers, shareholders and other stakeholders, and spells out the rules and procedures for making decisions on corporate affairs. While the intention behind these statements are admirable with respect to acknowledgement of stakeholder needs, the choice of the word "*should*" as opposed to the word "*must*" attaches a lower level of accountability or expected action as would be expected from company directors.

In 1999, OECD stated that corporate governance was "the *process by which companies are directed and controlled*". This definition, however, was updated in 2001. OECD extended their definition of corporate governance in 2001 to be; "*corporate governance refers to the private and public institutions, including laws, regulations and public institutions, which together govern the relationships, in a market economy, between corporate managers and entrepreneurs, on the one hand, and those who invest resources in corporations on the other hand*". Similarly, two prominent corporate governance activists Monk and Minow from the United States also described in 2001 the subject of corporate governance in a comparable way by the OECD approach where they assert that *corporate governance is also the association between multiple stakeholders to the performance and directions of organisations. The primary participants are the shareholders, the management and the board of directors* (Tricker 2009) However, in its 2004 update, the OECD describes what corporate governance involves and provides that the existence of "effective corporate governance is a necessary condition to enable effective running of a market economy" (OECD 2004, p. 11).

As mentioned above already, we can draw two important observations on the OECD's perception of the role of the company here. Firstly, it is assumed that the company serves purely as an agency for wealth-maximisation for all concerned. The shareholders' interests are assumed to be synonymous with those of the company and the role and interests of stakeholders are narrowly defined in terms of economic activity "wealth, jobs, and the sustainability of financially sound enterprises" (Hong 2011). Secondly, stakeholders are carefully defined in close legal terms: only rights protected by law—whether through contract or by statute—need be respected. Wider, non-statutory or non-contractual relationships are not considered in this framework. In the context of the banking industry, this may allow bank supervisors to be included in the corporate governance of banks because of financial law and regulation and therefore implies that bank regulation and supervision of bank governance can be treated as an external governance mechanism. Similarly, as Cobbaut and Lenoble define it; "corporate governance refers to a legal and de facto framework of rules and policies for the management and supervision of a company" (Cobbaut and Lenoble 2003, p. 35). Corporate governance thus refers to the relationships between the company's various stakeholders.

The importance of governance to ensure the economic health of a company is highlighted in the online encyclopaedia of corporate governance in their definition which focuses on the economics side of governance, "Corporate governance is a field in economics that investigates how to secure/motivate efficient management of corporations by the use of incentive mechanisms, such as contracts, organisational designs and legislation. This is often limited to the question of improving financial performance; for example, how the corporate owners can secure/motivate that the corporate managers will deliver a competitive rate of return". Consistent with the above definition, Shleifer and Vishny (1997, p. 737) state that "corporate governance deals with the means and the mechanisms regarding the manner in which corporate financiers guarantee their investment returns".

Producing a singular definition of corporate governance is not a simple thing to do. You can attempt to focus just on boundaries of a singular country, such as the United Kingdom, but even then, deciding a core meaning of the discipline is challenging and complex depending on the philosophical viewpoint of the author or stakeholder (e.g. government, policy maker, theorist, etc.). It seems that existing definitions of the subject fall along a spectrum with a narrow view at one end and more inclusive "broad" views placed at the other. The narrow view of corporate governance seems to restrict it as the relationship between a company and its shareholders. This is the traditional finance paradigm expressed in agency theory. At the other end of the spectrum, corporate governance may be seen as a web of relationships between a company and its owners, employees, customers, suppliers, bondholders, to name a few. This broader view is thus gradually attracting greater attentions and is brought to the forefront of policy and practice in the United Kingdom, United States and elsewhere.

The term "corporate governance" is susceptible to both broad and narrow definitions—and many of the codes in the European Union corporate governance structure identified do not even attempt to articulate what is encompassed by the term. Table 4.1 illustrates some of the selected definitions of Corporate Governance which includes examples of definitions used in codes emanating from both the EU Member States and pan- European and international sources.

Table 4.1 Selections of key definitions of corporate governance

No	*Corporate governance definition*	*Source*
1	"*Corporate governance is the system by which companies are directed and controlled*".	Cadbury Report, Report (UK)
2	"*'Corporate governance' refers to the set of rules applicable to the direction and control of a company*".	Cardon Report (Belgium)
3	"*[Corporate governance is] [t]he goals, according to which a company is managed, and the major principles and frameworks which regulate the interaction between the company's managerial bodies, the owners, as well as other parties who are directly influenced by the company's dispositions and business (in this context jointly referred to as the company's stakeholders). Stakeholders include employees, creditors, suppliers, customers and the local community*".	Nørby Report & Recommendations, Introduction (Denmark)
4	"*Corporate governance describes the legal and factual regulatory framework for managing and supervising a company*".	Berlin Initiative Code, Preamble (Germany)
5	"*Corporate Governance, in the sense of the set of rules according to which firms are managed and controlled, is the result of norms, traditions and patterns of behaviour developed by each economic and legal system.. ..*"	Preda Report, (Italy)
6	"*[T]he concept of Corporate Governance has been understood to mean a code of conduct for those associated with the company. ..consisting of a set of rules for sound management and proper supervision and for a division of duties and responsibilities and powers affecting the satisfactory balance of influence of all the stakeholders*".	Peters Report (Netherlands)
7	"*Corporate Governance is used to describe the system of rules and procedures employed in the conduct and control of listed companies*".	Securities Market Commission (CMVM) (Portugal)
8	"*[C]orporate governance. .. involves a set of relationships between a company's management, its board, its shareholders and other stakeholders. Corporate governance also provides the structure through which the objectives of the company are set, and the means of attaining those objectives and monitoring performance are determined*".	OECD Principles, Preamble

(continued)

Table 4.1 (continued)

No	*Corporate governance definition*	*Source*
9	"*Corporate governance comprehends that structure of relationships and corresponding responsibilities among a core group consisting of shareholders, [supervisory] board members and managers designed to best foster the competitive performance required to achieve the corporation's primary objective*".	Millstein Report to OECD, pp. 13

Source Created by the author using various reports, (Akuffo 2018)

The majority of the definitions articulated in the codes relate corporate governance to "control" of the company, of corporate management, or of company or managerial conduct. Perhaps the simplest and most common definition of this sort is that provided by the Cadbury Report (UK), which is frequently quoted or paraphrased. This widely accepted definition of the subject in the United Kingdom has not changed from 1992. Following the global financial crisis, the Walker Review (2009) report—A review of corporate governance in UK banks and other financial industry entities—describes corporate governance as "the role of corporate governance is to protect and advance the interest of shareholders through setting the strategic direction of a company and appointing and monitoring capable management to achieve this" (Walker 2009, p. 19). It was, however, very disappointing for the report to place emphasis on shareholder views on governance despite the UK government (i.e. tax payer funds) commissioning the report due to the global devastation caused by the financial crisis on businesses including stockholders, employees, households and the economy in general. The UK legislative guidance retains the Cadbury Committee's definition of corporate governance, which states that: *Corporate Governance is the system by which companies are directed and controlled[;] [b]oards of directors are responsible for the governance of their companies [and] [t]he board's actions are subject to laws, regulations and the shareholders in general meeting* (FRC 2010, para 2).

Under this definition, corporate governance is concerned with structures and the allocation of responsibilities within companies. It deals with the decision-making at the level of the board of directors and is therefore to be distinguished from the day-to-day operational management of the company by the senior management (FRC 2010, para 3). When reading it together with the UK Companies Act 2006 (c.46), Section 172, corporate governance also deals with the different internal and external governance mechanisms which ensure that all decisions taken by the board of directors are in line with the objectives of a company and its shareholders, taking into account the interests of other stakeholders. Further, this definition, by explicitly stating that the board's actions are subject to financial laws and regulations which focus on financial stability and market confidence, leaves room for potentially conflicting definitions for the banking industry that can be interpreted with either agency theory or stakeholder perspective.

Another related theme common to the definitions of corporate governance found in these codes concerns "supervision" of the company or of management. In addition, a number of definitions relate corporate governance to a legal framework, rules and procedures and private sector conduct. Finally, some of the codes (this is common in the definitions in the international codes) speak of governance encompassing relationships between shareholders, (supervisory) boards and managers.

However, it is interesting to note that definitions of corporate governance become more precise when the specific characteristics of individual industries are taken into account. Bank supervisors' perception of corporate governance, as embodied in the BCBS, (Principles for Enhancing Corporate Governance) is much wider. It regards corporate governance as encompassing the standards for decision-making within a company, the duties of directors and senior managers, the internal structure of the firm and the relationship between the corporation and its shareholders and other stakeholders. The BCBS guidance states that a bank's corporate governance involves: The manner in which the business and affairs of a bank are governed by its board and senior management, including how they: set the bank's strategy and objectives; determine the bank's risk tolerance/appetite; operate the bank's business on a day-to-day basis; protect the interest of depositors, meet shareholder obligations, and take into account the interests of other recognised stakeholders; and align corporate activities and behaviour with the expectation that the bank will operate in a safe and sound manner, with integrity and in compliance with applicable laws and regulations (BCBS 2010).

Such a concept of corporate governance goes beyond the Corporate Governance Code's and the OECD's definitions in three respects.

First, it has the regulatory objectives of financial stability and bank safety and soundness in mind; second, it implies that senior management is also responsible for corporate governance and the day-to-day operational management within the domain of corporate governance. Put differently, it implies that corporate governance also deals with substantive management issues and the pertinent decision-making by the board and senior management by, inter alia, requiring them to set up a risk management system. Third, it regards corporate governance as dealing with the internal structure of the firm, i.e. with internal structures below the level of the company's board and senior management.

It is important to note that each of the published definitions of corporate governance adopts a different view of the subject. The variations between the definitions illuminate the different perspectives taken by the authors. In fact, those who see corporate governance as principally concerning the activities of the shareholders, the board and management (Monk and Minow 2008) in rendering accountability has in fact occupied a strong emphasis comparatively. Other contributors on the other hand recognise the context in which corporate governance is practised and these include the regulators, auditors and the market institutions involved in the provision of capital (OECD 2001). With the widest focus are those who recognise that an understanding of corporate governance needs to involve all and every element that affects the exercise of power over corporations (Clarke 2004; Tricker 2009 and this book).

However, many of the "definitions" of corporate governance are merely descriptions of practices or preferred orientations. For example, many authors describe corporate governance in terms of a system of structuring, operating and controlling a company with a view to achieving long-term strategic goals to satisfy shareholders, creditors, employees, customers and suppliers, and complying with the legal and regulatory requirements, apart from meeting environmental and local community needs. Additionally, there is substantial interest in how external systems and institutions, including markets, influence corporate governance in offering effective accountability.

4.3 Exploring the Association Between Corporate Governance and Concept of Accountability

There has recently been a number of growing discussions within the academics, practitioners, and development communities about the different accountability typologies and its impact on corporate governance. This sub-section presents the academic and outlines prior literature regarding the nature and the relationship between accountability and corporate governance within the finance and accounting studies.

4.3.1 Overview of Concept and Definition

Accountability is one of the cornerstones of good corporate governance; however, it can be difficult for scholars and practitioners alike to navigate the myriad of different types of accountability. Accountability in this book is, however, considered to be a vital component of effective corporate governance overall to various stakeholders.

An important theme of corporate governance is the nature and extent of accountability of particular individuals in the organisation, and mechanisms that try to reduce or eliminate the principal–agent problem. A great deal of effort has been dedicated by many scholars to designating the "right" corporate accountees. In the days of the classic debate between Adolf Berle and Merrick Dodd during the early 1930s, the question had been formulated as "For whom are corporate managers trustees?' (Berle and Means 1932). This debate took place against the backdrop of the famous 1919 ruling in Dodge v. Ford in the USA (Licht 2002, p. 2) which squarely pointed out shareholders as the sole beneficiaries of the corporation, and hence, as accountees of corporate officers. Characterising the relationship between shareholders and corporate officers as one of trust has undergone several revisions over time in the USA, UK and in other common law jurisdictions.

The US Congress in 1909 passed a series of legislative acts that developed into the basis of the corporate income tax. With the ratification of the Sixteenth Amendment in 1916, the taxation of corporate profits became a law. As a result, simple bookkeeping developed into more complex accounting issues. The income tax requirement coupled with the financial audit created large amounts of organised information about the financial position of the business. Managers were now expected to use this financial information to better manage the corporation (Washburn 1996). However, the seminal ruling in the Michigan courts, *Dodge* v. *Ford Motor Company in 1919, indeed* set the legal tone for management responsibility and corporate governance. The court ruled that: "A business corporation is organized and carried on primarily for the profit of the shareholders". Mere ownership of a business gave way to the new concept of creating profits for owners. Managers were responsible for coordinating the business to achieve this goal (Grant 2003).

As the stock market plunged and the Great Depression unfolded, Berle and Means published their landmark book, *The Modern Corporation and Private Property.* Written in 1932, it drew widespread attention to the fact that shareholders were legal owners of a corporation, but managerial authority was left to professionally trained executives. The book focused on the fiduciary responsibility of the corporation and the separation of ownership and control. Corporations, by this time, had grown beyond the optimal means to carry on business, and had developed to become a "method of property tenure and a means of organizing economic life. [...] the corporation, within it there exists a centripetal attraction which draws wealth into aggregations of constantly increasing size, at the same time throwing control into the hands of fewer and fewer men" (Berle and Means 1967, p. 3). Separation of ownership from control thus paved the way to the development of a market-based control mechanism and the evolution of the nexus of contract philosophical framework of corporate governance. It is therefore assumed that the nexus of contracts theorists argued that due to the incomplete nature of contracts problems of expropriation arise, the agent theoretic model focused on the behavioural motivations of conflicts of interests (Dragomir 2008).

Any system that assumes the delegation of power can refer to this definition: "Accountability is a means of concretizing relations between institutions, delineating responsibilities, controlling power, enhancing legitimacy, and ultimately promoting democracy" (Fisher 2004, p. 510). The aim of devising accountability is creating trust in governance institutions. Seal and Vincent-Jones (1997, p. 410) argue that the need for trust is especially acute in shaping long-term relationships. Any organisation that claims sustainability cannot refrain from keeping business risk at moderate levels. Stanton (1997, p. 684) quotes "Rosenfield who perceives accountability as the justifiable holding of one to account for personal actions or to answer a charge, justifiability being conferred by an authority relationship between the persons concerned. Inside the corporation, the authority relations may be evaluated from the two angles: the shareholder-value maximisation theory, and stakeholder theory". Spira (2001, p. 739) considers that individuals and organisations are discharged of their accountability duties by providing timely information to interested parties.

Romzek and Dubnick (quoted by Licht 2002, p. 8) provide a representative description of accountability, as follows: "*A relationship in which an individual or agency is held to answer for performance that involves some delegation of authority to act; […] accountability is a generic form of social relationship found in a variety of contexts… Accountability does not necessarily imply the existence of democracy; rather, it suggests any form of governance conducted through some delegation of authority.*"

Accountability belongs to an important category of social norms that may collectively be called "norms of governance". Norms of governance prescribe legitimate modes of wielding power—that is, they deal with use and abuse of power (Licht 2002, p. 14). Accountability may be held as the trademark of corporate governance, and particularly of the two descendants of this field of study: agency theory and stakeholder theory.

Political scientist Robert Behn opens his book-length discussion of democratic accountability in the United States with the following questions:

> *What do we mean by 'accountability'? What exactly do we mean when we say that that we want 'to hold people accountable'? We talk this way all the time. We are always talking about holding someone accountable. Yet, when we say it—'we are going to hold people accountable'—what do we really mean?".* (Behn 2001)

However, Behn acknowledges his inability to offer a good definition and conjectures that neither the accountability holders—the politicians, the stakeholders, the auditors, the scholars, the lawyers, or the journalists—know exactly what it means to "hold someone accountable".

The notion of accountability is an amorphous concept that is difficult to define in precise terms. However, broadly speaking, *accountability* exists when there is a relationship where an individual or body, and the performance of tasks or functions by that individual or body, are subject to another's oversight, direction or request that they provide information or justification for their actions. Therefore, the concept of corporate accountability involves two distinct stages: *answerability* and *enforcement*. Answerability refers to the obligation of the firm, its directors, other agencies/stakeholders and public officials to provide information about their decisions and actions and to justify them to the public and those institutions of accountability tasked with providing oversight and supervision. Enforcement suggests that the public or the institution responsible for accountability can sanction the offending party or remedy the contravening behaviour. As such, different institutions of accountability might be responsible for either or both of these stages.

The concept of accountability in corporate governance can be classified according to the type of accountability exercised and/or the person, group or institution the public official answers to. That is, what is the ultimate mechanism of accountability for effective corporate governance? The present debate within the accounting and finance literature as to the content of different forms of accountability is best conceptualised by reference to opposing forms of accountability. Accountability cannot exist without proper accounting practices; in other words, an absence of accounting means an absence of accountability.

4.3.2 *Mechanisms of Accountability in Corporate Governance in Accounting Studies*

Corporate governance is the policies and procedures a company implements to control and protect the interests of internal and external business stakeholders. It often represents the framework of policies and guidelines for each individual in the business. Bigger organisations often use corporate governance mechanisms to manage their businesses because of their size and complexity. Companies that are publicly held are also primary users of corporate governance mechanisms. The conventional studies proposed from the perspective of scholars in finance and accounting streams have concentrated on a range of corporate governance mechanisms of accountability used in various organisations, where accountability has been construed merely as firm accountability to shareholders as postulated by agency theory (Brennan and Solomon 2008). These researchers have tended to emphasise on two key groups i.e. internal and external mechanisms to demonstrate accountability in corporate governance. The overall effectiveness of the governance system is determined by the combination of internal and external mechanisms. They both must function coherently and drive the desired behaviours. A modification in

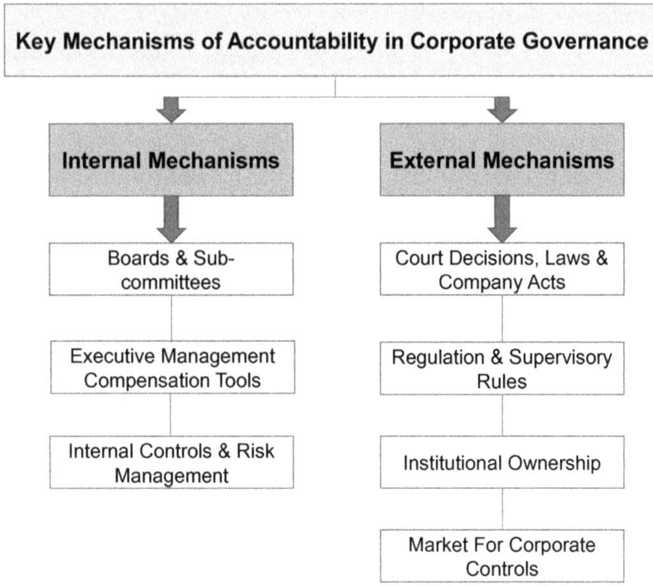

Fig. 4.1 Key mechanisms of accountability in corporate governance

one component would cause changes in the other. Figure 4.1 shows the current mechanisms of accountability in corporate governance in accounting studies. The three main internal company governance mechanisms are centred around boards or board performance, independents control functions and executive management compensation (Solomon 2007; Tricker 2009). In fact, each mechanism has its own set of vital, and unique, responsibilities. In many systems the activities of the three groups are reinforced by codes of conduct and best practices that are intended to promote proper behaviour.[1]

It is critical in accountable corporate governance for internal and external stakeholders including shareholders to have a fair, balanced and understandable assessment of the company's position and prospects so they can choose where and when to invest their capital. The board

[1] See further detail discussion by Banks E. (2004). *Internal Governance Mechanisms: Corporate Accountability*. In: Corporate Governance. Finance and Capital Markets Series. Palgrave Macmillan, London

needs to consider what accountability means and then address it and demonstrate its commitment. External corporate governance mechanisms include legal systems and regulations, shareholder monitoring, debt-holder monitoring, market for corporate controls, labour and product markets. Interestingly, while offering managerial accountability is not easy within corporate governance for either internal or external mechanisms, it should however be a process that helps businesses manage risks, protect existing value and enable further value-creation. A company's board is publicly accountable for its successes and challenges. This means demonstrating responsibility for its decision-making. But accountability is more than meeting regulatory requirements or explaining how things went wrong, it is about holding others to account and being accountable to others. While not all decisions can be shared outside the business, the right tone can be established for shareholders and wider stakeholders through the way a company communicates its strategy, risks and results. They should be able to understand a board's decision-making process: its responsibility, challenges and how it plans to address them. Informed stakeholders can therefore weigh up the risks and make their own judgements; the ill-informed can only react, or overreact, to events.

Moreover, several studies in accounting and accountability emphasise that balancing power in an organisation ensures that no one individual has the ability to overreach resources. Separating duties between board members, directors, managers and other individuals ensures that everyone's responsibility is well within reason for the organisation. The mechanisms of accountability also can separate the number of functions that one division or department completes within an organisation. Constructing well-defined roles also keeps the organisation flexible, ensuring that operational changes or new hires can be made without interrupting current operations. Additionally, the law in many national systems holds the boards and executive directors of corporations to certain standards in order to enforce proper accountability. These standards as many scholars argued revolve around attention to business, fidelity to corporate interests, and exercise of reasonable business judgment.

Various pieces of research have been completed looking at board effectiveness and the impact they can have on shareholder value and corporate profitability. The core essence of the work was regarding various attempts made to add to shareholder value by increasing the effectiveness of the board—these included things such as introducing a board of subcommittees, the impact of non-executive directors, separating the role of chief executive officer and the board chairman. One area of study that was completed by numerous accounting scholars (Byrd and Hickman 1992; Ezzamel and Watson 1997; Hermalin and Weisbach 1991; Kirkbride and Letza 2005 among others) where they focused on the impact of hiring non-executive directors combined with their task of monitoring firm management on behalf of their shareholders. Another investigation conducted by Dahya et al. in 2002 took the approach of looking at the interconnection of top executive turnover and financial performance with the aim of unpicking further the relationship between board of directors and management effectiveness. Overall, it has been determined that there is a positive correlation between the total non-executive directors on a board and the resultant financial performance of firms (e.g. Kaplan and Reishus 1990; Ferris et al. 2003). All the accounting research overwhelmingly is based on shareholder-centric agency theory which dominates scholarly work in accounting and finance research (Brennan and Solomon 2008).

The use of board of directors' subcommittees is another key area of mechanisms of board accountability in corporate governance frameworks for ensuring board effectiveness and improvement. A number of accounting studies that have examined this area includes for example, Main and Johnston (1993); Newman and Mozes (1999); Newman (2000) examined the mechanism of board remuneration committees and suggested that it improves board effectiveness. Also, the work of Ruigrok et al. (2006) investigated board effectiveness and nomination committees. The work of Jensen and Murphy (1990) and Core et al. (1999) examined the association between executive remuneration and financial performance. Other accounting research has even proposed that the mere presence of board remuneration committees influences the level and structure of senior executive pay (Conyon and Peck 1998), although some other works have found evidence to the contrary (Daily et al. 1998). Nonetheless, a number of academic scholars in accounting and finance have sought to criticise the measurement variables used for these studies. Brennan and Solomon (2008) infer that the use of "managerial turnover, proportion of non-executive directors, CEO duality and existence/composition of board subcommittees are crude proxies for board effectiveness' and calls have been made into studies to include a more appropriate method relating to firm performance, particularly measures of CEO competence and activity".

Another important external corporate accountability mechanism in directing and monitoring the behaviour of senior managers in corporations is via the use of "market for corporate controls". A multitude of governance studies in general have sought to focus on different forms, namely: "proxy contests, friendly mergers and takeovers and hostile takeovers" and their association with firm performance. One key example of such important research was provided by Jensen and Ruback (1983)—a seminal research which recognised corporate takeover as a disciplining mechanism over company management, again within the finance paradigm of agency theory. However, there are very limited studies in this area of governance that focuses on financial institutions. Another example of vital external accountability mechanism research for improving corporate governance is regarding the role of institutional investors and their emergent impact in monitoring and controlling corporate management (Coffee 1991; Karpo et al. 1996; Holland 1998; Faccio and Lasfer 2000). It is important to emphasise that the role of institutional investors in advancing the development of corporate governance has been very significant in the United Kingdom,[2] United States and the European Union (Solomon 2007; Monk and Minow 2004, 2008).

Demonstrating accountability—particularly in the annual report—gains stakeholder trust and earns capital; be it investment funds, supplier working capital or the commitment of employees and customers. Finance studies tend to rely on audits as a key component of accountable governance mechanisms in internal controls. Audits are an independent review of a company's business and financial operations. These corporate governance mechanisms ensure that businesses or organisations follow national accounting standards, regulations or other external guidelines. Shareholders, investors, banks and the general public rely on this information to provide an objective assessment of an organisation. Audits also can improve an organisation's standing in the business environment. Mechanisms of both transparency (alignment of interests between shareholders and management) and accountability tools, such as audit committees, internal audit and risk management (assuring the expected standard of financial reports) have long been major topics of study for accounting and finance specialists. A specific study that took place was by Cohen

[2] There are four vital types of institutional investors namely pension funds, life insurers, unit trusts and investment trusts with important influence in the corporate world (see Solomon 2007 for further discussion and literature)

et al. (2004) which looked at the impact of regulations (such as the stock exchange, the court, etc.), financial analytics, shareholders and furthered the links between corporate governance mechanisms and the quality of financial reports (Brennan and Solomon 2008).

Moreover, an area of widespread research has been regarding audit committees as board mechanisms—they serve to improve accountability in both accounting tasks in a firm and financial reporting (e.g. DeZoort and Salterio 2001; Gendron et al. 2004; Turley and Zaman 2007 and also DeZoort et al. 2002 offered a detailed literature review on the same topics). The effect of internal audit mechanism as an accountability measure has had limited research completed on it. Other finance scholars such as Raghunandan et al. (2001), Turley and Zaman (2007) and Gramling et al. (2005) have produced detailed works on this topic also. Again, these studies have extensively been based on an agency theory theoretical perspective.

Financial reporting, voluntary disclosures and accounting are all mechanisms of transparency that within governance research are normally approached from the agency theory angle where transparency is achieved by disclosures to shareholders. This transparency is vital in ensuring alignment of the interests of both shareholders and managers (e.g. Bushman and Smith 2001; Healy and Palepu 2001). Research has been completed looking at the impact that corporate governance has had on transparency and corporate disclosures. Some researchers have approached this from the perspective of the firm (e.g. Cheng and Courteney 2006) and others of the country concerned (e.g. Bushman and Smith 2001, 2003; Francis et al. 2003). There is a number of factors said to manipulate the level of both disclosure and transparency within corporate governance. These range across internal governance mechanisms (such as board independence, board of directors/committees, shared ownership) and also external mechanisms (such as the legal system of the country concerned). A key mechanism that was referenced within the corporate governance framework that can really show accountability is the systems of internal control within companies, more work would be beneficial to unpick this further. Other researchers, such as Linsley and Shrives (2006) have conducted work looking at other mechanisms such as assessment, management, disclosure and risk identification.

In departing from the shareholder-centric focus and moving towards a wider stakeholder-centric model of governance and accountability mechanisms, the hunger for more research on these newly positioned theoretical frameworks is increasing along with a desire for more studies on corporate governance and its accountability mechanisms to widen the scope of work available within the finance and accounting discipline. A number of academic works have been conducted to support the need for extending the scope of accountability mechanisms beyond the traditional agency theory, especially in the United Kingdom (Solomon 2007). Also, the 2003 Tyson Report in the United Kingdom for example, sought to broaden boardroom diversity and inclusivity, by encouraging non-executive directors to be drawn from more diverse backgrounds, representing a broader group of external constituencies. Furthermore, international work has also been established in moving forward towards the stakeholder accountability governance method. As Brennan and Solomon (2008, p. 11) offered—"The two King Reports (1994; 2002), produced in South Africa, represented a turning point in the international agenda for corporate governance reform, as they drew attention to the need for companies to act responsibly towards their diverse stakeholders. These reports laid the foundations for the more stakeholder-oriented code of best practice produced by the Commonwealth Association on Corporate Governance (CACG) (1999)". The Organisation for Economic Cooperation and Development (OECD) has influenced the area of accountability to stakeholders by establishing that the issues of the stakeholder need to be one of the chief principles when striving to deliver best practice corporate governance.

Solomon (2007) and Tricker (2009) have both looked into the movement within financial organisations towards an approach that is more stakeholder focused and the increased spotlight on financial services accountability to a wider set of stakeholders. Institutional investors are more commonly being utilised as a mechanism to enhance corporate governance in financial services and studies are now looking at their role and the increase of the use of stakeholder focused approaches also. The movement has extended further with financial companies broadening their scope of considerations even further. Freshfields Bruckhaus Deringer (2005) documented the elements of governance that are now starting to be considered by focusing on core groupings such as social, environmental and governance considerations under the topic of institutional investment. This is further evidenced in studies that focused on the corporate governance mechanism of socially responsible investment. These investments work to allow their investment firms to adapt their approaches in governance to be more inclusive of their stakeholders (e.g.

Solomon and Solomon 2006). This shift in focus in the financial service sector is inspiring more investigation in this wider area of accountability within corporate governance.

Conventionally in accounting studies, transparency has been more concentrated on shareholders rather than stakeholders. The transition away from agency theory frameworks towards stakeholder focused ones has led to increased studies within accounting of the topic of transparency mechanisms aimed at the inclusion of stakeholders. Examples of such transparency mechanisms include social, environmental and sustainability reporting and assurance with the aim to enhance firm accountability to wider stakeholders (e.g. Unerman et al. 2007).

However, other studies (especially, Sikka 2008) emphasise the question of "who" regarding the accountability and corporate governance in his essay. According to Brennan and Solomon (2008), Sikka's study made an important contribution to the understanding of "stakeholder accountability" in corporate governance inquiry by completely concentrating on the significance of 'workers' function inside the structures of corporate governance. Sikka (2008) begins on the assumption that these groups of vital stakeholders have been overlooked, both in terms of the academic inquiry, and in the practice of corporate governance. He concluded by emphasising accountability to stakeholders as a critical corporate governance function. Additionally, the research broadened corporate governance study alongside the aspect of corporate accountability, expanding the application of theoretical paradigm by adopting a political economy perspective on his research question and extending the method of research employing statistics available publicly (Brennan and Solomon 2008, p. 21).

4.4 The Nature of Discosure Studies in Corporate Governance

4.4.1 *Importance and Nature of Research Evidence*

Corporate governance disclosure has a pivotal role in the abovementioned argument. Thus, any definition of corporate governance needs to encompass fundamental values of transparency, accountability, fairness, and responsibility. The Association of Chartered Certified Accountants defines three main purposes of corporate governance which are: (1) to ensure the board, as representatives of the organisation's owners, protects resources and allocates them to make planned progress towards the organisation's defined purpose; (2) to ensure those governing and managing an organisation account appropriately to its stakeholders and (3) to ensure shareholders and, where appropriate, other stakeholders, can and do hold boards to account. In fact, the World Bank argued that inherent in all three of these factors is the requirement to transparently disclose the corporate governance structure, processes and issues faced by the company. Organisations need to demonstrate their authentic commitment to these values in order to create and sustain the confidence of investors, stakeholders, and society as a whole. Consequently, transparency about corporate governance is a vital element in accounting reporting (Abraham and Cox 2007).

It is important to note that the strength of an organisation's corporate governance systems and the quality of public disclosures are becoming increasingly important to business for a number of reasons. As sustainability becomes an ever more critical business issue, stakeholders are paying more attention to what is reported and how. The global financial crisis has sharpened the lens through which corporate governance structures are held to account and expectations around transparency are raising the bar for more comprehensive and proactive disclosures from forward-thinking organisations, as opposed to the release of corporate governance details or policies in a "reactive" fashion. A distinction is growing between those that maintain ongoing communications as part of an integrated approach to corporate governance, and those that produce isolated or single issue-based communications, for example, in response to legislation or as a risk management exercise. Organisations that see disclosing information on corporate governance as an opportunity to be transparent with stakeholders can potentially use reporting processes to drive improvements to their structures and processes internally (but good reporting doesn't necessarily lead to good governance, as has been demonstrated in the economic downturn in 2007/2008).

Generally, the existence of the right corporate governance structure at a financial organisation contributes to enhancing trust among the diverse stakeholders that are interested in the institution's performance. This is because a good governance system builds the various appropriate mechanisms for aligning management's objectives and goals with those of the shareholders and other stakeholders. Equally, an insufficient disclosure of corporate governance structures at banking and other financial organisations may generate a perceived image of lack of ability of senior directors to appropriately manage its underlying liabilities and assets. This could spark a steady exodus of deposits to rival organisations triggering a run on the banking firm in extreme situations.

"Disclosure" encapsulates the variety of information sources that are issued by firm. This includes items like the cash flow statements, balance sheets, profit and loss accounts, annual reports and the Operating and Financial Review (OFR).[3] Also covered underneath the disclosure umbrella is the voluntary communications a company may issue—something would be classed as a voluntary disclosure if it is outside of the mandated minimum (Core 2001). Examples of voluntary disclosures would be the AGM, press releases, information published on websites, management forecasts, etc. (Healy and Palepu 2001). To achieve an effective system of corporate governance that is accountable, transparency is a core component (OECD 2004). Disclosures to stakeholders is one of the best methods to attain this (Solomon 2007). To have a proficient capital market, disclosure is also a vital function.

In the stewardship concept, it has been recognised for many years that accounting is required to monitor the relationship between shareholders and management. Accounts have always been used to support investors with their decision making. It is believed by many that auditing and accounting were brought in as a mechanism to monitor dealings in the investment community. The research conducted by Watts and Zimmerman (1986) specifically focused on the use of financial accounting reporting to reduce the "information asymmetry". They discussed the agency theory approach of Jensen and Meckling (1976), inter alia, and showed that accounting plays a contracting role, as accounting is used in the nexus of contracts, aimed at monitoring managers. Inefficiencies in the market for information have resulted in the need for mandatory disclosure by companies.

Risk governance is a significant component of corporate governance disclosure, specifically within financial institutions. Within accounting and finance research, risk disclosure, found in annual financial statements of accounts, has increased its position in studies of accounting and regulatory systems across the breadth of the world (Abraham and Cox 2007; Linsley and Shrives 2006; Elzahar and Hussainey 2012). These authors utilised different measures within their data—e.g. Abraham and Cox

[3] The equivalent of the OFR in the USA is the MDA part of the financial statement reporting.

(2007) used the number of independent directors on company boards and the level of risk being reported, whereas the work of Elzahar and Hussainey (2012) compared both the company size and the amount of risk disclosure. This difference in approach may explain the reason for the mix of results identified and examples of inconsistency.

Research conducted by the United Nations that looked at countries within the OECD, determined that for risk reported, the internal accounting standards need to be bolstered. Currently, there appears to be "no consistent global set of generally accepted risk management accounting principles and reporting standards" (UNCTAD 2010) which can make risk disclosure somewhat difficult. The legal systems among many countries do not currently differ which also complicates the exact disclosure requirements on risk. An example where this has attempted to be mitigated, is in the United Kingdom, where they are utilising the comply or explain principle to their disclosures of corporate governance. Interestingly, although there is a legal requirement for corporations to complete financial reports, anyone failing to comply or misrepresenting information, face civil as opposed to criminal charges. The Sarbanes-Oxley Act (2002), as introduced in the United States, attributes more personal liability to directors and their disclosures. In the context of UK legislation, firms that do not disclose according to the guidelines would struggle to both attract investors and keep their listing on the stock market. This should be a good enough incentive to encourage directors to maintain respectable accounting processes.

Governance reporting is an element of corporate disclosure that has been to an extent ignored and also not at the forefront of the United Kingdom's development of corporate governance. A step towards improving this reporting area and clarifying what firms should be aware of when completing a disclosure of governance-related information stems from the collaboration between Independent Audit Limited[4] and the ACCA,[5] developed with the aim of addressing this issue. There are two elements to the resulting report (Independent Audit Limited 2006)—research-based accounts on current perceptions of governance reporting

[4] This independent organisation specialises in helping boards strengthen their leadership and control.

[5] The Association of Certified Chartered Accountants (ACCA) is the global body for professional accountants founded in 1904.

and also introducing a viable structure for disclosing corporate governance information.

4.4.2 *Empirical Surveys on Measuring Quality, Contents and Levels of Details Accounting Disclosure Reporting*

4.4.2.1 *Overview of the Method of Content Analysis in Accounting Studies*

The prior studies by accounting scholars describe two general approaches to content analysis, namely mechanical and interpretative technique in analysing corporate governance and disclosures. Details of methodological and literature can be found in the work of Akuffo (2018) and Campbell et al. (2010). However, this section provides a brief overview of the two methods of disclosure studies. The aim of the "mechanical" method is to capture and explain a proxy assumed to carry meaning and reporting intent (e.g. Beck et al. 2010). These studies are characteristically "form oriented", meaning the emphasis is on either a volumetric or frequency capture and semiotic assumptions tend to be supplied. Smith and Taffler (2000) contrasted this with "meaning orientation" suggesting that "form orientated" content analysis involves "routine counting of words or concrete references" while "meaning orientated" analysis "focuses on the underlying themes in the texts under investigation" (p. 627). In this regard, meaning orientation has a greater interpretative element than in the mechanical assumptions of form orientation. Also, it can be argued that mechanical studies provide information about disclosure volumes and/or frequencies and help to draw associations between different variables that might impact on disclosure behaviour. Typical mechanical data capture is by word counts, sentence counts, (summed) page proportions, frequency of disclosure, and high/low disclosure ratings. In most cases, the semiotic assumption applies in that "the volume of disclosure signifies the relative importance of those disclosures (to the discloser)". Additionally, it is evident from Table 5.1B that mechanical content analysis approaches have been dominant in the prior literature, with a minority reporting mainly interpretative methods.

On the other hand, we observed that interpretative analysis characteristically endeavours to take meaning by disaggregating narrative into its constituent parts and then describing the contents of each disaggregated component (e.g. Campbell et al. 2010; Raar 2002; Wiseman 1982). The purpose of this type of interpretative study is to increase better understanding of how and what is communicated (e.g. Aerts 1994, 2005) and hence placed importance with regard to the quality, richness or qualitative character of the narrative. The technique leans therefore towards interpretation of text rather than attempting to record the mechanics of its conveyance. These types of studies characteristically look for an understanding of how meaning is being understood and the effects of the narratives on users.

4.4.2.2 Studies Measuring Quality and Reporting Details in Accounting Disclosures

The measure used to capture the actual contents of narratives is important when researchers are interested in understanding disclosure practices (e.g. Hammond and Miles 2019; Toms 2002). While it is generally accepted that "mechanical" content analysis has a clear limitation in terms of reliability of findings (e.g. Wiseman 1982), there is less agreement on how the content analysis can be used to capture information content on qualitative dimensions. The weight or the metric used to measure the quality of disclosure is quite debatable and contentious in the accounting research and is generally regarded as an arduous job for most researchers. According to Aburaya, this arduous task "can be attributed to the unresolved theoretical debate around the concept of quality itself, and consequently, the difficulty of determining a clear and accepted disclosure quality measurement. However, in addition to the way in which quality is defined, data source, reliability issues, concerns and statistical inaccuracy examined are also highlighted in the literature (Hammond and Miles 2019)" (Aburaya 2012, p. 94). In fact, in corporate governance studies, the metric used to assess or compute the quality of corporate governance will broadly hang on the investigators' notion of defining quality that befits the aim of the research.

A huge volume of studies exists in social accounting and finance literature covering the type, features and the quality of disclosures (Gray et al. 1995a, b; Beattie et al. 2004; Solomon 2007; Tricker 2009). A selection of academic studies summarising the areas and the disclosure metric used are presented in Table 4.1a. However, the work of Beattie et al. (2004) implied that the research approach in disclosure studies in social and environmental accounting can be observed in two standard methods of evaluating disclosures, namely: "the use of subjective analyst disclosure quality ranking and the use of researcher-constructed disclosure indices

Table 4.1a Particular academic research measuring quality of disclosure reporting

Researcher name & year	*Quality measure and area of disclosure*	*Type of quality measure*
Wiseman, J. (1982)	The nature of environmental disclosures	Index created by the author Ordinal ranking—used a four-point rating score (0–3) measure
Guthrie, J.E. and Matthews, M.R. (1985)	Social responsibility disclosure	Index created by the author Used four dimensions of themes as a measure
Freedman and Stagliano (1992)	Reporting of social indicators	Index created by the author Four element index to measure quality
Patten (1995)	Reporting of social indicators	Index created by the author Two-dimensional rating index—presence or absence of a range of issues
Gray et al. (1995b)	Reporting of social and environmental indicators	Index created by the author 3 quality category index
Gamble et al. (1995)	Environmental disclosures	Index created by the author A weighted score based on a ten-point scale
Robertson and Nicholson (1996)	Reporting of social responsibility indicators	Index created by the author
Walden and Schwartz (1997)	Environmental disclosure	Index created by the author A dichotomous indices within a category—presence or absence of an issue
Hughes et al. (2001)	Environmental disclosures	Index created by the author 0-4 rating scale based on Wiseman (1982)

(continued)

Table 4.1a (continued)

Researcher name & year	*Quality measure and area of disclosure*	*Type of quality measure*
Raar (2002)	Environmental disclosure	Index created by the author A seven-point weight scale used (1-7)
Toms (2002)	Environmental disclosure	Index created by the author Ordinal rankings (0–5 qualitative score metric)
Hooks et al. (2002)	General disclosure	Index created by the author 0–5 weighted score used
Milne et al. (2003)	Triple bottom line reporting	Analyst disclosure quality ranking A score in 0–4 range used
Beretta and Bozzolan (2004)	Risk disclosure	Index created by the author Four different but complimentary dimensions
Beattie et al. (2004)	Voluntary disclosure	Index created by the author Four-dimensional framework for analysing narratives of main theme subtopic
Hammond and Miles (2019)	Reporting of social indicators	Index created by the author The use of dichotomous disclosure indices.
Al-Tuwaijiri et al. (2004)	Environmental disclosure	Index created by the author Weighted 0–4 scale for assigning of quality indicator based on an ordinal ranking index.
Chapman and Milne (2004)	Triple bottom line reporting	Analyst disclosure quality ranking Reporting items are score on a scale of 0–4

(continued)

Table 4.1a (continued)

Researcher name & year	*Quality measure and area of disclosure*	*Type of quality measure*
Hasseldine et al. (2005)	Environmental disclosure	Index created by the author Used a 0–5 qualitative scale
Van der Laan Smith et al. (2005)	Reporting of social and environmental indicators (external ratings vs. quality and information content)	Index created by the author Presence or absence through a dichotomous disclosure index
Van Staden and Hooks (2007)	Environmental disclosure	Index created by the author A dichotomous disclosure index and an ordinal ranking disclosure index (5-point scoring scale)
Gibson and O'Donovan (2007)	Environmental disclosure	Index created by the author
Raar (2007)	Reporting of social and environmental indicators	Index created by the author A ranking system of 7-point scale used
Gruning (2007)	General disclosure	Index created by the author 0–5 scoring model to measure seven categories
Beretta and Bozzolan (2008)	Forward-looking disclosure	Index created by the author A multi-dimensional analysis of categories
Clarkson et al. (2008)	Voluntary environmental disclosures	Index created by the author Used seven broad categories in GRI based on dichotomous index –presence or absence of an item.

(continued)

Table 4.1a (continued)

Researcher name & year	*Quality measure and area of disclosure*	*Type of quality measure*
Plumlee et al. (2009)	Voluntary environmental disclosures	Index created by the author Used GRI guidelines to assess the presence or absence of a disclosure
Moroney et al. (2009)	Environmental disclosure	Index created by the author Adopt a GRI for seven categories—presence or absence of an item based on a dichotomous index.
Bozzolan et al. (2009)	Forward-looking disclosure	Index created by the author A dichotomous index based on two different index measures.
Moneva and Cuella (2009)	Environmental disclosures	Index created by the author Use five categories of items
Campbell et al. (2010)	Voluntary and environmental reporting	Index created by the author 0–5 scoring scale used
Mouselli and Hussainey (2010)	General disclosure	Index created by the author
Sun et al. (2010)	Environmental disclosure	Index created by the author 0–3 quality scale used
Plumlee et al. (2010)	Voluntary environmental disclosures	Index created by the author Adopt a GRI score framework
Delmas and Blass (2010)	Environmental disclosure	Analyst disclosure quality ranking A dichotomous index based on GRI' weighted score.

(continued)

Table 4.1a (continued)

Researcher name & year	*Quality measure and area of disclosure*	*Type of quality measure*
Eugster and Wagner (2011)	Voluntary disclosure	Analyst disclosure quality ranking Used a six-point grading score
Glaum1 et al. (2011)	General disclosure	Analyst disclosure quality ranking A binary score (0–1) was used
Magness and Bewley (2011)	Environmental reporting	Index created by the author
Acerete et al. (2011)	Mandatory environmental disclosure	Index created by the author
Siddique et al. (2011).	Environmental disclosure	Index created by the author
Liu et al. (2011)	Environmental disclosure	Index created by the author
Clarkson et al. (2011)	Voluntary environmental disclosure	Index created by the author

Source Adapted by the author using various reference sources
Explanation note (a) Dichotomous disclosure index: Assigning a numerical score founded on the incidence (existence or non-existence) of information items within a category of the contents
(b) Dichotomous disclosure indices: Assigning a numerical score founded on the incidence (existence or non-existence) of information items within the categories of contents, by referring to more than one index
(c) Ordinal disclosure index: Assigning a numerical score with a weighted allocation to different disclosure items within the categories of the contents, that is centred regarding apparent significance on individual element to various groups of users

where the amount of disclosure is used as a proxy for disclosure quality" (Aburaya 2012, p. 101). However, during the critical reviewing of the prior research, we note that the studies were overwhelmingly focused on corporate environmental reporting practices and quality characteristics in general firms rather than banking institutions.

The academic work conducted by Wiseman (1982) focused on assessing the precision and disclosures reporting quality content that was presented in the financial statement annually. This research particularly focuses on environmental disclosure dimensions using a four-rating scoring system (3, 2, 1 & 0) to determine the level of quality disclosure content. Wiseman's research conclusion disclosure was based on the scoring constructed on either the presence or absence and the degree of specificity of each of the information items (Aburaya 2012). Rating score 3 represented the highest disclosure quality and zero represents the least or non-disclosure of a category content.

In a similar study conducted, that used a four dimension rating index according to Aburaya (2012), "Guthrie and Matthews (1985) measured both the scope and the degree of social responsibility reporting in the annual financial reports of Australian companies using four dimensions, namely: (i) Theme, (ii) Evidence, (iii) Amount and (iv) Location. A method of recording and quantification of the four dimensions was used. However, these methods did not attempt to capture the qualitative features or characteristics of the data. A particular link to quality measurement is the method of quantification, where data are classified into monetary, non-monetary and declarative. Moreover, a new category was introduced into the measurement process, that of news type where the assessment included whether the statements reflect well, badly or neutrally on the reporting entity" *(*Aburaya 2012, p. 95). Although, this research does not explicitly measure quality, the interpretation of the conclusion was based on the notion of quantification of quality information items reported in the annual statement.

Furthermore, a key piece of work that looked at modes of creating an information database to investigate both environmental and social reporting by companies based in the United Kingdom, classified the quality assessment groupings as follows—"(i) evidence—whether the nature of the disclosed information is monetary, non-monetary quantitative, or declarative, (ii) news—whether the news communicated by the disclosure is good, bad, or neutral and (iii) auditability—whether the information disclosed is verified by an independent third party or not" (Gray et al. 1995b). Aburaya (2012) reflected on this work and the internal debate of the authors regarding the possibility that assessing quality of data shared could, in a small way, lessen the information that would be lost from the more commonly seen approach of obtaining such a large amount of disclosures.

Using a six framework of disclosure scoring index, Hooks et al. (2002), conducted their research to investigate and evaluate disclosure quality in financial statements in New Zealand from stakeholder responsibility and accountability standpoint. The information categories in the annual reports disclosed were assigned a score ranging from 0 to 5. The lowest quality score was assigned a weighted score of 0, while the highest information quality item was scored a maximum 5. Similarly, Milne et al. (2003) used a 5-level scoring index measure to investigate the level of detail and comprehensiveness of corporate environmental reporting based on 50 individual disclosure information elements.

Furthermore, using an improvement in prior methodological approach to disclosure index measures, Beretta and Bozzolan (2004) investigated and assessed risk disclosures from both quality and the amount of information items reported. However, according to Aburaya (2012) Ph.D. research, they commented on the same 2004 investigation from Beretta and Bozzolan and the detail of their framework that is constructed around four quality dimensions. Each has a specific function to perform that interlinks and is of benefit to the other—they are "the content of information disclosed; the economic sign attributed to expected impacts; the type of measures used to quantify and qualify the expected impacts; and the outlook orientation of the disclosure". Although these dimensions provided interesting areas of study, one criticism that has come to light is regarding the singular method for measuring the quality as they opted to join the quality and quantity of information disclosed together.

Also using a dichotomous approach, but as an alternative to capturing the incidence of the set of disclosure issues in qualitative description, Van der Laan Smith et al. (2005) defined disclosure quality according to whether it contained numerical terms. This numerical perspective on quality has been adopted in several studies, e.g. Adams et al. (1998), Patten (1995) and Toms (2002). Numerical matters have been taken in conjunction with other elements that the researchers have believed to signify aspects of disclosure quality, but there has been a wide variation in the way these items have been analysed. For instance, while Adams et al. (1998) and Patten (1995) included a presentation of quantifiable terms as a second dichotomous index after identifying the presence or absence of predetermined disclosure issues, others have integrated these numeric aspects by devising an increasing ordinal inclusion scale, whereby at each level a new item is added until all the desired items have been covered (Table 4.1b).

Table 4.1b Key prior studies in accounting showing the range of methods employed

Author	*Research question(s)*	*Method*	*Tool*	*Approach*
Wiseman (1982)	Relationship between environmental disclosure and environmental performance	Analysis of document	Two-dimensional Disclosure Index: 4 main themes and 18 categories & information content score	Mechanical combined with interpretative
Harte and Owen (1991)	Disclosure practises of perceived good reporters in the United Kingdom	Analysis of document	Dichotomous disclosure index	Mechanical
Ness and Mirza (1991)	Environmental disclosures in the oil industry and agency theory	Analysis of document	Disclosure index based on prior framework	Mechanical
Patten (1991)	Examine the effect of Exxon Oil spill on the environmental disclosures	Analysis of document	Disclosure Index based on Wiseman (1982)	Mechanical
Gray et al. (1995a, b)	Describe CSR reporting practise within United Kingdom	Analysis of document	Dichotomous disclosure index based on Ernst & Ernst	Mechanical
Buhr (1998)	How did company react to changes in legislation? How are abatement activities presented?	Triangulation/mixed method	Historical analysis, interviews and Analysis of document	Mechanical
Kolk (1999)	Analysis of different benchmark tools	Benchmark study	UNEP/Sustainability guidelines	Mechanical

(continued)

Table 4.1b (continued)

Author	*Research question(s)*	*Method*	*Tool*	*Approach*
Unerman (2000)	Complement to Milne & Adlers (1999) paper on method application	Analysis of document (multiple media)	Number of pages	Mechanical
Wilmhurst and Frost (2000)	Perception of importance of environmental issues and actual environmental disclosure	Analysis of documents	Volume count (sentences)	Mechanical
Cormier and Gordon (2001)	Relationship between company disclosure, size and ownership	Analysis of documents	Disclosure index based on Wiseman, 1982	Mechanical
Toms (2002)	Environmental reputation through disclosure quality	Analysis of documents	Analysis of survey	Mechanical
Campbell (2003)	Environmental disclosures as a means of legitimising corporations	Analysis of documents	Volume count (sentences)	Mechanical
Milne et al. (2003)	Triple Bottom Line reports in NZ and how they score with their reporting	Benchmark study	UNEP/Sustainability guidelines	Mechanical
Chapman and Milne (2004)	Reporting quality in NZBCSD	Benchmark study	UNEP/Sustainability guidelines	Mechanical

(continued)

Table 4.1b (continued)

Author	*Research question(s)*	*Method*	*Tool*	*Approach*
Patten and Crampton (2004)	Exploration of use of webpage to communicate environmental information to stakeholders	Analysis of documents (multiple media)	Disclosure index based on Wiseman (1982)	Mechanical
Hasseldine et al. (2005)	Environmental reputation management through disclosures	Based on Toms (2002)	Empirical	Mechanical
Buhr and Reiter (2006)	Company's disclosure as a measure of contribution and reflection on discourse of environmentalism	Discourse analysis	Framing following Eder (1996)	Interpretative
Coupland (2006)	Role of stand-alone reports for non-financial information disclosures	Discourse analysis	Disclosure categories initially deducted from literature, but then evolved inductively	Interpretative
Van Staden and Hooks (2007)	External ranking vs. quality and information content of environmental disclosures	Benchmark study	UNEP/Sustainability guidelines and other studies	Mechanical

Source Adapted from Campbell et al. (2010)

4.5 Gaps in Prior Research on Corporate Governance and Accountability in Accounting and Finance

4.5.1 *Measurement of Disclosure Quality in Corporate Governance Studies*

As discussed previously in this chapter, a large number of prior studies that have been conducted from accounting, economics and finance perspectives emphasised the relevance of corporate governance reporting by firms. It is noted from these studies that there are a range of elements that influenced disclosure practices in order to ensure a transparent report. Despite the existence of large literature in this area, the concepts of measuring and evaluating disclosure quality in governance still remain unresolved and contentious. From the prior research reviewed, there is limited understanding and agreement among these researchers regarding what metric to use to evaluate corporate governance disclosure consistently. This methodological shortcoming has also been highlighted by other governance researchers (Beattie et al. 2004; Beretta and Bozzolan 2008).

The findings from the empirical chapters of this book also adds support to the Campbell et al. (2010) study that "caution should be exercised in claiming that any content analysis method is capable of measuring 'quality' per se because fitness for purpose in a research ('this being the usual technical definition of quality, see for example, Slack, Chambers, Johnston and Betts 2009') can only be assessed by considering supporting evidence from information users perspective". The implication for this book is that, in addition to interpretive interrogation, it introduces a scale of information content akin to a qualitative scale which is capable of describing the level of information details contained in each coded piece of information.

4.5.2 *Causation and Endogeneity Problems*

Empirical evidence using various techniques has documented these relationships at the level of the country, the sector, and the individual firm and from the investor perspectives. Some of these studies suffer from econometric raised by endogeneity: that is, firms markets, or countries may adopt better corporate governance and perform better. However, the relationship is not from better corporate governance to improved performance; rather it is either the other way round or because some other factors drive both better corporate governance and better account for performance.

The literature on corporate governance examines the efficacy of alternative structures of ownership and the boards of directors and various other governance structures. While there is increasing evidence of the failure of certain governance structures to control and motivate managers to increase firm performance, the empirical evidence to date is mixed and gives little coherent evidence for the shape of an optimal governance structure. One explanation is that existing theories have not been sufficiently complete to include all major determinants of good corporate governance. Perhaps there will never be one optimal governance structure because no two firms, two markets, two legal regimes or two cultures are exactly the same, resulting in a highly complex issue of corporate governance in financial institutions. Ultimately governance structure is determined by a combination of the above factors and their dynamics. A more likely and useful outcome of the ongoing debate and research, perhaps, might be the increasing focus on stakeholder interest and concerns, and identification of some widely accepted guiding principles, rather than trying to find some specific mechanisms which are universally applicable, for effective corporate governance.

4.5.3 *Lack of Studies with Longitudinal Focus*

From the literature reviewed, minimal consideration has been paid to using longitudinal analysis to study within a particular sector of the corporate governance disclosures. It has also been noted that a focus on banks corporate governance within the United Kingdom is very rarely conducted. Hence, one overriding motivation for undertaking this piece of investigation work for this book was to research and explore corporate governance disclosures in the banking industry in the United Kingdom on a longitudinal basis.

An analysis of the literature discovered very few pieces of research that were undertaken using a longitudinal analytical approach when looking at disclosures in bank corporate governance (e.g. bank risk disclosures). These were either short or long-term pieces of research that spanned up to twelve years (i.e. 3–6 years or 10–12 years). However, the prior longitudinal studies considered, highlighted the fact that minimal emphasis has been given to either quality governance discussion or intra-sectoral disclosures (e.g. Hill and Short 2009; Abdelghany 2005; Poshakwale and Courtis 2005; Ismail and Rahman 2011; Helbok and Wagner 2006; Taylor et al. 2010). Also, two other elements are commonly neglected—quality features of corporate governance and limited emphasis in addressing stakeholder issues concerning the banking industry. Hence, the empirical research evidence in this book strive to examine and analyse the quality of corporate governance disclosure (including risk management disclosure aspects) in UK banks using a twelve-year-period timeframe.

4.5.4 *Lack of In-Depth Intra-sector Studies*

Most studies found from the literature in the field of corporate governance reporting have largely focused on comparative studies for inter-countries (for example, Poshakwale and Courtis 2005; Yong et al. 2005; Bischof 2009). To date, to the best of my knowledge, no preceding academic research has looked into the banking industry corporate governance disclosures by seeking to compare specific bank's individual approaches historically. Despite the work completed by some researchers on this area, they have tended to particularly examine only risk reporting in banking (for example, Bischof 2009). This is particularly important given the nature of systemic effect and the interrelation among banks (e.g. the case of Northern Rock and RBS in 2007/2008 in the United Kingdom; Lehman Brothers and Bear Stern failure in 2008 in the US and the immediate panic that followed and caused the global banking crash). Despite this limitation pre financial crisis of 2007/2008, the Walker Report 2009 in the United Kingdom offered a detailed review of corporate governance in the UK banking and other financial industry entities.

4.5.5 *Lack of Focus on Consistent Use of Governance Categories and Findings*

Various pieces of research into corporate governance have also adopted diverse forms of categorisation when conducting their study. This is most evident in the area of risk and risk management aspects of corporate governance as well as the use of performance metrics to account for corporate governance. Other previous studies often select just one category within governance (for example, a single category such as board size, board meeting, board compensation, etc.). Although there are an increasing number of disclosure studies that follow the approach of Meek et al. (1995), there are no criteria for the classification of categories or the items under each category.

However, the approach of Meek et al. (1995) and by using more than three categories may help to explain the disclosure practices and provide a better understanding of the need of several stakeholders. Such an extension is more important in the case of listed banking institutions that seek to enhance market transparency. In addition, limited emphasis has been given to combining the majority of categories of mechanisms of accountability in corporate governance. Thus, this book will strive to evaluate the quality of corporate governance disclosures that cover the majority, if not all, of the main categories of governance disclosure.

4.5.6 *Lack of Consistent and Conclusive Overall Findings*

Another key reproach regarding prior academic work on corporate governance reporting and each of the mechanisms of accountability are mainly drawn from the lack of consistent and definite research findings. These well-known limitations of inconsistency may be attributed to a number of factors, namely (a) limited standardised model (b) data sources variety employed and (c) non-existence of unified academic theoretical viewpoint to analyse the requisite associations being investigated (Tricker 2009; Solomon 2007; Monk and Minow 2008).

4.6 Conclusion

Based on the above review and discussions, the following key points can be identified and summarised:

One of the problems with the current debate on corporate governance is that there are many different, and often conflicting, views on the nature and purpose of the firm. This debate ranges from positive issues concerning how institutions actually work; to normative issues concerning what should be the firm's purpose and how to define governance. While there have been considerable attempts in the prior literature to define corporate governance in accounting and finance, definitions of corporate governance tend to vary widely (Tricker 2009; Solomon 2007). They tend to fall into two categories. The first set of definitions concerns itself with a set of behavioural patterns: that is, the actual behaviour of corporations, in terms of such measures as performance, efficiency, growth, financial structure and treatment of shareholders and other stakeholders. The second set concerns itself with the normative framework: that is, the rules under which firms are operating, with the rules coming from such sources as the legal system, the judicial system, financial markets, and factor (labour) markets. However, for studies of single countries or firms within a country, the first type of definition is the most logical choice. It considers such matters as how boards of directors operate the role of executive compensation in determining firm performance, the relationship between labour policies and firm performance, and the role of multiple shareholders. For comparative studies, the second type of definition is the more logical one. It investigates how differences in the normative framework affect the behavioural patterns of firms, investors and others.

The subject of "corporate governance" has been employed broadly in a variety of means. In the economics debate concerning the impact of the subject on accountability and firm accomplishment, there are two different models of the corporation: the shareholder model and the stakeholder model. In its narrowest sense (shareholder model), corporate governance often describes the formal system of accountability of senior management to shareholders. In its widest sense (stakeholder model), corporate governance can be used to describe the network of formal and informal relations involving the corporation. More recently, the stakeholder approach emphasises contributions by stakeholders that can contribute to the long-term performance of the firm and shareholder value, and the shareholder approach also recognises that business ethics and stakeholder relations can also have an impact on the reputation and long-term success of the corporation. Therefore, the difference between these two models is not as stark as it first seems, and it is instead a question of emphasis.

The prior literature indicates that there is lack of any consensus regarding the definition of corporate governance and is also reflected in the debate on governance reform. This lack of consensus leads to entirely different analyses of the problem and to the strikingly different solutions offered by participants in the reform process. Therefore, having a clear understanding of the different models can provide insight and help us to appreciate the different sides of this debate within banking and other financial institutions. An understanding of the issues involved can also provide the basis from which to identify good corporate governance practices and to provide policy recommendations.

Most recent research finds a stronger relationship between firm performance and performance-based compensation for executives and boards of directors but is not clear what an optimal pay-for-performance tradeoff should be, especially in banking. A great deal of theory and empirical evidence supports the idea that market for corporate control addresses governance problems of inefficient firms in general and banking in particular. However, apart from the United States and to a lesser extent, the United Kingdom, these external governance mechanisms studies are almost non-existent, let alone common with the EU and developing countries.

Increasing corporate governance researches suggest that the extent of legal protection for investors in a country is an important determinant in developing financial markets. There is empirical evidence that the quality of minority shareholder rights and legal enforcement help reduce corporate earning management (to mask firm performance) by insiders, and that firm value is positively correlated with protection of minority shareholders. Better investor protection also means higher liquidity (in terms of bid-ask spread and trading volume) of stocks.

The literature has identified several channels through which corporate governance affects the individual firm (firm performance) as well as the country (via growth and development). There is a vast body of literature devoted to evaluating the relationship between corporate governance and performance, measured by valuation, operating performance or stock returns. Despite the large number of papers, there is no consensus yet. Furthermore, this line of research is plagued by the endogeneity problems and resolving this endogeneity has not been easy. Approaches such as fixed effects or instrumental variables fail to credibly establish causality, while difference-in-difference studies of exogenous legal and regulatory changes appear to be more reliable. While some studies argue that the causality runs from governance to performance, a number of studies demonstrate reverse causality. The question of the nature of causality is still open. This book proposes and recommends randomised experiments as one approach that might be useful in resolving the causality problems; however, they are not easy to implement. The emerging evidence shows that corporate governance is likely to emerge endogenously and thus be dependent on specific characteristics of the firm and its environment. More research is needed to fully understand which governance provisions are important for which types of firms and in which types of environments. Finally, accountability is considered as an integral part of corporate governance disclosure practices. However, limited attention has been paid in the literature to examine this issue in the banking sector systematically and qualitatively. Drawing on stakeholders' theory, the investigation used in this book contributes to the development of a framework to enable a detailed analysis of the role of the quality of accountability disclosure in corporate governance with special reference to the banking sector.

References

Abbott, L. J., Parker, S., & Peters, G. F. (2004). Audit committee characteristics and restatements. *Auditing: A Journal of Practice and Theory*, *23*, (1), 72–86.

Abdelghany, K. E. (2005). Disclosure of market risk or accounting measures of risk: An empirical study. *Managerial Auditing Journal, 20*(8), 870–871.

Abraham, S., & Cox, P. (2007). Analysing the determination of narrative risk information in UK FTSE 100 annual reports. *British Accounting Review, 39*(3), 221–240.

Aburaya, R. K. (2012). *The relationship between corporate governance and environmental disclosure: UK evidence.* Durham thesis, Durham University.

Adams, C. A., Hill, W., & Roberts, C. B. (1998). Corporate social reporting practices in Western Europe: Legitimating corporate behaviour? *British Accounting Review, 30*(1), 1–21.

Akuffo, J. A. (2018). *Corporate governance and bank accountability: The role of accountability in improving the quality of corporate governance disclosures in bank annual report, A UK perspective.* DBA Thesis, Grenoble Ecole De Management.

Beattie, V., McInnes, W., & Fearnley, S. (2004). A methodology for analysing and evaluating narratives in annual reports: a comprehensive descriptive profile and metrics for disclosure quality attributes. *Accounting Forum, 28*(3), 202–231.

Beck, A. C., Campbell, D., & Shrives, P. J. (2010). Content analysis in environmental reporting research: Enrichment and rehearsal of the method in a British-German context. *The British Accounting Review, 42*(3), 207–222.

Behn, R. D. (2001). *Rethinking democratic accountability.* Washington, D.C.: Brookings Institution Press.

Beretta, S., & Bozzolan, S. (2004). A framework for the analysis of firm risk communication. *The International Journey of Accounting, 39*(3), 265–288.

Beretta, S., & Bozzolan, S. (2008). Quality versus quantity: The case of forward-looking disclosure. *Journal of Accounting, Auditing and Finance, 23*(3), 333–375.

Berle, A., & Means, G. (1932). *The modern corporation and private property*. New York: Macmillan.
Berle, A. A. Jr., & Means, G. C. (1967). *The modern corporation and private property* (Rev. Ed.). New York: Harcourt, Brace and World.
Bischof, J. (2009). The effects of IFRS 7 adoption on bank disclosure in Europe. *Accounting in Europe, 6*(2), 164–193.
Bozzolan, S., Trombetta, M., & Beretta, S. (2009). Forward-looking disclosures, financial verifiability and analysts' forecasts: A study of cross-listed European firms. *European Accounting Review, 18*(3), 435–473.
Brennan, N., & Solomon, J. (2008). Corporate governance, accountability and mechanisms of accountability: An overview. *Accounting, Auditing and Accountability Journal, 21*(7), 885–906.
Bushman, R. M., & Smith, A. J. (2001). Financial accounting information and corporate governance. *Journal of Accounting and Economics, 32*, 237–333.
Bushman, R. M., & Smith, A. J. (2003, April). Transparency financial reporting and corporate governance. *New York Federal Reserve Bank's Economic Review, 9*(1), 65–87.
Byrd, J., & Hickman, K. (1992). Do outside directors monitor managers? Evidence from tender offer bids. *Journal of Financial Economics, 32*, 195–221.
Cadbury Report. (1992). *Report of the committee on the financial aspects of corporate governance*. London: Gee.
Cardon Report. (1998). *The report of the Belgium commission on corporate governance*. Brussels: Brussels Stock Exchange.
Campbell, D., Beck, A. C., & Shrives, P. J. (2010). Content analysis in environmental reporting research: Enrichment and rehearsal of the method in a British-German context. *The British Accounting Review, 42*(3), 207–222.
Cheng, E. C. M., & Courteney, S. M. (2006). Board composition, regulatory regime and voluntary disclosure. *The International Journal of Accounting, 41*(3), 262–289.
Clarke, T. (2004). *Theories of corporate governance: The philosophical foundations of corporate governance*. Oxon, NY and Canada: Routledge.
Cobbaut, R., & Lenoble, J. (2003). *Corporate governance: An institutionalist approach*. The Hague: Kluwer Law International.
Coffee, J. C. Jr. (1991, October). Liquidity versus control: The institutional investor as corporate monitor. *Columbia Law Review, 91*(6), 1277–1368.
Cohen, J., Krishnamurthy, G., & Wright, A. M. (2004). Corporate governance mosaic and financial reporting. *Journal of Accounting Literature, 23*, 87–152.
Conyon, M. J., & Peck, S. (1998). Board control, remuneration committees, and top management compensation. *Academy of Management Journal, 41*, 146–157.

Dahya, J., McConnell, J. J., & Travlos, N. G. (2002, February). The Cadbury committee, corporate performance, and top management turnover. *Journal of Finance, 57*(1), 461–483.

Daily, C. M., Johnson, J. L., Ellstrand, A. E., & Dalton, D. R. (1998). Compensation committee composition as a determinant of CEO compensation. *Academy of Management Journal, 41*, 209–220.

DeZoort, F. T., & Salterio, S. E. (2001). Effects of corporate governance experience and financial reporting and auditing knowledge. *Auditing: A Journal of Practice & Theory, 20*(2), 31–47.

DeZoort, F. T., Hermanson, D. R., Archambeault, D. S., & Reed, S. A. (2002). Audit committee effectiveness: A synthesis of the empirical audit committee literature. *Journal of Accounting Literature, 21*, 38–75.

Dragomir, V. D. (2008). Accounting in the name of global corporate governance a historical perspective. *Accounting and Management Information Systems*, 16–28, Bucuresti. ISSN 1583-4387.

Elzahar, H., & Hussainey, K. (2012). Determinants of narrative risk disclosures in UK interim reports. *Journal of Risk Finance, 13*(2), 133–147.

Ezzamel, M., & Watson, R. (1997). Wearing two hats: The conflicting control and management roles of non-executive directors. In K. Keasey, S. Thompson & M. Wright (Eds.), *Corporate governance: Economic, management and financial issues*. Oxford, UK: Oxford University Press.

Faccio, M., & Lasfer, M. A. (2000). Do occupational pension funds monitor companies in which they hold large stakes? *Journal of Corporate Finance, 6*, 71–110.

Ferris, S. P., Jagannathan, M., & Pritchard, A. C. (2003). Too busy to mind the business? Monitoring by directors with multiple board appointments. *Journal of Finance, 58*(3), 1087–1112.

Fisher, E. (2004). The European Union in the age of accountability. *Oxford Journal of Legal Studies, 24*(3), 495–515.

Francis, J. R., Khurana, I. K., & Pereira, R. (2003). The role of accounting and auditing in corporate governance and the development of financial markets around the world. *Asia-Pacific Journal of Accounting and Economics, 10*, 1–31.

Freshfields Bruckhaus Deringer. (2005, October). *A legal framework for the integration of environmental, social and governance issues into institutional investment*. UNEP Finance Initiative, Produced for the Asset Management Working Group of the UNEP Finance Initiative.

Gendron, Y., Bédard, J., & Gosselin, M. (2004). Getting inside the black box: A field study of effective audit committees. *Auditing: A Journal of Practice & Theory, 23*(1), 153–171.

Gramling, A. A., Maletta, M. J., Schneider, A., & Church, B. K. (2005). The role of the internal audit function in corporate governance: A synthesis of the extant internal auditing literature and directions for future research. *Journal of Accounting Literature, 23*, 194–244.

Grant, G. H. (2003). The evolution of corporate governance and its impact on modern corporate America. *Management Decision, 41*(9), 923–934.

Gray, R., Kouhy, R., & Lavers, S. (1995a). Constructing a research database of social and environmental reporting by UK companies. *Accounting, Auditing & Accountability Journal, 8*(2), 78–101.

Gray, R., Kouhy, R., & Lavers, S. (1995b). Corporate social and environmental reporting: a review of the literature and a longitudinal study of UK disclosure. *Accounting, Auditing & Accountability Journal, 8*(2), 47–77.

Hammond, K., & Miles, S. (2019). Assessing quality assessment of corporate social reporting: UK perspectives. *Accounting Forum, 28*(1), 61–79.

Healy, P. M., & Palepu, K. G. (2001). Information asymmetry, corporate disclosure, and the capital markets: A review of the empirical disclosure literature. *Journal of Accounting and Economics, 31*(1–3), 405–440.

Hermalin, B. E., & Weisbach, M. S. (1991). The effects of board composition and direct incentives on firm performance. *Financial Management, 20*(Winter), 101–112.

Helbok, G., & Wagner, C. (2006). Determinants of operational risk reporting in the banking industry. *Journal of Risk, 9*(1), 49–74.

Hooks, J., Coy, D., & Howard, D. (2002). The information gap in annual reports. *Accounting, Auditing and Accountability Journal, 15*(4), 501–522.

Holland, J. (1998). Private disclosure and financial reporting. *Accounting and Business Research, 28*(4), 255–269.

Ismail, R., & Rahman, R. A. (2011). Institutional investors and board of directors' monitoring role on risk management disclosure level in Malaysia. *IUP Journal of Corporate Governance, 10*(2), 37–61.

Jensen, M., & Murphy, K. J. (1990). Performance pay and top-management incentives. *Journal of Political Economy, 98*, 225–264.

Jensen, M., & Ruback, R. S. (1983). The market for corporate control: The scientific evidence. *Journal of Financial Economics, 11*, 5–50.

Kaplan, S., & Reishus, D. (1990). Outside directorships and corporate performance. *Journal of Financial Economics, 27*, 389–410.

Karpo, J. M., Malatesta, P. H., & Walkling, R. A. (1996). Corporate governance and shareholder initiatives: Empirical evidence. *Journal of Financial Economics, 42*, 365–395.

Kirkbride, J., & Letza, S. (2005, July). Can the non-executive director be an effective gatekeeper? The possible development of a legal framework of accountability. *Corporate Governance: An International Review, 13*(4), 542–549.

La Porta, R., Silance, F. L. D., Shleifer, A., et al. (1997). Legal determinants of external finance. *Journal of Finance, 52*(3), 1131–1150.

Letza, S., Kirkbride, J., Sun, X., et al. (2008). Corporate governance theorising: Limits, critics and alternatives. *International Journal of Law and Management, 50*(1), 17–32.

Letza, S., Sun, X., & Kirkbride, J. (2004). Shareholding versus stakeholding: A critical review of corporate governance. *Corporate Governance: An International Review, 12*(3), 242–262.

Licht, A. N. (2002). Accountability and corporate governance. *SSRN Electronic Journal.*

Linsley, P. M., & Shrives, P. J. (2006). Risk reporting: A study of risk disclosures in the annual reports of UK companies. *The British Accounting Review, 38*(4), 387–404.

Main, B. G. M., & Johnston, J. (1993). Remuneration committees and corporate governance. *Accounting and Business Research, 23*, 351–362.

Mallin, C. (2010). *Corporate governance* (3rd ed.). Oxford: Oxford University Press.

Meek, G. K., Roberts, C. B., & Gray, S. J. (1995). Factors influencing voluntary annual report disclosures by the US, UK and Continental European multinational corporations. *Journal of International Business Studies, 26*(3), 555–572.

Monk, R. A. G., & Minow, N. (2001). *Corporate governance* (2nd ed.). Chichester: John Wiley & Sons Ltd.

Monk, R. A. G., & Minow, N. (2004). *Corporate governance* (3rd ed.). Chichester: John Wiley & Sons Ltd.

Monk, R. A. G., & Minow, N. (2008). *Corporate governance* (4th ed.). Chichester: John Wiley & Sons Ltd.

Newman, H. A. (2000). The impact of ownership structure on the structure of compensation committees. *Journal of Business Finance and Accounting, 27*(5–6), 653–678.

Newman, H. A., & Mozes, H. A. (1999). Does the composition of the compensation committee influence CEO compensation practices? *Financial Management, 28*(3), 41–53.

Norby Report. (2001, December). *The Nørby committee's report on corporate governance in Denmark—Recommendations for corporate governance in Denmark.*

Patten, D. M. (1995). Variability in social disclosure: A legitimacy-based analysis. *Advances in Public Interest Accounting, 6*, 273–285.

Peters Committee. (1997, June). *Corporate governance in the Netherlands—Forty recommendations, secretariat committee on corporate governance.* Amsterdam.

Pirson, M., & Turnbull, S. (2011). Corporate governance, risk management, and the financial crisis: an Information processing view. *Corporate Governance: An International Review, 19*(5), 459–470.

Poshakwale, S., & Courtis, J. K. (2005). Disclosure level and cost of equity capital: Evidence from the banking industry. *Managerial and Decision Economics, 26*(7), 431–444.

Preda Report. (1998). *Report on code of conduct: Committee for the corporate governance of listed companies*. Italy: Borsa Italiana S.p.A.

Raar, J. (2002). Environmental initiatives: Towards triple-bottom line reporting. *Corporate Communications: An International Journal, 7*(3), 169–183.

Raghunandan, K., Read, W. K., & Rama, D. V. (2001). Audit committee composition gray directors and interaction with internal auditing. *Accounting Horizons, 15*(2), 105–118.

Rattanatippo, P. (2013). *Risk disclosures in the annual reports of UK Banks*. Newcastle University Business School.

Ruigrok, W., Peck, S., Tacheva, S., Greve, P., & Hu, Y. (2006). The determinants and effects of board nomination committees. *Journal of Management and Governance, 10*(2), 119–148.

Seal, W., & Vincent-Jones, P. (1997). Accounting and trust in the enabling of long-term relations. *Accounting, Auditing & Accountability Journal, 10*(3), 406–431.

Security Market Commission (CMVM). (2007). *CMVM recommendations on corporate governance code*. Portugal: Security Market Commission.

Shleifer, A., & Vishny, R. W. (1997). A survey of corporate governance. *Journal of Finance, 52* (2), 735–782.

Sikka, P. (2008). "Corporate governance": What about workers? *Accounting, Auditing, Accountability Journal, 21*(7), pp. X–X O/S.

Smith, M., & Taffler, R. J. (2000). The chairman's statement: A content analysis of discretionary narrative disclosures. *Accounting, Auditing & Accountability Journal, 13*(5), 624–647.

Solomon, J. (2007). Corporate *governance and accountability* (3rd ed.). Hoboken: Wiley.

Solomon, J. F., & Solomon, A. (2006). Private social, ethical and environmental disclosure. *Accounting, Auditing and Accountability Journal, 19*(4), 564–591.

Spira, L. (2001). Enterprise and accountability: Striking a balance. *Management Decision, 39*(9), 739–748.

Stanton, P. (1997). Users's rights to published accounting information: Nature, justification and implications. *Accounting, Auditing & Accountability Journal, 10*(5), 684–701.

Tandelilin, E., Kaaro, H., Mahadwartha, P. A., & Supriyatna (2007). *Corporate governance, risk management and bank performance: Does type of ownership matter?* Final Report of an EADN Individual Research Grant Project, EADN Working Paper.

Taylor, G., Tower, G., & Neilson, J. (2010). Corporate communication of financial risk. *Accounting & Finance, 50*(2), 417–446.
Tomasic, R. (2011). The financial crisis and the haphazard pursuit of financial crime. *Journal of Financial Crime, 18*(1), 7–31.
Toms, J. S. (2002). Firm resources, quality signals and the determinants of corporate environmental reputation: Some UK evidence. *The British Accounting Review, 34*(3), 257–282.
Tricker, B. (2009). *Corporate governance: Principles, policies and practices* (1st ed.). New York: Oxford University Press Inc.
Tse, T. (2011). Shareholder and stakeholder theory: After the financial crisis. *Qualitative Research in Financial Markets, 3*(1), 51–63.
Turner Review. (2009). *The Turner Review: A regulatory response to the global banking crisis*. London: Financial Service Authority.
Turley, S., & Zaman, M. (2007). Audit committee effectiveness: Informal processes and behavioural effects. *Accounting Auditing & Accountability Journal, 20*(5), 765–788.
Unerman, J., Bebbington, J., & O'Dwyer, B. (2007). *Sustainability, accounting and accountability*. London: Routledge.
United Nations Conference on Trade and Development (UNCTAD). (2010, October). *Corporate governance in the wake of the financial crisis, selected international reviews.* New York and Geneva: United Nations.
Van der Laan Smith, J., Adhikari, A., & Tondkar, R.H., (2005). Exploring differences in social disclosures internationally: A stakeholder perspective. *Journal of Accounting and Public Policy, 24*(2), 124–151.
Walker, S. D. (2009). *A review of corporate governance in UK banks and other financial industry entities.* Final recommendations,
Washburn, S. A. (1996). Challenge and renewal: A historical view of the profession. *Journal of Management Consulting, 9*(2), 47–53.
Williamson, O. E. (1984). Corporate governance. *Yale Law Journal, 93*(7), 1197–1230.
Wiseman, J. (1982). An evaluation of environmental disclosures made in corporate annual reports. *Accounting, Organizations and Society, 7*(1), 53–63.
Yeoh, P. (2010). Causes of the global financial crisis: Learning from the competing insights. *International Journal of Disclosure and Governance, 7*, 42–69.
Yong, H. H. A., Chalmers, K., & Faff, R. (2005). Asia pacific banks' derivative and risk management disclosures. *Asian Review of Accounting, 13*(1), 15–44.

CHAPTER 5

To Blame? The Less Talked About Cause of the 2007–2009 Financial Crisis

5.1 Introduction

The 2008 Great Recession was triggered by the 2007 financial crisis. Corporate governance has become an increasingly critical issue after the corporate scandals which occurred all over the world and its specific role in the stability of financial intermediaries was highlighted by the severe crisis which hit the financial markets from the summer of 2007. In fact, for financial intermediaries, the governance system is even more important not only because intermediaries are basically in the business of risk acceptance but also due to their special role within the economy in the aggregation and transfer of financial resources. Regulation may impact on financial risk taking by financial intermediaries by way of the decision-making process envisaged in the various possible legal structures set forth by the law.

A number of research investigations have now confirmed that the recent financial crisis is the most severe crunch after "The Great Depression" of the 1930s. Several researchers and reports reviewed the causes of this global financial crisis. Many scholars directly implicate corporate governance flaws as one of the main reasons for causing the global crisis, while other factors play only a supplementary role. Several deficiencies in the mechanisms of accountability within corporate governance structure

J. A. Akuffo, *Corporate Governance and Accountability of Financial Institutions*, Palgrave Studies in Accounting and Finance Practice, https://doi.org/10.1007/978-3-030-64046-0_5

and processes led to the collapse of many financial institutions and triggered the crisis. Many banking and financial institutions did not pay due attention to corporate governance before and during the crisis. Indeed, the key paradox of this collapse in governance was that it happened largely in a number of complex and established financial institutions in well-developed capital markets and in advanced countries (for example, America, the European Union and the United Kingdom).

This chapter will explore and examine the implication of ineffective corporate governance and the various mechanisms of accountability, which contributed to the collapse of a variety of banking and other financial institutions, specifically linked to the financial crash of 2007–2008. It will investigate the reasons of the failure in the corporate governance industry and financial markets during the crisis by looking at the various academic evidence produced after the banking crisis. Following the crisis, a number of governments and banking authorities around the world, including the UK, have investigated several banks and other financial organisations over claims related to poor corporate governance practices and breaches. The deficiencies that were identified, including the cost of the crisis, will also be covered in this chapter. These include, inadequacy of risk management in addressing corporate governance, compensation and misalignment of enticement arrangement in financial institutions, lapses in board behaviour and competence, the ineffectiveness of oversight of governance structures, gaps in disclosure and accounting standards, misleading information provided by rating agencies and lack of active shareholder engagement in scrutinising boards of directors.

5.2 The Cost/Impact of the Global Financial Crisis

The 2008 Great Recession was triggered by the impact of the 2007 financial crisis. The Credit market instability did in fact trounce the banking system internationally, forced a severe asset write-down of more than a third of a trillion dollars by mid-2008, squeezing lending everywhere and instigating a harsh slowing of the world economy. It is now acknowledged that the financial crisis of 2007–2008 was a crisis truly global in nature that affected all regions and countries of the world (Clarke 2010). In fact, the scale and reach of this crisis was worrisome, and much bigger than the earlier regional specific crises in Asia, Japan and the United States, and was only comparable to the Great Depression. The fall of share prices on a single day was even more than the Great Depression of the 1930s (Cheffins 2009). According to the International Monetary Fund (IMF), the estimated potential losses from this crisis were approximately $1400 billion up to the end of October 2008 (see Fig. 5.1a). The global crisis was initiated in the latter part of 2006 and by the end of 2008 engulfed the entire world. There were several macro- and micro-economic perspectives of this crisis (UNTACD 2010) as illustrated in the text below:

> *"Expansionary monetary policy with falling interest rates caused asset price booms, particularly in the U.S. housing sector. This was accompanied with a rapid expansion of lending and a corresponding decline in underwriting standards and increase in risk, fuelled in part by the unregulated growth of the so-called 'shadow banking system.' This side of the financial system developed between 2000 and 2008 and consists of institutions and legal entities that provide financial intermediation without taking deposits. As such, they are not subject to the same regulatory oversight as institutions that do take deposits. These institutions used short-term credit to invest heavily in sub-prime mortgage-backed securities, which became increasingly risky as housing*

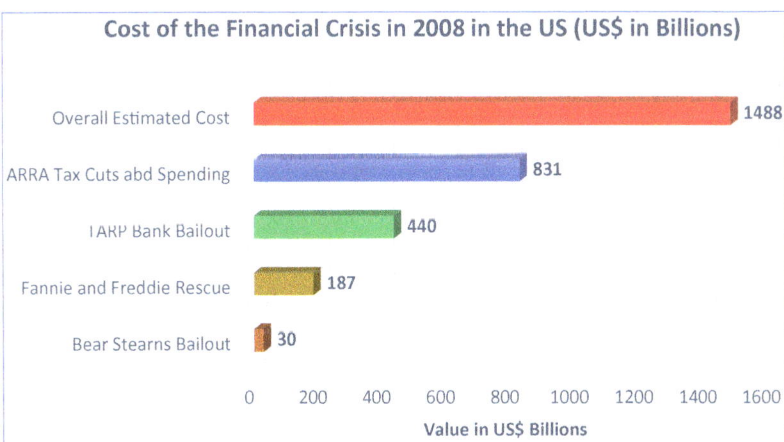

Fig. 5.1a Cost of the crisis (*Source* Adapted from US Congressional Budget Office)

prices began to fall in the US after mid-2006. In the absence of regulatory oversight, the risk inherent in these assets were not adequately rated yet had become increasingly dispersed throughout the global financial system. Being highly leveraged and holding what became known as 'toxic assets', large financial institutions in the shadow banking system began to fail as default rates began to rise. Global credit markets contracted with the decline in confidence: the record high interest rates that banks used to lend to each other almost halted inter-bank lending. This caused a global liquidity crisis and a subsequent decline in world trade triggering, through various feedback loops, a recession which has impacted real economies globally".

Source Adopted from UNCTAD (2010, pp. 1–2)

The financial crisis of 2008 has been described as the worst economic catastrophe, and this happened notwithstanding the UK Bank of England, the EU Central Bank and the US Federal Reserve and Treasury Department's concerted efforts to stop it. The crisis steered us to the Great Recession, where housing prices plummeted more than the price drop during the Depression. The cost for example, to the United States was so severe that more than two years after the recession had ended, the US unemployment rate was still nearly 10%, and in addition does not include hard working employees who had given up efforts in seeking work (see Fig. 5.1b). The cost of the crisis has not only affected shareholders and investors, but also national governments, taxpayers and the public at large in many respects. In the United Kingdom for example, according to the Parliamentary Commission on Banking Standard report:

> Banks in the UK have failed in many respects. They have failed taxpayers, who had to bail out a number of banks including some major institutions, with a cash outlay peaking at £133 billion, equivalent to more than £2,000 for every person in the UK. (Parliamentary Commission on Banking Standards report 2013, p. 82)

The knowledge that the taxpayer bailed out of several financial institutions including banks during the financial crisis casts a long shadow over the public's view of banking and many national governments attitude to their reform's agenda post crisis. Although, it can be observed that the impact of particular nation-wide banking disasters in the past have been more severe—for example, the failure of the US banking system between

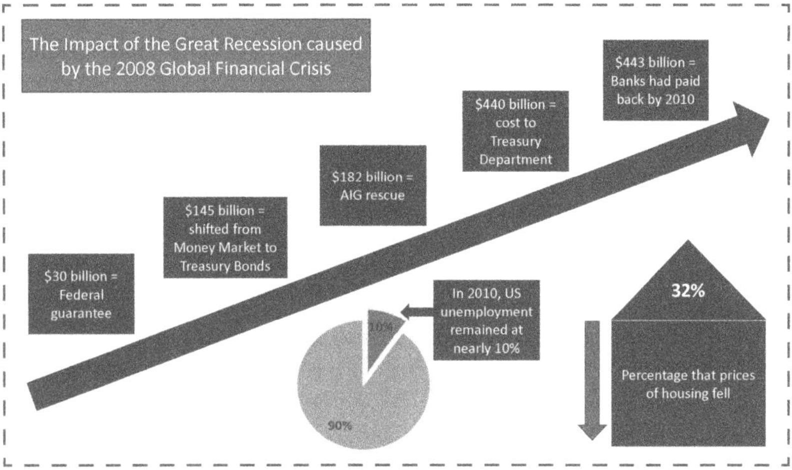

Fig. 5.1b Extract of US impact of the crisis (*Source* Created by Author using US Congressional Budget Office information)

1929 and 1933. Nonetheless, what is distinctive about the impact of this crunch is that severe financial difficulties did emerge concurrently in several different countries, and that its economic impact was felt and to some extent is being felt all over the world as a result of the increased interconnectedness of the global economy (Turner 2009).

The foremost indication that the US economy was in difficulty happened probably in the latter part of the year 2006 when housing prices started to fall. At the start of fall, there were not many market observers and analysts who recognised there were too many US homeowners with dubious credit, and financial intermediaries including banking firms had approved individuals to take out loans for 100% or more with respect to the value of their new homes. A few economists and financial market analysts now hold responsible the Community Reinvestment Act, which had pressed banking firms to make investments in subprime areas, but that was not the principal cause of the crisis.

In fact, some regulators and finance scholars arguably blamed "The Commodity Futures Modernization Act" in the United States. This Act permitted financial institutions and particularly, banks to take part in trading profitable derivatives that these institutions sold to stockholders, investors and financiers. These mortgage-backed securities needed home loans as collateral, and the derivatives generated a limitless demand for more and more mortgages. Banks, hedge funds and other financial institutions around the world not only owned the mortgage-backed securities, but they were also in pension funds, mutual funds and corporate assets. The opacity around these practices by banking firms in slicing up the original mortgages and repackaging and selling them in tranches enabled the derivatives to be viewed as nearly impossible to value and price. Insurance firms also complicated the market by insuring these derivatives and created risky insurance products which were then sold to institutional investors and pension funds around the world.

Although there is no yet agreed overall cost and impact of the crisis, the impact and the degree of the overall cost of the 2008 financial crisis can be evaluated in one way by observing the different stages of the timeline from 2006 to 2009. The various points of significant events as they occurred have been summarised and highlighted in Fig. 5.2. The cost of the crunch has been in many respects enormous nationally and internationally. The crisis caused the worldwide financial systems to come to a crushing freeze: leading to an abrupt departure of international liquidity which ran on to cause a devastating dip in the global economy. This disaster was in fact saved only by the sudden and well-coordinated national governments and international organisations intervention on a massive scale. The global economy would have gone into a depression if such a swift concerted effort had not occurred.

In the decade before the financial crisis, financial industry around the world went through several key significant developments and changes that led to the creation of the new global financial system with unique characteristics, when amalgamating with macroeconomic imbalances, aided in creating an unsustainable credit boom and asset price inflation.[1] However, those characteristics did play a critical part in strengthening the gravity of the financial crisis and in transmitting financial system problems into real economy effects. According to Turner (2009), there were several elements that contributed to the extended length and brevity of the crisis, two of these are listed below:

[1] The real drivers of financial innovation, development and regulatory changes are beyond the scope of this study. See Turner (2009) report for detailed analysis and evaluation.

Key event information and significant dates
Oct-Dec 2006: • US housing market slows down • Rise in bankruptcies by subprime lenders as result of delinquency rate rise on US subprime mortgages
Feb 2007: • HSBC declare that additional money needs to be put by to cover bad loan in US subprime credit portfolios • The third biggest US subprime lender declares expectation of losses in last quarter • The Fed ignores Alan Greenspan's public warning of a recession
April 2007: • US Fed ignores market warning signs but the Stock Market disapproves • Fannie Mae and Freddie Mac issued commitment to help subprime mortgage holders to keep their homes • The US Durable Goods Orders Forecast a Recession
June 2007: • Interest rates are raised by European Central Bank by a quarter point to 4% • Shock announcement of loss by Bear Stearns as result of bad bets on securities backed by subprime loans. $4 billion of assets are sold to cover investor redemptions and expected margin calls • 2 large hedge funds collapse
July 2007: • Interest rates are raised by Bank of England by a quarter point to 5.75% • Standard & Poor announce a cut in ratings, around $12 billion that are associated with subprime loans • In 6 weeks, credit spread skyrockets by a full % point from a record low in June • Credit spreads rise due to statement from Bear Stearns regarding two hedge funds with subprime exposure having little value. As a result of this, S&P drops ratings by 8 notches on certain top-rated mortgage bonds • US subprime listed as main cause for earning losses by German bank IKB.DE. A record high is reached in credit spreads as it hits above 500 basis points
Aug 2007: • The Fed maintains interest rates notwithstanding stricter credit conditions • The ECB put in 95 billion euros of one-day funds to money markets due to interbank lending freezing as concerns about banking firm's subprime exposure increases • The US Fed, Germany's Bundesbank, and Bank of Canada injected into their banking systems additional liquidity • Direct discount rates for loans to banks were reduced by half a percentage point by the Fed causing shockwaves in the market as the expected change is normally a quarter point. The aim of this brave move was to return liquidity and confidence • Bank of England lends £314 million to Barclays Bank as part of its standing lending facility. The reason for this is that banks had stopped lending to each other. 9 days later, Barclays Bank requested an emergency fund of £1.6 billion from the BoE again
Sep 2007: • Northern Rock (British mortgage lender) requests emergency financial assistance from the BoE. News of this move led to widespread panic causing a run on the bank's deposits • Alistair Darling, the British Finance Minister, made a public announcement that the British government will guarantee all Northern Rock deposits • The Fed reduces its discount rate and Federal funds target rate by half a % point. This was a calculated attempt to counteract the effect of the ongoing financial market unrest • The ECB publicises loaning 3.9 billion euros to an unnamed bank/s needing the funds • The London Interbank Offered Rate (LIBOR) makes an unexpected deviation from the fed funds rate **signalling the start of the economic crisis**
Oct 2007: • USB AG (Swiss Bank) announces a loss of assets write down of $3.4 billion which is their first quarterly loss in 9 years. • Citigroup (US bank) also announces they estimate their third-quarter net income will decrease by 60%

Fig. 5.2 Timeline of key event dates from 2007–2009 in the financial crisis (*Source* Created by the Author)

- JPMorgan Chase & Co, Citigroup and Bank of America propose plans to create a fund which pools assets from stressed Special Investment Vehicles (SIVs) to avoid the selling of these assets which could destabilise the credit markets further
- A further loss and write-down of $6.5 billion is announced by Citigroup relating to subprime debt and leveraged loans
- A larger loss and asset write-downs associated with subprime CDOs and leveraged loans was declared by Merrill Lynch (US Investment bank) - $8.4 billion. This resulted in the bank's largest quarterly loss in their history and the imminent departure of CEO Stan O'Neal

Nov 2007 -

- The US Treasury invent $75 billion super fund by persuading JP Morgan Chase, Citigroup and Bank of America to set it up to provide liquidity in the market
- The US federal government guaranteed the superfund and encourage financial institutions to take up more subprime loans

Dec 2007 -

- The Fed create another innovative instrument called the 'Term Auction Facility' (TAF) to maintain liquidity in the financial market
- The first two $20 billion auctions are held on the 11th and 20th of December by the Fed
- Mortgage foreclosure rates double

Jan 2008 -

- The Federal Open Market Committee (FOMC) starts to lower the fed funds rate to try to stop the struggling housing market
- Significant increase in US foreclosure rate (57% more than previous 12 months)

Feb 2008 - USB

- The US President (George Bush) signs Tax Rebate to aid the struggling economy
- The US housing market continues to nose-dive
- Northern Rock taken over by the UK Government

Mar 2008 -

- The US Federal Reserve starts bailout programmes
- Fed announces its Term Auction Facility programme ($50 billion)
- The Fed announce $200 billion Treasury notes to rescue bond dealers in the financial market to keep up liquidity which has dried out
- Bear Stearns declare bankruptcy
- The panic in the market force the Federal Reserve to hold its first emergency meeting in 30 years
- The Fed fund rate was lowered significantly by the Federal Open Market Committee
- The US regulators encouraged Fannie Mae and Freddie Mac to take on a significant amount of subprime mortgage debt ($200 billion)

April/May 2008 -

- The FOMC lowered the Fed fund rate
- The US Fed injected $50 billion into the market
- The liquidity problem in the financial market exacerbates
- The US Fed auctions a further $150 billion into the market under its Term Auction Facility

June 2008 -

- A further deterioration of liquidity in the financial market by large financial institutions
- The US Fed auctions $1.2 trillion total into the financial market
- The Federal Reserve lends $225 billion to the market under its Term Auction Facility

July 2008 -

- IndyMac Bank declares bankruptcy and was closed by the Office of Thrift Supervision
- Liquidity problems worsen, and mark-to-market losses declared by large institutions trading books
- The US House of Congress enacts the Housing and Economic Recovery Act
- The US creates a new regulator - the Federal Housing Finance Agency for regulating Fannie Mae and Freddie Mac
- Funding and liquidity problems worsen in the US, the UK and across Europe

Fig. 5.2 (continued)

Aug 2008 -

- The Fed allows the Federal Housing Finance Agency to guarantee $300 billion loans
- Both Freddie Mac and Fannie Mae turn to the US Government for more bailout funds
- Funding shortages and liquidity in the market seriously worsens triggering several large financial institution bankruptcies

Sep 2008 -

- The US Treasury nationalises Fannie Mae and Freddie Mac under conservatorship
- Lehman Brothers file for bankruptcy protection
- Bradford & Bingley are nationalised by the UK Government
- Dexia are bailed out by Belgium, France and Luxemburg
- American International Group (AIG) and Washington Mutual are nationalised by the US Government
- Fortis are partially nationalised by governments of Belgium, Holland and Luxemburg
- The Bank of America announces its plan to buy ailing giant US investment bank Merrill Lynch
- The US Treasury Secretary and the Fed Chair meets with US Congress to discuss bailouts and the financial crisis. Following this, they went on to submit legislation to Congress
- The Stock Market crashes Congress rejects the bailout request

Oct 2008 -

- The UK Government takes majority stake in Royal Bank of Scotland
- Swiss Government bails out Union Bank of Switzerland (UBS)
- Landsbanki HF fails and rescued by UK Government and the EU
- The Fed injects to AIG another $38 billion in exchange for fixed income securities
- The US Congress passes $700 billion bailout bill
- Global Stock Market collapses irrespective of central banks actions
- Several central banks in a number of countries coordinate to create a global action plan to rescue the financial system globally

Nov 2008 -

- The US Fed starts to restructure its financial aid packages for the market
- The automobile companies in the US seek government bailouts
- The Fed creates the Term Asset-Backed Securities Loan Facility to help credit card companies
- The US Government rescues Citigroup
- Wachovia files for bankruptcy and is bought by Wells Fargo
- The FDRC agrees up to $1.3 trillion in loans guarantee that banks have made to one another
- The US Treasury partners with the Fed to use part of the TARP funds to remedy the consumer credit market freeze

Fig. 5.2 (continued)

- "*The massive growth and increasing complexity of the securitised credit model, underpinned by inadequate capital requirements against trading books, which facilitated unsustainable growth in credit extension to households and to some parts of the corporate sector.*
- *Extensive commercial bank involvement in trading activities, which meant that falling asset prices have had a large and rapid effect on bank profitability, and in turn on perceptions of their credit worthiness, creating a collapse in bank funding liquidity*".

The shockwaves that went through the banking systems worldwide were so enormous that it impaired the ability of several financial institutions to extend credit to the real economy. It has played and is still playing a key part in worsening the economic recession, which in turn undermines banking system strength in a self-reinforcing feedback loop (Turner 2009).

The impact of the recession really started to emerge in March 2008. The decision of investors of Bear Stearns to sell off their shares proved to initiate a domino effect due to the nature of their belief that the company had too many worthless and toxic assets. JP Morgan Chase was contacted by Bear Stearns to request financial rescue; in the end, the US Federal Reserve Bank were required to make a deal by guaranteeing $30 billion for the deal to go through. The extent of the damage was unknown to the Federal Reserve and they initially thought that the subprime mortgage crisis would not reach any further than the housing sector itself. The primary sources for the subprime mortgage crisis were not fully appreciated by the Fed either until further through the crisis. As financial institutions fully appreciated the magnitude of the need to absorb any loss, it led to heightened alarm within the banking industry and an abrupt halt to interbank lending. The reason for this move to stop these transactions was because of the fear of being stuck with collateral that are backed by worthless mortgages. This led to the sudden increase of the London Interbank Offer Rate.

The impact of credit rating agency downgrades also severely affected the worsening of the liquidity situations of many financial institutions in the financial markets. A key example of the effect of the sudden bond downgrades can be observed in 2008 September by AIG case regarding asset write-down loss.

5.3 The 2007/08 Banking Crisis and Lapses in Accountability of Corporate Governance Mechanisms

Corporate governance has become an increasingly critical issue after the corporate scandals which occurred all over the world, and its specific role in the stability of financial intermediaries, was highlighted by the severe crisis which hit the financial markets from the summer of 2007. The crisis is attributed to the collapse of trust that happened between banking firms the year before the 2008 financial crisis. This was triggered by the subprime mortgage crisis due to the unregulated use of derivatives in the financial market. This occurred on the presumption that the US institutions such as Freddie Mac and Fannie Mae guaranteed mortgages even though they were subprime. The housing industry's downward spiral turned into the financial market disaster since several financial intermediaries and other financial institutions invested heavily in mortgage-backed derivatives.

A number of research investigations have now confirmed that the recent financial crisis was the most severe crunch after "The Great Depression" of the 1930s (Blundell-Wignall et al. 2008; Cheffins 2009; Kirkpatrick 2009; Clarke 2010; Lang and Jagtiani 2010). Several researchers and reports reviewed the causes of this global financial crisis (Clarke 2010; Laeven et al. 2010; Lang and Jagtiani 2010; Tarraf 2010; UNCTAD 2010; Yeoh 2010). Many of these scholars implicate corporate governance as one of the main reasons for global crisis, while other factors play only a supplementary role (Kirkpatrick 2009; Fetisov 2009).

Several deficiencies in the mechanisms of accountability within corporate governance structure and processes led to the collapse of many financial institutions and triggered the crisis. Many banking and financial institutions did not pay due attention to corporate governance before and during the crisis. Indeed, the key paradox of these collapses in governance was that it happened largely in a number of complex and established financial institutions in well-developed capital markets and in advanced countries (for example, America, the European Union and the United Kingdom). As an example, some of the failed and bailed out institutions are listed in Fig. 5.3.

However, a number of investigations and research have been conducted to examine the implication of ineffective corporate governance and the various mechanisms of accountability, which contributed to the collapse of a variety of banking institutions, specifically linked to the financial crash of 2007–2008. The key prevalent points of their deductions are outlined and discussed in the following sub sections below.

5.3.1 *Inadequacy of Risk Management in Addressing Corporate Governance*

The nature of financial intermediation is an intrinsically risky business, and the risks that these institutions face are indeed numerous and multifaceted. The concept of conventional banking exists from the so-called transformation of key short-term risks into long-term risks. These significant risks incorporate market, credit, compliance, operational, liquidity

United Kingdom

a) Northern Rock – The UK Government took over the bank in February 2008.

b) Bradford & Bingley – Taken into public ownership by UK Government in September 2008.

c) Halifax Bank of Scotland – Taken over by Lloyds Banking Group in January 2009.

d) Royal Bank of Scotland– UK Government took majority stake in RBS in October 2008.

Continental Europe

a) Dexia – Bailed out by Belgium, France and Luxemburg to the tune of $9bn in September 2008

b) Fortis – Partially nationalised in September 2008, with Belgian, Dutch and Luxemburg governments investing $16bn in the bank.

c) Hypo Real Estate – German Government has provided capital injections to prop up HRE over a period of time since September 2008, and now owns a 90% stake.

d) Union Bank of Switzerland – Bailed out by Swiss Government in October 2008.

e) Landsbanki HF - The collapse of Landsbanki HF in October 2008 and was propped up by both UK Government and the EU.

United States

a) Lehman Brothers – Filed for bankruptcy protection on 15 September 2008.

b) Citigroup – Massive United States Government bailout in November 2008.

c) Bear Stearns – Distress sale to JP Morgan Chase in March 2008.

d) Merrill Lynch – Distress sale to Bank of America in December 2008 – now Bank of America Merrill Lynch

e) Wachovia – Bought by Wells Fargo in November 2008 after government had attempted to force a sale to Citigroup.

f) American International Group (AIG) – Bailed out (or 'nationalised') by United States Government 16 September 2008.

g) Washington Mutual – Taken over by the Government and distress sale to J.P. Morgan on 28 September 2008.

h) Freddie Mac – (Government Sponsored Enterprise) taken over by US Government on 7 September 2008.

i) Fannie Mae – (Government Sponsored Enterprise) taken over by US Government on 7 September 2008."

Fig. 5.3 Examples of failures of major financial institutions (*Source* Adapted from UNCTAD 2010)

and reputational, among others (BCBS 2010a, b). As a result, management of these risks have been a major cause of concern for banking supervisors and regulation for more than a century now. One major conclusion drawn from a number of studies found that a dearth of "effective risk governance" was discovered as the highest on the catalogue of governance failures that contributed significantly to the banking crisis in 2007/08 (OECD 2009a, b; UBS 2008; Moxey and Berendt 2008; UNCTAD 2010; Walker 2009). The UNCTAD report published in 2010, asserts that "*risk governance is generally defined as board and management oversight of risk and the attendant configuration of internal risk identification, measurement, management, and reporting systems*" (UNCTAD 2010). The publication also concluded that "*understanding the bank's risk composition and market position is key to the board's ability to set strategic direction and risk policy, provide management oversight, respond to developing challenges and opportunities, and effectively measure institutional performance based on the return of those risks and allocated capital*". Nevertheless;

a. Board of directors displayed a lack of detailed knowledge of their company's risk profile and as such failed to adequately evaluate its appropriateness.
b. Executive directors of several financial organisations failed to both champion and include vital components that would serve to most effectively identify and manage their risks.
c. There was a failure recognised that many departments (accountable for reporting on risk) did not have the required status to effectively draw the attention of boards of directors about the existence of serious risks to enable them to manage the situation effectively.

Kirkpatrick (2009) suggested that there were certain inherent deficiencies in the system. Deficient corporate governance processes attributed to the failures of risk management systems and effective internal controls in many of the failed banks. Boards of failed banks did not take into consideration the risk factors before approving the company strategy. Company's disclosures about the foreseeable risk factors and about systems for monitoring and managing risk were noticeably lacking in many banks. The accounting and regulatory environment was not even efficacious. It seems that history keeps repeating itself given that many of the failures or problems described above had been encountered well before the start of the financial and banking crisis. For example, one of the key primary causes of the collapse of Baring was attributed to weaknesses in corporate governance and risk management where "a lack of understanding at board level of the nature and complexity of derivative market, leading to board members placing blind faith in a young trader" (Solomon 2013).

However, it is important to emphasise that beside prudential regulation, there is a role for corporate governance in constraining excessive risk-taking behaviours by financial institutions. It transpired, subsequent to the collapse of Barings and Enron, corporate governance and its mechanisms of accountability (whether in practices, policies or procedures) inclined to react in a reflexive way to events occurring. Ironically, corporate governance advancement around the world does not appear to follow a proactive development and focus by policy makers and governments. Looking through time, it almost appears that it requires a major crisis to take place to promote the improvement of fresh recommendations and enactment of new corporate governance laws. For example, the United States did create the Dodd-Frank Act specifically aimed at reforming the financial industry in the United States and to a large extent globally. Similarly, the United Kingdom reacted following the global financial crisis by producing the Walker Review and recommendations (2009), the Kay Review and its proposals (2012) and Corporate Governance Stewardship Code (2012) with a clear intention to avert a reappearance of the financial sector disaster.

5.3.2 Compensation and Misalignment of Enticement Arrangements in Financial Institutions

The design and the use of appropriate directors' incentive and rewards structure has been one of the tenets of corporate governance accountability mechanisms as postulated by both agency theory and stakeholder in the running of a firm. Some of the compensated structures are well defined and to some extent prescribed under both legal and mandatory disclosure requirements for financial institutions. In addition, the theoretical work has on numerous occasions drawn attention to the danger of inducement packages that might give confidence to excessive risk taking. Yet another major conclusion drawn from a number of studies after the recent financial crisis found misalignment of rewards and compensation arrangements for these failed financial institutions. It has been acknowledged particularly, at the G20[2] that one of the causes of the financial crisis was the inadequately devised senior managerial compensation packages that led to excessive risk taking in financial institutions. It has been established that the norm of practice of good governance necessitates that boards of directors in organisations must attempt to bring into line senior directors and boards of directors' compensation with the longer-term interests of their firm and its stockholders.

In the last two decades, this general good practice norm was construed in the United States and other parts of the world to mean greatly increased usage of equity-based and uneven remuneration packages that includes short-term share options. Nevertheless, it can be observed from the 2010 UNCTAD reports that "{the financial crisis has increased scepticism over the structure and use of incentive-based compensation. In banks (particularly failed ones), executives were seen to "reach for short-term yield" at the expense of long-term firm stability and value. This problem was compounded by the short-term nature of incentive structures, particularly those designed for the traders and business lines dealing with financial products most centrally implicated in the financial crisis. In some cases, the relatively high proportion of variable pay comprising remuneration packages required companies to issue bonuses even when the business was not profitable}".

Again Kirkpatrick (2009) stated that remuneration systems were not aligned to the company's risk appetite, strategy and long-term sustainability of the company. Buiter (2009) pointed out that there was very little transparency regarding off-balance-sheet items of complex financial products, and the risk financial institutions were carrying for the shareholders of the company. Further, the author agreed that the remuneration structure of banking professionals allowed them to take extreme risk with focus on short-term profit.

5.3.3 *Lapses in Board Behaviours and Competence*

Board chairmanship plays the significant task of maintaining objectivity and effective leadership of boards for both financial and non-financial

[2]The G20 at 2009 Pittsburgh summit advocated for 'stricter rules for risk-taking, improved corporate governance mechanisms that align compensation with long-term performance, and called for superior transparency in corporate governance'.

institutions. In fact, notwithstanding the significance given to board composition and its leadership by financial regulators and principles of corporate governance (UNCTAD 2010) to ensure board objectivity, the financial crisis has exposed severe deficiencies in board behaviours and practices within a number of key financial institutions (UNCTAD 2010; FSA 2009a, b). The role of board chairmanship and the requisite behaviours of board members came under severe scrutiny during and immediately after the crisis from the UK, the European Union and the United States. Several policy makers and government regulators blame a number of board directors' performance and their chairmanship directly for ineffective board performance and leadership issues (Walker 2009).

Yeoh (2010) studied many financial institutions during the financial crisis. He directed attention to severe lapses in transparency and disclosure norms and raised a number of valid questions about the role of non-executive directors in the running of financial institutions. Two key large financial institutions—Bear Sterns and Lehman Brothers—were engaged in opaque financial reporting and lacked transparency in communication with shareholders. Yeoh (2010) also suggested that non-executive directors of financial institutions lacked sufficient time, knowledge and expertise to deal with complex financial products. This important finding has also been corroborated by several financial scholars and regulator's investigations in a number of countries. Additionally, Pirson and Turnbull (2010, 2011) suggested that directors and boards of Anglo-American corporate governance systems did not perform their responsibilities well. Boards failed to keep check on risk management systems and directors could not control the excessive risk-taking behaviour of management. Non-executive and independent directors did not raise any significant questions on remuneration and incentive systems of executives.

5.3.4 *Lack of Active Shareholder Engagement in Scrutinising Board of Directors*

There have been several reforms that have been introduced and implemented in the decades before 2006 in order to bolster the role of shareholders in the setting of senior directors pay as part of a broader theme concerning corporate governance. This is to make sure that shareholders accomplished their ability as promoters of managerial accountability. The crisis of 2008 highlighted a serious deficiency in activating shareholders as efficient corporate governance and accountability mechanisms for financial institutions and particularly banking. Several financial market observers and regulators offer debates and findings over shareholders engagement, roles, rights and their passivity during the run-up to the crisis. "According to good corporate governance practice, shareholders have a number of basic rights and obligations. These include the right to appoint directors, the right to make key corporate decisions, and the right to obtain information about the company in order to inform their decision-making and prevent management from taking decisions that are contrary to their interests" (UNCTAD 2010). This means that institutional investors, where they owned the bulk of shares, need to play a well-informed and very active role in monitoring the board of directors. In other words, according to UNCTAD report, "they should participate in the governance process, engage with company management and vote their shares responsibly" (UNCTAD 2010). However, in the United States, the UK and elsewhere, in the run up to and during the crisis, shareholders of financial institutions are rarely able to veto board members or propose new ones in annual meetings.

Notwithstanding this, there has been ample evidence in the United States and elsewhere, that indicates that these stockholder elementary rights are often ignored, violated and also not fulfilled by institutional investors (Bebchuck and Fried 2004; FSA 2009a, b; UNCTAD 2010). These research reports maintained that "board independence alone does not appear to have been able to control excessive risk-taking by banks, the growth of executive compensation, and ultimately, the riskiness of the banking sector during the crisis".

5.3.5 *The Ineffectiveness of Oversight Governance Structure*

The crisis uncovered severe gaps in supervision and regulation of the banking system, both on a national scale and internationally. This has led to an improved focus on a number of macro-prudential structures to monitor movements in systemic risk over time and between institutions (ICB 2011). Maintaining effective bank corporate governance needs suitable supervision, regulation and enforcement powers. In conjunction with regulation provisions relating to liquidity and adequacy of capital against the risk profile of financial institutions, most financial supervisors are intensively interested in the effectiveness of the corporate governance of the entity. In an ideal world, financial regulation or supervision and corporate governance of a financial institution needs to be equally supporting each other. However, they were demonstrably insufficient and, non-existent in several cases from the experience of the crunch (FSB 2011a, b). The evidence from the 2007/08 banking crisis from numerous government enquiries largely affirmed this assertion. In the UK, the FSA investigation regarding the supervision of Northern Rock, "noted inadequate staff resources and training so that its risk-based system of supervision was not effective". The report noted that "we cannot provide assurance that the prevailing framework for assessing risk was appropriately applied in relation to Northern Rock, so that the supervisory strategy was in line with the firms' risk profile" (FSA 2011). It reports further that "under-resourcing was also an issue, the internal report noting shortages of expertise in some fundamental areas, notably prudential banking experience and financial data analysis. These are important deficiencies in view of the demands placed on supervisors" (FSA 2011). Additionally, Keasey and Veronesi (2008) in their investigation regarding the reasons why the Northern Rock bank collapsed suggested that the prevailing tripartite supervisory structure in the UK "(HM Treasury, Bank of England and FSA) had the role of intervening ex post rather in a more alert role in order to avoid the disruption".

Furthermore, the then UK Financial Service Authority (FSA) in its final report entitled "The Failure of the Royal Bank of Scotland" highlighted a number of areas that collectively contributed to the collapse of the bank. Specifically, they stated that some of the key concerns were mainly attributed to the poor standard of the senior management decisions, deficits in bank regulations and a flawed supervisory approach to the banking institutions (FSA 2011, p. 21). As discussed in Sect. 5.2 regarding events leading up to the crisis, both regulators and financial institution management did not understand or focus on proper and judicious management of liquidity standards and risks of banks.[3] In fact, "they placed insufficient emphasis on managing the risk that funding sources might cease to be available, including a complete halt of the wholesale financial markets". This was a key trigger for several bank failures internationally, as well as in the United Kingdom during the financial crisis.

[3] 'In response to the crisis, in 2008 the BCBS published its Principles for Sound Liquidity Risk Management and Supervision, to promote stronger governance, risk management, disclosure and robust supervision of banks' liquidity management frameworks'.

The crisis also has underscored the importance of interconnectedness of large cross-border banking and other financial institutions, as well as the concern that a number of financial institutions are deemed to be "too big to fail" (ICB 2011; FSB 2011a, b).

Following the crisis, there have been important developments in the United States, the United Kingdom and internationally to improve not only the stability of the financial system but also significant improvements in the corporate governance rules and guidelines for financial institutions. Key instruments or measures that have been implemented or are being considered for reforms include tougher liquidity and capital rules, greater cross-border co-ordination on banking supervision and conducts, and improved resolution for larger systemic important financial institutions, among others (ICB 2011). The International Monetary Fund, the Financial Stability Board and the Bank for International Settlement have been working jointly to develop and implement effective macro-prudential rules and structures to toughen the resilience of the financial system. The specific measures that have been considered covers "loss-absorbency requirements, collating data and techniques for identifying systemic risk; and developing relevant corporate governance arrangements; and an effective macro-prudential toolkit for the use of such tools" (ICB 2011; FSB 2011a, b). The overriding objective of these new measures are to enable banking firms and national supervisors to coordinate, harmonise, extend and report more frequently on information that is used to monitor and deal effectively with systemic risks.

5.3.6 Gaps in Disclosure and Accounting Standards

The crisis in the financial sector has confirmed that the robustness, crystal clear accountable governance norms and practices must be entrenched in all firms, alongside a reassessment of the disclosures of a number of key governance mechanisms of accountability such as board level training and expertise, risk management and remuneration structures. The quality of disclosure of financial accounting information to stakeholders is a key requirement for effective and better corporate governance. It is established that sound corporate governance is predominantly essential in corporate financial reporting as it is a key determining factor in safeguarding confidence in capital markets through the provision of financial and other information of the upmost quality. The task of better corporate governance demands elevated accounting standards and financial reporting, particularly for financial institutions. Corporate disclosure to stakeholders is the principal means by which organisations can be transparent (Solomon 2007). Transparency is an essential element of a well-functioning system of accountable corporate governance (OECD 1999, 2004). Disclosure is critical to the functioning of an efficient capital market. The term "disclosure" refers to a whole array of different forms of information produced by companies, such as the annual report which includes the director's statement, Corporate Governance Statements, the Operating and Financial Review (OFR), assurance statement by independent qualified accountants and auditors, the profit and loss account, balance sheet, cash flow statement and other mandatory items. It also includes all forms of voluntary corporate communications, such as management forecasts, analysts' presentations, the AGM, press releases, information placed on corporate websites and other corporate reports, such as stand-alone environmental or social reports. Voluntary disclosure is defined as any disclosure above the mandated minimum.

The nature of both the mandatory and voluntary disclosures of this information provided by listed and non-listed firms are regulated by several national and international bodies. It is important to emphasise that the disclosure intention, as set out by the various supervisory and regulators, pay attention particularly, to the fundamental relationships and obligations between boards, auditors and shareholders. For example, the external auditor is supposed to add value by reporting on his independent assessment of whether certain aspects of the corporate governance statement abides by or conforms with defined corporate reporting standards. Such measures will indisputably make stronger the practices of corporate governance within individual organisations. The disclosures of these practices remain certainly a key element as it permits financiers, stakeholders and others to shape their individual opinion in relation to the way a company is controlled or governed. However, a number of accounting authorities and regulators have identified this as a major inadequacy following the banking crisis (UNCTAD 2010; FSA 2011; FSF 2008 and FRC 2014). For example, in the research investigation on OECD economies by UNCTAD, it indicated "that the readability of the risk disclosures is difficult or very difficult and that there is generally no consistent global set of generally accepted risk management accounting principles and additional guidance available for risk disclosures in the annual report (van Manen 2009)" (UNCTAD 2010, p. 73). In response to the crisis and the weaknesses implicated, the Financial Stability Forum in 2008 offered encouragement to various financial institutions to create vigorous risk disclosures by employing the foremost disclosure practices that were proposed by the Senior Supervisors Group.

Additionally, the accounting regulators in the United States and the "Financial Accounting Standard Board" have identified the following gaps in financial reporting disclosures affecting governance; (a) lack of disclosures regarding consistency of generally accepted risk management accounting principles in annual reports; (b) disclosure and misuse of off-balance-sheet information; and (c) lack of consistency in the valuation of assets disclosure standards and methodologies to shareholders and regulators (UNCTAD 2010, p. 73). The US regulators and members of both the US Senate and House of Representatives also clearly blame these gaps as a key contributor to the cause of the credit crunch and subsequent collapse in the financial system globally. Also, several market observers and regulators were wary in the financial markets that different banks employed very different valuations for the same asset adding to market opacity and reduced integrity.

The quality and the role of accurate provisions of high standard accounting information to key stakeholders is not new to major global crisis. Following the Enron scandals in 2001 and 2002, the Financial Accounting Regulatory Authority in the United States (i.e. Financial Accounting Standard Board), introduced a number of rule changes and disclosure requirements that effectively strengthened the possibility for not misusing off-balance-sheet entities, and yet the problem re-emerged once again during the financial crisis in 2007/08.

A number of Prudential standards in the OECD jurisdictions encouraged financial intermediaries to "engage in regulatory arbitrage by taking mortgages and other assets off the balance sheet and to finance them separately in conduits, or Qualified Special Purpose Entities" (QSPE).[4] This allowed them to economise on banks' regulatory capital while booking fees from the transaction. A key importance highlighted in the establishment of this guide was to be fully transparent with shareholders. An example where this proved problematic was when Citibank failed to disclose to both the board and shareholders the full risk associated with

[4] "Qualified Special Purpose Entities is a device created in the mid-1990s to permit off-balance-sheet treatment for securitisation of financial instruments. The criterion is that the off-balance-sheet entity should be able to function independently from the originator".

their use of off-balance CDO security. This resulted in $25 billion having to be put back on the balance sheet in November 2007. Similarly, during the financial crisis, a number of financial institutions had to bring back some of the off-balance-sheet securities and derivatives that resulted in both credibility and reputational loss to the entities.

5.3.7 *Misleading Information Provided by Rating Agencies*

Traditionally and until the global financial crisis, Credit Rating Agencies (CRA) seem to operate somehow saliently but as powerful actors in the financial industry and as reliable caretakers that provide appropriate independent risk assessment and quality assurance to numerous financiers for government and corporate securities globally. The key task of Credit Rating Agencies is to assess debt issuers and specific debt issues that can be described here as; (a) by evaluating default probabilities (e.g. corporate and sovereign bonds, commercial paper, state and municipal bonds) using private and public information provided by the issuers and (b) by notifying financial markets of their valuation through the issuing of bond ratings. The significant role of determining the future creditworthiness of certain borrowers and securities regarding the specific date gives assurance to both investor and issuers in their belief that rating agencies have specialised skills with relation to assessing credit and default risk (Han et al. 2010; Chemrat 2014). As a result, CRAs make known essential additional information about a firm to the financial and the credit markets in the form of ratings and "thus help reduce information asymmetry between the issuing firm and potential investors in the new debt issue"—as discussed, a key role performed by financial institutions. According to Turner—"*It is a valuable role since (i) good investment practice should seek diversification across a wide spread of investments; and (ii) it is impossible for all but the very largest investing institutions to perform independent analysis of a large number of issuing institutions*" (Turner 2009).

Some global rating agencies control around 80% of the global credit ratings market (*Wall Street Journal* 2003). Agencies with this level of influence include both Standard & Poor and Moody's. Interest rates paid on its price, security and yield are all affected by the ratings that are assigned by the credit rating agencies. There is an inverse relationship between higher ratings provided by the rating agencies for a creditor, and a low probability of default risk associated with the creditors.

The value of information that is being provided by Credit Rating Agencies came under severe scrutiny during the financial crisis in 2008/09 period (Walker 2009). In fact, while boards of financial institutions are primarily responsible for the weaknesses and failure of risk assessment and management and remunerations, other aspects of the corporate governance framework by credit rating agencies have also played a role for the crisis. Many of the CRAs were accused of providing false, misleading and poor disclosure information regarding several financial institutions and many of the financial product ratings they were offering Hoogeboom 2010; Sinclair 2010. The criticisms stem from the fact that many financial institutions and investors depended heavily prior to the crisis on bond and other securitised product ratings for credit, loans and asset investment decisions to various creditors. A number of regulatory bodies, namely the International Organisation of Securities Commissions, the US Security and Exchange Commission and the Financial Stability Forum have started to recommend mechanisms for strengthening of the voluntary code for CRAs to follow in their assessment process for underwriting work. These recommendations came about as most rating agencies were partially implicated for contributing to the global financial crisis due to lapses in underwriting standards, culture and practices (FSF 2008; Turner 2009). For example, in the UK, the FSA investigation concluded that "*poor credit assessments by CRAs have contributed both to the build-up to and the unfolding of recent events. In particular, CRAs assigned high ratings to complex structured subprime debt based on inadequate historical data and in some cases flawed models*" (UNCTAD 2010).

There are several prior academic literatures indicating that corporate governance factors affect corporate bond yields. For example, the studies conducted by Liu and Jiraporn (2010), Bradley and Chen (2010), and Bhojraj and Sengupta (2003) suggested in their conclusions that corporate governance affects the costs of debt. Additionally, Miller and Puthenpurackal (2005) and Petrasek (2010) research suggests that global bond issuance reduces the cost of corporate debt due to the higher liquidity of global bonds. These studies have been collaborated following the crisis by various studies and investigations. The Eurozone and the US bond market crisis in 2008 that led to various countries' and individual large firms defaults and losses were due to sudden bond rating downgrades that were previously assigned higher ratings (Nanto et al. 2009; Reavis 2009; Turner 2009). Tables 5.1a and 5.1b perfectly illustrate the magnitude of the impact of credit rating agency downgrades.

Table 5.1a Corporate finance cumulative default rates 1981–2008 (%) of Standard & Poor

Bond rating type (%)	*Years after the issue of security*		
	5	*10*	*15*
AAA	0.3	0.6	0.7
AA	0.3	0.8	1.2
A	0.7	1.9	2.9
BBB	2.4	5.2	7.7
BB	9.1	16.0	19.3
B	20.6	28.4	33.1
CCC/C	44.9	50.4	52.9

Source Adapted from Turner (2009)

Table 5.1b Global structured finance 1-year transition rates of largest CRAs

Bond rating type (%)	*Financial crisis year 2007*			*Financial crisis year 2008*		
	Downgrade	*Upgrade*	*Stable*	*Downgrade*	*Upgrade*	*Stable*
AAA	1	n/a	99	23	0	77
AA	4	4	92	35	2	63
A	11	4	84	37	2	61
BBB	20	3	77	40	1	58
BB	21	2	77	45	2	54
B	11	2	87	56	1	44
CCC	35	1	33	79	1	21

Source Adapted from Turner (2009)

A key example of the effect of the sudden bond downgrades by credit rating agencies during the financial crisis, can be seen with the cumulative asset write-down loss of $93.4 billion experienced by Merrill Lynch (US$26.1billion), AIG (US$33.2billion) and Citigroup (US$34.1billion) in October 2008 (Benmelech and Dlugosz 2010).

5.4 Conclusion

The subprime mortgage crisis in the United States began in the year 2007, once the housing industry's asset boom collapsed. It was noticeable and at the time customary practice that with the previous years' increasing home values and low mortgage rates, several participants in the market bought houses not as places to live in, but as investment vehicles. Government backed financial institutions in the United States like Fannie Mae and Freddie Mac guaranteed mortgages, even if they were subprime or those lent to people who wouldn't normally qualify for housing loans. Since the financial industry heavily invested in mortgage-backed derivatives, the housing industry's downturn became the financial industry's catastrophe. The 2008 Great Recession was triggered by the 2007 financial crisis.

The result of the financial crisis has moved forward the vital role of corporate governance to the top of the agenda for corporate boards, governments and regulators around the world, specifically in the areas of risk management, supervisory functions and executive compensation. It has been acknowledged and confirmed by a number of reports and particularly, by the G20, that one of the causes of the financial crisis was the inadequate devised senior managerial compensation packages that led to excessive risk taking in financial institutions. The discussions and assessment made in this chapter in relation to the causes of the financial crisis internationally indicate that not only supervisory and regulatory limitations at the global and national levels are to blame, but also was due to structural deficiencies of corporate governance practices in relation to the board of directors and risk management standards prevalent in several large financial institutions.

The influence and the effect of the worldwide financial crisis on the global economic system has helped to emphasise the interconnectedness of the health of large global financial corporations and the effect on the livelihood of many ordinary people. Although the causes that are attributed to the crisis are complex in nature and the solutions that have been proposed are multidimensional, corporate governance and its various accountability mechanisms still feature convincingly.

References

BCBS. (2010a). *Principles for enhancing corporate governance*. Basel: Basel Committee on Banking Supervision.

BCBS. (2010b). *Basel III: International framework for liquidity risk measurement, standards and monitoring*. Basel: Basel Committee on Banking Supervision.

Bebchuck, L. A., & Fried, J. (2004). *Pay without performance: The unfulfilled promise of executive compensation*. Harvard University Press.

Benmelech, E., & Dlugosz, J. (2010). The credit rating crisis. *NBER Macroeconomic Annual, 24*, 161–207.

Bhojraj, S., & Sengupta, P. (2003). Effect of corporate governance on bond ratings and yields: The role of institutional investors and outside directors. *The Journal of Business, 76*(3), 455–475.

Blundell-Wignall, A., Atkinson, P., & Lee, S. (2008). The current financial crisis: Causes and policy issues (white paper). *Organization for Economic Co-operation and Development: Financial Market Trends, 2008*(2), 1–21.

Bradley, M., & Chen, D. (2010). Corporate governance, credit condition, and the cost of debt. *SSRN Electronic Journal.*

Buiter, W. (2009). *Lessons from the global financial crisis for regulators and supervisors*. London: Financial Markets Group, London School of Economics and Political Science.

Cheffins, B. R. (2009). *Did corporate governance 'fail' during the 2008 market meltdown? The case of the S&P 500* (ECGI Law Working Papers No. 124/2009).

Chemrat, O. (2014). *'Credit rating agencies', liability in the light of the global financial crisis of 2008–2009*. Central European University.

Clarke, T. (2010). Recurring crises in Anglo-American corporate governance. *Contribution to Political Economy, 29*(1), 9–32.

Fetisov, G. (2009). Measures to overcome the global crisis and establish a stable financial and economic system. *Problems of Economic Transition, 52*(5), 20–34.

Financial Reporting Council (FRC). (2012). *The UK stewardship code*. London: Financial Reporting Council.

Financial Reporting Council (FRC). (2014). *Guidance on risk management internal control and related financial and business reporting*. London: Financial Reporting Council.

Financial Service Authority (FSA). (2009a, September). *Reforming remuneration practices in the financial services, Consultation Paper*. London.

Financial Service Authority (FSA). (2009b, March). *The Turner review: A regulatory response to the global banking crisis*. London.

Financial Stability Board (FSB). (2011a, November). *FSB issues international standard for resolution regimes*. Press release.

Financial Stability Board (FSB). (2011b). *Effective resolution of systemically important financial institutions*.

Financial Stability Forum (FSF). (2008, April). *Report of the financial stability forum on enhancing market and institutional resilience*. New York.

Han, S. H., Pagano, M. S., & Shin, Y. S. (2010). *Rating agency reputation, the global financial crisis, and the cost of debt*.

Hoogeboom, Q. (2010). *The role of credit rating agencies in the subprime crisis of 2008–2009*.

Holland, J. (2010). Banks, knowledge and crisis: A case of knowledge and learning failure. *Journal of Financial Regulation and Compliance, 18*(2), 87–105.

Independent Commission on Banking (ICB). (2011, September). *Final report recommendations*.

Kay Review. (2012, July). *The Kay Review of UK equity markets and long-term decision making*. Final Report.

Keasey, K., & Veronesi, G. (2008). Lessons from the northern rock affair. *Journal of Financial Regulation and Compliance, 16*(1), 8–18.

Kirkpatrick, G. (2009). The corporate governance lessons from the financial crisis. *Financial Markets Trends, OECD: Financial Regulation and Compliance, 16*(1), 8–18.

Lang, W. W., & Jagtiani, J. A. (2010). The mortgage and financial crises: The role of credit risk management and corporate governance. *Atlantic Economic Journal, 38*(2), 295–316.

Liu, Y., & Jiraporn, P. (2010). The effect of CEO power on bond ratings and yields. *Journal of Empirical Finance, 17*4), 744–762.

Miller, D. P., & Puthenpurackal, J. (2005). Security fungibility and the cost of capital: Evidence from global bonds. *Journal of Financial and Quantitative Analysis, 40*(4), 849–872.

Moxey, P., & Berendt, A. (2008, November). *Corporate governance and the credit crunch*. ACCA Discussion Paper. London: ACCA.

Nanto, D. K., et al. (2009). *The global financial crisis: Analysis and policy implications*. CRS.

OECD. (1999). *OECD principles of corporate governance*. Paris: OECD Publishing.

OECD. (2004). *OECD principles of corporate governance*. France: Organisation for Economic Co-operation and Development.

OECD. (2009a). *The financial crisis, reforms and exit strategies*. France: Organisation for Economic Co-operation and Development.

OECD. (2009b). *Business ethics and OECD principles: What can be done to avoid another crisis*. France: Organisation for Economic Co-operation and Development.

Parliamentary Commission on Banking Standards. (2013). *Changing banking for good. First report of sessions 2013–14* (Vol. II). House of Commons.

Petrasck, L. (2010). Multimarket trading and the cost of debt: Evidence from global bonds. *SSRN Electronic Journal*.

Pirson, M., & Turnbull, S. (2010). The future of corporate governance: Network governance—A lesson from the financial crisis. *SSRN Electronic Journal*.

Pirson, M., & Turnbull, S. (2011). Corporate governance, risk management, and the financial crisis: An information processing view. *Corporate Governance: An International Review, 19*(5), 459–470.

Reavis, C. (2009). *The global financial crisis of 2008–2009: The role of greed, fear and oligarchs*.
Solomon, J. (2007). *Corporate governance and accountability* (3rd ed.). John Wiley and Sons Ltd.
Solomon, J. (2013). *Corporate governance and accountability* (4th ed.). West Sussex: Wiley.
Tarraf, H. (2010). Literature review on corporate governance and the recent financial crisis. *SSRN Electronic Journal*.
Turner Review. (2009). *The Turner review: A regulatory response to the global banking crisis*. London: Financial Service Authority.
Sinclair, T. J. (2010). *Credit rating agencies and the global financial crisis*. Economic.
UBS. (2008, April 18). *Shareholder report on UBS's write-downs*.
United Nations Conference on Trade and Development (UNCTAD). (2010, October). *Corporate governance in the wake of the financial crisis, selected international reviews*. New York and Geneva: United Nations.
Walker, S. D. (2009). *A review of corporate governance in UK banks and other financial industry entities*. Final recommendations.
Yeoh, P. (2010). Causes of the global financial crisis: Learning from the competing insights. *International Journal of Disclosure and Governance, 7*, 42–69.

CHAPTER 6

Why? Examining and Understanding the UK Financial System and Its Regulatory Framework for Corporate Governance

6.1 Introduction

The UK banking and other financial sectors have become progressively more diverse in scope and international in orientation. Its international character is increasingly indicated by the significant number and sizeable assets of foreign banks operating in London in both commercial and investment banking. The UK banking industry represents an important and essential component of the overall output of the United Kingdom.

Thus, this chapter provides an understanding of the nature of the UK banking sector and corporate governance in the United Kingdom. An analysis and discussion of the background circumstances seek to provide useful understanding of the conclusions observed in this study. This chapter outlines an overview of the UK financial and banking sector and sets out its importance in an international context. Using a stakeholder perspective, this chapter also aims to set the scene of the contextual analysis for understanding the relationship between the industry corporate governance and accountability framework applicable to the United Kingdom.

J. A. Akuffo, *Corporate Governance and Accountability of Financial Institutions*, Palgrave Studies in Accounting and Finance Practice, https://doi.org/10.1007/978-3-030-64046-0_6

6.2 Why the United Kingdom Is a Major International Financial Centre

To attempt to measure and assess the potential impact of the size of the UK banking system on financial stability, it is important to identify what factors may have led the UK banking system to its current size, and which of them could have a significant influence and affect its future growth. This subsection of the chapter identifies a number of possible factors, namely: comparative advantage; the benefits from clustering in financial hubs; historical factors; and the implicit subsidy associated with "too big to fail" (TBTF) banks (Bank of England 2013a, b). The first three of these factors are closely related to the international nature of the UK banking system.

Firstly, the benefit of comparative advantage being enjoyed by the United Kingdom could explain why there is a financial centre in the United Kingdom? One explanation may be that the United Kingdom is able to produce banking and other financial services more efficiently than other countries. In other words, it may have a comparative advantage in providing international financial and banking services. The sources of this advantage may include the United Kingdom's central time zone location between the United States and Asia, its openness to trade and capital flows, its language and its robust legal and regulatory structure (Carney 2013; Bush et al. 2014). A useful resource to view can be found in the International Monetary Fund (IMF) World Economic Outlook (October 2014) and OECD report, it is also cited in the Bank of England Quarterly report by Bush, Knott and Peacock (2014). The reports provided some supporting evidence that openness has been an important factor in the growth of financial centres. It looks at the measure of financial openness—the ratio of gross capital flows[1] to world GDP. It also presents a measure of the cross-country variation in banking system size relative to GDP. When the ratio is low, banking systems across the world are similarly sized. But when it is high, some are much larger than others and also shows that when financial openness has been high, there has been a tendency for financial activity to cluster in a few large international financial centres and vice versa. This is consistent with the fall in UK banking

[1] Variation in financial system size is measured as the coefficient of variation of financial sector output shares of GDP. Gross capital flows are shown as a percentage of worlds GDP. The sample includes all OECD member countries excluding Luxembourg.

system size relative to GDP since the 2008–2009 crisis: over the past four years it has shrunk by 100% of GDP on a residency basis.

Second, the United Kingdom maintains the benefit of the global financial hubs in the banking sector due to a significant number of factors. One factor behind the existence of international financial centres, including the United Kingdom, is likely to be the gains from clustering, when firms and people locate near one another in cities and industrial clusters (Glaeser 2010).[2] United Kingdom is both home and host to large domestic and international financial institutions (IMF 2011, 2012). International foreign bank subsidiaries and branches hold half of UK banking assets, while according to the Financial Stability Board (2013, p. 46) "UK-owned banks have over half of their assets outside the country. Overall, these institutions hold over £12 trillion of assets in the United Kingdom and globally, equal to just over eight times GDP, of which UK banks account for assets equivalent to five times GDP". The UK insurance industry is the third largest in the world, after the United States and Japan. The United Kingdom is an important host to the global funds industry and to derivatives business and plays a significant role in cross-border trading and clearing (Table 6.2). Hence, the International Monetary Fund in its 2011 report suggested that the "financial institutions in the United Kingdom and its market infrastructure are broadly wide open to stresses originating from somewhere else in the world and also act as a conduit of shocks domestically and to the global financial system (IMF 2011)". Also, see details in Table 6.3.

Third, the United Kingdom is a major global hub for international wholesale finance. Within the United Kingdom, the importance of London is core to its international position. London is a dominant factor worldwide in most segments of financial markets (see Table 6.5 in the Appendix). In particular, UK markets, infrastructure, and UK-based institutions have a large or dominant role across a broad range of global cross-border financial operations. Thus while US equity and bond markets are larger, they are more domestically focused, whereas London markets are dominant in secondary market trading of international bonds or foreign equity listings. London markets—closely related with international banking activities, foreign exchange and derivative markets in

[2] The benefits of clustering include higher productivity and wages and competitive advantage in the world trade for industries within the agglomeration (Crafts and Wolf 2013).

particular—are also the most important globally, and some specialist insurance functions serving internationally active firms are located there (notably in transportation). Finally, and directly related with the presence of these markets and functions, much of the critical infrastructure of global finance—in the form of central counterparties (CCPs)—is in London (BIS 2011; IMF Stability Report 2012; TheCityUK 2012 Banking Report[3]).

Fourth, according to the International Monetary Fund (IMF 2012), "*it is no surprise that location data from the Bank of International Settlements on cross-border holdings shows the UK is "central" to the global financial network in the sense of having many large connections to other centres, including other well-connected financial centres. But the UK is also central in the sense of lying on the path between other nodes, reflecting its role as a financial centre where a bank from a second country raises money in a third country to lend to a fourth. On this measure of centrality, the UK exceeds all other financial centres including the United States*" (IMF 2012, Spill over Report). The report was based on using information from the Bank of International Settlements global financial locational network analysis. The IMF argued for this reason, a shock to a link with the United Kingdom can spread through the financial network faster than shocks to links unconnected to the United Kingdom. For example, the IMF identifies two UK banks as having high potential to generate spillovers. These UK institutions are also among the most susceptible to spillovers from others and are more likely to be affected in times of market stress, including dislocations in funding markets or a generalised sell off in broader asset markets. A freeze in wholesale funding markets would hit UK banks particularly hard, which in fact can exacerbate their deleveraging both in the United Kingdom and outside. By contrast, a sovereign shock would affect the United Kingdom only indirectly through stress and deleveraging of foreign banks (Bush et al. 2014).

The financial crisis of 2007/08 revealed major fault lines in the UK financial sector and its regulatory and governance framework (IMF 2011), in dealing with systemic shock posed by interrelated banks. The heavy reliance on market discipline and the assumption of a wide dispersion of risks proved to be inadequate. Substantial risks posed by large, complex and interconnected financial institutions crystallised, exposing weaknesses

[3]TheCityUK is the industry-led body representing UK-based financial and related professional services.

in the oversight framework that had enabled the expansion of their reach and complexity, both domestically and internationally (IMF 2011a). Additionally, in the UK spillover report (IMF 2012), the IMF highlighted that the UK financial sector function played an intermediating role in worldwide savings and providing market/legal infrastructure for financial services. The UK financial system thus serves as a global public good, warranting the highest quality supervision and regulation.

Lastly, another possible factor behind the growth in the United Kingdom and other banking systems is that they have benefited from an implicit government subsidy. This is an example of a market friction—something which, according to economic theory, leads to the over or undersupply of goods or services relative to the amount that would be most beneficial for society. The implicit government subsidy arises because some banks effectively receive insurance from the government without fully paying for it. Specifically, unlike with most other firms, holders of certain banks' debt have historically not faced sufficient risk of loss because they expect the government to prevent banks from failing, as they did in a number of cases in the recent financial crisis. To the extent that banks and creditors do not pay for this guarantee, it can be considered an implicit subsidy (Noss and Sowerbutts 2012). Estimates of the extent of the implicit subsidy vary by sample period and the estimation method used, but it is material on most measures. For instance, a study by the IMF (2014) suggests that in 2011–2012 the implicit subsidy was in the range of US$20 billion to US$110 billion for major UK banks, US$15 billion to US$70 billion for major US banks, and US$90 billion to US$300 billion for major euro-area banks (IMF 2014; and BOE calculations and cited in Bank Of England Quarterly report by Bush, Knott and Peacock 2014). To try to make the implicit subsidy estimates more comparable across regions, the authors used estimates of the implicit subsidy value for G-SIBs in the euro area, the United Kingdom and the United States from 2011 to 2012. The report shows a proxy for the subsidy per unit of asset for major banks in each region. This proxy is only a partial picture—for example, it covers only the global systemically important banks (G-SIBs)[4]—but on the face of it, it suggests that the scale of the implicit subsidy in the United Kingdom was no bigger than in the euro area and therefore it is unlikely to explain why

[4] See detail on BCB 2011, Global Systemically Important Banks: Assessment Methodology and the Additional Loss Absorbency Requirement.

the United Kingdom has a much larger banking system as a share of GDP. However, according to Bank of England, there is some evidence that implicit (and explicit) government guarantees lead banks to overinvest in risky assets (for example, see Marques et al. 2013; Gropp et al. 2013). Hence, micro-prudential regulation—implemented in the United Kingdom by the Prudential Regulation Authority—aims to mitigate this, in part, by ensuring that banks have sufficient levels of capital and liquidity to reflect the risks that they take. And macro-prudential policy—carried out in the United Kingdom by the Financial Policy Committee—aims to ensure the resilience of the financial system as a whole (see Farag et al. 2013; Tucker et al. 2013).

6.3 The Structure of Banking (Deposit-Taking) Institutions

This section describes and outlines the current structure of the UK banking environment, institutions and the overall functions.

6.3.1 General Functions of the Financial Services Sector

The financial system provides a range of services that support the real economy. It is convenient to distinguish three main types of financial service:

1. **Payment, settlement and transaction services**: These services include the provision of deposit and custody accounts, as well as services to support the efficient settlement of payments between households and companies.
2. **Intermediation**: Household savings are typically pooled in deposit accounts, pension funds or mutual funds. They are then transformed into funding for households, companies or government.
3. **Risk transfer and insurance**: Deposit accounts allow households and companies to insure themselves against liquidity shocks, while securitisation, derivatives and other insurance contracts facilitate the dispersion of other financial risks within the economy. For example, foreign exchange derivatives allow companies to protect their international revenues from fluctuations in foreign exchange rates; and securitisation markets package and disperse banks' loan exposures.

6.3.2 *The Size and Number of Banks in the United Kingdom*

How big is the UK banking sector? The banking system size is often measured by the sum of assets held by banks on their balance sheets (Bush et al. 2014). These assets include loans to households and companies, as well as securities, such as bonds and equities, and other assets. How different types of assets are measured, among other factors, can have a material impact on estimates of banking system size. Banking assets are often expressed as a share of nominal GDP. While there is no mechanical link between the two variables, this gives a measure of the size of a banking sector relative to overall economic activity. The UK banking sector consists of UK incorporated banks and foreign banks operating in the United Kingdom. According to the IMF (2011), the United Kingdom is both home and host to systemically important financial institutions (SIFIs). The "UK banking sector" could be defined in several ways (Table 6.1):

- one focused purely on the UK-based assets, either from UK banks or foreign banks' operations in the United Kingdom (I + II + III);
- one focused on all assets of UK-owned banks, in the United Kingdom and abroad (I + IV + V); or
- a combination of both. Conceptually, there is no consensus definition, and various analyses of the UK banking sector may include or exclude any of the items above, depending on the focus.

UK incorporated banks consist of both UK and foreign-owned banks authorised by the Financial Services Authority (FSA) under the Financial Services and Markets Act 2000 (FSMA). They include commercial

Table 6.1 Possible definitions of the UK banking sector

United Kingdom	*Abroad*
UK-owned banks (I)	Foreign branches of UK-owned banks (IV)
Branches of foreign-owned banks (II)	Foreign subsidiaries of UK owned banks (V)
Subsidiaries of foreign-owned banks (III)	

Source IMF Spill over Report (2011)

banks, investment banks and other UK banks such as London headquarters of banks operating abroad, private banks and banks operated by retail companies. The number of UK incorporated banks declined to 157 in 2011 from 189 a decade earlier (Table 6.2). This was due to a fall in the number of UK-owned incorporated banks. During this period the number of foreign-owned UK incorporated banks increased from 77 to 85. UK incorporated banks consist of UK and foreign-owned banks authorised by the Financial Services Authority (FSA) under the Financial Services and Markets Act 2000 (FSMA). These mainly include commercial banks, investment banks, branches of foreign-owned banks and banks operated by retail companies.

On the other hand, foreign banks in the United Kingdom are authorised by the Financial Services Authority (FSA) or their home country within the European Economic Area (EEA), to open branches in the United Kingdom. London is a major centre for international banking and many foreign banks have located branches and representative offices there. At the end of March 2011 there were 251 foreign banks that were physically located in the United Kingdom, with the majority of these located in the City of London. Most of these banks were from Japan, Germany, United States, Italy and Switzerland.

The banking industry within the United Kingdom represents the fourth biggest in terms of financial institutions assets in the world. Detail is provided in Table 6.3 to show the system structure in the United

Table 6.2 Overview of the number of banks in the United Kingdom

Number of banks in the UK	*Year on year trends*					
Year end–March	*1990*	*1995*	*2000*	*2009*	*2010*	*2011*
Incorporated in the UK	289	224	189	159	156	157
UK owned	209	142	112	71	70	72
Foreign-owned [1]	80	82	77	88	86	85
Incorporated outside the UK	259	301	242	166	162	192
UK branch of an EEA firm [2]	115	102	115	82	79	86
UK service of an EEA firm	–	44	–	5	7	26
Outside the EEA [3]		155	127	79	76	80
Total authorised banks	548	525	369	325	318	323
Foreign banks physically located in the UK [1] + [2] + [3]	195	339	319	249	241	251

Source Adapted from Bank of England, Financial Services Authority

Table 6.3 Structure of UK banking system (in GBP millions)

Date	*Firm*	*Total assets*		*Total sterling assets*		*Sterling loans and advances*	
		Amount	*Proportion (%)*	*Amount*	*Proportion (%)*	*Amount*	*Proportion (%)*
Dec-10	UK owned MFIs	5,968,217	49.20	2,602,367	71.00	1,987,967	70.90
	Non-UK owned MFIs	6,169,746	50.80	1,062,145	29.00	815,570	29.10
		12,137,963	**100**	**3,664,512**	**100**	**2,803,537**	**100**
Dec-11	UK owned MFIs	6,384,494	47.20	2,637,824	72.00	2,175,867	73.40
	Non-UK owned MFIs	7,156,072	52.80	1,027,610	28.00	786,531	26.60
		13,540,566	**100**	**3,665,434**	**100**	**2,962,398**	**100**
Dec-12	UK owned MFIs	5,953,424	47.80	2,684,131	72.60	2,289,625	75.90
	Non-UK owned MFIs	6,498,745	52.20	1,010,551	27.40	728,063	24.10
		12,452,169	**100**	**3,694,682**	**100**	**3,017,688**	**100**

Source Adapted from Bank of England (2012b)

Kingdom. UK banking sector assets are the fourth largest in the world and include large domestic and foreign-owned financial institutions. The latter—consisting of both foreign branches and subsidiaries—account for one half of banking assets in the United Kingdom, while UK-owned banks have over half of their assets outside the country. Overall, these institutions hold over GBP 12 trillion of assets in the United Kingdom and globally, equal to just over eight times GDP, of which banks resident in the United Kingdom account for assets equivalent to five times GDP. Foreign branches alone account for one-third of UK resident banks' assets.

Additionally, the financial sector in the United Kingdom is broadly dominated by very few but large institutions in terms of products and services that are offered, although there are several hundred operated in the sector. The leading five banks within the United Kingdom according to their market capitalisation[5] are: "HSBC Holdings plc, Lloyds Banking Group plc, Barclays plc, Standard Chartered plc, and the Royal Bank of Scotland Group plc". These five remain at the forefront regarding business banking markets and personal account markets (apart from Standard Chartered Group). However, the loan and savings market face mounting rivalry from other large corporate intermediaries (for example life insurance firms).

6.3.3 UK Bank Lending, Funding and Other Assets

Banks' assets consist of a small amount of cash to meet normal deposit withdrawals; short term or easily realisable bills (both Treasury and commercial), investments, claims under sale and repurchase agreements, but the major part of the banks' assets is lending. UK-owned and incorporated banks hold significant assets abroad, while foreign bank subsidiaries and branches hold more than half of UK-based banking sector assets (Fig. 6.1). There are a number of key observations of the IMF Spill over report for the United Kingdom in 2011 which can be noted in the following summary:

Firstly, UK-based banking assets are dominated by foreign banks, which hold more than half the total banking assets in the United Kingdom. Of this amount, European banks hold more than half (54%), while US banks account for 15%. Second, UK-owned and incorporated banks represent a small share of UK-based banking sector assets. The top five UK banks (HSBC, RBS, Barclays, LBG, and SCB) hold 22% of UK-based banking sector assets, while foreign-owned and UK incorporated banks (e.g. Santander UK) own an additional 27%. Third, only two of the six major UK-owned and incorporated banks have a strong domestic focus. Specifically, LBG and Nationwide operate almost exclusively within UK borders.

[5] "According to the OFT, the top 5 retail banks (HSBC, Barclays, Lloyds Banking Group, Royal Bank of Scotland and Santander UK jointly making up to approximately 85% of the PCA markets" (Slaughter and May 2014, p. 856).

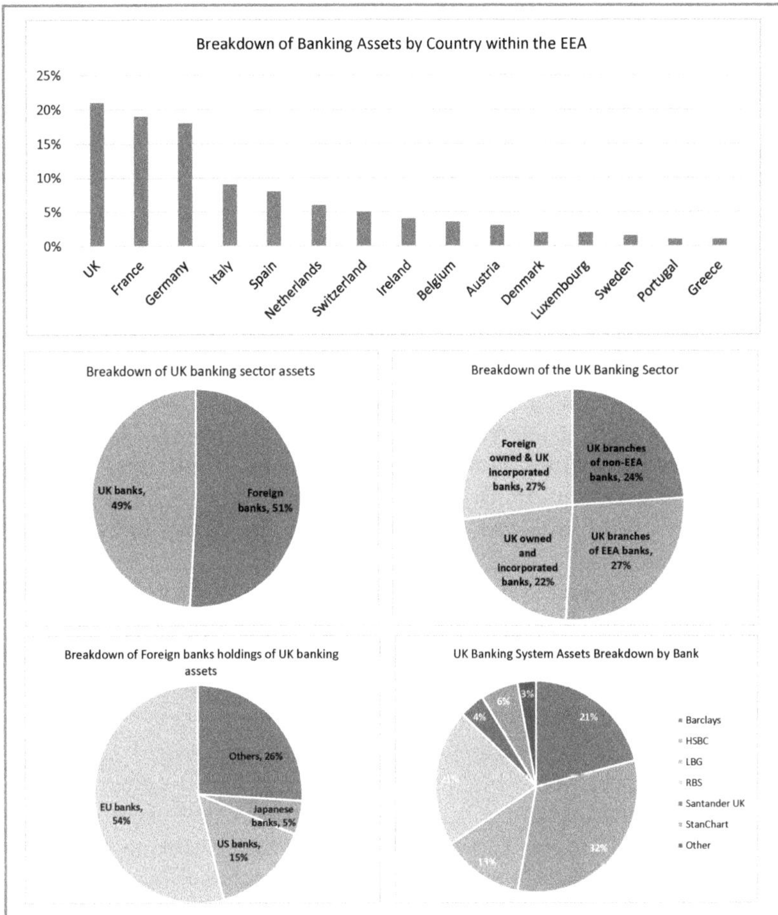

Fig. 6.1 Overview of the UK Banking Sector (*Source* IMF Spill over Report 2011, TheCityUK 2012; EBF; and Estimates from various annual reports of Banks)

Conversely, the remaining four major UK-owned and incorporated banks have more diversified geographic profiles. Fourth, UK-owned and incorporated banks hold significant assets abroad. For example, SCB has less than 5% of its business in the United Kingdom, while HSBC Holdings Plc has significant operations in the Asian region and other emerging market countries (Fig. 6.1). Separately, Barclays has increased its exposure to the United States, following its acquisition of the Lehman Brothers franchise. Fifth, the UK-based portion of UK-owned and incorporated banks' assets is less than half of those banks' total assets. The five major UK banks hold 40–45% of United Kingdom based banking sector assets. According to the British Bankers' Association, the Herfindahl index for the share of total assets of the five largest credit institutions shows that the United Kingdom is only the twenty-third most concentrated EU market.

Similarly, it can be highlighted that foreign banks primarily use London as their international funding and trading platform. London is a major financial hub, offering a broad range of financial and support services, a deep talent pool, comprehensive market infrastructure, all located in a convenient time zone. For these reasons, it is an attractive place for foreign banks to conduct their international investment banking operations (IMF 2011 Spillover Report). There are fewer foreign banks providing traditional loans to the UK economy. Santander UK (a foreign-owned, UK incorporated bank) is a prime example of a foreign bank that grew through the acquisition of local banks to expand its presence in the UK retail market (BOE 2010). Irish banks are also active in the UK retail market, as are Australian and German banks, lending either to UK households or corporates.

Furthermore, the structure of the UK banking system has important policy implications with regard to effective corporate governance, from both regulatory and supervisory perspectives. For instance, European Economic Area banks hold 27% of UK-based banking assets. Set up as branches in the United Kingdom (through "pass porting" rules), they remain under the supervision of their home authority, and the UK authorities have very limited oversight powers over them. Conversely, many UK-owned banks have significant activities outside the United Kingdom while the UK authorities retain consolidated supervision powers over these groups, individual subsidiaries are also subject to host country supervision and local regulations. The banking system in the United Kingdom is particularly concentrated. Partly because of their size and interconnectedness, four UK-owned banks are on the Financial Stability Board's list of global systemically important banks, which requires them to have more capital (which can absorb losses when economic conditions deteriorate). What I have described above has been confirmed in the IMF report (2011) titled United Kingdom: Financial System Stability Assessment, where the importance of the United Kingdom as a key global financial centre is illustrated using key facts regarding the UK Bank Lending and Funding structures.

Moreover, the UK banking system evolved intensively after 2000 in ways that made it more vulnerable to adverse shocks. The banks became larger, highly complex and leveraged and relied increasingly on short-term wholesale funding (Fig. 6.2). However, according to the IMF, the trading book displaced loans as the most important balance sheet asset, reducing the importance of net interest income (IMF 2011a).[6] Financial activity was concentrated in a small set of institutions highly interconnected to other developed financial systems. Actual leverage was greater than was apparent, in part because regulatory requirements did not capture key risks.

6.3.4 *UK Largest Banks and Consolidation After Financial Crisis in 2007/08*

The number of UK incorporated banks has been on a downward trend since the mid-1990s (as observed in Table 6.2) despite the conversion of a number of building societies into banks and an increase in the number of new entrants into the market. The largest banks are the major high street banks (see Table 6.4 in Appendix 3 for details). These banks dominate the UK current account market and account for over half of credit cards and personal loans. Branch networks remain an important point of service delivery for banks. Technology is having a major impact on banking in creating new ways in which banks are delivering services to their customers.

The competitive pressures on banks' margins have kept the focus on cost control as a strategic priority. This has resulted in the reduction of the branch network. Many banks are seeking to reduce costs through a combination of outsourcing and offshoring. Operations have in some cases been centralised, allowing lower unit processing costs. Staff numbers

[6] The increasing involvement by banks in leveraged trading activities in the lead-up to the crisis is largely seen to have played an important role in the financial stress many experienced. A survey by the FSA of 10 investment banks suggests that some $240 billion of losses on trading positions between January 2007 and March 2009 were attributable to structured credit products, mostly linked to the U.S. housing market.

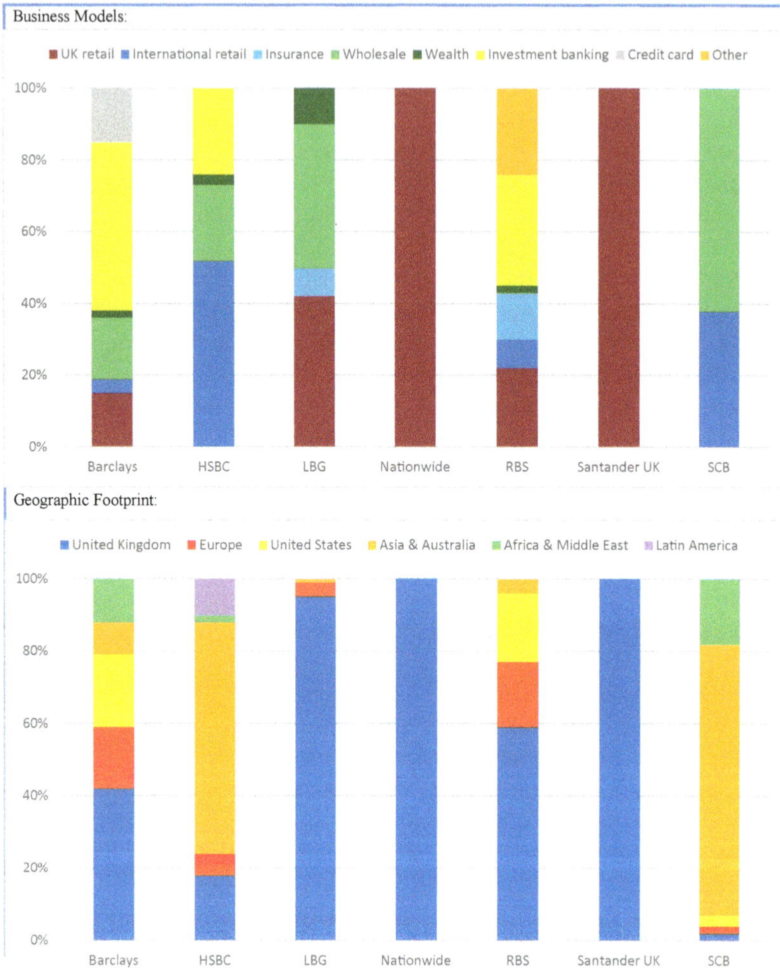

Fig. 6.2 UK Banks: Differentiated Geographic and Business Models (As at end-2010, in percent of individual banks' revenues) (*Sources* Adopted from Bloomberg; individual banks' Annual Reports; IMF 2011 staff estimates)

have been reduced in some branches and the profile of the work carried out by branch staff has been more oriented towards sales. During the past decade the number of branches in the United Kingdom fell by over a quarter, to below 10,000. The Post Office role as a banking distribution channel has been expanding given that it is the largest cash handler in the United Kingdom. A number of banks have established partnerships with the Post Office, which allow their customers to use these offices for their basic banking needs. More than 95% of the 8,438,000 Basic Bank Accounts at the end of 2010 were accessible at Post Office counters.

However, it is interesting to note that, the UK Government intervened after the financial crisis, through the injection of capital into a number of major banks, to attempt to stop a full breakdown of the banking industry to safeguard key stakeholders (such as depositors) and keep key operational functions running.

6.4 The Structure of the Financial Market in the United Kingdom

The composition of the United Kingdom financial markets (both the primary and secondary markets) are viewed by several participants as the major worldwide markets for dealing in a range of assets such as shares, stocks, bonds, derivatives trading currencies and commodities. As discussed already above, the financial services industry of the United Kingdom is a major player (see Table 6.5 in Appendix 4 for further detailed evidence) in the global financial market with regard to strong domination and leaderships on key services, classes of assets and product markets (FSB 2013; TheCityUK 2013). For example, according to the Financial Stability Board report issued in December 2013, the "United Kingdom was the biggest exporter of financial services worldwide" (FSB 2013, p. 49). Hence, occurrences impacting on other nations can have a substantial consequence on the UK markets. Following the financial crisis, the UK government proposed new supervisory structure of the financial markets (see Sect. 6.5) to focus more on a robust shareholder protection and conduct of the market (FSB 2013).

6.4.1 *The Insurance Market in the United Kingdom*

According to the Financial Stability Board report issued in 2013, the insurance market in the United Kingdom "is the largest in Europe and the third largest in the world, accounting for 7% of total worldwide premium income (2011 figures). It employs 290,000 people and contributes GBP 10.4 billion in taxes" (FSB 2013, p. 49; TheCityUK 2013). It consists of insurance companies, the Lloyd's market, intermediaries and various specialist support professions and services. The London Market is a distinct, separate part of the UK insurance and reinsurance industry based in central London. It consists mostly of general insurance and reinsurance and predominantly involves high exposure risks. The London Market is the world's leading market for internationally traded insurance and reinsurance. It is the only place where all of the world's twenty largest international insurance and reinsurance companies are active.

The UK insurance market's strong international position is indicated by (a) being the largest source of both insurance funds and pensions in Europe; (b) UK companies feature prominently in rankings of the world's largest insurance companies and (c) the 19% marine insurance premiums transacted on the London Market in 2011 was higher than in any other country. London accounts for around a 10% share of total world reinsurance.

6.4.2 *The Fund Management Industry in the United Kingdom*

The fund management industry plays a significant role within the UK financial market. Again, according to the FSB (2013) peer review report "the UK asset management industry is a world-leading industry in the management of third-party assets. These assets are managed on behalf of a wide range of clients, of whom the major ones are estimated to be: pension funds (approx. GBP 2 trillion), insurance funds (approx. GBP 1.8 trillion) and mutual funds (GBP 525 billion mutual funds). The United Kingdom is estimated to be the second largest manager of assets globally (with around 8% market share), albeit significantly behind the United States (approximately 50% market share). The United Kingdom is Europe's leading fund manager, managing c.33% of all assets under management in Europe and is estimated to have the highest ratio of assets managed to GDP of any country globally (272%)" (FSB 2013, pp. 50–51).

Additionally, the report confirms the UK's dominant position in this industry within the European Union market in the particular area of "alternative asset management, with approximately 18% of global hedge fund assets managed in the United Kingdom (which is around 80% of the assets managed in Europe)" (FSB 2013, p. 51).

6.4.3 *The Structure of the Payment and Settlement System in the United Kingdom*

The majority of transactions are still made in cash although the proportion is falling steadily. Technology has become increasingly important for the remaining transactions which include cheques, automated payments and plastic cards. The clearing process involves the transmission and settlement of payments between accounts held at different banks or different branches of the same bank. Payment systems can broadly be divided into clearing networks and plastic card networks. Clearing networks in the United Kingdom include: Bankers Automated Clearing Services (BACS) for direct debits, direct credits and standing orders; real time gross settlement which is cleared by the Clearing House automated Payments Scheme (CHaPS) and the Cheque and Credit Clearing Company (CCCL). Plastic card networks cover debit, credit and ATM cards.

The number of non-cash transactions made in the United Kingdom including credit and debit cards, direct debits, standing orders and cheques has risen nearly threefold from 4.7bn in 1990 to 14.5bn in 2011 (BOE 2012a). Again, according to FSB (2013, p. 51) "Inter-bank payment systems handled 7 billion transactions with a value of GBP 69.2 trillion in 2011, of which GBP 68.5 trillion were electronic and GBP 705 billion were paper transactions (mainly cheques). The card and ATM networks handled 9.4 billion purchases in the United Kingdom with a total value of GBP 474 billion and facilitated cash acquisition of GBP 199 billion". The management of risks associated with the payment systems remain a significant challenge for the UK regulator. In regard to corporate governance arrangement in the United Kingdom, the Bank of England maintains the oversight accountability for the management of "systematically important inter-bank payment systems".

6.4.4 *Financial Sector Contribution to UK Economy*

The UK banking sector is a crucial and integral part of the UK economy. Its core business of taking deposits from one set of customers and lending to a largely different set provides an essential market mechanism for distributing funds to where they are most required and providing a return to those wishing to hold assets in liquid form. A modern economy could not operate without this mechanism, but its "value" is difficult to measure statistically. The categories of indicators can be used to measure the banking sector contribution to the UK economy in particular and the financial sector in general are (1) Contribution to Gross Domestic Product and Employment, (2) Contribution to Business and Household, (3) Contribution to Current and Capital Accounts and (4) Contribution to general Tax Revenues. Details of these important contributions are discussed in Appendix 6 and 7.

6.5 Financial Sector Supervision and Bank Regulation in the United Kingdom

The financial services industry plays a key role in the UK economy. It provides a range of services including banking, insurance, pensions and advisory services to businesses and households. It is worth an estimated £234.2 billion (7.7% of UK gross domestic product) and employs over a million people (The Office for National Statistic 2017). A crucial role of regulation is to prevent crises or to mitigate their effect. The financial sector is subject to much closer supervision than, say, manufacturing because banks are critical to the operation of the economy. Banks are important in a way no other kind of firm is important. Close supervision is needed because bank failures have a wide-ranging external effect on depositors, taxpayers, other financial institutions, businesses and the economy as a whole. Financial regulation is effective when it addresses these external effects or "externalities", either by making banks and other financial firms pay for the consequences of their actions, or by restricting their actions so as to avoid the most damaging effects of financial failure, or at the least cost in terms of reduced competitiveness, discouragement of innovation or encouragement of avoidance. The term "regulation" is used here to refer to the rules that govern the behaviour of financial intermediaries, and "supervision" for monitoring and enforcement of the rules. In the United Kingdom most financial supervision and banking regulations fall into three broad categories, namely:

A. Micro-prudential supervision and regulation that checks that individual financial firms and banking institutions are complying with financial regulation. It involves the collection and analysis of information about the risks that the firms take, their systems, and their personnel. Because micro-prudential supervision uses firm-specific information to generate a picture of risk and its management, it is often referred to as "bottom-up supervision" approach.

B. Macro-prudential supervision and regulation that is concerned with the aggregate effect of individual firms' actions. A lending decision which appears sensible at an individual bank may engender system-wide risk if it is taken by every bank. Because it aims to generate an overall picture of the functioning of the financial sector, macro-prudential supervision is often referred to as "top-down supervision".
C. Conduct-of-business supervision that is concerned with consumer protection, inter-firm transactions and behaviours, insider trading and other matters including measures against money-laundering.

In this regard bank regulation and supervision in the United Kingdom thus provides an external framework of rights and obligations in which a bank operates so that it can undertake regulated activities in the financial marketplace. In order to aid compliance with this external framework, bank regulators incorporate formal mechanisms of internal self-regulation into their regulatory and supervisory framework. The purpose of this is to utilise effective corporate governance in banks to reduce the likelihood of risks becoming unmanageable such that competitiveness and the drive for profitability do not adversely threaten the stability of the bank and the financial industry. This next section details and analyses the UK corporate governance and bank regulatory and supervisory system.

6.5.1 *The UK Regulatory Framework for Corporate Governance*

6.5.1.1 *The Overview of Structure and Sources of UK Corporate Governance Regimes*

The United Kingdom has developed a market-based approach that enables the board to retain flexibility in the way in which it organises itself and exercises its responsibilities, while ensuring that it is properly accountable to its shareholders. This is done primarily through non-legal requirement and operates via "comply or explain" approach. There are a variety of foundations that form part of the United Kingdom supervisory and regulatory structure for corporate governance, as illustrated in the Fig. 6.3.

According to the London Stock Exchange (LSE), this encompasses the following; "(a) Key legislation, mainly based upon the Companies Act 2006; (b) the Listing Rules (the LR); (c) the Disclosure and Transparency Rules (the DTR) and the Prospectus Rules (the PR), which are created and administered by the Financial Services Authority as the UK Listing Authority (UKLA); (d) the UK Corporate Governance Code (the

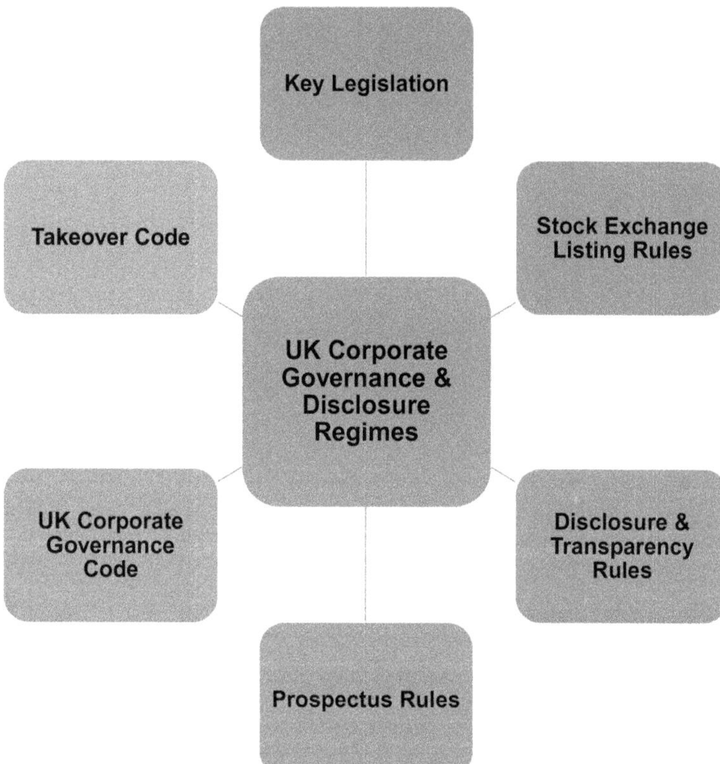

Fig. 6.3 Sources of UK corporate governance regimes

Code) and the UK Stewardship Code, which are the responsibility of the Financial Reporting Council[7] (FRC); and the (e) Takeover Code, which is issued and administered by the Takeover Panel" (London Stock Exchange 2012, p. 17). The Financial Services Authority (FSA) is accountable for the Listing Rules, which comprise the obligations that issuers of securities admitted to the UK Official list have to meet (including a number relating to corporate governance) and is also the UK Competent Authority for the *Prospectus, Transparency and Market Abuse Directives.*

It can be noted that in the United Kingdom, it is the law and rules under regulations that set up fundamental "standards of conduct and transparency, while the non-statutory codes of practice use self-regulation as a means of maintaining good corporate governance" (LSE 2012). In general, the impact of this structural framework of regulation as suggested by the LSE is "to create a principle-based system of corporate governance, based on proportionality, flexibility and targeting, that cannot be achieved through a 'one size fits all' approach. The 'comply or explain' approach to corporate governance under the LR and DTR, a listed company must report to its shareholders on how it has applied corporate governance guidance and, where it has not applied the guidance as envisaged, provide an explanation as to why it has not done so" (London Stock Exchange 2012, p. 17).

The next job for shareholders is to make the choice of whether they believe the organisations corporate governance practices are acceptable or not. The FRC introduced the "comply or explain" approach as an option to move away from the more traditional stringent rules-based structure (i.e. the US system). However, it is accepted by the FRC if an individual organisation decides to employ an approach that is deemed more suited to their specific context and ways of working. The key merit of the use of the United Kingdom "comply or explain" method is to enable stockholders and boards of directors to have the ultimate accountability to make judgements about the appropriateness of their corporate governance policies and practices, rather than an external regulator. This will result in the need for companies to report their reasoning to shareholders should any question regarding their departure from following of the code be cited. The requirements from the Financial Reporting Council code

[7] The Financial Reporting Council (FRC) is the UK's independent regulator for corporate reporting and governance, with responsibility for the content of the *UK Corporate Governance Code.*

guidance, state that firms must strive to provide evidential proof of how they are working to align to the expected code provisions and achieving good corporate governance standards. Additionally, the Companies Act in Section 168 provides shareholders the ability to appoint and dismiss individual directors, while Sections 303 to 305 gives them the right to call a general meeting of the company. The Code also specify that firms included in the FTSE 350 index must put all their directors forward for re-election each year or provide explanation why they have not done so (LSE 2012).

6.5.1.2 The United Kingdom Corporate Governance Code

There are five core segments of the UK Corporate Governance Code: (1) leadership, (2) effectiveness, (3) accountability, (4) remuneration and (5) relations with shareholders. Each of the main segments of the Code are organised into different requirement and guideline headings that comprise of; "(a) Main Principles; (b) Supporting Principles and (c) Code provisions. The Main Principles set out broad tenets of good corporate governance practice; the Supporting Principles and more detailed Code provisions expand on the Main Principles" (LSE 2012).

Extract summary of the Main Principles of UK code of governance:

Leadership	"Every company should be headed by an effective board that is collectively responsible for the long-term success of the company. The chairman is responsible for leadership of the board and the chief executive for the running of the company's business. The board should include non-executive directors whose role it is to constructively challenge and help develop proposals on strategy
Effectiveness	The board and its committees should have the appropriate balance of skills, experience, independence and knowledge of the company to enable them to discharge their respective duties and responsibilities effectively. The updated Code will incorporate a requirement that the board consider board diversity, including gender, when making new appointments
Accountability	The board is responsible for maintaining sound risk management and internal control systems. The board should establish formal and transparent arrangements for considering how they should apply the corporate reporting and risk management and internal control principles, and for maintaining an appropriate relationship with the company's auditor

(continued)

(continued)

Remuneration	Levels of remuneration should be sufficient to attract, retain and motivate directors of the quality required to run the company successfully. A company should avoid paying more than is necessary and a significant proportion of executive directors' remuneration should be linked to performance. There should be a formal and transparent procedure for developing policy on executive remuneration
Relations with Shareholders	There should be a dialogue with shareholders based on the mutual understanding of objectives. The board should use the Annual General Meeting (AGM) to communicate with investors and encourage their participation In the 'comply or explain' section of the Preface to the Code, the FRC states that the Main Principles are the core of the Code and that the way they are applied should be the central question for a board as it determines how it is to operate according to the Code The Code is not a rigid set of rules, and the FRC has drafted the Supporting Principles broadly to give companies the flexibility of deciding their own method of implementation. In addition, the Code reflects the fact that some provisions are more applicable to companies of a certain size than others. For example, B.7.1 on the annual re-election of directors applies only to companies in the FTSE 350, and B.1.2 on the composition of the board and C.3.1 on the audit committee distinguish between companies that are in the FTSE 350 and those that are not"

Source Adopted from London Stock Exchange Corporate Governance for Main Market and AIM Companies 2012, p. 18

In order to apply to be admitted to the London Stock Exchange, all firms are required to list their securities on the UKLA Official List. The scope of the expected level for a firm to "comply or explain" is determined by the manner of that particular organisation's listing securities. "Listing categories" are specified (eight since April 2010), outlining the listing prerequisites for both issuer and security types, especially in the areas of corporate governance requirements (LSE 2012). This influenced the corporate governance reporting that is being disclosed publicly by listing premium firms on the stock exchange. It is important to note that there is now a widespread expectation from many investment firms for compliance with the code to be specified by investing companies, or for explanations to be provided if they are not adhering to the code of corporate governance in their annual report.

6.5.2 *The UK Financial Regulatory Framework Applicable to Banks*

As already discussed in the previous sections, the systemic importance, size, and complexity of the UK financial markets necessitate the highest quality regulatory and supervisory framework. Domestic and global shocks transmit through the United Kingdom and may be amplified in transmission. Thus, according to the IMF proportionally intense supervision—commensurate with the importance of the UK's global role—is necessary to ensure domestic and global financial stability (IMF 2011). The following subsections describes the United Kingdom supervisory and regulatory frameworks that govern the banking industry.

6.5.2.1 *The Financial Services and Markets Act: The Statutory Regime*

The primary statute governing banking is the "Financial Services and Market Act 2000" (FSMA 2000[8]—referred to as FSMA in this book). The FSMA introduced a new structure for the regulation of the financial services industry in the United Kingdom, which came into effect from midnight on 30 November 2001. It established a new regulatory regime, replacing a number of self-regulatory organisations with a single statutory regulator, the Financial Services Authority (FSA) and established a system that instituted "on a risk-based" method for every financial institution regulation and supervision. Under the FSMA 2000, it is an offence for a person to engage in "regulated activities" in the United Kingdom unless he is authorised to do so or is "exempt from the authorisation requirement". Also, the nature of regulated activities is defined in secondary legislation". Its specified legislative purposes are: "*are to maintain confidence in the financial system, to promote public awareness, to provide appropriate consumer protection, and to reduce financial crime. Financial Services Authority (FSA) as a single regulator of the financial services industry with responsibility, inter alia, for banking supervision and regulation of the investment services and insurance industries*"

[8] "The FSMA received Royal Assent on June 14, 2000. The FSMA repealed existing financial services legislation, including the Banking Act of 1987, the Financial Services Act of 1986, and the Insurance Companies Act of 1982" (Alexander 2004, pp. 42).

(Alexander 2004, p. 17). The FSA is thus responsible for regulation of banks including authorisation, supervision and enforcement.

However, in order to meet its legal aims, the Financial Service Authority was; "*delegated with the legislative authority to adopt rules and standards to ensure that the statutory objectives are implemented and enforced. In so doing, the FSA must have regard to seven principles, which include "the desirability of facilitating innovation in connection with regulated activities;" "the need to minimise the adverse effects on competition that may arise from anything done in the discharge of those functions;" and "the desirability of facilitating competition between those who are subject to any form of regulation by the Authority*" (Alexander 2004, p. 17). In fact, the Financial Service Authority discreated a supervisory structure that primarily stresses "ex ante preventative strategies, including front-end intervention when market participants are suspected of not complying with their obligations" (Alexander 2004, p. 17).

Moreover, with FSMA 2000 regime according to Alexander (2004) "regulatory resources are redirected away from reactive, post-event intervention towards a more proactive stance emphasising the use of regulatory investigations and enforcement actions, which have the overall objective of achieving market confidence and investor and consumer protection. In devising regulations, the FSA is required to conduct a cost–benefit analysis of the regulations' impact on financial markets (FSMA 2000, p. 155 (2) (a))" (Alexander 2004, p. 17). The Act also established "a single authorisation process and a new market abuse offense that imposes civil liability, fines, and penalties for the misuse of inside information and market manipulation" (FSMA 2000, c.8 at & 118).

The FSA's main functions will be forming policy and setting regulation standards and rules (including the authorisation of firms); approval and registration of senior management and key personnel; investigation, enforcement and discipline; consumer relations; and banking and financial supervision. The FSMA requires the FSA to adopt a flexible and differentiated risk-based approach to setting standards and supervising banks and financial firms. The FSA has authority to enter into negotiations with foreign regulators and governments regarding a host of issues, including agreements for the exchange of information, coordinating implementation of EU and international standards, and cross-border enforcement and surveillance of transnational financial institutions.

According to Alexander (2004, p. 17–18); "the FSMA sets out a framework to protect the integrity of nine of the United Kingdom's recognised investment exchanges, including the London Stock Exchange, the London Metal Exchange, and the London International Financial

Futures Exchange. The FSA has the power to scrutinise the rules and practices of firms and exchanges for anti-competitive effects. Moreover, the FSA has exercised its statutory authority to create an ombudsman and compensation scheme for consumers and investors who have complaints against financial services providers for misconduct in the sale of financial products".

6.5.2.2 The Structure of the Financial Service Authority Corporate Governance

The introduction of the FSMA 2000 act had a large effect on the standards for corporate governance for banking organisations in the United Kingdom, as it set high levels of expectation regarding the conduct of those in senior positions within the companies. This was in response to the need to maintain higher levels of executive behaviour and the core need for information transparency and accountability within disclosures to all stakeholders. According to Alexander 2004, "the FSA has adopted comprehensive regulations that create civil liability for senior managers and directors for breaches by their firms, even if they had no direct knowledge or involvement in the breach or violation itself. For example, if the regulator finds that a firm has breached rules because of the actions of a rogue employee who has conducted unauthorised trades or stolen client money, the regulator may take action against senior management for failing to have adequate procedures in place to prevent this from happening" (Alexander 2004, p. 18).

1. *Operating a High-Level Principle*

The Financial Service Authority established a regulatory principle based on some specific requirements for directors in financial institutions. A selection of eleven principles of business that is applicable to every individual of every level and all organisations in the United Kingdom financial sector. They are often invoked as a means to aid the introduction of new supervisory rules and guidelines for the financial industry, and to assess potential candidates applying for approved person status.

The second principle outlines that "[a] firm must conduct its business with due skill, care and diligence. The FSA back then interprets this principle as setting forth an objective, reasonable person standard for all persons involved in the management and direction of authorised financial firms" (Alexander 2004, p. 18; FSA 2001). The reasonable person standard also applies to Principle Nine, which provides a basic framework for internal standards of corporate governance by requiring that a financial firm "organise and control its internal affairs in a responsible manner". Regarding employees or agents, the firm "should have adequate arrangements to ensure that they are suitable, adequately trained and properly supervised and that it has well-defined compliance procedures" (FSA 2001).

2. *Implementation of Senior Management Arrangements, Systems and Controls*

Regulation of "activities" of both individuals (with particular positions of influence) and firms was the legislative objective of the FSMA 2000 act. In enforcing this legislative duty, the Financial Service Authority split these individuals into two categories: "(1) members of governing bodies of firms, such as directors, members of managing groups of partners, and management committees, who have responsibility for setting the firm's business strategy, regulatory climate, and ethical standards; and (2) members of senior management to whom the firm's governing body has made significant delegation of controlled functions. Controlled functions include, inter alia, internal audits, risk management, leadership of significant business units, and compliance responsibilities" (FSA 2004). The delegation of controlled functions likely would occur in a number of contexts, but would occur particularly in companies that are part of complex financial groups (Alexander 2004).

The FSA is required to regulate in a way that recognises senior managements' responsibility to manage firms and to ensure the firms' compliance with regulatory requirements. FSA regulations are designed to reinforce effective senior management and internal systems of control. At a fundamental level, firms are required to "take reasonable care to establish and maintain such systems and controls as are appropriate to [their] business" (FSA 2004). However, the FSA requires for a key role to be adopted by senior managers to oversee the implementation of better corporate governance structures within their individual organisations. For example, emphasis must be placed in areas such as internal risk and control systems and ensuring higher standards of accountability. This area was one of the failures that were severely criticised in the aftermath of the financial crash of 2007/08.

3. *The Need for Authorisation*

A key function of the FSA as part of its regulatory approach to the financial services is the operation of the authorisation regime in the United Kingdom. In circumstances where deposits are lent to third parties or interest on deposits or assets are used to either partially or completely fund activities, the acceptance of the deposit becomes a regulated activity (Slaughter and May 2014).

Banks must therefore obtain authorisation under the FSMA 2000 for them to be able to operate their business. The legal basis for the operation of this authorisation structure and procedures were derived from the FSMA 2000 act. The Financial Service Authority has the power to penalise or prevent individuals who has not been approved by the regulator from completing regulatory activities. Punishment for breaches of authorisation may take the form of a civil fines or be escalated to a criminal offence.

Also, in pursuit of the decision for authorisation, the Financial Service Authority assesses individuals regarding their fitness to carry on financial duties in the industry. Three core elements are judges within this process—i.e. competence, financial soundness and finally honesty (FSA 2004). This is known as the "honesty, integrity, and reputation" requirement. The FSA requires the applicant to have competence and capability—that is, the necessary skills to fulfil the functions that are assigned or expected. Finally, an applicant must be able to demonstrate financial soundness. These are objective standards that must be fulfilled to engage in the banking or financial business.

In addition, a firm or an individual applying for authorisation must submit a business plan detailing its intended activities, with a level of detail appropriate for the level of risks. The FSA will determine whether employees, the company board, and the firm itself meet the minimum requirements set out in the Act. It is a core function of the FSA authorisation process that the regulator satisfies itself that the applicants and their employees are capable of identifying, managing, and controlling various financial risks and can perform effectively the risk management functions.

6.5.2.3 *The Interaction of Company Law and Corporate Governance Regime*

The law provides the structure for the internal regulation of companies, such as the duty of directors' to be open about their dealings and it also provides a mechanism of control; for example, the ability for shareholders to dismiss the directors and to exercise control of the company through the articles and meetings. There are two main sources of corporate governance regulation in the United Kingdom—laws and regulation of various kinds and rules and self-regulatory codes with some legal underpinnings. In the United Kingdom, the common law has long played an important part in regulating companies, as in areas such as shareholder rights and directors' fiduciary duties.

From the mid-nineteenth century onwards, there have been various statutory interventions, some of a piecemeal kind, others major initiatives, consolidations, and reforms. In practice, the legislature has tended to intervene periodically when significant problems have been perceived or when there is a felt need for consolidation of existing legislation. In fact, the main legal regulations that affect companies until the financial crisis occured in 2007/08 are as follows:

Name of legal regulation	*Contains rules/guidance on*
Companies Act 2006	Registering, administration and operating Companies within the United Kingdom
Model articles of association	Interaction between the shareholders & directors
Company Directors Disqualification Act 1986	Behaviour and conduct of directors. Breach of its rules may lead to disqualification of directors
The Criminal Justice Act 1993 and Money Laundering Regulations 2007	Criminal activities such as money laundering and insider dealing
Insolvency Act 1986 (amended by the Enterprise Act 2002)	Individual and corporate insolvency and administration-the alternative to winding up
Stock Exchange Listing Regulations 1984	Listing rules such as admission and disclosure requirement
EU Council Directives 2004/25 and 2004/109	Takeovers (2004/25) and transparency requirement for listed companies (2004/109)

However, these regulations are often circumvented, and loopholes may be found that allow unscrupulous directors to bend the rules. To that extent, the law has been unsuccessful and must be supplemented by a strong corporate governance standard. The Code is neither law nor regulation, but best practice recommendations for good corporate governance for only firms that are listed. However, the "Listing Rules" interact with the Code, and listed companies must include a section in their financial statements published annually, which explains how they have "complied with the Code" or why they have not done so. Since mid-2003, the Combined Code has come within the domain and oversight of the FRC, the statutory body, which regulates accounting and auditing. Subsequent to this change, the Council initiated a review of the original Turnbull report and made a small number of amendments, including a recommendation that boards confirm that they have taken action remedying any significant failings in their organisation internal control structures.

In fact, we have already seen that in the United Kingdom, corporate governance is contained in the Combined Code. Some critics have described it as "soft law" due to the fact that companies may avoid compliance with the code if they explain why. This leaves a problem, what can be done if a company avoids compliance with the code? Is there any way of enforcing it? Without any legal force, nothing can be done. At present, the government or any of its bodies (such as the FSA) cannot interfere. Only the shareholders can take action against board of directors. The Stock Exchange listing rules will enforce the "comply or explain" procedure, but this will not stop non-compliance providing it is disclosed. However, if enough companies continue with non-compliance, the government may step in and make rules legally binding. As companies tend to prefer voluntary codes, this threat might be enough to ensure compliance in most organisations. According to Alexander (2004) the FSA "considers compliance with the Code to be an important issue for investor consideration. Although the Combined Code is technically voluntary in a legal sense, public companies listed on the London Stock Exchange and other regulated exchanges are required to state in their annual reports whether they comply with the Code and must provide an explanation if they do not comply. … the combined code is not a legal requirement under UK financial regulation. For example, it is not part of the FSA's banking regulation regime or the Listing Rules for the capital markets. It has therefore not been subject to FSA investigations and enforcement. It should be recalled that the Cadbury Report recommended that the combined code be applicable to all companies – listed and unlisted" (Alexander 2004, p. 13).

6.5.2.4 *The Regulatory Rule Pertinent to Banks Corporate Governance*

i. **The New Financial Supervisory Structure After 2012**

Prior to the financial crisis in 2007–2008, the UK FSA had been operating what came to be called a principles-based regulatory approach following a deregulation philosophy that was widely supported by the industry, policy makers and many commentators. (It was also referred to as a "light touch", though this was not a term that was generally used by the FSA). It involved a risk-based supervision philosophy. The authorities have since indicated that, in hindsight, the crisis demonstrated that supervisors had placed too much confidence in banks' internal risk management and governance systems (IMF 2011, 2012; HM Treasury 2009a). The engagement of the FSA with firms had been neither as frequent nor as probing as it should have been. A number of commentators were also critical of how the tripartite arrangements worked in practice during the early stages of the crisis, including coordination and information sharing (Turner 2009; Walker 2009; OECD 2009).

However, in 2010, the new government released a white paper proposing major changes in regulatory and supervisory responsibility, and formal implementation of a macro prudential overlay on traditional micro-prudential regulation and supervision. Under the proposals the FSA is to be split into: (i) a Prudential Regulator Authority (PRA) regulating banks, banking groups, insurance companies and larger broker-dealers, and (ii) Consumer and Markets Authority (CMA), taking over the FSA's conduct of business mandate, including wholesale markets, market enforcement, market infrastructure, Anti-Money Laundering/Counter-Terrorism Financing Act, and prudential regulation of smaller dealers, asset managers, financial advisors, and so on. The PRA is to become a semi-autonomous subsidiary of the Bank of England (BoE) with the BoE being given authority over certain macro-prudential tools. The legislation implementing these changes is to be in place by year-end 2012.

The United Kingdom government introduced a new system of financial supervisory structures that became effective from the beginning of April 2013. The new make-up of the regulation gave the Bank of England new substantial accountability and responsibilities over the UK financial industry as represented in Fig. 6.4. As mentioned above already, the enactment of the new law created "a macro-prudential authority, the Financial Policy Committee (FPC) within the BoE to monitor and respond to systemic risks; transferred responsibility for significant micro-prudential regulation to a focused new regulator, the Prudential Regulation Authority (PRA), established as a subsidiary of the BoE; and created a new conduct of business regulator, the Financial Conduct Authority (FCA)" (FSB 2013, p. 14). The responsibility for supervision of banks in the United Kingdom is split between the Prudential Regulation Authority and the Financial Conduct Authority. Authority for macro-supervision of banks regarding the identification and mitigation of risk, financial disparities and exposures affecting the entire financial system in the United Kingdom sits within the Financial Policy Committee accountabilities. Figure 6.4 provides an overview of the managerial and regulatory structure in the UK banking industry.

Adaptations to the regulatory landscape were driven by failings pre-crisis (i.e. prior to 2007/08). The aim for these structural changes was to ultimately bolster the resilience of the system of financial regulation in the United Kingdom, in particular corporate governance and accountability. Weaknesses were identified in the previous mechanism of financial supervision that were provided by the then regulators. It was stated by authorities both nationally and internationally, that individual regulators within the United Kingdom did not have the power to intervene autonomously in response to identification and monitored systemic

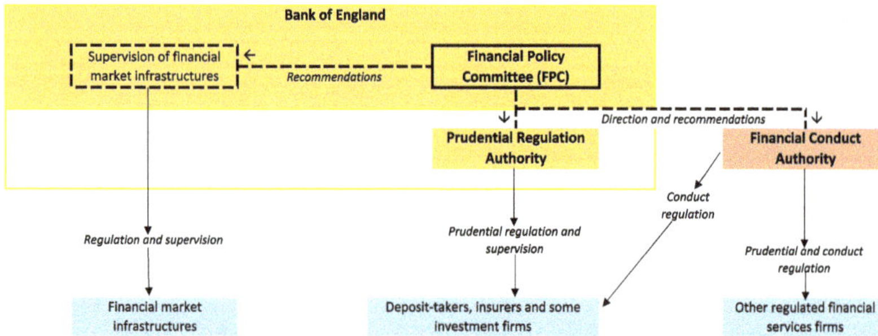

Fig. 6.4 Stylised diagram of the new UK regulatory framework (*Source* Adapted from Financial Stability Board report 2013)

failures. The Bank of England, while possessing the accountability for financial stability, reflected that they did not have all the means to fulfil its obligations as expected (FSB 2013). Further, in support of its financial stability objective, the Bank will be accountable for regulation of some of the areas of financial market infrastructures, involving the supervision of central counterparties and securities settlement systems, to help ensure that these important institutions are resilient. This responsibility will sit alongside the Bank's existing responsibilities for overseeing recognised payment systems.

The New Statutory Decision-Making Bodies for UK Banks
From April 2013, the Bank will have two new statutory decision-making bodies: the PRA Board, responsible for micro-prudential supervision and regulation; and the FPC, responsible for macro-prudential supervision and regulation (Fig. 6.5). These are in addition to the Monetary Policy Committee (MPC) and its existing responsibilities for monetary policy, and the Bank's responsibilities for liquidity provision and resolution.

The Bank of England's statutory responsibilities in relation to monetary stability—that is, to maintain price stability and, subject to that, to support the Government's economic policies remain unchanged under the new law. Among the statutory objectives, market confidence and financial stability are the most relevant to corporate governance-related requirements under the FSMA 2000 (FSMA 2000 (c.8), section 3.1). The

Monetary policy	**Monetary Policy Committee** *Created in 1997* Responsible for maintaining price stability and, subject to that, supporting the economic policy of the Government, including its objectives for growth and employment.
Micro prudential regulation	**Prudential Regulation Authority** *Created in 2013* Responsible for promoting the safety and soundness of PRA-authorised persons, and, specifically for insurers, contributing to securing an appropriate degree of protection for those who are or may become policyholders.
Macro prudential regulation	**Financial Policy Committee** *Created in Interim form in 2011, statutory form in 2013* Responsible for identifying, monitoring and taking action to remove or reduce systemic risks with a view to protecting and enhancing the resilience of the UK financial system. And, subject to that, supporting the economic policy of the Government, including its objectives for growth and employment.

Fig. 6.5 Major statutory decision-making responsibilities of the Bank of England (*Source* Created by Author using Financial Stability Board report 2013 and HM Treasury UK Government Reform Bill)

establishment of the FPC is an important step in developing mechanisms to mitigate systemic risk. For the FPC to be credible, it will be important to set realistic expectations of what macro-prudential regulation can achieve, especially in its early stages of implementation. A range of macro-prudential tools should be considered, given uncertainties regarding their effects and the nature of future risks.

The Prudential Regulation Authority is the United Kingdom's main regulator for deposit-takers (banks, building societies and credit unions), insurers and designated investment firms.[9] It derives its responsibilities and its powers from the "Financial Services and Markets Act 2000" (as revised by the Financial Services Act 2012), and the relevant EU Directives for which it is a competent authority.[10] The PRA is a part of the Bank of England and responsible for the regulation and supervision of all "systemically important firms"—meaning any organisation that present a potential risk to the financial system were they to fail.

The PRA currently holds responsibility for the regulation of 1700 of all banks, building societies, insurers, credit unions and major investment firms with the aim of ensuring that any failure would not undermine the stability of the financial system. These firms are included in the 26,000 firms whose conduct is regulated by the FCA. It also sets standards and supervises financial institutions at the level of the individual firm.

The FSMA issued a statutory objective to the Prudential Regulation Authority to promote "the safety and soundness[11] of firms (including banks)", and within this it focuses primarily on the harm that they can cause to the stability of the UK financial system (Prudential Regulation Authority 2013). A stable financial system, that is resilient in providing the critical financial services the economy needs, is a necessary condition for a healthy and successful economy, as demonstrated by the costs imposed by the 2007–2008 financial crisis on society at large. In terms of

[9] Most investment firms are prudentially regulated by the FCA. However, the PRA regulates a small number that could bring about substantial risks with regard to the financial system stability.

[10] Specifically, the Capital Requirements Directive, the Financial Conglomerates Directive, the Markets in Financial Instruments Directive and the Deposit Guarantee Schemes Directive.

[11] "Safety and soundness" involves firms having resilience against failure now and in the future, and avoiding harm resulting from the disruption to the continuity of financial services, either in the course of business or in the event of failure.

corporate governance perspective, the PRA's regulatory decision-making is rigorous and well documented, consistent with public law. Its most significant supervisory judgements are taken by its board.

An effective framework for financial stability needs to combine firm-specific supervision with work to safeguard, improve and develop to protect and enhance the resilience of the entire financial system. The PRA therefore works closely with the rest of the Bank of England, including, crucially, the FPC, which is able to make recommendations and give directions to the PRA. The PRA also cooperates closely with the rest of the Bank on, for example, market intelligence and oversight of critical financial infrastructure, and with the Bank's Special Resolution Unit on resolution and operational resilience. The PRA also engages with the boards and senior management of firms in forming its decisions, using this dialogue both to ensure that it takes account of all relevant information in reaching its judgements, and to communicate clearly the rationale for them. Firms should not, however, approach their relationship with the PRA as a negotiation.

The PRA cooperates closely with the Financial Conduct Authority (FCA), which is the conduct regulator for PRA-authorised firms and the conduct and prudential regulator for many other UK firms. As set out in the Memorandum of Understanding between the two authorities, this coordination recognises their separate, independent mandates and statutory objectives. Reflecting the international nature of the banking industry and capital markets, and in particular the United Kingdom's membership of the single market in EU financial services, the PRA plays a full and active role with its counterparts globally and in the European Union in developing and implementing prudential standards and in supervising international firms.

The FCA in the United Kingdom is now in control of regulating the "conduct of business of all FSMA regulated firms (including banks and other PRA-authorised firms), as well as conduct of business regulation in respect of wholesale and retail financial markets, and the market infrastructure that supports those markets" (Slaughter and May 2014, p. 859). They are in charge of the conduct regulation for 26,000 companies and the prudential regulation of around 23,000 firms, and in December 2013 had 2783 full-time equivalent employees. Some firms whose conduct is regulated by the FCA are not required by law to be prudentially regulated. The delivery of its functions must therefore be carried out in a manner that complies with its statutory objectives and within the parameters in which the FCA is authorised to act.

However, under the act, there is a "strategic objective" for the Financial Conduct Authority to make sure that UK markets are functioning effectively. According to Slaughter and May (2014), the following operational objectives support this aim: "(a) Securing an appropriate degree of protection for consumers; (b) Protecting and enhancing the integrity of the UK financial system; (c) Promoting efficiency and choice in the market for financial services; and (d) Promoting effective competition in the interests of consumers in the markets for regulated financial services or services provided by investment exchanges" (Slaughter and May 2014, p. 859).

The statutory regulatory framework under the conduct of business rules and guidance cover a number of specific areas, namely: (1) Banking conduct of business rules, (2) Mortgage regulation, (3) Consumer Credit Act 1974 (as amended), (4) Investment business, (5) Payment services. The details of the individual areas listed here are beyond the scope of this particular book.

ii. **Regulatory Approach to Governance and Bank Management**

The FSMA denotes that if an individual is responsible for carrying out particular functions within banks in the United Kingdom, they are subject to an "approved persons" procedure of authorisation. The next section will outline the regulatory framework used in this instance, which are divided between the Financial Conduct Authority and the Prudential Regulation Authority. The section also examines briefly how the regulation have changed the way they interact with the financial services firm and individuals to achieve their regulatory and governance objectives.

Using Approved Persons Regime

Firms and individuals must be authorised to carry out regulated activities and compliance functions. Who are the appropriate individuals to be designated with ultimate accountability for bank's compliance with rules and guidance on corporate governance? Under Section 2 (3) (b) of the FSMA 2000 (c.8), the then FSA is required to take into consideration senior management responsibility. One of the FSA's (now FCA) Principles of Good Regulation states that a bank's senior management is responsible for its activities and regulatory compliance. This principle is thus designed to secure a proper regulatory intervention by holding senior management[12] responsible for governance arrangements, risk management, and internal controls. Apart from senior management responsibility for bank governance, the board of directors of a bank is also responsible collectively for the bank's compliance with regulations. However, the board of directors, under the FSMA 2000 (c.8) itself, cannot directly bear regulatory obligations.

Approval is required from the PRA or FCA for anyone aiming to fulfil certain "controlled functions" within regulated firms. "Controlled functions fall broadly into two categories: functions involving the exercise of significant influence over the conduct of a firm's regulatory affairs, known as 'significant influence functions' (SIFs), and functions involving dealing directly with customers of the firm or their property, known as 'customer dealing functions" (Slaughter and May 2014, p. 861).

Qualification of Approved Persons

As part of its authorisation process, both the Financial Conduct Authority and the Prudential Regulation Authority will grant approval provided an applicant meets criteria to ensure the person is "fit and proper" to perform controlled functions. "The PRA and the FCA both apply a 'fit and proper test for approved persons', which includes a number of factors that the regulators will take into account when assessing the fitness and propriety of an individual to perform a particular controlled function. The most important of these factors is concerned with the individual's: (1) Honesty, integrity and reputation; (2) Competence and capability; and (3) Financial soundness. In addition, a firm must employ approved persons with the skills, knowledge and expertise necessary for the discharge of the responsibilities allocated to them ('the competent employees rule'). This also includes achieving a good standard of ethical behaviour. The PRA and the FCA provide guidance on the training and supervision that employees, including approved persons, will require in order to ensure compliance with the competent employees rule" (Slaughter and May 2014, p. 863).

Enforcing Accountability of Approved Person Obligations

Enforcement involves using regulatory power to deter firms and individuals from breaking rules and to act against firms/individuals when they do. In terms of corporate governance, both the FCA and the PRA have

[12] Senior management in this context comprises all approved persons with significant influence functions (e.g. executive and non-executive directors as well as senior managers).

the power (under Section 63 of the FSMA) to withdraw the approval of an individual if the person is deemed no longer fit and proper to complete all tasks. Upon consideration of the need to withdraw a particular approval, "the relevant regulator must have regard, inter alia, to the criteria for fitness and propriety, any failures to comply with the Statements of Principle and Code of Practice for Approved Persons (APER)... and the qualifications and training of the approved person. Moreover, the PRA and the FCA have powers under Section 56 of the FSMA to issue prohibition orders, prohibiting approved persons from carrying on any controlled functions" (Slaughter and May 2014, p. 864).

Supervision of "Senior Persons" Administration for Banks
Supervision activity assesses risks that firms and individuals pose to the regulators' objectives. Following the 2008 financial crisis and the lesson learnt especially within the United Kingdom, a new structure was established within the Banking Reform Act to aid the supervision of executive directors. This new act replaces the current "Significant Influence Functions" with the newly designed "senior persons regime".

The main characteristics of the new framework are: "(a) Conditional approvals: the regulators will have the power to grant senior person approvals subject to specified conditions, or for only a limited time period; (b) 'Reversal of the burden of proof': where either regulator takes action against an approved senior person for misconduct, the relevant individual will be required to demonstrate that they took all reasonable steps to prevent the contravention occurring or continuing; and (c) Licensing regime: the senior person's regime provides for a licensing framework for those individuals in banks who are not carrying out controlled functions but who, nevertheless, could cause serious harm to the bank or its customers" (Slaughter and May 2014, p. 865). The major implication of this new law if implemented fully will be to significantly improve corporate governance practices and behaviour within large banking firms.

6.5.3 UK Prudential Regulation and Mechanisms

Managing risks in financial services requires a range of regulatory interventions. There are also many rationales for "prudential regulation" and one example is to reduce the risks to consumers and the taxpayer from the failure of providers which could undermine the stability of the overall financial system. In 2008 the government intervened financially in the financial sector, providing support which at its height totalled £1162 billion (HM Treasury Annual Report and Account, 2011/12). By forcing financial institutions to hold a reasonable quantity and quality of capital reserves, good quality prudential regulations should reduce the need for future governments to provide so much support.

However, prudential regulation as set out by the European Union and the United Kingdom Prudential Regulation Authority encompass three main areas:

1. Policies and key rules on firms' resilience covering such areas as capital adequacy, liquidity and leverage in order to maintain an effective regulatory framework for financial stability;
2. Supervisory assessment and interventions in order to reduce the probability of a firms' failure and ensure that, if a firm does fail, it does so in an orderly manner; and
3. Policies and mechanisms to support resolution in order to reduce the impact of a firm's failure on the financial system as a whole.

Following the financial crisis of 2007/08, the UK government decided to reform the regulatory system. This section outlined some of the relevant prudential policies, tools and mechanisms that affect supervision, governance structure and management of banks and financial institutions in United Kingdom. This includes "(a) the regulation of capital requirements; (b) the types of regulatory capital; (c) group supervision of banking boards and governments; (d) liquidity requirements; (e) ring fencing; and (f) recovery and resolution regime for banking firms in the United Kingdom" (Slaughter and May 2014, pp. 866–872). The detail of all the new requirements set out under the new prudential regulation is considered out of scope for this book.

6.6 European Banking Supervisory and Corporate Governance Framework

All of the European jurisdictions have companies acts that regulate the activities of companies. The corporate governance framework for listed companies in the European Union is a combination of legislation and "soft law" (i.e. corporate governance codes that contain "recommendations" for good and responsible governance where companies are required to report to their shareholders on a comply or explain basis). EU legislation requires that institutions have robust governance arrangements, including a clear organisational structure with well-defined, transparent and consistent lines of responsibility, effective risk management processes, control mechanisms and gender-neutral remuneration policies. The internal governance should be appropriate to the nature, scale and complexity of the institution. The main responsibility for internal governance lies with the management body, which is subject to specific suitability requirements. Guidelines on internal governance/outsourcing has been published by the European Banking Authority (EBA) and, also joint guidelines regarding the assessments to judge the management body members and function holders' level of fitness were published with the European Securities and Market Authority (ESMA). European establishments created a multi-layered system which included both micro- and macro-prudential authorities, this system is called the European System of Financial Supervision (ESFS). The aforementioned ESMA is part of this and was part of setting it up along with other institutions based in Europe, and the core aim of the ESFS is that the financial supervision within the EU jurisdiction remains both clear and consistent. The ESFS key purpose is to, firstly to deliver sufficient protection for financial consumers, and second, to enforce the following of any of their rules that are aimed at the financial sector. The second part serves to ensure that confidence is maintained within the system and that financial stability is protected. The core European Supervisor Authorities (ESA's) that make up the ESFS are:

- European Systemic Risk Board (ESRB)
- National competent/supervisory authorities of each Member State
- ESMA and EBA (European Banking Authority)
- European Insurance and Occupational Pensions Authority (EIOPA)

Individual financial institutions are under the eye of national supervisory authorities, whereas the ESAs are working to enhance operational workings of the internal market. The method taken to achieve this is making certain that the European regulation and supervision is efficient, fit-to-purpose and ensures complete harmonisation across the continent. The Joint Committee (made up of EIOPA, ESMA, EBA and the 2 other ESAs) exists to ensure cross-sectoral consistency and united stances when it comes to supervision of financial conglomerates. They will also work together on any other issues that occur cross-sector. Across Europe, macro-prudential oversight of financial markets is undertaken by the European Systemic Risk Board (ESRB). Prevention and mitigation of EU systemic financial stability risk (regarding to macro-economic changes) is its core aim. There are many activities that the ESRB complete. These include identifying and prioritising risk, the issuance of warnings, recommendations, and monitoring follow-up, collecting/analysing pertinent information and updating the Council with timely assessments regarding any urgent circumstances. The ERSB also works alongside other members of the ESFS and directs any necessary actions with other international financial corporations, (for example the Financial Stability Board (FSB) and the International Monetary Fund (IMF). As part of the work that the ESMA adds to that of the ERSB, data and stress tests are undertaken in close coordination with both the ESRB and the other ESAs.

6.7 US Financial Industry Corporate Governance Supervisory Framework

The financial services industry is the United States is highly regulated. Companies in the United States including financial institutions are governed by legal systems relating to corporate governance concerns. These comprises of state laws and federal statutory rules and regulations of multiple government agencies (including regulations promulgated by the Securities and Exchange Commission) and a series of codes of various self-regulating authorities ranging from the New York Stock Exchange to the accounting industry. The supervisory arrangement is fairly complicated, with numerous regulatory agencies and overlapping responsibilities. This framework is often perceived as overwhelming and confusing, and it has its costs and complications as there is no monopoly supervisor for governance (Chartered Institute for Securities & Investment 2013). Figure 6.6—shows an overview of the US Financial Services Industry Regulatory & Corporate Governance Regimes. One key example of such regulatory complexity, a commercial bank's holding company is usually regulated by the Federal Reserve, while the primary safety-and-soundness regulator for the bank itself is the federal Office of the Comptroller of the Currency (OCC), or one of the 50 state bank regulators that have jurisdictions on corporate governance matters at state level. There are five federal regulators of depository institutions, as well

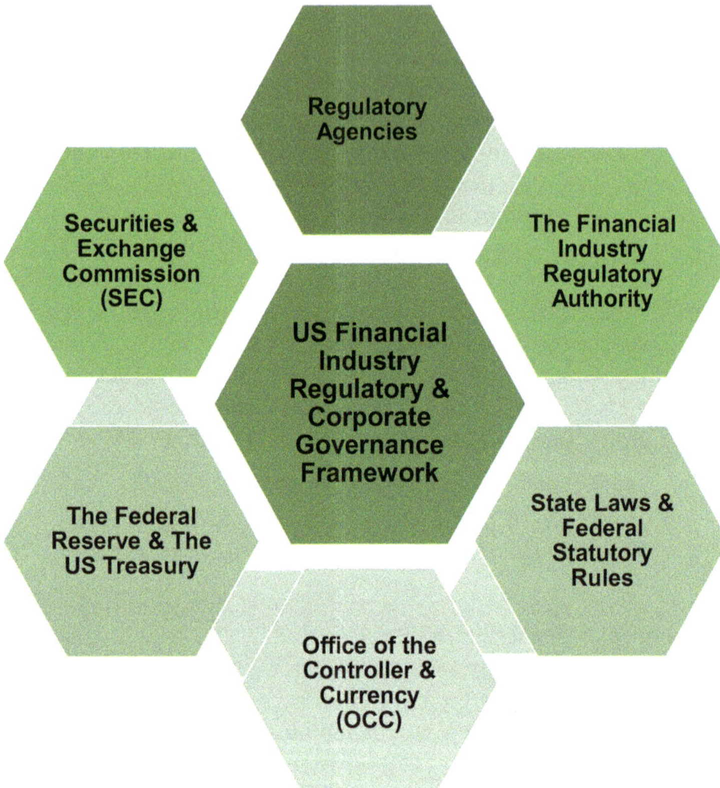

Fig. 6.6 Overview of US Financial Services Industry Regulatory and Corporate Governance Regimes (*Source* Created by the Author)

as one or more regulators in each of the 50 states. The states also regulate lenders and mortgage originators that are not depositories. There is a separate federal agency that has the responsibility for regulating Fannie Mae, Freddie Mac, and the Federal Home Loan Bank System.[13]

[13] Fannie Mae and Freddie Mac are government sponsored enterprises that provide a secondary market in home mortgages in the US. They purchase mortgages from the lenders who originate them; they hold some of these mortgages and some are securitised—sold in the form of securities, which they guarantee.

There are two federal regulators of the securities markets and financial instruments, as well as 50 state regulators. The supervision of insurance companies is exclusively the domain of the 50 states. Pension funds are regulated by two federal agencies, and, again, the 50 states have a legal claim on governance issues. However, since the mid 2011, the OCC assumed responsibility for the ongoing examination, supervision, and regulation of federal savings associations and rule-making for all savings associations, state and federal. Additionally, The SEC oversees the key participants in the securities world, including securities exchanges, securities brokers and dealers, investment advisers and mutual funds. The Securities and Exchange Commission supervisory and governance concerned is primarily with promoting the disclosure of important market-related information, maintaining fair dealing, and protecting against fraud.

The enactment of Dodd-Frank legislation has transformed the US Financial regulation and supervisory framework. It is currently reforming banking sector corporate governance and its accountability instruments. The Board of Governors of the Federal Reserve at the time of writing this book contains new proposals and rulemakings is sending signals that indicates a major and further prescriptive approach to the supervision of corporate governance for significant bank holding companies and significant foreign banking organisations with US operations (FBOs) than what many believe traditionally has been the case. This approach should also be expected to apply to systemically significant non-bank financial companies (Non-bank SIFIs) designated by the Financial Stability Oversight Council. In addition, Dodd-Frank has allowed regulators to expand their toolkit for dealing with perceived corporate governance failings, and so non-compliance with the new governance requirements may lead to greater supervisory consequences including increased penalties that may be imposed if those responsibilities are not met.

6.8 Conclusion

The financial services industry is worth an estimated £234.2 billion and therefore plays a key role in the UK economy, particularly the banking sector. Managing risks in financial services requires a range of regulatory interventions. Conduct regulation aims to protect consumers from unfair practices from providers. Prudential regulation aims to protect consumers and taxpayers from risks that are associated with financial system stability.

The size of a banking system is huge and is often measured by the sum of assets held by banks on their balance sheets. These assets include loans to households and companies, as well as securities, such as bonds and equities, and other assets. How different types of assets are measured, among other factors, can have a material impact on estimates of banking system size and its impact on the economy should a crisis occur? While different definitions produce different sizes, there are three key features of the UK banking system that emerge regardless of the definition used. First, the UK banking system is big. Looking at a sample of countries comprising the United States, Japan and the ten largest European Union countries, the United Kingdom has the largest banking sector on a residency basis. Second, foreign banks are a particularly large part of the UK banking system. This is arguably its defining feature. Third, non-loan assets constitute a high proportion of total UK banking assets. Only around half of UK-owned banks' assets are loans to non-bank borrowers. The United Kingdom is both home and host to large domestic and international financial institutions. International foreign bank subsidiaries and branches hold half of UK banking assets.

The UK banking system evolved extensively after 2000 in ways that made it more vulnerable to adverse shocks. The banks became larger, highly complex and leveraged, and relied increasingly on short-term wholesale funding (IMF 2013). The trading book displaced loans as the most important balance sheet asset, reducing the importance of net interest income (IMF 2013). Financial activity was concentrated in a small set of institutions highly interconnected to other developed financial systems. Actual leverage was greater than was apparent, in part because regulatory requirements did not capture key risks. However, the 2007–2008 financial crisis revealed major fault lines in the UK financial sector and its regulatory framework. The heavy reliance on market discipline and the assumption of a wide dispersion of risks proved to be inadequate (Turner 2009). Substantial risks posed by large, complex and interconnected financial institutions crystallised, exposing weaknesses in the oversight framework that had enabled the expansion of their reach and complexity, both domestically and internationally (IMF 2013).

The UK banking sector is big by any standard measure and, should global financial markets expand, it could become much bigger. Against that backdrop, this chapter has examined a number of issues related to the size and resilience of the UK banking system, including why it is so big and the relationship between banking system size and financial stability.

There are a number of potential reasons why the UK banking system has become so big. These include benefits to clustering in financial hubs; having a comparative advantage in international banking services; and historical factors. It may also reflect past implicit government subsidies.

Evidence from the recent global financial crisis suggests that bigger banking systems are not associated with lower output growth and that banking system size was not a good predictor of the crisis (after controlling for other factors). On the other hand, larger banking systems may impose higher direct fiscal costs on governments in crisis. For example, in 2008 the UK government intervened financially in the financial sector, providing support which at its height totalled £1162 billion (HM Treasury Annual Report and Account, 2011–2012). That said there are aspects of banking sector size that were not considered in this research but that might have a bearing on financial stability, such as the possibility that the banking system becomes more opaque and interconnected as it grows in size and the link between banking system size and the rest of the financial system. However, this book is particularly interested in the aspects that fundamentally affect corporate governance mechanisms and disclosure reporting. This chapter has outlined the new regulatory regime that has been established in the United Kingdom. Following the passage of the Financial Services Act 2012 the ground was set for the abolition of the Financial Services Authority and the creation of three new regulatory bodies: the Financial Conduct Authority, the Prudential Regulation Authority and the Financial Policy Committee. This new regime came into being on 1 April 2013. The chapter also provided an overview of the regulatory and oversight regimes in the EU and the United States with regard to corporate governance.

Financial Conduct Authority has an overarching strategic objective to ensure that the relevant markets function well. It also has three operational objectives, namely: (1) Consumer protection; (2) Integrity and (3) Competition. The FCA will take a more proactive approach, including taking action early, before consumer detriment occurs. Prudential Regulation Authority is responsible for advocating the "safety and soundness" of systemically important organisations, comprising insurers, and ensuring policyholders are protected in the event of a firm's failure. Its approach to regulation and supervision has three characteristics: Judgement-based: using judgement in determining whether financial firms are safe and sound. Forward-looking: assessing firms not just against current risks, but also against those that could plausibly arise in the future. Focused:

focusing on those issues and companies presenting the biggest threat to the stability of the system and policyholders.

Financial Policy Committee is accountable for horizon scanning for emerging risks to the financial system as a whole and providing strategic direction for the entire regulatory regime. It also has the authority and "tools" to employ to counteract systemic risk. These tools could include imposing leverage limits on banks or enforcing particular capital requirements for given asset classes. The Bank of England is now in charge of micro-prudential and macro-prudential regulation, on top of its existing responsibilities for monetary policy. However, there are numerous areas where the regulators' work overlaps and they are legally required by the legislation to coordinate their activities effectively. The FCA is operationally independent of the government but accountable to HM Treasury. The PRA is also accountable to HM Treasury. The PRA has the power of veto over the FCA in certain circumstances. The regulators also have to coordinate with other UK and international organisations with related responsibilities. The supervisory framework derived from the FSMA highlights the vital task fulfilled by the regulator in protecting the wellbeing of stakeholders and more generally ensuring efficient and sound financial and banking systems for the benefit of the public. Regulation frameworks in the United Kingdom pay specific attention to the link between the enticement mechanism for risk-taking and the internal corporate governance regimes of banking institutions.

References

Akuffo, J. A. (2018). *Corporate governance and bank accountability: The role of accountability in improving the quality of corporate governance disclosures in bank annual report, A UK perspective.* DBA Thesis, Grenoble Ecole De Management.

Alexander, K. (2004). *Corporate governance and banking regulation* (Working Paper). CERF Research Programme in International Financial Regulation, Cambridge, 17, pp. 2–38.

Balluck, K. (2015). Investment banking: Linkages to the real economy and the financial system. *Bank of England Quarterly Bulletin, 55*(1), 4–22.

Bank of England (BOE). (2010). *The financial stability report* (Issue No. 28). Bank of England.

Bank of England (BOE). (2012a). *The financial stability report* (Issue No. 32). Bank of England.

Bank of England (BOE). (2012b). *Monetary financial institutions (MFIs) in the UK that feed into the national accounts. Bankstats table: Monetary financial institutions' balance sheets, income and expenditure*. Bank of England.

Bank of England (BOE). (2013a). *The financial stability report* (Issue No. 33). Bank of England.

Bank of England (BOE). (2013b). *The financial stability report* (Issue No. 34). Bank of England.

Barker, K., & Ridgeway, A (2014). National Accounts and balance of payments. *National Statistics Quality Review*, Series 2, Report 2.

Breckenridge, J., Farquharson, J., & Hendon, R. (2014). The role of business model analysis in the supervision of insurers. *Bank of England Quarterly Bulletin, 54*(1), 49–57.

BCBS. (2010). *Principles for enhancing corporate governance*. Basel Committee on Banking Supervision.

Bush, O., Knott, S., & Peacock, C. (2014). Why is the UK banking system so big and is that a problem? *Bank of England Quarterly Bulletin, 54*(4), 385–395.

Carney, M. (2013). *The UK at the heart of a renewed globalisation*. Bank of England, London. Available at www.bankofengland.co.uk/publications/Documents/speeches/2013/speech690.pdf.

Chartered Institute for Securities & Investment (CISI). (2013). *UK regulation and professional integrity, study material*. London: Chartered Institute for Securities & Investment.

City of London Corporation and PwC. (2017, November). *Total tax contribution of UK financial services: Tenth edition* (pp. 6–9). City of London Corporation.

Crafts, N., & Wolf, N. (2013). *The location of the UK cotton textiles industry in 1838: A quantitative analysis* (CEPR Discussion Paper No. 9626).

Farag, M., Harland, D., & Nixon, D. (2013). Bank capital and liquidity. *Bank of England Quarterly Bulletin, 53*(3), 201–215.

Financial Reporting Council (FRC). (2009, March). *Review of the effectiveness of the combined code-call for evidence*. London.

Financial Service Authority (FSA). (2009, March). *The turner review: A regulatory response to the global banking crisis*. London.

Financial Service Authority (FSA). (2001). *FSA code of best practice handbook*. London: Financial Service Authority.

Financial Service Authority (FSA). (2004). *FSA handbook*. London: Financial Service Authority.

Financial Stability Board (FSB). (2009a, September). *FSB principles for sound compensation practices-implementation standards*. New York.

Financial Stability Board (FSB). (2009b, September). *Financial stability board issues implementation standards on compensation*. New York.

Financial Stability Board (FSB). (2013, September). *Peer review of the United Kingdom*. Review Report, New York.

Financial Stability Board. (2014). *Adequacy of loss-absorbing capacity of global systemically important banks in resolution*. Consultative document.

Financial Stability Forum (FSF). (2008, April). *Report of the financial stability forum on enhancing market and institutional resilience*. New York.

Financial Stability Forum (FSF). (2009, April). *FSF principles for sound compensation practices*. New York.

FSMA. (2000). *Financial services and markets act 2000 (c8)*. Parliament of the United Kingdom.

Glaeser, E. (2010). *Agglomeration economics*. NBER: University of Chicago Press.

HM Treasury. (2009a, November). *A review of corporate governance in UK banks and other financial industry entities: Final recommendations*. London.

HM Treasury. (2009b/a, July). *A review of corporate governance in UK banks and other financial industry entities: Walker review*. London.

HM Treasury. (2009, November). *Government introduces financial services bill, press release*. London.

HM Treasury. (2009, July). *Reforming financial markets, White Paper presented to parliament by the chancellor of the exchequer*. London.

Hoggarth, G., Hooley, J., & Korniyenko, Y. (2013). *Which way do foreign branches sway? Evidence from the recent UK domestic credit cycle* (Bank of England Financial Stability Paper No. 22).

International Monitoring Fund (IMF). (2011). *United Kingdom: Financial system stability assessment*. Washington, DC: IMF Country Report.

International Monitoring Fund (IMF). (2012). *Spillover report*. IMF Country Report, Washington, DC.

International Monitoring Fund (IMF). (2013). *United Kingdom: Financial system stability assessment*. IMF Country Report, Washington, DC.

International Monitoring Fund (IMF). (2014, April). How big is the implicit subsidy for banks considered to important to fail?, Chapter 3 in *Global financial stability report: Moving from liquidity- to growth-driven markets*.

London Stock Exchange (LSE). (2012, September). *Corporate governance for main market and AIM companies*. London: White Paige Ltd.

Mallin, C. (2010). *Corporate Governance* (3rd ed.). Oxford: Oxford University Press.

Marques, L. B., Correa, R., & Sapriza, H. (2013). *International evidence and government support and risk taking in the banking sector* (IMF Working Paper No. 13/94).

Noss, J., & Sowerbutts, R. (2012). *The implicit subsidy of banks* (Bank of England Financial Stability Paper No. 15). Bank of England, London.

Organisation for Economic Co-operation and Development (OECD). (2009, June). Corporate governance and the financial crisis: Key findings and main messages. *Financial Market Trends*.

Prudential Regulation Authority (PRA). (2013). *Policy statement: Conducting statutory investigations*. Bank of England.

Slaughter and May. (2014). *The Banking Regulation Review* (5th ed.). London: Gideon Roberton.

Solomon, J. (2013). *Corporate governance and accountability* (4th ed.). West Sussex: Wiley.

The Office for National Statistics. (2017, October). *UK balance of payments—The pink book time series dataset*. ONS, London.

TheCityUK. (2012a). *Key facts about UK-based financial and related professional services*. London.

TheCityUK (2012b). *Global banking report*. London.

TheCityUK. (2013). *Key facts about UK-based financial and related professional services*. London.

TheCityUK. (2018). *Key facts about UK-based financial and related professional services*. London.

Tricker, B. (2009). *Corporate governance: Principles, policies and practices* (1st ed.). New York: Oxford University Press Inc.

Tse, T. (2011). Shareholder and stakeholder theory: After the financial crisis. *Qualitative Research in Financial Markets, 3*(1), 51–63.

Tucker, P., Hall, S., & Pattani, A. (2013). Macroprudential policy at the Bank of England. *Bank of England Quarterly Bulletin, 53*(3), 192–200.

Turner Review. (2009). *The Turner review: A regulatory response to the global banking crisis*. London: Financial Service Authority.

Walker, S. D. (2009). *A review of corporate governance in UK banks and other financial industry entities*. Walker Review, Final recommendations.

World Bank. (2012). *Global financial development report 2013: Rethinking the role of the state in finance*. Washington, DC: World Bank.

CHAPTER 7

A Review of Corporate Governance and Accountability Mechanisms in UK Financial Institutions—What Is Working and What Is Not?

7.1 Introduction

The relationship between corporate governance and accountability are mutually facilitative, inclusive and interdependent. Corporate governance involves corporate fairness, transparency disclosure and accountability. The consensus among finance and accounting scholars suggest that corporate accountability is the extent to which a company is transparent in its corporate activities and responsive to those it serves. Hence, accountability is both a key element as well as requirement for corporate governance, fortifying it by providing a transparent template governing the critical decision-making, procedures and activities. In fact, because corporate directors and executives are often perceived as being accountable for corporate performance and firms' legal and ethical behaviours, their accountability is also an integral part of corporate governance. Moreover, board of directors in the traditional sense, represents shareholders' interests and as such, monitor and control the opportunistic behaviour of managers; thus, in the presence of effective accountability, agency cost can be reduced. Financial institutions corporate governance has been recognised as multidimensional, very complex in character and can be embodied in a variety of systems. For example, this can take the form of

J. A. Akuffo, *Corporate Governance and Accountability of Financial Institutions*, Palgrave Studies in Accounting and Finance Practice, https://doi.org/10.1007/978-3-030-64046-0_7

firm legislation, supervisory structures, stock exchange admission requirements, standards and best practice guidelines as well as individual firm policies.

This chapter will explore empirically the role of banking and other financial institution boards of directors, corporate governance function and the mechanisms it uses to offer accountability to stakeholders. The method of evaluation applied in this chapter devised by the author is capable of both mechanical in operation and interpretive examination of the accountability mechanisms of financial institutions' corporate governance disclosures.

7.2 Approach to Evaluating Corporate Governance Document Contents

A large number of prior studies that have been conducted from accounting, economics and finance perspective emphasised the relevance of corporate governance reporting by firms. We note from these studies that there are a range of elements that influenced disclosure practices (Adams 2002: Gray et al. 2001; Aburaya 2012) in order to ensure a transparent report. Despite the existence of large literature, the concepts of measuring and evaluating disclosure quality in governance still remain unresolved and contentious, particularly for financial institutions. From the prior research reviewed, there is limited understanding and agreement among these researchers regarding what metric to use to evaluate corporate governance disclosure consistently. This methodological shortcoming has also been highlighted by other governance researchers (Beattie et al. 2004; Beretta and Bozzolan 2008). The assessment outlined in this chapter also adds support to the Campbell et al. (2010) study that "caution should be exercised in claiming that any content analysis method is capable of measuring 'quality' per se because fitness for purpose in a research ("this being the usual technical definition of quality, see for example Slack, Chambers, Johnston and Betts 2009)" can only be assessed by considering supporting evidence from information users perspective. The implication for this study is that in writing this book, in addition to interpretive interrogation, it introduces a scale of information content akin to a qualitative scale which is capable of describing the level of information details contained in each coded piece of information.

The assessment employs a content analytical framework that is principally interpretive and qualitative.[1] The approach used here seeks to show the overall results as an aggregate for all the 19 corporate governance category mechanisms for all the companies under the period of investigation. The empirical study examined and evaluated the disclosure of corporate governance narrative and information in the annual reports of the following six banks: (1) HSBC; (2) HBOS; (3) RBS; (4) Barclays; (5) Lloyds and (6) Standard Chartered Bank. The findings and analysis presented in this chapter includes an overall view of the findings for all six sample banks in 72 annual reports that were published between 2001 and 2012. The main aim and objective of this chapter is to answer two specific objectives/questions for the research:

1. To understand and assess the overall quality of corporate governance disclosure levels and its accountability categories provided by listed UK banks in their annual reports on a longitudinal basis.
2. To identify the corporate governance accountability categories which are most and least disclosed within the UK banking firms' annual reports on a longitudinal basis.

To provide answers to the research questions raised above, the corporate governance scoring system was used to evaluate and analyse the different aspects of the governance variables adopted for the study. Investigation that is based on content analysis needs well-defined and correct occurrences underneath the inquiry. It is based on a verifiable and specific element related to the firms' circumstances and has adopted five different levels (0–4 point scale) of disclosure content or character used as coding categories of content measurement. The highest score type 4 represents the best (or highest) quality disclosure while scores of type 1 indicate least/lowest disclosure with little information disclosure of the category. Following this taxonomy, disclosure score type 4 is a genuine, detailed explanation unique to the company. Disclosure with a level of narrative details or explanation over and above a mere mention, were classified as score type 2 quality disclosures. The distinction between score 1 and

[1] Content analysis entails an approach to an analysis of a systematic reading of documents, texts, images and symbolic matter, not necessarily from an author or user perspective. It is a flexible technique that can be employed to a variety of media. For detailed discussion, see Akuffo (2018).

score 2 disclosures was clear in the majority of the cases, but where the distinction was debatable, disambiguation rules were applied. Figure 7.1a provides disclosure quality explanations coded as scale types 0–4. Whereas a score 1 disclosure is (merely) a mention of a given subcategory, a score type 2 code provides the reader with more narrative information on that subcategory. Score type 0 occurs when there is a non-disclosure in the annual report and no explanation is provided. However, the omission of any type of disclosure explanation or mention is regarded a purely objective fact and does not suffer from any subjective judgement in the scoring classification. As mentioned above, the selection of the twelve-year sample period facilitated an assessment of whether the corporate governance narrative and information provided remained static or evolved over time. In addition, the analysis was performed to facilitate the assessment of the quality of the corporate governance disclosures, and hence, to suggest how corporate governance reporting by banks may be improved. The following sections outline the findings of the analysis of the longitudinal data by all years and all banks. This chapter presents analysis by information for all the sample banks over the twelve-year period.

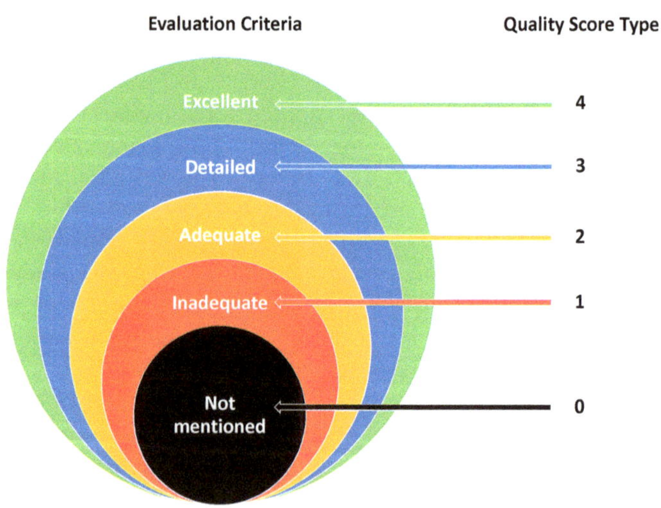

Fig. 7.1a Criteria of scoring method (*Source* Devised by author, Akuffo 2018)

7.3 Presentation of Overall Disclosure Findings and Analysis

Corporate governance is the system by which companies are directed and controlled. Boards of directors are responsible for the governance of their companies. The shareholders' role in governance is to appoint the directors and the auditors and to satisfy themselves that an appropriate structure is in place. The responsibilities of the board include setting the company's strategic aims, providing the leadership to put them into effect, supervising the management of the business and reporting to shareholders on their stewardship. Since 1992, there has been a code on corporate governance in the United Kingdom which has acted as a guide to a number of key components of effective board practice and has been based on the underlying principles of all good governance including accountability, transparency and the success of a company or group over the longer term. A fundamental aspect of corporate governance reporting and disclosure in the United Kingdom is that of "comply or explain". The various corporate governance codes have not been a rigid set of rules and companies have been able to explain their reasons for non-compliance with certain aspects of it.

This section of the chapter presents the overall findings and analysis of the assessment of the quality of corporate governance disclosures conducted over the twelve-year period in the United Kingdom sample large financial institutions (i.e. banks). Corporate governance and the mechanisms of accountability narrative disclosures from the annual reports are classified into the following five main categories (groups): (1) Corporate governance in context disclosure; statement of compliance for codes and standards and statement of non-compliance explanation for not adhering to codes and standards; (2) Board Leadership disclosure; board responsibilities and responsibilities of the board chairman; (3) Board Effectiveness disclosure; board size, board meetings, board compositions, non-executive directors independence, board evaluation, board committees working activities and board refreshment; (4) Board Accountabilities disclosure; risk management and internal control, internal audit, external audit and audit committees scrutiny activities; and (5) Performance or results disclosure; key performance indicators, code of ethics or conduct, whistle-blowing policies and practices, penalties and breaches. The following sections discuss details of the evaluation results and analysis based on the research approach and methodology employed.

7.3.1 *Presentation of Main Theme Findings and Analysis*

The constructed indicators used to assess disclosure quality within corporate governance in this study reflect on both the overall quality level, and the level found within each individual category as have been publicly disclosed by these financial institutions. The provision of sufficient and detailed information disclosed publicly plays an important role in supporting stakeholder decision-making. The results displayed in Table 7.1 illustrate the overall findings for the study for each level of detail analysed. Additionally, Figs. 7.1b, 7.2, and 7.3 present the results of the overall quality of corporate governance disclosure across the various categories examined between the years 2001–2012. The data in Fig. 7.1b presents the ranking of total index score disclosed (from the most or best corporate governance disclosure to the least disclosed) by governance category (in all years and in all banks) per annual report for the entire sample period. It, however, shows the proportion that was made with regard to each of the categories towards the mean quality disclosure. Findings suggest that despite the large amount of significant effort by the UK authorities to advance the development of rules and codes of compliance, there are large variations in the performance of the banks in this study. The total overall proportion of disclosure of corporate governance quality level score achieved as a percentage of maximum expected score over the twelve-year period of study was 39% (as a proportion of required maximum quality score expected) for all companies in all years of the items in the checklist that are disclosed. This suggests a growth in the mean of the quality of corporate governance during the timeframe of the research.

The average overall corporate governance disclosure quality over the period under investigation is considered to be low and relatively poor. This is perhaps a surprise result given the fact that the Combined Code of best practice has been in existence since 2003. Although the UK corporate governance code operates under the principle of "comply or explain" for all listed companies, it is mandated under the stock exchange Listing Rules for all UK quoted banking institutions.

Additionally, the highest quality score disclosure achieved is 69%, and the lowest quality score disclosed is 0%. These findings demonstrate that there exists a huge disparity or differences regarding the disclosure quality of the corporate governance reporting customs and practices among the

Table 7.1 Overall descriptive analysis of the quality of corporate governance categories

Corporate governance disclosure item		*Total score achieved*	*Maximum expected score*	*(%) minimum score achieved*	*(%) maximum score achieved*	*(%) mean score achieved*
Main category score	**Governance in context**	**184**	**576**	**17**	**52**	**34**
Subcategory scores	Statement of compliance	118	288	33	52	41
	Statement of non-compliance explanation	66	288	17	33	27
Main category score	**Board leadership**	**256**	**576**	**31**	**65**	**45**
Subcategory scores	Board responsibilities/role of board	132	288	38	63	46
	Responsibilities/role of board chairman	124	288	31	65	43
Main category score	**Board effectiveness**	**852**	**2016**	**31**	**69**	**42**
Subcategory scores	Board size	114	288	31	50	40
	Board meetings	124	288	33	63	43
	Board balance/composition	135	288	40	56	47
	Non-executive directors independence	120	288	33	54	42
	Board evaluation	114	288	31	63	40
	Committees working activities	152	288	4	69	53
	Board refreshment	93	288	25	44	32
Main category score	**Accountability**	**573**	**1152**	**29**	**67**	**50**
Subcategory scores	Risk management and internal control	158	288	50	63	55
	Internal audit	150	288	48	60	52
	External audit	130	288	42	50	45

(continued)

Table 7.1 (continued)

Corporate governance disclosure item		*Total score achieved*	*Maximum expected score*	*(%) minimum score achieved*	*(%) maximum score achieved*	*(%) mean score achieved*
	Audit committees scrutiny	135	288	29	67	47
Main category score	**Performance**	**274**	**1152**	**0**	**69**	**24**
Subcategory scores	Key performance Indicators	139	288	40	69	48
	Code of ethics	73	288	10	38	25
	Whistle-blowing	19	288	0	17	7
	Breaches and penalties	43	288	4	21	15
Overall corporate governance disclosure score for all categories		2139	5472	0	69	39

Source Akuffo (2018)—DBA Thesis by the Author

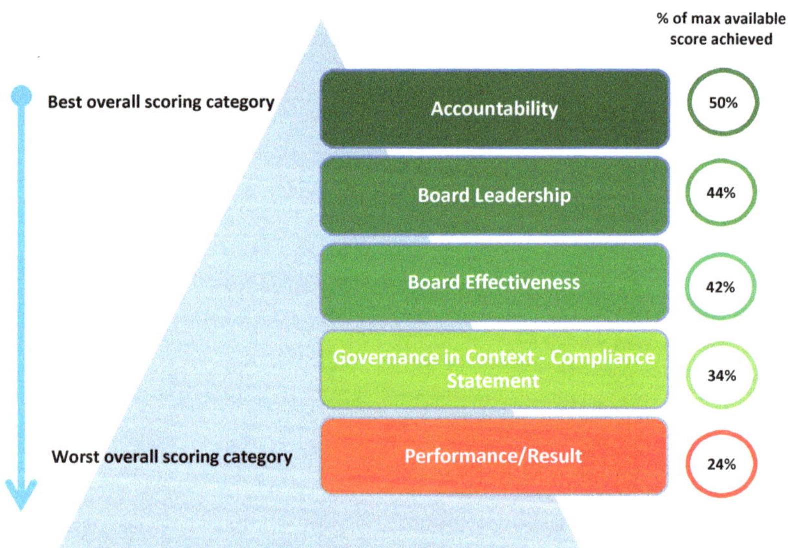

Fig. 7.1b Overall ranking of disclosure scoring for main categories (2001–2012)

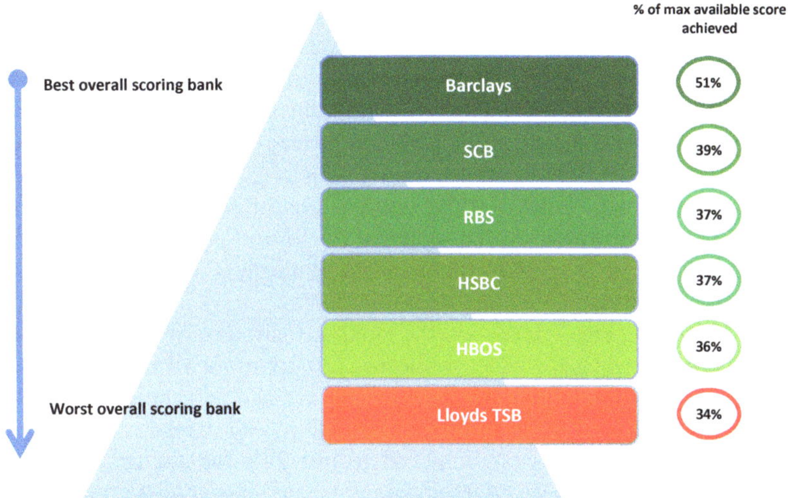

Fig. 7.2 Overall ranking of disclosure quality scoring per bank (2001–2012)

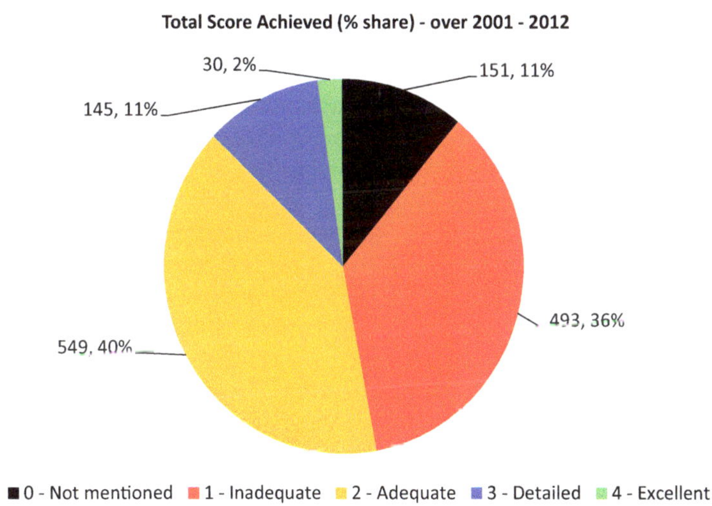

Fig. 7.3 Display of overall disclosure of quality level as a percentage of the maximum score available

firms in this study. It could be interpreted that selecting a set of organisations, all of whom operate with such a variety of different governance practices/disclosure approaches, could be a potential reason for this set of results. The highest average achieved within main category of board effectiveness and performance is 69% over the twelve-year period. This serves to illustrate that at the minimum, one of the chosen organisations fulfilled the disclosure requirements at the highest level of corporate governance. Conversely, the lowest awarded score for disclosure quality is 0% meaning that even the lowest expected level of disclosure was not reported by at least one company.

Furthermore, Fig. 7.1b shows the ranking analysis of overall findings of the main corporate governance disclosure categories for all sample companies over the sample timeframe. The overall average percentage scores for the main criteria category groups across all the six banks ranged from 50% disclosure quality score achieved to just 24% for disclosure quality over the period. The level of disclosure regarding narrative with accountability achieved the maximum quality score awarded which was 50%. Considering the level of expectation in the banking industry to effectively convey the highest level of detail to its stakeholders to ensure transparency regarding the decision-making of senior directors, the highest score being just 50% is surprising. This seems to confirm some of the claims made within the literature that banking institutions are opaque regarding information disclosure. However, the lowest score of 24% was awarded for the performance category. This finding within the results is expected given that there is no agreement within the literature about performance disclosure mechanisms. Secondly, it is somewhat surprising given the fact that there is overwhelming literature indicating the contrary to this result. One possible explanation for this result is due to variables chosen to measure this category. Additionally, there is a lack of both voluntary and mandatory regulation guidance, and to some extent variable quality of verification to be reported in annual reports (Hammond and Miles 2004).

Figure 7.2 portrays the ranking analysis of the overall findings of the corporate governance disclosure score achieved per company over the sample timeframe. The overall scores against the total 19 criteria (subcategories) grouped into five main categories for the entire 72 annual reports among the sample companies ranges from 34 to 51%, with disclosures from Barclays Bank achieving the highest average of all the 19 corporate governance subcategories with 51% disclosure quality score overall. Standard Chartered has the second highest with a quality score of

39% disclosure quality achieved. Lloyds TSB performed relatively poorly with 34% overall disclosure quality score achievement over the twelve-year period. The result confirms that within the UK banking sector, there is a great deal of variability in both the way and manner that banking firms are reporting how corporate governance disclosure in the annual reports is used to demonstrate information disclosure, and accountability to various stakeholders. We explore in-depth, individual companies' longitudinal findings using evaluation spotlight 1—Barclays PLC and spotlight 2—Lloyds, to support the overall findings and interpretation of this result.

7.3.2 *Findings of Overall Analysis of Quality Level Scores*

Following the disclosure of corporate governance content categorisation, the content was evaluated and analysed in terms of the level of information provided combined with the detail of the disclosure. This approach is broadly in line with similar prior studies (Beratta and Bozzolan; Campbell et al. 2010; Cross and Djajadikerta 2004). In completing the assessment, the author has scored each company for each of the 19 subcategory items within the five main themes of the corporate governance checklist/index using a five-point scoring system. This research study is based on verifiable and a specific element related to the firms' circumstances and has adopted five different levels (0–4 point scale) of disclosure content or character used as coding categories of content measurement. The highest score, type 4, represents the best (or highest) quality disclosure while scores of type 1 indicate least disclosure with little information disclosure of the category. The purpose of this is to capture all relevant meanings from a narrative form to enable a better interpretation of the phenomenon. The originality of this method of scoring represents an improvement of the current scoring being used in literature presently.

Figure 7.3 shows the analysis and breakdown of overall findings of disclosure quality level score achieved for all sample companies for all years and for all the categories and subcategories. The results indicate that there is still significant progress to be made on overall quality narrative of corporate governance disclosures in annual reports for the sample banks in the United Kingdom, as well as the individual category groups, whose scores ranged from 0 to 100%. Overall, 51% of the sample banks gave a combined score of adequate and detailed quality disclosure information in the annual reports to support their stakeholders' decisions, but 36%

gave inadequate or less meaningful corporate governance information disclosure year-on-year.

In terms of information disclosure volume per quality score type, Fig. 7.3 shows very clearly that overall the majority of the corporate governance disclosure narratives were made purely in an explanation form, at Type 2 quality score level, with a total score achievement of 40% (as a proportion of the total score achieved) over the twelve-year period. This is closely followed by 36% disclosure score Type 1 level over the sample years. Information quality score Type 3 and Type 4 for the entire twelve years was 11 and 2%, respectively. Although the United Kingdom has been in the forefront in advocating the need for transparency in corporate governance reporting over the past two decades (i.e. publication of the UK Cadbury Report in 1992), this finding confirms that there is still a need for improvement to the disclosure reporting of corporate governance mechanisms of accountability in the UK banking institutions.

The findings also support the conclusion that corporate governance disclosure reporting in annual reports has become proportionately more concerned with the narrative of box-ticking or standard boilerplate disclosures, rather than firm context-specific, detailed and meaningful information for stakeholders. This conclusion confirmed previous findings by the UK Financial Reporting Council (2010, 2012) as well as the Walker Report (2009) regarding bank corporate governance, despite the use of alternate original methods of investigation.

7.3.3 *Finding of Overall Long-Term Trend and Evaluation*

Banking business operations are mainly characterised and often viewed as driven by opacity and increased complexities within an organisation. A key objective of reporting is to promote transparency and accountability by enhancing the quality of disclosure, by reducing information asymmetry. Good quality corporate governance disclosures have a number of potential benefits for stakeholders (Lajili and Zeghal 2005; Linsley and Shrives 2005). It must, however, be recognised that disclosure in itself would not enhance transparency if it appears to lack useful and meaningful information for shareholders, depositors, market analysts, regulators and other stakeholders. Thus, this study has investigated how the sample banks disclosed corporate governance issues with regard to information richness on a longitudinal basis.

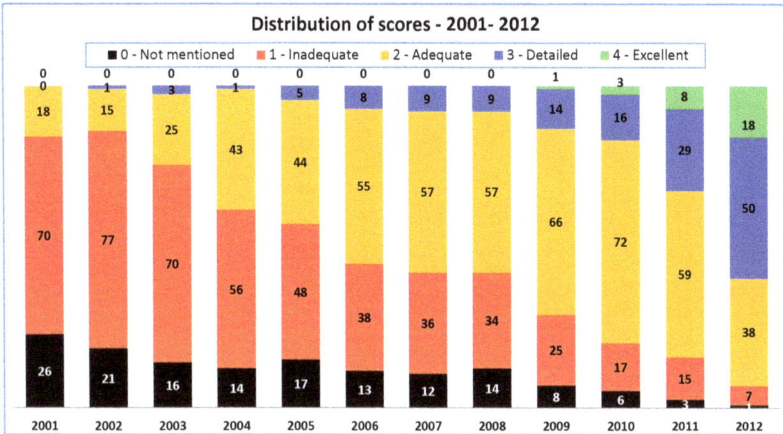

Fig. 7.4 Display of the number of quality disclosure score levels (type 0–4)

Figure 7.4 summarises the results of the disclosure content scale in a year-by-year basis and shows that significant differences were found at some quality levels. It indicates the pattern of disclosure quality within the timeframe analysed. For type 1 disclosures (inadequate), there was a consistent decrease in disclosure in the overall sample from 2002 to 2012, indicating a trend towards more detailed and company-specific reporting on corporate governance related themes. Type 2 (adequate) disclosures recorded a steep increase in the number of score information from 2003 to 2010. These findings could reflect a trend towards more improved accountability in the quality of disclosure reporting.

However, the level of these disclosure types decreased in 2011 and 2012. Type 4 (excellent) corporate governance disclosures were rare. However, over the twelve years of study, their increased appearance in the annual report proved to be significant between 2009 and 2012. Overall, one might be tempted to conclude from this data finding that the quality of reporting is improving over time but in actual fact, the very low level of type 4 disclosures and the frequency of type 4 disclosures across the sample banks suggest that there is ample room for major improvement.

However, the results in Fig. 7.5 display the percentage of the maximum allocated scores awarded for each of the corporate governance categories

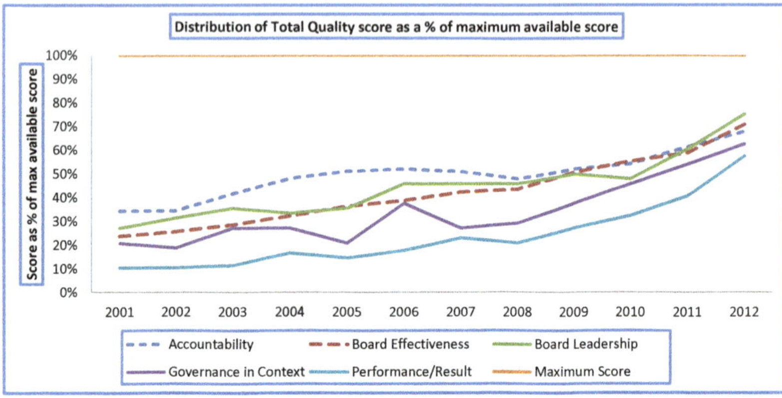

Fig. 7.5 Display of year-on-year of disclosure quality achieved per main category

for all sample companies over the sample period. The figure also corroborates that there has been an increase in the level of quality of disclosures within every category in the twelve-year cycle.

In order to establish whether there have been differences in the quality of disclosure within the time period, the content data was analysed using the sum of the information content scale over the period. Thematic analysis from Fig. 7.6 shows that the majority of disclosures were recorded in the category that included information for board effectiveness. Overall, the performance and result category shows the most improvement in disclosure scores (with 49%) over the sample period.

Figure 7.7 displays the year-on-year total corporate governance disclosure score awarded for all sample banks. We can observe from Fig. 7.7 that the number of quality disclosures in the bank's annual reports has been increasing steadily over time for all banks until 2007, with a slight fall in 2008. However, the rate of increase from 2009 to 2012 has been significant. The total average lowest category disclosed was 106 in 2001 and the average highest was 305 in 2012. The growth observed across the time period highlights the banks' heightened awareness of the expectations of improvements within their annual reports. The development of guidance from major accounting bodies, standard setters and bank regulators (such as Financial Service Authority and Financial Reporting Council in the United Kingdom) displays a link with these improvements

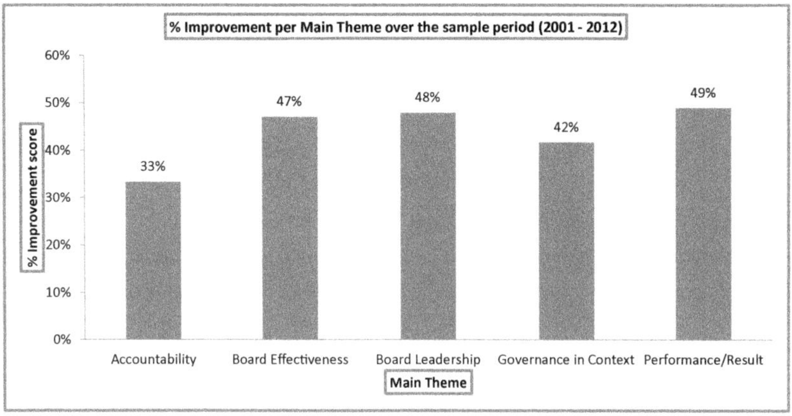

Fig. 7.6 Display of overall percentage improvements per main category (2001–2012)

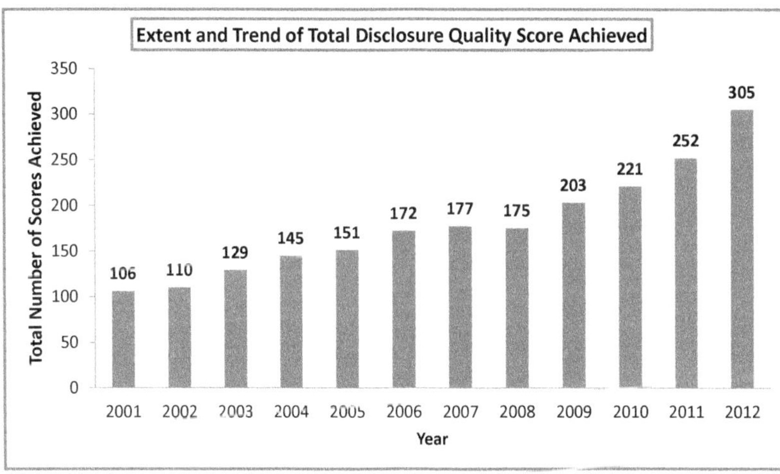

Fig. 7.7 Display of year-on-year total corporate governance disclosure quality score achieved

to standards of disclosure. Additionally, the introduction (and use) of the revised Combined Code (2003 and 2010) of Corporate Governance in the United Kingdom can be linked to the observed increase in corporate governance responsibilities disclosure. We can conclude from this observation that this document issued by financial supervisory regulators had a tangible impact on levels of disclosure quality (Fig. 7.8).

Evaluation Spotlight 1—Barclays PLC

The total overall proportion of disclosure of corporate governance quality level score achieved as a percentage of maximum expected score over the twelve-year period of study was 51% (as a proportion of required

Bank Profile: Barclays

Year	2001	2002	2003	2004	2005	2006	2007	2008	2009	2010	2011	2012	Total	Maximum	% of Maximum
Governance in Context - Compliance Statement															
COC,Statement of Compliance	1	1	2	2	2	2	2	2	2	2	3	4	25	48	52%
CONC,Statement of Non-compliance explanation	2	1	3	2	0	2	0	0	0	0	1	2	13	48	27%
Sub-total	3	2	5	4	2	4	2	2	2	2	4	6	38	96	40%
Board Leadership															
LE1.1 ,Board Responsibilities/Role	1	3	3	1	2	2	3	3	3	2	3	4	30	48	63%
LE1.2 ,Responsibilities/Role of board chairman	2	2	3	3	2	2	2	3	3	2	3	4	31	48	65%
Sub-total	3	5	6	4	4	4	5	6	6	4	6	8	61	96	64%
Board Effectiveness															
BE1 ,Board Size	1	1	1	2	1	2	2	2	2	2	2	2	20	48	42%
BE2,Meetings	1	1	1	2	1	3	3	3	3	4	4	4	30	48	63%
BE3 ,Board Balance/composition	2	2	2	2	2	2	2	2	2	3	3	3	27	48	56%
BE4,Non-Executive Directors independence	2	2	2	2	2	2	2	2	2	2	3	3	26	48	54%
BE5,Board Evaluation	1	1	1	2	3	2	3	3	3	3	4	4	30	48	63%
BE6,Committees working activities	2	2	2	2	2	3	3	3	3	3	4	4	33	48	69%
BE7,Board Refreshment	1	1	1	1	1	2	2	3	2	2	3	3	22	48	46%
Sub-total	10	10	10	13	12	16	17	18	17	19	23	23	188	336	56%
Accountability															
ACC1. ,Risk management and internal control	2	2	2	2	2	2	3	3	3	3	3	3	30	48	63%
ACC2.,Internal audit	2	2	2	2	2	3	3	3	3	2	2	3	29	48	60%
ACC3.,External audit	2	2	2	2	2	2	2	2	2	2	2	2	24	48	50%
ACC4.,Audit committees scrutiny	2	2	2	2	3	3	3	3	3	3	3	3	32	48	67%
Sub-total	8	8	8	8	9	10	11	11	11	10	10	11	115	192	60%
Performance/Result															
PERF1. ,Key performance Indicators	2	2	2	2	2	2	2	3	4	4	4	4	33	48	69%
PERF2. ,Code of ethics	1	1	0	1	1	2	2	1	1	1	2	2	15	48	31%
PERF3.,Whistle blowing	0	0	0	0	0	0	2	1	1	1	1	2	8	48	17%
PERF4. , Breaches and penalties	0	0	0	0	0	1	1	1	1	1	2	3	10	48	21%
Sub-total	3	3	2	3	3	5	7	6	7	7	9	11	66	192	34%
Grand Total	27	28	31	32	30	39	42	43	43	42	52	59	468	912	

Score/colour	0	1	2	3	4
Description	Not mentioned	Inadequate	Adequate	Detailed	Excellent

Fig. 7.8 Barclay's year–on-year disclosure results of the quality of corporate governance

maximum quality score expected) for the corporate governance disclosure specification elements. This indicates an improvement in the corporate governance mean score quality within the reported inquiry timeframe. Additionally, the highest level of quality disclosure score achieved for Barclays is 69%, and the lowest quality level score is 17%. This finding suggests that there exists significant differences in the quality of the corporate governance systems within Barclays. However, this result also reveals that the highest quality score of 69% is awarded to the main category of "Board Effectiveness" (i.e. subcategory—"Board committee working activities"), and the "Performance" category (i.e. subcategory—"Key Performance Indicators"). Conversely, the lowest quality disclosure score achieved of 17% is disclosed in a different section within the "Performance" category, indicating that the subcategory item of "Whistle-blowing" has provided the lowest quality score.

The findings as observed from the table above also illustrate that over the time period there has been a steady improvement in the overall number of categories of corporate governance disclosed by Barclays bank. The least amount of corporate governance disclosure categories was 27 in the year 2001 and the greatest amount of disclosure categories was 59 in the year 2012.

Furthermore, another volumetric measure was employed to reflect the longitudinal trend of the categories disclosures. The graph below shows the trend of the proportion of disclosure of each of the categories measured as a proportion of total quality score achieved over the expected maximum score for the period (Fig. 7.9).

It is interesting to note that there has been a significant improvement in the quality score for all 5 main categories between the year 2010 and 2012. The number of disclosures increased dramatically in 2011 and 2012. However, this study found that the overall trend in the amount of quality disclosure suggests the presence of variabilities and changeover in specific corporate governance categories and subcategories. The observed yearly trend of disclosure analysis indicates a noticeable expansion in the amount of quality disclosure for key performance indicators in the years 2008 to 2012, statement of compliance for 2011 and 2012, and board effectiveness in 2005, 2006, 2007 and 2010 to 2012 category.

Although the results for Barclays have remained stable in the overall average disclosure narrative in the various corporate governance disclosures over the period, some of the subcategories have clearly significantly increased after 2007. Two reasons can be attributed to this. Firstly, it

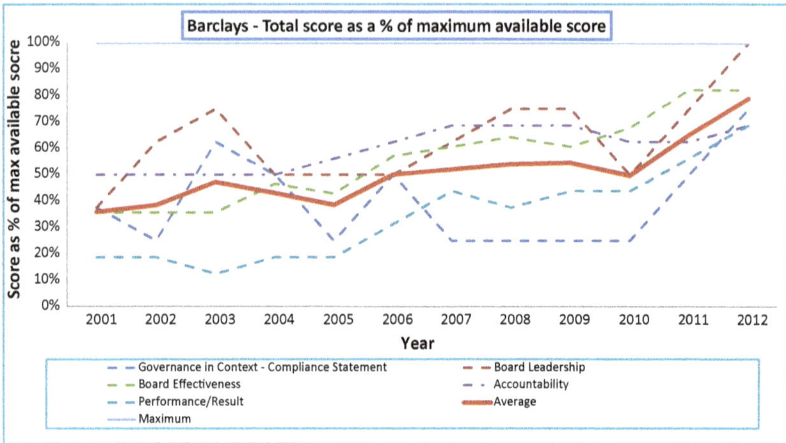

Fig. 7.9 Display of year-on-year main categories total disclosure trends by Barclays

could be the consequences of the financial crash in 2007–2008 that affected a number of major domestic and international banking firms including Barclays. Secondly, the UK Corporate Governance Code that had been introduced in 2003 was revised in both 2008 and 2010 in order to improve best practice disclosures (Fig. 7.10).

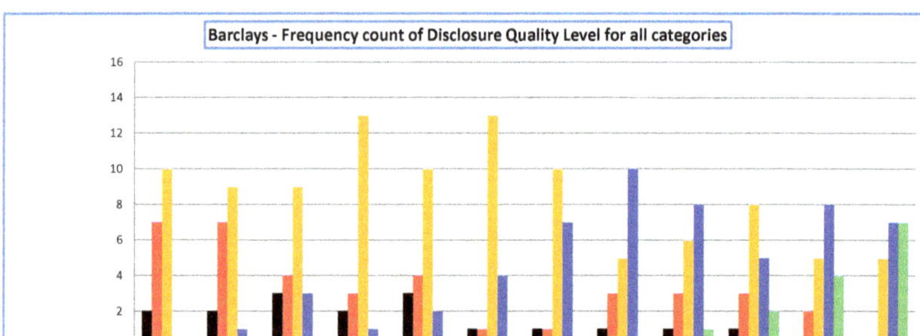

	2001	2002	2003	2004	2005	2006	2007	2008	2009	2010	2011	2012
Not mentioned- 0	2	2	3	2	3	1	1	1	1	1	0	0
Inadequate - 1	7	7	4	3	4	1	1	3	3	3	2	0
Adequate - 2	10	9	9	13	10	13	10	5	6	8	5	5
Detailed - 3	0	1	3	1	2	4	7	10	8	5	8	7
Excellent - 4	0	0	0	0	0	0	0	0	1	2	4	7

Fig. 7.10 Level of occurrence of quality disclosure levels disclosed by Barclays

The rate of occurrence with regard to the disclosure quality levels was computed and tallied for all the corporate governance subcategories of Barclays in order to distinguish the quality levels in all the disclosure items over the period of study. This level of analysis permits deeper investigation to examine both the level of development over the timeframe as well as the degree of information quality. It can be observed from this graph that the overall total regularities of quality disclosure were of Type 2 level (i.e. Adequate) with 45% (103/228) of the total scores achieved over the twelve-year period. In addition, the overall disclosure result illustrates that "Excellent" quality (i.e. score type 4) with 6% (14/228) only started to improve since 2009. In general, the conclusion drawn from these findings support the investigation arguments regarding the significant task of quality corporate governance disclosures in shaping the manner in which banking firms are accountable to the concerns of numerous stakeholders using the annual financial statement report. However, the study highlights that further steps could be taken by boards and policymakers to enhance the quality and usefulness of corporate governance disclosures contained in the annual report for stakeholders.

Spotlight Evaluation 2: Lloyds TSB

The total overall proportion of disclosure of corporate governance quality level score achieved as a percentage of maximum expected score over the twelve-year period of study was 34% (as a proportion of required maximum quality score expected) in all years for the corporate governance disclosure specification categories elements. Also, the highest level of quality disclosure score achieved for Lloyds TSB is 54% and the lowest quality level score is 6%. This finding is similar to the results found in Barclays, HSBC and HBOS and also suggests that there was substantial divergence in the quality of the corporate governance systems reporting habits by Lloyds TSB. However, this result also reveals that the highest quality score of 54% is awarded to the main category of both 'Accountability' (i.e. subcategory items on 'Risk Management & Internal Control'), and 'Performance' category (i.e. subcategory item 'Key Performance Indicators') (Fig. 7.11).

Conversely, the lowest quality disclosure score achieved of 6% is disclosed in another subdivision of the performance category, indicating that the subcategory item on whistle-blowing has provided the lowest quality performance. The findings show that the number of corporate governance category items disclosed by Lloyds TSB has been increasing

Bank Profile: Lloyds TSB

Year	2001	2002	2003	2004	2005	2006	2007	2008	2009	2010	2011	2012	Total	Maximum	% of Maximum
Governance in Context - Governance Statement															
COC,Statement of Compliance	1	1	1	1	1	1	1	2	2	2	2	2	17	48	35%
CONC,Statement of Non-compliance explanation	0	0	1	1	0	1	1	1	1	2	2	2	12	48	25%
Sub-total	1	1	2	2	1	2	2	3	3	4	4	4	29	96	30%
Board Leadership															
LE1.1 ,Board Responsibilities/Role	1	1	1	1	1	1	1	2	2	2	2	3	18	48	38%
LE1.2 ,Responsibilities/Role of board chairman	1	1	1	1	2	2	2	2	2	2	2	3	21	48	44%
Sub-total	2	2	2	2	3	3	3	4	4	4	4	6	39	96	41%
Board Effectiveness															
BE1 ,Board Size	1	1	1	1	1	1	1	1	2	2	2	1	15	48	31%
BE2,Meetings	1	1	1	1	1	1	1	1	1	2	2	3	16	48	33%
BE3 ,Board Balance/composition	1	1	1	2	2	2	2	2	2	2	2	2	21	48	44%
BE4,Non-Executive Directors Independence	1	1	1	1	1	2	2	2	2	2	2	3	20	48	42%
BE5,Board Evaluation	1	1	1	1	2	2	1	1	1	2	1	3	17	48	35%
BE6,Committees working activities	1	1	2	2	2	2	2	2	2	2	3	3	24	48	50%
BE7,Board Refreshment	0	1	1	1	1	1	1	1	1	1	1	2	12	48	25%
Sub-total	6	7	8	9	10	11	10	10	11	13	13	17	125	336	37%
Accountability															
ACC1. ,Risk management and internal control	1	2	2	2	2	2	2	2	2	2	3	4	26	48	54%
ACC2.,Internal audit	2	2	2	2	2	2	2	2	2	2	2	2	24	48	50%
ACC3.,External audit	1	1	1	1	2	2	2	2	2	2	2	2	20	48	42%
ACC4.,Audit committees scrutiny	1	1	1	1	1	1	1	1	1	1	2	2	14	48	29%
Sub-total	5	6	6	6	7	7	7	7	7	7	9	10	84	192	44%
Performance/Result															
PERF1. ,Key performance Indicators	1	1	1	2	2	2	2	2	2	2	2	3	22	48	46%
PERF2. ,Code of ethics	0	0	0	0	0	0	0	0	1	1	1	2	5	48	10%
PERF3.,Whistle blowing	0	0	0	0	0	0	0	0	0	1	1	1	3	48	6%
PERF4. , Breaches and penalties	0	0	0	0	0	0	0	1	1	1	2	3	8	48	17%
Sub-total	1	1	1	2	2	2	2	3	4	5	6	9	38	192	20%
Grand Total	15	17	19	21	23	25	24	27	29	33	36	46	315	912	

Score/colour	0	1	2	3	4
Description	Not mentioned	Inadequate	Adequate	Detailed	Excellent

Fig. 7.11 Lloyds TSB year-on-year disclosure results of the quality of corporate governance

gradually over time. The lowest number of categories was 15 disclosed in 2001 and the highest number was 46 in 2012.

Furthermore, in order to further understand the degree of change over the period under study with regard to the categories, a longitudinal analysis was employed by the use of a volumetric measure to chart the trend of the categories of disclosure. Figure 7.12 exhibits the trend of the proportion of disclosure of each of the categories measured as a proportion of total quality score achieved over the expected maximum score for the period.

It can be seen that there has been a significant improvement in the quality score for all 5 main categories between 2001 and 2012. Again, the amount of quality disclosures that has increased represents a consistent

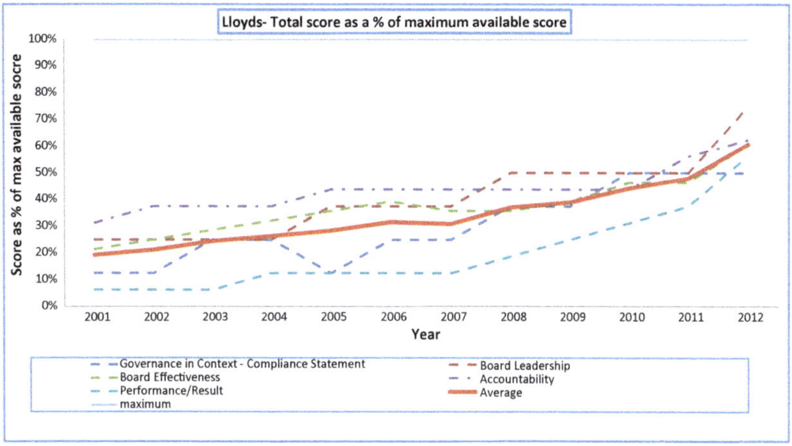

Fig. 7.12 Display of year-on-year main categories total disclosure trend by Lloyds

and steady year-on-year improvement, except between 2011 and 2012, where the increase is considered to be significant. However, although this study has discovered a growth in the volume of quality disclosures, the results mask the variances within some of the subcategories. The observed patterns of longitudinal disclosure indicate a steady improvement in the volume of quality disclosure for board effectiveness with a particular point of increase between 2011 and 2012, for board leadership in 2012, performance for 2012, and also for accountability in 2011 and 2012.

Furthermore, it can be noted from the trend analysis of results in the overall average disclosure narrative in the various corporate governance disclosures over a longitudinal period, some of the subcategories have clearly undergone a substantial interchanging growth period after 2005 that affected the quality of disclosure. The impact of the banking crisis in 2007 does not appear to have affected the disclosure reporting in the annual report for Lloyds as might have been expected. However, the revised version United Kingdom Corporate Governance Code that was introduced in 2010 did seem to affect some disclosure items. Accountability was the most disclosed quality corporate governance category in the annual report over the sample period with an overall score of 44% (i.e. total quality score as a percentage of maximum score expected). This indicates that accountability disclosure was the largest area of focus of corporate governance by Lloyds senior management and hence the reason for the provision of more narrative disclosures to its important stakeholders. The category that has the least disclosure score rating from the annual reports over the period was performance or results category with a quality disclosure score of 20% overall (Fig. 7.13).

The occurrence of different quality disclosure levels was computed and tallied for all the corporate governance subcategories of Lloyds TSB with the aim of gaining further insights regarding the information quality levels in all the governance disclosure specification dimensions over the study timeframe. Also, this level of analysis facilitates deeper investigation to examine the level of improvement that has occurred over the twelve-year period. It can be observed that the overall level of occurrence of quality disclosure was mainly disclosed on quality score level 1 with 43% (97/228) of the total scores achieved. Overall, the disclosure result shows no growing trend of high quality of information content (i.e. score type 4) with a 0% (1/228) quality scores achieved. Additionally, the combined information quality level 1 (Inadequate) and level 0 (Not mentioned) were over half (55%) of the overall disclosed information in Lloyds annual reports over the study timeframe.

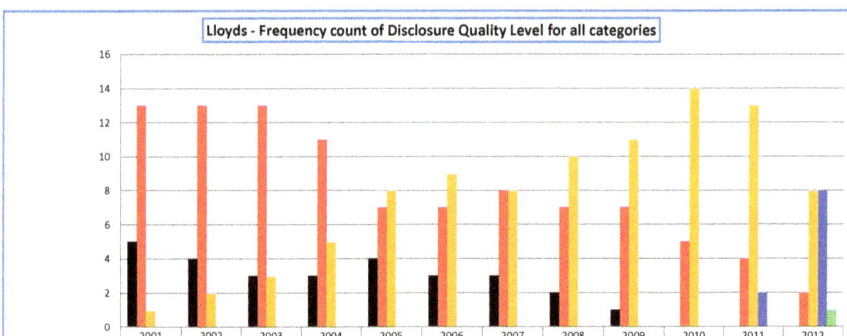

	2001	2002	2003	2004	2005	2006	2007	2008	2009	2010	2011	2012
Not mentioned- 0	5	4	3	3	4	3	3	2	1	0	0	0
Inadequate - 1	13	13	13	11	7	7	8	7	7	5	4	2
Adequate - 2	1	2	3	5	8	9	8	10	11	14	13	8
Detailed - 3	0	0	0	0	0	0	0	0	0	0	2	8
Excellent - 4	0	0	0	0	0	0	0	0	0	0	0	1

Fig. 7.13 Level of occurrence of quality disclosure levels disclosed by Lloyds TSB

7.4 Conclusion

The mechanisms of accountability in corporate governance is very much an evolving area. Much of the advancement of corporate governance in financial institutions seems to broadly be propelled by the desire to offer greater accountability and transparency to the financial markets after damage caused by corporate collapse and financial scandals. The evaluation presented here forms the first part of the empirical work on the assessment of the quality of corporate governance disclosure reporting in the annual reports of the top six UK-listed banking firms over the period 2001–2012. We have used the findings to demonstrate the significance of "good" corporate governance and the various mechanisms of accountability for financial institutions. The illustration of spotlights 1 and 2 used in this chapter showcases the disparity that still exists within financial institutions. Although only two spotlights were covered, additional analysis of further companies (such as HSBC, Halifax Bank of Scotland etc.) affirm the conclusions that have been drawn elsewhere in this book. The five-point scoring system (Score Type 0–4) enabled clear judgements to be presented regarding the overall disclosure category/subcategory items quality level. It highlighted core areas of focus that different organisations need to further develop in order to ensure full transparency with their stakeholders. The surprising decline in some categories despite the financial crash putting a sharper focus on some of these elements continues to form an area of confusion. With the illusion of increased effort and disclosure, a closer look has exposed contradicting results for some.

There has been an increasing level of interest in the quality of disclosure in annual reports (Bayou et al. 2011), which has intensified following the failures of several large companies (for example, Enron, WorldCom, Tyco Corporation, Bear sterns, Northern Rock). However, the nature of disclosure is reliant on the standard, volume and frequency of divulged information as well as the richness offered by additional information (Beretta and Bozzolan 2004). In terms of the quality of disclosure, narrative components with sufficient information are able to convey messages for stakeholders' clarification, validation and effective decision-making about their investment. It is also able to offer useful insights into corporate governance reporting. The findings include the observation that information diversity has been broadened over time. The study also notes the dominance of repetitive narratives (or boilerplate) with little disclosure containing comparative or detailed specific contextual information relating to the individual organisation. However, the study highlights that further steps could be taken by boards and policymakers to enhance the quality and usefulness of corporate governance disclosures contained in the annual report for stakeholders.

In conclusion, the overall results reinforce the study's general arguments that corporate governance plays an important role in determining how banking firms mitigate agency problems and respond to the needs and interests of various stakeholders and, hence, in determining the quality of corporate governance disclosures in the annual reports. In this regard, the sound bank corporate governance systems (i.e. process, policies and practices) serve as both monitoring and accountability mechanisms, by which bank managers' opportunistic behaviours and manipulations are controlled and banks made to respond to the informational needs of stakeholders, thereby reducing information asymmetry or information gaps. In other words, the stakeholder theoretical framework adopted by the current study is thus supported by the current study's findings. However, non-disclosure or not mentioning some corporate governance features indicates the need for some attention either in revising the principles of the corporate governance codes or in demonstrating their application.

However, the empirical results of previous studies cannot be directly compared with the results of the current study because of the time period and the different types and number of information items measured. As the above discussion attests, the results of the current study can be seen as primary evidence, taking into account the development of disclosure practices by listed banks over a long period of time as opposed to the short term (i.e. 1 or 2 years) period used in previous studies to investigate corporate governance. Also, very few previous empirical disclosure studies have focused on the extent of banking disclosure, since most of the prior earlier disclosure studies have excluded banks and other financial institutions from their samples.

The findings confirm the importance of accentuating information quality disclosure to enhance corporate governance by focusing on financial institutions, in particular banking firms. Overall, the result of the findings presented in this chapter encourages broader approaches to corporate governance and accountability research beyond the traditional and primarily quantitative approaches of prior research. The findings also depart from the previous studies that overwhelmingly used agency theory to investigate corporate governance practices by especially using a single metric to evaluate accountability to stakeholders.

References

Aburaya, R. K. (2012). *The relationship between corporate governance and environmental disclosure: UK evidence*. Durham thesis, Durham University.

Adams, C. A. (2002). Internal organisational factors influencing corporate social and ethical reporting: Beyond current theorising. *Accounting, Auditing and Accountability Journal, 15*(2), 223–250.

Akuffo, J. A. (2018). *Corporate governance and bank accountability: The role of accountability in improving the quality of corporate governance disclosures in bank annual report: A UK perspective*. DBA Thesis, Grenoble Ecole De Management.

Bayou, M. E., Reinstein, A., & Williams, P. F. (2011). To tell the truth: A discussion of issues concerning truth and ethics in accounting. *Accounting, Organization and Society, 36*(2), 109–124.

Beattie, V., McInnes, W., & Fearnley, S. (2004). A methodology for analysing and evaluating narratives in annual reports: A comprehensive descriptive profile and metrics for disclosure quality attributes. *Accounting Forum, 28*(3), 202–231.

Beretta, S., & Bozzolan, S. (2004). A framework for the analysis of firm risk communication. *The International Journey of Accounting, 39*(3), 265–288.

Beretta, S., & Bozzolan, S. (2008). Quality versus quantity: The case of forward-looking disclosure. *Journal of Accounting, Auditing and Finance, 23*(3), 333–375.

Campbell, D., Beck, A. C., & Shrives, P. J. (2010). Content analysis in environmental reporting research: Enrichment and rehearsal of the method in a British-German context. *The British Accounting Review, 42*(3), 207–222.

Cross, T. A., & Djajadikerta, H. G. (2004). An examination of voluntary environmental disclosures in New Zealand and Australia: A research framework. *15th International Congress on Social and Environmental Accounting Research (3rd Australasian CSEAR Conference)*. Sydney: CSEAR.

Financial Reporting Council (FRC). (2010). *The UK corporate governance code*. London: Financial Reporting Council.

Financial Reporting Council (FRC). (2012). *The UK corporate governance code*. London: Financial Reporting Council.

Gray, R., Javad, M., Power, D. M., & Sinclair, C. D. (2001). Social and environmental disclosure and corporate characteristics: A research note and extension. *Journal of Business Finance Accounting, 28*(3–4), 327–356.

Hammond, K., & Miles, S. (2004). Assessing quality of corporate social reporting: UK perspectives. *Accounting Forum, 28*(1), 61–79.

Lajili, K., & Zeghal, D. (2005). A content analysis of risk management disclosures in Canadian annual reports. *Canadian Journal of Administrative Sciences, 22*(2), 126–141.

Linsley, P. M., & Shrives, P. J. (2005). Transparency and the disclosure of risk information in the banking sector. *Journal of Financial Regulation and Compliance, 13*(3), 205–214.

Walker, S. D. (2009). *A review of corporate governance in UK banks and other financial industry entities.* Final recommendations.

CHAPTER 8

Power! Qualitative Corporate Governance Disclosures in UK Financial Institutions

8.1 Introduction

This chapter will explore empirically an in-depth analysis of the assessment of the quality of corporate governance disclosures in financial institutions and its mechanisms of accountability narrative disclosures from their annual reports. The finding here adds to the existing accounting literature in understanding the different level of quality disclosures in financial institutions on a longitudinal basis. The presentation of the evidence in this chapter is classified into the following five main governance categories of disclosures: (1) Corporate governance in context disclosure; statement of compliance for codes and standards and statement of non-compliance explanation for not adhering to codes and standards; (2) Board Leadership disclosure; board responsibilities and responsibilities of the board chairman; (3) Board Effectiveness disclosure; board size, board meetings, board compositions, non-executive directors independence, board evaluation, board committees working activities and board refreshment; (4) Board Accountabilities disclosure; risk management and internal control, internal audit, external audit and audit committees scrutiny activities; and (5) Performance or results disclosure; key performance indicators, code of ethics or conduct, whistle-blowing policies and practices; penalties and breaches.

J. A. Akuffo, *Corporate Governance and Accountability of Financial Institutions*, Palgrave Studies in Accounting and Finance Practice, https://doi.org/10.1007/978-3-030-64046-0_8

Corporate governance is the system by which companies are directed and controlled. Boards of directors are responsible for the governance of their companies. The shareholders' role in governance is to appoint the directors and the auditors and to satisfy themselves that an appropriate structure is in place at least from the theoretical perspective. The responsibilities of the board include setting the company's strategic aims, providing the leadership to put them into effect, supervising the management of the business and reporting to shareholders on their stewardship. Since 1992, there has been a code on corporate governance in the United Kingdom which has acted as a guide to a number of key components of effective board practice and has been based on the underlying principles of all good governance including accountability, transparency and the success of a company or group over the longer term. A fundamental aspect of corporate governance reporting and disclosure in the United Kingdom is that of "comply or explain". The various corporate governance codes have not been a rigid set of rules and companies have been able to explain their reasons for non-compliance with certain aspects of it, while in the United States the nature and requirement of corporate governance are much more based on prescriptive rules and laws.

8.2 Findings Per Dimension of Main Corporate Governance Themes

This section seeks to address the book objective that intends to identify the governance categories and subcategories (i.e. mechanisms of accountability) that are most disclosed, and those that are least disclosed within the UK financial institutions sample for the empirical investigation. It also addresses whether the level of disclosure among the companies varies across different company's corporate governance categories/subcategories as reported.

To substantiate the selected approach for this analysis, initially the level of disclosure for each category score achieved by each company has been analysed, followed by the analysis of the type of quality level score achieved by each company for the entire sample period. Each singular sub-quality of disclosure was scrutinised to enable a more detailed picture of the organisation's disclosure strategy to be produced. This was done both collectively and independently to allow an in-depth analysis. In this regard, the breakdown of the quality of the disclosure of corporate governance provides an improved overall understanding of the relationship between quality disclosure and governance. The aim of this improved granularity within the breakdown of the analysis of each category in this study is to depart from the current limitations within the existing literature, regarding the "one size fits all" measurement approach to corporate governance performance (as previously discussed within the literature).

8.2.1 *Disclosure of Corporate Governance in Context Findings*

This subsection of the Corporate Governance Disclosure findings deals with the detail of disclosure regarding the quality of narrative explanations of corporate governance in contextual environments provided in the annual reports. Two subcategory measures are used to collect information in the annual reports, namely; (1) statement of compliance for codes and standards and (2) statement of non-compliance explanation for not adhering to codes and standards. The qualities of information disclosed in both subcategories are measured using the information content scale type of 0–4 quality score cumulatively for the sample period 2001 to 2012. The following two subsections present the main findings as obtained from the company's annual reports.

8.2.1.1 *Statement of Compliance for Codes and Standards Disclosure*

Figures 8.1a and 8.1b portray the results for the sample banks used for the study regarding the assessment of statement of compliance for codes and corporate governance standards narratives disclosed in the annual reports. Figure 8.1a shows the total average disclosure quality score for each bank as a percentage or as proportions of the total maximum score available for the twelve-year period. Figure 8.1b shows the distribution of Statement of Compliance disclosure score type achieved per financial institution over the sample period.

The constructed index measure used to assess this category was in line with the requirements from the UK Financial Reporting Council regarding the reporting of corporate governance disclosures in annual financial statements. In essence, the "UK legislation and regulations establish basic standards of conduct and transparency, while the non-statutory codes of practice use self-regulation as a means of maintaining good corporate governance" (LSE 2012, p. 17). Within the United Kingdom, the overall effect of the regulatory framework for effective

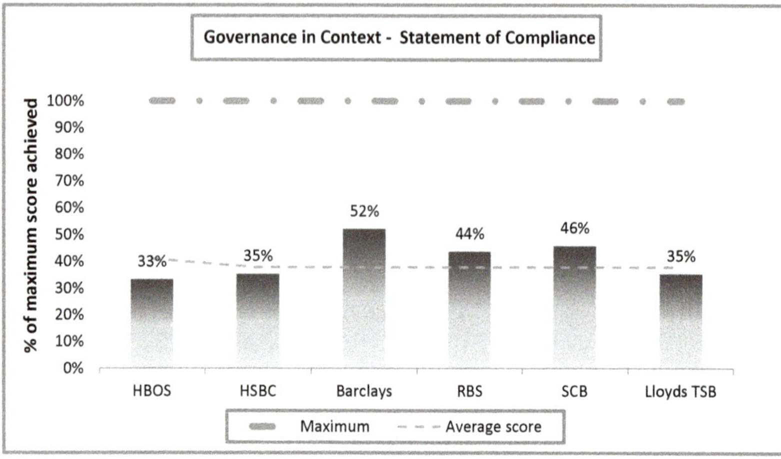

Fig. 8.1a Display of statement of compliance disclosure score (2001–2012)

	HBOS	HSBC	Barclays	RBS	SCB	Lloyds TSB
0 - Not mentioned	0	0	0	0	0	0
1 - Inadequate	8	9	2	5	5	7
2 - Adequate	4	2	8	5	4	5
3 - Detailed	0	0	1	2	3	0
4 - Excellent	0	1	1	0	0	0

Fig. 8.1b Display of distribution of statement of compliance disclosure scores (2001–2012)

corporate governance "is to create a principles-based system of corporate governance, based on proportionality, flexibility and targeting, that cannot be achieved through a "one size fits all" approach. The "comply or explain" approach to corporate governance under the UK LR and DTR, states that a listed company must report to its shareholders on how it has applied corporate governance guidance, where it has not applied the guidance as envisaged, and provide an explanation as to why it has not done so" (LSE 2012, p. 17). For listing companies, it is up to shareholders (or where applicable, direct stakeholders) to offer judgement as to whether their firm has fully disclosed sufficient details on the practice of corporate governance adopted or not. The result from the findings in this investigation seems to support the narrative assertion that there is no "one size fits all" approach to the reporting of corporate governance in the United Kingdom. Additionally, the data confirms the important role played by governance reporting requirements demanded by financial supervisors or governance authorities over regulated firms or listed firms (for example, FRC 2012).

The number of financial institutions assessed here are all UK-listed firms and provide the overwhelming majority of various financial service products in the United Kingdom. The finding shows (Fig. 8.1a) that overall reported rates of the explanations provided for corporate governance in the UK context remain fairly average and, to some extent, very poor among the sample banks over the twelve-year period. Barclays Bank had the highest quality disclosure index score (with 52%) for statement of compliance with the relevant Code provisions. HBOS provided the least explanations (33% in Fig. 8.1a) detailing how they have applied the principles from the code of corporate governance and also on how they have conformed to the requirements of the code. The 33% score is well below the overall average of 41% disclosure score achieved for the sample period.

Regarding the distribution of the quality of the information types disclosed over the period, the results confirm that overall, out of the total of 72 frequency counts of quality score achieved that were recorded for this category over the twelve-year period, 50% (36/72) were regarded as inadequate disclosures (type 1 quality score), 38.9% (28/72) recorded as adequate disclosures (type 2 quality score), 8.3% (6/72) described as detailed disclosures (type 3 quality score) and only 2.8% (2/72) portray excellent disclosures (type 4 quality score). Although, this result cannot be compared directly to any other prior research in UK banking, it, however, contradicts the result from Grant Thornton's best practice report on corporate governance for 2012, which stated that 86% of listed financial companies claim to have provided "more" explanations in the same year (Grant Thornton 2012).

8.2.1.2 Statement of Non-compliance for Codes and Standards Disclosure

As discussed in the previous section and also in chapter five, in the United Kingdom, it is important that where listed companies do not follow a Code provision, a clear explanation is provided so that their shareholders can assess whether they are content with the governance arrangements that the company has put in place. In terms of explanation quality in the annual report, the disclosure code states that "an alternative to following a provision may be justified if good governance can be achieved by other means. A condition of doing so is that the reasons for it should be explained clearly and carefully to shareholders". The empirical study reviewed the selection of disclosure explanations in the 72 annual reports over the sample period to assess the extent to which the companies provided this information.

Figures 8.2a and 8.2b portray the overall findings of the narrative regarding the provision of the statement of non-compliance disclosure quality score for the sample banks. The standard of disclosure explanations vary considerably among the companies. It can be noted that Standard Chartered Bank provided more quality information explanations and reasons for their non-compliance statement, with reference to the relevant code of best practice of corporate governance with 33% score achieved in relation to the expected maximum score (with the sample

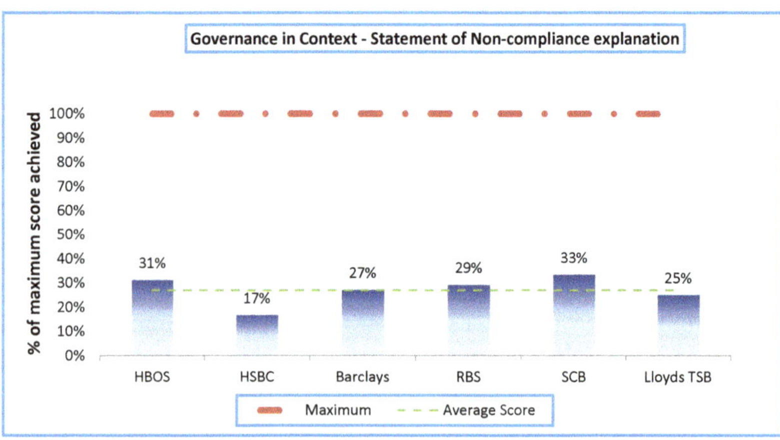

Fig. 8.2a Overall statement of non-compliance disclosure quality scores

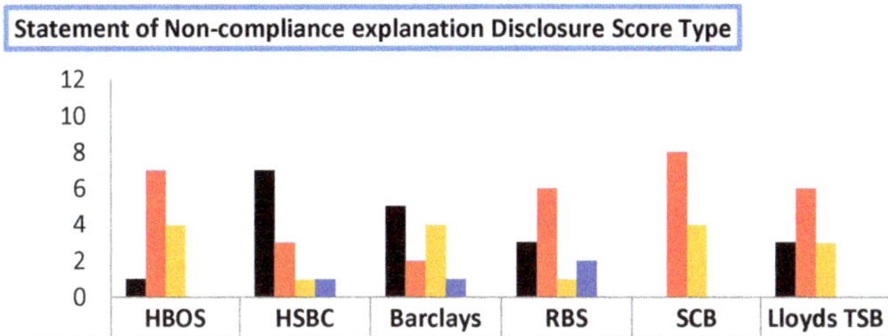

	HBOS	HSBC	Barclays	RBS	SCB	Lloyds TSB
0 - Not mentioned	1	7	5	3	0	3
1 - Inadequate	7	3	2	6	8	6
2 - Adequate	4	1	4	1	4	3
3 - Detailed	0	1	1	2	0	0
4 - Excellent	0	0	0	0	0	0

Fig. 8.2b Distribution of statement of non-compliance disclosure quality score type

average of 27%) compared with the lowest score achievement of 17% for HSBC.

Furthermore, with respect to the distribution of the quality of the information types disclosed over the period, the results confirm that overall, out of the total of 72 frequency counts of quality score achieved, 26.4% (19/72) were regarded as "not mentioned" disclosures (type 0 quality score), 44.4% (32/72) recorded as inadequate disclosures (type 1 quality score), 23.6% (17/72) described as adequate disclosures (type 2 quality score) and only 5.6% (4/72) portrayed detailed disclosures (type 3 quality score). Again, this result contradicts the result from Grant Thornton's best practice report on corporate governance for 2012, which stated that 73% (69% in 2011) of listed companies claim to have provided detailed explanation reasons to support non-compliance disclosure in the year 2012 (Grant Thornton 2012).

8.2.2 Disclosure of Board Leadership Findings

This subsection of the Corporate Governance Disclosure findings deals with the role of the board, division of responsibilities and the role of the chairman and non-executive directors. Since the financial crisis of 2007–2008 and other recent financial scandals, there is increasing emphasis

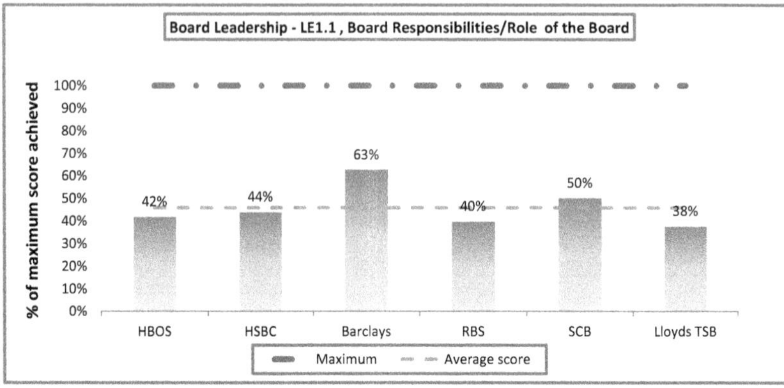

Fig. 8.3a Board leadership—Disclosure of board responsibility/role of bank boards of directors (2001–2012)

on the way boards carry out their role, the behaviours they display and the culture they promote for their respective companies. This message was reinforced in the UK "Financial Reporting Council 2011 Guidance on Board Effectiveness". The UK code of best practice guidance on corporate governance states that "every company should be headed by an effective board that is collectively responsible for the long-term success of the company. The chairman is responsible for leadership of the board and the chief executive for the running of the company's business. The board should include non-executive directors, whose role it is to constructively challenge and help develop proposals on strategy" (LSE 2012, pp. 18). The checklist measure adopted in this study includes the reporting requirements as stated above but also added subsequent qualifiers to capture the narratives in the disclosure in more details. Figures 8.3a, 8.3b and 8.4a, 8.4b portray the main findings for the total annual corporate governance reporting for the sample banks covering both pre and post financial crisis period.

8.2.2.1 *The Role of Bank Board of Directors Disclosure*

As noted in the literature, the duties of bank boards are very complex and imply arbitrating between stakeholders and constituencies (i.e. regulators, shareholders, depositors, employees). Shareholders have widely diverging views and the notion of acting in the best interest of the

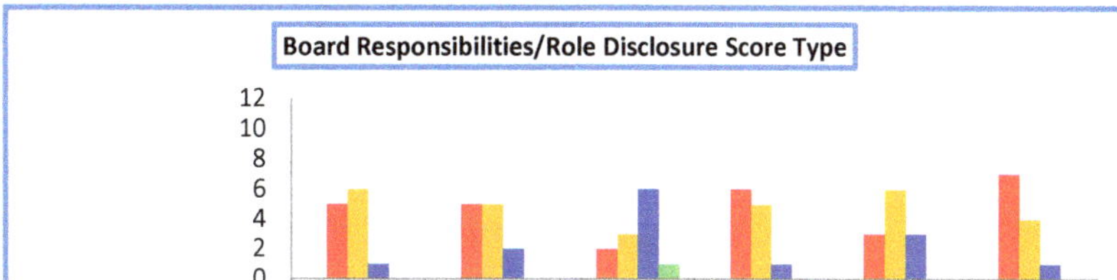

	HBOS	HSBC	Barclays	RBS	SCB	Lloyds TSB
0 - Not mentioned	0	0	0	0	0	0
1 - Inadequate	5	5	2	6	3	7
2 - Adequate	6	5	3	5	6	4
3 - Detailed	1	2	6	1	3	1
4 - Excellent	0	0	1	0	0	0

Fig. 8.3b Distribution of disclosure quality level of board responsibility/role of bank boards of directors (2001–2012)

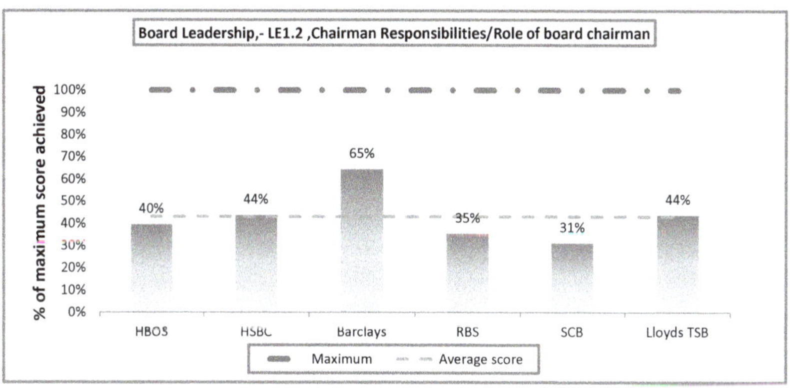

Fig. 8.4a Board leadership—Disclosure of Chairman Responsibility/Role of Boards Chairman (2001–2012)

company is not clear cut (OECD 2009a, b) as well as the format on how the information is communicated in bank annual reports. This section will address the question of what the role of directors is and to whom they are accountable. This is intended to help understand how they can fulfil their tasks more effectively to their stakeholders. The board has been formally defined as "the link between the shareholders of the firm

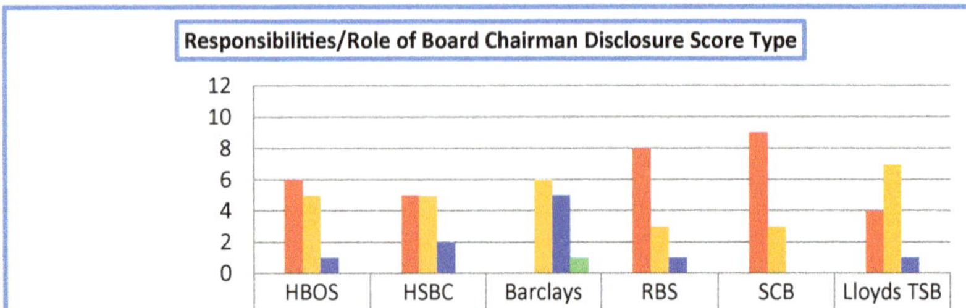

	HBOS	HSBC	Barclays	RBS	SCB	Lloyds TSB
0 - Not mentioned	0	0	0	0	0	0
1 - Inadequate	6	5	0	8	9	4
2 - Adequate	5	5	6	3	3	7
3 - Detailed	1	2	5	1	0	1
4 - Excellent	0	0	1	0	0	0

Fig. 8.4b Distribution of disclosure quality level of Chairman Responsibility/Role of Board Chairman (2001–2012)

and the management entrusted with undertaking the day-to-day operation of the organization" (Stiles and Taylor 2001, p. 4). The board duties outlined in the OECD Principles (1999) also emphasises overseeing management, but more explicitly states the duties of "fulfilling its accountability obligations to the company and to the shareholders".

The board of directors is regarded as an integral part of the governance in any publicly held organisation because of its fiduciary duty to monitor the activities of management and provide strategic directions on behalf of both its shareholders and relevant key stakeholders (Cadbury Report 1992; BCBS 1999). Adams and Mehran (2003) provide empirical evidence to show that the BOD in banks plays a relatively higher role than boards in manufacturing companies. As established in the literature review section, the fiduciary duty of the board is a valuable device in the banking context because of the nature of the high level of information asymmetry in prevailing banks (Macey and O'Hara 2003) as well as different stakeholders' level of interest. The following three criteria were used to evaluate the disclosure details on the effectiveness of board leadership narratives that have been disclosed within the sample banks' financial statement reports:

A statement of how the board operates, including a high level statement of which types of decisions are to be taken by the board and which are to be delegated to management should be included in the annual report; (2) A statement in the annual report that describes the actual activities undertaken by the board as well as matters reserved for it and (3) A statement in the annual report that provide the names of the chairman, the deputy chairman (where there is one), the chief executive, the senior independent director and the chairmen and members of the board committees.

The author outlined the findings from the evaluation of the narratives in the twelve-year study below as per the corporate governance checklists used for the study in this section.

The results of the empirical findings shows (Fig. 8.3a) that Barclays bank disclosure achieved more (top) quality and meaningful information in their annual reports for the sample period with 63% score achieved (as a proportion of total expected maximum score) regarding the disclosure quality narratives for the role of bank boards. The least disclosed bank was Lloyds TSB with 38% disclosure achievement score over the twelve-year period. This finding also indicates that there is variability within the UK banking sector regarding the narrative disclosure standard within the listed UK banking firms' annual reports.

Regarding the distribution of the quality of the information types disclosed over the period, the results confirm that overall, out of the total of 72 frequency counts of quality scores achieved that were recorded for the board leadership category over the twelve-year period, 38.9% (28/72) were regarded as inadequate disclosures (type 1 quality score), 40.3% (29/72) recorded as adequate disclosures (type 2 quality score), 19.4% (14/72) described as detailed disclosures (type 3 quality score) and only 1.4% portray excellent disclosures (type 4 quality score). This finding further adds support to the prior literature regarding agency problems in banking (Flannery et al. 2004; Hopt 2013; Ciancanelli and Gonzalez 2000; Mehran et al. 2011).

In disclosing the duties and role of bank boards in annual reports, the best practice example is that the board has overall responsibility for the banking institutions, including providing oversight over executive management, approving the strategic objectives, approval of risk management strategy, corporate values and corporate governance. In this regard, it would be useful for policymakers and regulators to define clearly respective responsibilities of the board members as a collective to be disclosed in the annual report which could be then reviewed by shareholders, depositors and/or supervisory regulators.

8.2.2.2 *The Role of Bank Board Chairman Disclosure*

The role of board chairman is an important part of ensuring effective internal corporate governance and accountability, especially for financial institutions. The best practice requirements for corporate governance in the United Kingdom maintain that "the chairman is responsible for leadership of the board and ensuring its effectiveness on all aspects of its role" (UK Corporate Governance Code, main principle A.3). The chairman is responsible for setting the board's agenda and ensuring that adequate time is available for discussion of all agenda items, in particular strategic issues. The chairman should also promote a culture of openness and debate by facilitating the effective contribution of non-executive directors in particular and ensuring constructive relations between executive and non-executive directors. The chairman is responsible for ensuring that the directors receive accurate, timely and clear information. The chairman should set out how they have ensured effective communication with shareholders.

Board chairmanship involves whether or not a firm's CEO is also the board of directors' chairman/chairperson. This is because a central role of the chairman is to monitor top management behaviour; this sort of CEO "duality" is likely to seriously hinder management accountability (Baliga et al., 1996) and may inhibit the board's ability to function properly as an independent body. The previous literature overwhelmingly used the presence of, or absence of, a board chairman or the CEO, as a proxy for measuring board effectiveness. Agency theory advocates the separation of these two positions to protect shareholders. Duality as argued by many scholars hamper the board's ability to effectively monitor and discipline top management because board members are more likely to have emotional, attitudinal and functional dependencies on the CEO and top management. However, based on stakeholder theory, the criteria used in this book offers a different and a much broader criteria measure to assess the role of board chairman as a corporate governance mechanism of accountability to stakeholders.

The following two criteria were used to evaluate the effectiveness of board chairman narratives among the sample banks' yearly report statements: *(1) A statement of disclosure of the extent to which the features of governance discussed in the Chairman's statement in the annual report?*

and (2) A statement of disclosure of how the Chairman describes the key features of the governance found within the governance reports in the annual report section.

The author outlined the findings from the evaluation of the narratives in the twelve-year study below as per the corporate governance checklists used for the investigation in this section.

The result of the empirical findings shows that Barclays bank disclosed more quality and meaningful information in their annual reports for the sample period with 65% disclosure score achieved (Fig. 8.4b) regarding the disclosure quality for the role of board chairman. The least disclosure bank was Standard Chartered Bank with 38% disclosure achievement score over the twelve-year period.

Regarding the distribution of the quality of the information types disclosed over the period, the results confirm that overall, out of the combined total of 72 quality scores achieved that were recorded for the board chairman subcategory over the twelve-year period, 44.4% (32/72) were regarded as inadequate disclosures (type 1 quality score), 40.3% (29/72) recorded as adequate disclosures (type 2 quality score), 13.8% (10/72) described as detailed disclosures (type 3 quality score) and only 1.4% portrayed excellent disclosures (type 4 quality score). Again, this result finding adds to the growing calls for better disclosure reporting and provision of meaningful information in financial institutions' annual reports to improve transparency and accountability to stakeholders.

Overall, the research findings of the board leadership corporate governance category also confirms that the most informative disclosures within the bank annual report from the discussion of the chairman statements included detail of the following: (1) the bank culture and the values they intend to instil in the business; (2) an overview of their governance structure and framework; and (3) the key governance objectives and focus of the board of directors for the following year.

8.2.3 Disclosure of Board Effectiveness Findings

The effectiveness of a board of directors (their attitude, viewpoint and skillset) is intrinsically linked with the scope of the increasing quality of bank corporate governance. This can be demonstrated in the level of information that is provided in the bank financial statements annually.

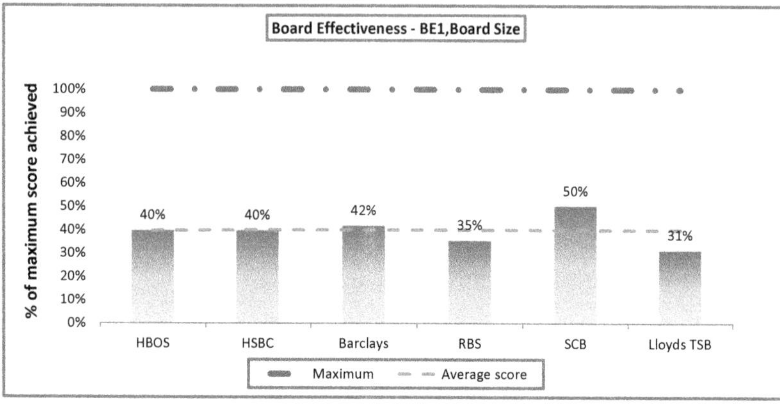

Fig. 8.5a Board effectiveness—Board Size disclosures

Within the United Kingdom, "the Code principle and associated provisions dealing with board balance and independence[1] address the balance of executive and non-executive directors on the board, board size, balance of skill and experience, refreshment of board committees and board independence – key essential elements of good bank governance" (Irish Stock Exchange 2012, p. 16).

This subsection of the Corporate Governance Disclosure results deals with the findings from the 7 subcategories used to measure the quality of board effectiveness disclosures in the sample banks annual reports for the twelve-year period (see Appendix 2 for detail criteria description). These subcategories are (1) Board size; (2) board meetings; (3) composition of the board; (4) Non-Executive Directors' Independence; (5) Board evaluation; (6) Board committees working activities; and (7) Board refreshment.

The main findings from the longitudinal assessment and analysis for board effectiveness are presented from Figs. 8.5a, 8.5b, 8.6a, 8.6b, 8.7a, 8.7b, 8.8a, 8.8b, 8.9a, 8.9b, 8.10a, 8.10b, 8.11a, 8.11b, and 8.12. It was expected that the boards and its committees should disclose and discuss openly the appropriate balance of skills, levels of experience, status of independence and company knowledge to complete all required

[1] "Main and supporting principle (A.3) and Code provisions A.3.1 to A.3.3" (UK Corporate Governance Code).

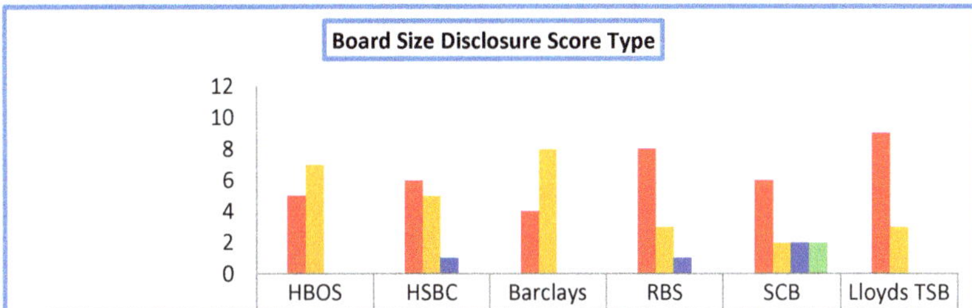

	HBOS	HSBC	Barclays	RBS	SCB	Lloyds TSB
0 - Not mentioned	0	0	0	0	0	0
1 - Inadequate	5	6	4	8	6	9
2 - Adequate	7	5	8	3	2	3
3 - Detailed	0	1	0	1	2	0
4 - Excellent	0	0	0	0	2	0

Fig. 8.5b Distribution of disclosure quality level of board size (2001–2012)

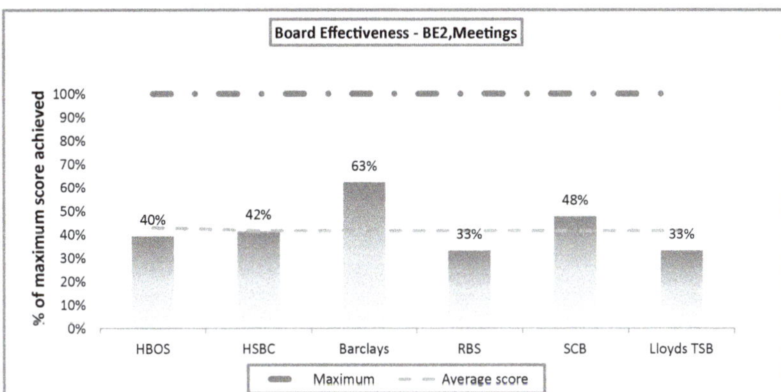

Fig. 8.6a Board effectiveness—Board composition disclosures

roles effectively, and justification of its board size, especially for banking firms in their annual reports. Based on the findings of the empirical work presented here, this section in addition highlights examples of incidents where improvements could be made to both the quality and level of reporting detail to aid comprehension of shareholders, regulators, depositors and other stakeholders.

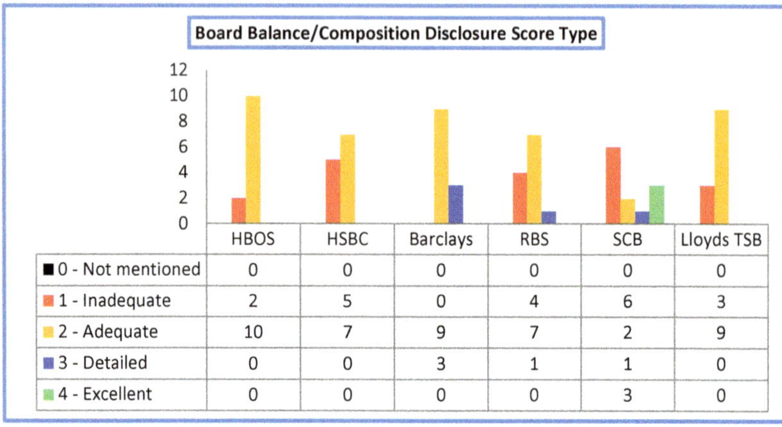

	HBOS	HSBC	Barclays	RBS	SCB	Lloyds TSB
0 - Not mentioned	0	0	0	0	0	0
1 - Inadequate	2	5	0	4	6	3
2 - Adequate	10	7	9	7	2	9
3 - Detailed	0	0	3	1	1	0
4 - Excellent	0	0	0	0	3	0

Fig. 8.6b Distribution of disclosure quality level of Board Composition (2001–2012)

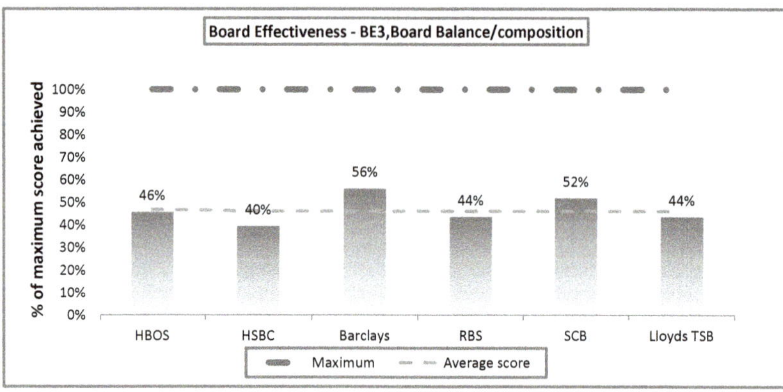

Fig. 8.7a Board effectiveness—Board meetings disclosures

8.2.3.1 Board Size Narrative Disclosures

Board size denotes the overall number of directors who make up the board (Aburaya 2012). Board size is an important factor of market-based corporate governance since there are drawbacks when boards are either too small or too large. The findings from the Walker Review, confirmed that the boards of listed banks in the United Kingdom were in fact larger

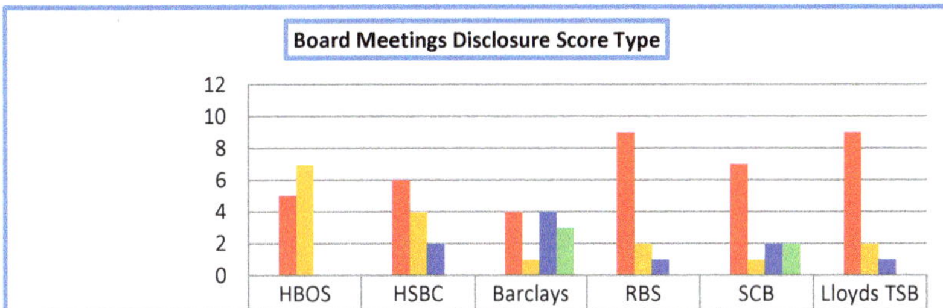

	HBOS	HSBC	Barclays	RBS	SCB	Lloyds TSB
0 - Not mentioned	0	0	0	0	0	0
1 - Inadequate	5	6	4	9	7	9
2 - Adequate	7	4	1	2	1	2
3 - Detailed	0	2	4	1	2	1
4 - Excellent	0	0	3	0	2	0

Fig. 8.7b Board effectiveness—Board meeting disclosures quality breakdown

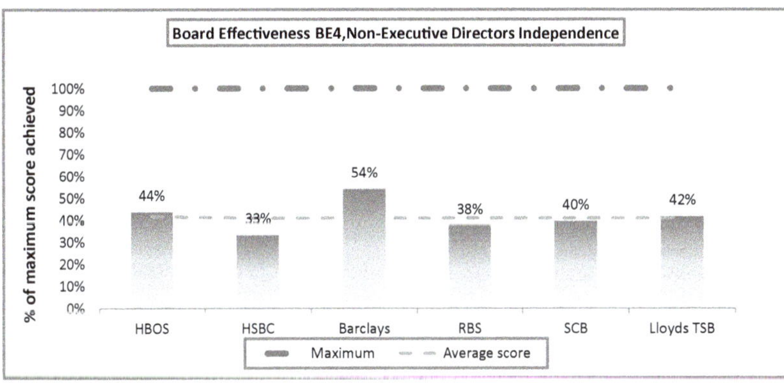

Fig. 8.8a Board effectiveness—Non-executive directors independence disclosures

than the boards of other listed firms. This was reflected on as challenging due to "a widely held view that the overall effectiveness of the board, outside a quite narrow range, tends to vary inversely with its size" (Walker 2009, p. 41). As observed from the literature, while it may find this to be true for ordinary companies (Hermalin and Weisbach 2003), banks

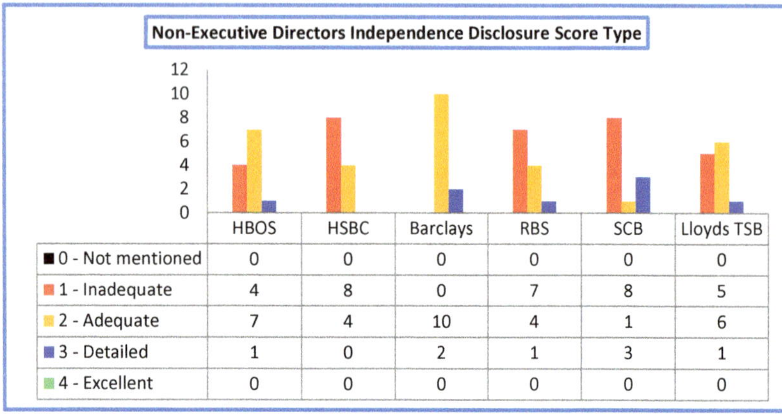

	HBOS	HSBC	Barclays	RBS	SCB	Lloyds TSB
0 - Not mentioned	0	0	0	0	0	0
1 - Inadequate	4	8	0	7	8	5
2 - Adequate	7	4	10	4	1	6
3 - Detailed	1	0	2	1	3	1
4 - Excellent	0	0	0	0	0	0

Fig. 8.8b Distribution of disclosure quality level score of non-executive directors (2001–2012)

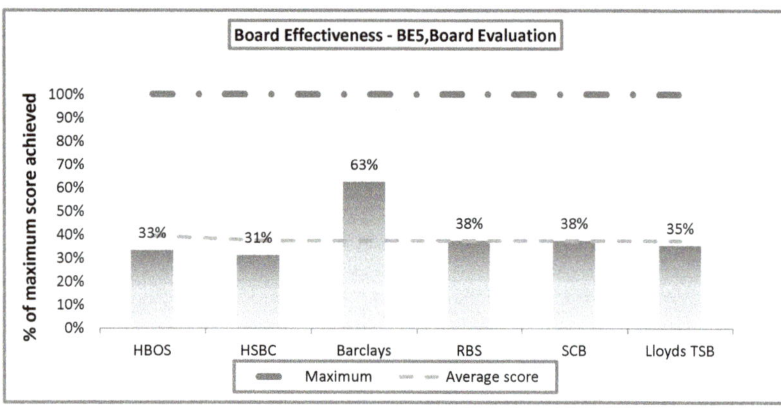

Fig. 8.9a Board effectiveness—Board evaluation disclosures

contradict this as the evidence does not support this assertion for them (Adams and Mehran 2003; Belkhir 2009).

In the United Kingdom, the corporate governance requires that every board of directors should examine its size, with a view to determining the impact of the number upon effectiveness, and undertake, where appropriate, programmes to reduce the number of directors to a number which

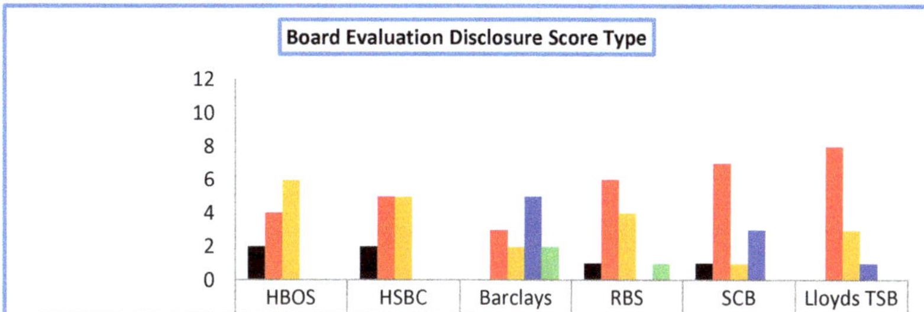

	HBOS	HSBC	Barclays	RBS	SCB	Lloyds TSB
0 - Not mentioned	2	2	0	1	1	0
1 - Inadequate	4	5	3	6	7	8
2 - Adequate	6	5	2	4	1	3
3 - Detailed	0	0	5	0	3	1
4 - Excellent	0	0	2	1	0	0

Fig. 8.9b Distribution of board evaluation disclosures quality level score (2001–2012)

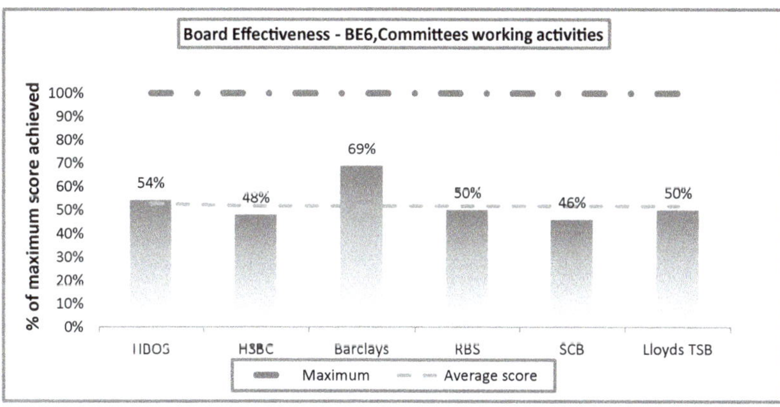

Fig. 8.10a Board effectiveness—Board committees working activity disclosures

facilitates more effective decision-making. The following two criteria were used to assess effectiveness of board size narratives disclosed in the sample banks' financial statement reports: "*(1) A statement that describe the evaluation process of the board size; (2) A statement of disclosure of the person or committee responsible for this evaluation; (3) Disclose how often the size of*

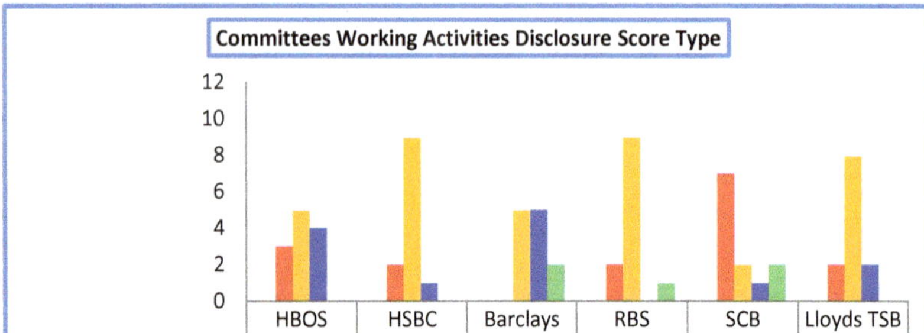

	HBOS	HSBC	Barclays	RBS	SCB	Lloyds TSB
0 - Not mentioned	0	0	0	0	0	0
1 - Inadequate	3	2	0	2	7	2
2 - Adequate	5	9	5	9	2	8
3 - Detailed	4	1	5	0	1	2
4 - Excellent	0	0	2	1	2	0

Fig. 8.10b Board effectiveness–Board Committees working activities disclosures

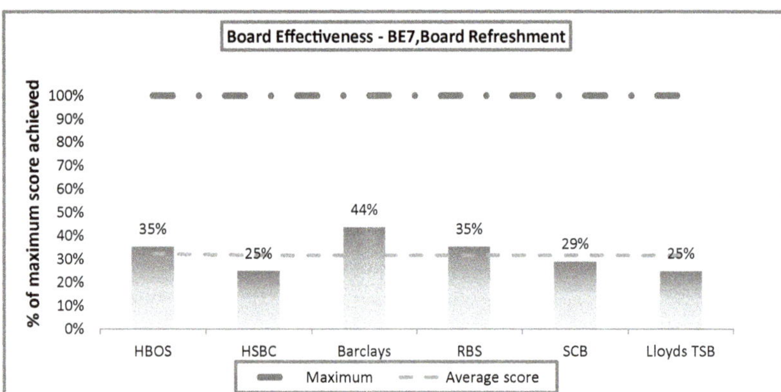

Fig. 8.11a Board effectiveness—Board refreshment disclosures

the board is reviewed and (4) Statement outlining the rationale for the size of its present board and structure, explaining why the company believes it to be appropriate and provide details of any planned or anticipated changes

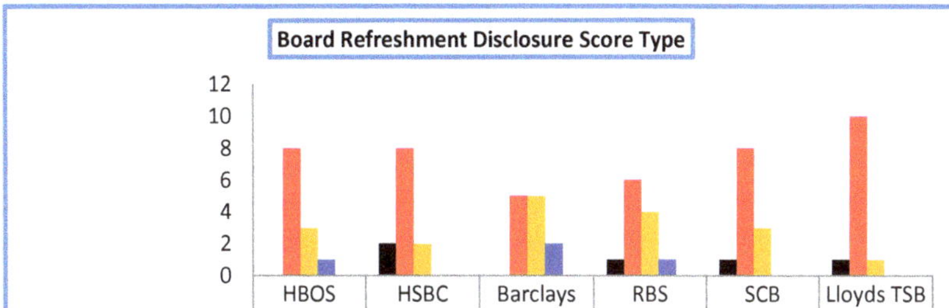

	HBOS	HSBC	Barclays	RBS	SCB	Lloyds TSB
0 - Not mentioned	0	2	0	1	1	1
1 - Inadequate	8	8	5	6	8	10
2 - Adequate	3	2	5	4	3	1
3 - Detailed	1	0	2	1	0	0
4 - Excellent	0	0	0	0	0	0

Fig. 8.11b Board effectiveness—Board refreshment disclosures score type

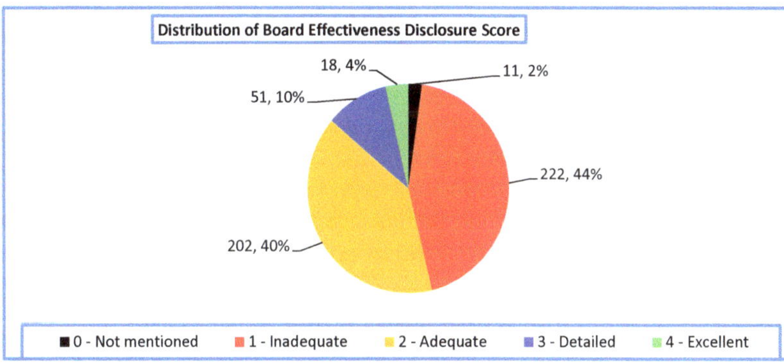

Fig. 8.12 Distribution of board effectiveness disclosure scores

to the board size”. The author outlined the findings from the evaluation of the narratives in the twelve-year study below as per the corporate governance checklists used for the study in this section.

The overall average performance disclosure and explanation regarding effectiveness of board size for the sample banks over the twelve-year period was 40% quality score achieved. The highest disclosure in this category was Standard Chartered Bank with a quality overall achievement score of 50%. Lloyds TSB performs poorly with a disclosure quality score of 31% (Fig. 8.5). Interestingly, the findings observe that detailed consideration is not commonly given within reports to the reasons for the number of directors verses non-executive directors that make up the board or the number of selected individuals. Between 2001 and 2006, the overwhelming majority of the disclosure narratives in the bank's annual report were regarded as inadequate disclosure (i.e. type 1 score) for board size disclosure explanations. That is a box-ticking exercise or uninformative explanation which captures examples where the information offered did not disclose the required level of relevant discussion or information needed.

Furthermore, the findings show that the overall division scores for quality of disclosure across the timeframe selected illustrates that the majority of the sample banks disclosed inadequate information with 52.8% (38/72) score achieved, compared with adequate score of 38.9% (21/72); detailed score of 5.6% (4/72); and excellent disclosure information score of 2.7% (2/72) in their annual reports for the longitudinal time period.

8.2.3.2 Board Balance/Composition Disclosures

A board should be structured in such a way as to ensure that the interest of all stakeholders may be represented fairly and objectively. Board composition, or the proportion of executive directors versus non-executive directors, has a strong implication on corporate governance because the board is essentially the "guardian" of the principal interest of stakeholders (i.e. as postulated by stakeholder's theory). Many researchers believe that effective boards should be composed of a greater proportion of non-executive directors (Borokhovich et al. 1996; Mizruchi 1983; Zahra and Pearce 1989) because the non-executive directors can make more exhaustive and profound evaluations of strategic decisions and management behaviour than executive directors (Baysinger and Butler 1985). The general argument is that non-executive directors should be competent, committed and have character. UK Corporate Governance Code, main principle B.1 requires that "*the board and its committees should have the appropriate balance of skills, experience, independence, and knowledge of the company to enable them to discharge their respective duties and responsibilities effectively*" (LSE 2012).

However, using the criteria as defined in the corporate governance checklist in appendix 2, the findings from the evaluation of the narratives in the twelve-year study are portrayed in Figs. 8.6a and 8.6b. The overall average performance disclosure and explanation regarding effectiveness of board composition narrative in the annual report for the sample banks over the twelve-year period was 47% (out of the maximum expected score of 100%) quality score achieved. The highest information quality disclosure in this category was Barclays Bank with a quality overall achievement disclosure score of 56%. This was followed by Standard Chartered Bank with 52% quality score achieved. HSBC performs poorly with a disclosure quality achievement score of 40% (Fig. 8.6a).

Figure 8.6b portrays the result of the overall frequency count of disclosure quality level scores for board composition for all companies over the twelve-year period. The overall findings show that the majority of the sample banks disclosed adequate information with 61.1% score (44/72) achieved, compared with inadequate disclosure information score of 27.8% (20/72); detailed disclosed score was a mere 6.9% (5/72); and information disclosed that was recorded for excellent disclosure had a score of 4.2% (3/72). None of the sample firm information disclosed were assessed as "type 0" (No Disclosure) score. However, the result in both Figs. 8.6a and 8.6b indicates that there are substantial disparities in the manner in which the board composition disclosures are narrated among the observed banking firms in the United Kingdom.

Diversity on boards, especially of non-executive board members including recent gender balance on boards is of key corporate governance in the financial service sector. Arguments in favour of diversity remain valid even in the light of arguments favouring greater expertise of boards of banking institutions. Empirical evidence as observed from the literature highlights the benefits of diversity for corporate governance in terms of efficiency and better monitoring (see Hagendorff and Keasey 2012; Higgs Report 2003). However, the lack of detailed or excellent disclosure narratives regarding board compositions information from this finding would make it hard for stakeholders to effectively monitor these institutions, especially institutional shareholders and supervisory regulators.

Details of a board's balance and its independence disclosure can prove difficult for companies to provide in situations where directors have been selected by government or stockholders which could result in a lack of understanding of firms' context for investors (i.e. for Bailout banks such

RBS and Lloyds banking group). Generally, the selection of candidates for non-executive positions in financial institutions seems to have drawn on a too narrow pool of people (see Walker 2009). It is suggested that the addition of greater detail regarding selected director's prior experience and what they uniquely bring to the board would greatly enhance stakeholders' understanding as most of the information currently being provided in the reports are somewhat ambiguous and insignificant. This is most relevant when directors are not part of any board committee structures.

8.2.3.3 *Board Meetings Disclosure*

The frequency of board meetings has been recognised as a key measure of an effective corporate governance mechanism in a number of national and international Codes of Best Practices, as well as from the academic literature studies. The UK Code does not advise on the frequency of boards and their committees meetings; it merely specifies that "the board should meet sufficiently regularly to discharge its duties effectively". There should be a formal schedule of matters specifically reserved for its decisions. Figures 8.7a and 8.7b display the findings from the assessment and evaluation of the sample banks annual report over the twelve-year period.

The overall average performance disclosure and explanation regarding effectiveness of board meeting narrative for the sample banks over the twelve-year period was 43% quality score achieved. The highest narrative disclosure in this category with the most meaningful and quality explanations in the annual reports was Barclays Bank with a quality overall score of 63% from the maximum expected scores of 100%. Standard Chartered Bank had the second highest disclosure quality score of 48%. Both RBS and Lloyds TSB perform poorly with the least disclosure quality score of 33% (Fig. 8.7a). There was no disclosure quality score type 0 as per the corporate governance index constructed in this study. According to Fig. 8.7b, 40/72 (55.5%) of the disclosure information relating to their board meetings in their annual reports were regarded as inadequate (i.e. Type 1 disclosure). This result confirms that disclosure information regarding the narratives for board meetings in the annual report over the twelve-year period is not informative and reliable enough for stakeholder decision-making.

Further to the above, 17/72 (23.6%) disclosed adequate information score over the period, while 10 (13.8%) disclosed detailed and meaningful information. Only five (7%) of the entire disclosure on board meeting information were regarded as excellent (score type 4 disclosure). Additionally, detailed analysis of the information relating to board meetings reveals that, of the five excellent disclosed board meeting information, Barclays Bank recorded the highest disclosure with three (60%) score achieved and Standard Chartered bank disclosing 40% of the excellent board meeting information over the twelve years. However, helpful and meaningful disclosures explained both how many meetings were originally planned and the number of, and the reasons for, unscheduled meetings. The best (i.e. excellent; Type 4 score) disclosures were presented in a tabular form with both quantitative and narrative explanations.

8.2.3.4 Non-executive Directors Independent Scrutiny Disclosure

The role of non-executive directors in executing independent judgement for financial institution boards has recently been the subject of much debate after the recent financial crisis. The financial crisis of 2008 revealed serious flaws and shortcomings in boards performance at a number of financial institutions (see for instance, OECD 2009a, b; Kirkpatrick 2009; Walker 2009). This in particular, for different reasons, meant non-executive directors were not in a position to form objective and independent judgements on management decisions. Hence, in many instances they failed to act as an effective check on, and challenge to, executive directors/managers.

Figure 8.8a displays the total overall findings of Non-Executive Directors' independent disclosure quality explanation distributed over the sample years, 2001–2012 for the banking firms evaluated. The empirical finding shows that overall; Barclays had the highest distribution of quality disclosure score with 54%, followed by HBOS (44%); Lloyds TSB (42%); SCB (40%); RBS (38%) and the least quality disclosure information being HSBC with 33% which is below the sample average of 40% for the twelve-year period. Non-executive director scrutiny of executive management actions and behaviours is considered to be an important component of good corporate governance. As already discussed in the literature review section, non-executive directors can play an important role in monitoring the performance of management and limit managerial opportunity (Fama 1980; Fama and Jensen 1983) from both agency and stakeholders' theory perspective.

Despite this, independent directors' quality disclosures were relatively poor across the majority of the companies, 44% (32/72) providing only basic information or inadequate score (Fig. 8.8b). This is often limited to a commentary on appointments with little or no discussion around board constructive challenges, scrutiny of management performance or desirable characteristics. These findings are consistent with the literature review findings in the sense that there is no clear consensus concerning whether or not non-executive directors play a useful corporate governance role.

The notion of independence of boards constitutes an essential tenet that has been preserved in every code of corporate governance standards, and firms are encouraged to place significant emphasis in its disclosure. For example, "provision A.3.2 of the United Kingdom corporate governance code requires that at least half of a company's board (excluding the Chairman) should comprise of independent non-executive directors and provision A.3.1 requires that boards identify in the annual report the non-executive directors determined by the board to be independent". Despite this emphasis, the analysis from the findings in this inquiry suggests that most companies have a long way to go to provide meaningful disclosures in this area. Detailed disclosures were only 11% (8/72) of the quality score, although there are signs of improvement. The overall level of information in this category that was provided is judged to be inadequate and insufficient for stakeholders' acceptance.

8.2.3.5 *Board Evaluation Disclosures*

The UK Corporate Governance Code required that "the board should undertake a formal and rigorous annual evaluation of its own performance and that of its committees and individual directors". However, it does not require companies to disclose the outcome of those reviews. Figures 8.9a and 8.9b portray the overall findings regarding board performance evaluation disclosure explanation and discussion information. The constructed corporate governance index measure used here is based on the demand for firms or companies to provide information in their published statements with regard to conducting board evaluations and performance (as specifically required by UK Code provision A.6.1) as well as the outcomes of the evaluations. The findings show that overall, Barclays had the highest distribution of quality disclosure information score with 63%, followed jointly by Standard Chartered and RBS with (38%) each; Lloyds TSB (35%); HBOS with 33% and the least quality disclosure information being HSBC with 31% which is below the sample average of 40% for the twelve-year period.

The findings from the assessment indicate that, with few exceptions, board evaluation narratives/explanations that were provided in various reports were weak from the sample banks in this study. The majority of the bank's annual report sections regarding this governance subcategory simply repeat or echo the same information requirement that are covered by the United Kingdom corporate governance "Code provision A.6" and offer no meaningful discussions and actions. This finding collaborates or is in line with similar findings and concluding observations by the Walker Report (Walker 2009) regarding the UK banking firms' corporate governance. The Walker review revealed that not all boards have hitherto given the evaluation process the attention and seriousness that it deserves and recommended an enhanced rigour to promote disclosure in this regard. We also note that the procedure for the board evaluation standard ways of working was hardly ever discussed in the disclosure in the annual reports.

Performance evaluation is an effective way of assessing the board's performance and bringing issues to light where remedial action can be taken. It is recommended that best practice currently indicated that an external evaluation should be carried out every three years with an internal assessment being carried out every year. The vast majority of the reports reviewed show that independent consultants or external independent firms were rarely employed to carry out board of directors' evaluations. Given the significance of this area in corporate governance, bank supervisors and key stakeholders will need to demand more qualitative disclosure information from banks' boards.

Furthermore, the findings demonstrate that the overall spread of scores for quality of disclosure within the timeframe selected shows that the majority of the sample banks disclosed inadequate information with 46% score (33/72), compared with an adequate score of 29% (21/72); detailed score of 13% (9/72); and excellent disclosure information score of 4% (3/72) in their annual reports for the longitudinal time period.

As noted in previous sections, there has been a notable increase in the number of banks disclosing more information since 2008 in general and in particular, the identity of external facilitators they used in the evaluation as well as the outcomes and actions for follow ups.

8.2.3.6 Board Committees' Workings

A number of prior studies, as noted in the literature, suggest that enriched standards of corporate governance are correlated with board committees. The responsibilities that the board committee complete are improved through the introduction of particular dedicated committees (Zahra and Pearce 1989, Irish Stock Exchange 2012; Walker 2009). Corporate governance subcategory findings from the empirical study with respect to board committees' activities working disclosures are presented in Figs. 8.10a and 8.10b. Disclosures relating to the board itself are covered within the prior Sect. (8.2.2 board leadership). The current segment looks into board operation models (with particular focus on how it fulfils its responsibilities) and how these are communicated to relevant stakeholders and shareholders within the annual financial report. As noted in the literature and many international Codes of Best Practice reporting, it has become a more widely accepted practice to partition boards into different working committees to support the functioning of the main board more effectively. The most acknowledged board committees that are enshrined in most corporate governance legislation and guidance are the nomination committee, the audit committee and the remuneration committee. The corporate governance checklist constructed in this book was meant to capture how these three board committees' activities and information are communicated in the annual report. We note, however, that banks often have additional board committees (for example HSBC and Standard Chartered created a stand-alone risk committee in 2010).

The features of board committees are anticipated to have a tangible effect on the level of corporate governance reporting and improve the transparent monitoring of stakeholders. The result confirms or shows that this is the highest performance subcategory of corporate governance within the main category disclosures in the annual report over the twelve-year period with an overall disclosure narrative quality score of 52% longitudinally, which illustrates that most companies from the sample would support the creation/disclosure of the committees in question. The best disclosure category bank was Barclays with an overall average score of 69% (Fig. 8.10a). The least disclosure bank was Standard Chartered with a score of 46%, showcasing a vast variability within results regarding the provision of board committee information within reports under the study. The overall findings of the different levels of quality scores show that the majority of the sample banks disclosed adequate information with 53% score (48/72) compared with inadequate disclosure information score of 22% (16/72); detailed disclosed score of 18% (13/72); and excellent disclosure score of 7% (5/72).

However, these findings can be seen as somewhat expected when taking into consideration the development and publication in 2003 of the Combined Code of corporate governance in the United Kingdom (revised in both 2010 and 2012). The evidence from the assessment of the sample banks discovers that disclosure regarding the work of the committees by boards could stand to be enhanced with the aim to aid disclosure of better levels of detail in the information provided to stakeholders.

Additionally, the results of this study show that, information provided by the sample banks over the twelve-year cycle that can be categorised either as excellent (type 4 quality score) or detailed (type 3 level) were not adequately described. The findings observed that banks, rather than providing specific and detailed information regarding the work and activities of the nomination committee, were instead opting to provide simplistic and generalised overviews of their duties year on year. Examples of details being left out include the advertising and use of consultants being employed and the manner by which new directors are appointed. It is interesting to note the absence of such justifications when considering the fact that the constructed checklist to measure this is clearly stated within the requirements of the Combined Code to achieve best practice disclosure, especially when firms are listed on the London Stock Exchange. Furthermore, a number of investigations by numerous regulators and researchers criticised banks' remuneration policies and lack of effective board committees' work as a contributing factor of the global financial crisis in 2007–2008 (Turner Report 2009; Walker 2009; FSA 2009a, b; UNCTAD 2010). Findings from this category particularly seem to corroborate this notion. Hence, more disclosures will need to be improved in the remuneration areas within published financial statements to enable both shareholder and stakeholder scrutiny.

8.2.3.7 Board Refreshment

The quality of disclosure and explanation for board refreshment subcategory had the lowest overall average score of 32% for the entire sample period. Barclays had the highest disclosure quality score of 44% achievement. Both HSBC and Lloyds TSB performed poorly with a joint quality score of 25% disclosure score (Fig. 8.11a) achieved. The assessment found that the subject of board refreshment or renewal were not adequately addressed in the financial reports and failed to clearly set out how boards are working to meet the governance requirements demanded by either legislation or voluntary codes. Furthermore, the results of the different levels of quality score measure show that the majority of the sample banks disclosed inadequate information with 63% score (45/72), compared with adequate disclosure information score of 25% (18/72); detailed disclosed score was a mere 6% (4/72); and excellent disclosure had a score of 0%. 7% (5/72) of the disclosures provided no useful information or did not disclose at all any board refreshment information (Fig. 8.11b).

The UK Code of best practice reporting requires that, when a company is "proposing a non-executive for re-election, boards confirm that, following formal performance evaluation, the individual's performance continues to be effective and to demonstrate commitment to the role" (Irish Stock Exchange 2012, p. 17). Given the fact that this was clearly not met within the disclosure observed over the sample period, this finding would recommend a strong improvement regarding the level of detail shared re the rationale for re-election or continued service of board independent directors. Additionally, the findings from the assessment note the predominance of repetitive usage of typical wording in the annual reports such *as "The director continues to be effective and challenge the executives on the board*". This is regarded as meaningless and uninformative and recommends that improvements are made in code provisions or best practice guidance to ensure better information is delivered to shareholders and stakeholders that are appropriate regarding specific firm context.

8.2.4 Disclosure of Accountability Findings

This subsection of the corporate governance disclosure deals with a number of specific areas of narrative disclosures, namely: (a) internal control & management of risk (b) audit committee scrutiny and (c) external auditors. Four subcategories were constructed to measure overall disclosure quality as well as trend over the sample time period for all firms. The findings from the study are presented in each of the subcategory sections.

The corporate governance main and subcategories criteria constructed to measure the effectiveness of board of directors accountability using stakeholders theoretical lenses are largely drawn from the UK Corporate Governance Code main and supporting principle provisions and evidence found from the empirical literature on banking disclosures. It aimed at avoiding one-size-fits-all approach to corporate governance as found in prior governance studies in accounting. According to the United Nation Conference on Trade and Development (UNCTAD 2010) "the board should establish formal and transparent arrangements for considering how they should apply the corporate reporting and risk management and internal control principles, internal audit independence and for maintaining an appropriate relationship with the company's external auditor". The following sections outline the findings from the disclosure narratives provided in the sample firms' annual reports over the sample period.

8.2.4.1 Risk Management and Internal Control Disclosures Information

Financial and banking institutions' effective risk management is crucial for the sustainable success of their operations. Banks profits are usually sourced from risk-taking activities. Risk management is therefore not about eliminating risk but rather ensuring optimal risk-taking without endangering the viability of the financial institutions. The financial crisis in 2008 demonstrated failure of risk management and weakness in internal controls in financial institutions can have significant consequences, not just for shareholders, but also for depositors and for the economy. However, existing evidence shows that such weaknesses in governance aspects were due to inadequate oversight of risk and definition of risk appetite by boards, and firms did not have a comprehensive and systemic approach to risk management, with appropriate internal controls (Kirkpatrick 2009; G20 2009a, b, 2011; Turner Report 2009; Walker 2009). These weaknesses therefore contributed to the call for strengthening bank corporate governance frameworks in the area of risk reporting and enhance disclosure reporting practices in financial institutions (BCBS 2010; Walker 2009).

Banking firms need to give detailed and genuine insight into their risk management and control operations, rather than just ticking the compliance boxes of disclosure requirements for these crucial areas in their annual reports. The corporate governance index used to determine this subcategory is mainly drawn from the UK code of best practice disclosure requirement. Interestingly, for listed banks, it is a mandatory requirement supported by legislation under the listing rule from the London Stock Exchange and FSA Disclosure Rules and Transparency Rules (DTR).

Figure 8.13a reflects the quality disclosure of risk management and internal control information in the 72 annual reports of the six companies as a proportion of total expected maximum score. According to the diagram, Barclays bank obtained the highest score of 63% (30/48) which was recorded with regard to risk management and internal control information. The result also finds that both HBOS and HSBC had the lowest

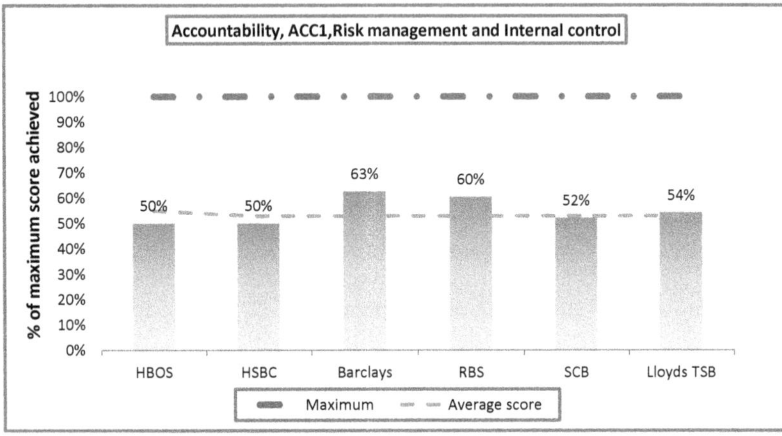

Fig. 8.13a Board accountability—Risk management and internal control disclosure information achieved as a proportion of maximum score available

joint disclosure score achieved of 50% (24/48) of information quality within this subcategory. This result is below the 55% total average score achieved within this subcategory for the sample period under the study.

In assessing internal control effectiveness in annual reports within the United Kingdom, the Turnbull guidance put the spotlight on both risk management and internal control in 1999 and revised in 2005. Since then the emphasis on these two aspects of governance has gathered momentum. While all sample banks disclosed and claimed full compliance disclosure in their annual report section with Turnbull, between 2001 and 2008, all the sample banks offered little or no detailed insight to readers. The disclosures in the reports tend towards the boilerplate, merely confirming the existence of appropriate systems and practices. The majority of the company's annual disclosures enable real understanding of their systems and how their boards measure their effectiveness. This figure has barely altered between 2001 and 2007 (see spotlight 1 and 2 for specific banks examples). With a growing focus on risk management and both the FRC and BIS seeking greater transparency, the emphasis needs to move from acknowledging that the annual internal controls review took place towards revealing actual risk management practices and the role internal control plays in mitigating risks specifically applied to individual banking institutions.

An overall finding for the twelve-year period suggests that the quality of risk management and internal control disclosures in the annual report have barely improved (i.e. the disclosure narratives have been little more than "boilerplate" repeated year-after-year. This finding is consistent with other disclosure quality findings in the United Kingdom (Walker report in 2009 and Turner report in 2008; Accounting Standard Board, 2009 (i.e. part of FRC in 2009 findings). However, there has been considerable improvement in the amount of information provided since 2009. All the sample banks provided detailed disclosure in 2011 (100% type 3 disclosure) and 50% excellent disclosure for 2012.

While most of the sample banks set out their risks clearly in the annual report sections, they often struggled to explain their risk management processes and disclosure of control weaknesses with about 11% overall count of quality scores providing unhelpful disclosures. This result could also be attributed to the lack of stand-alone risk committees for the majority of the sample banks over the majority of the study period. Perhaps it is suffice to note that the often scant attention paid by these firms to the quality of disclosure for internal control and risk management makes the FRC's forthcoming review particularly timely. About 22% (16/72) of the overall disclosures provided detailed descriptions of their processes covering: (i) risk management roles and responsibilities; (ii) reporting, monitoring and mitigation of risk; (iii) how risk management is embedded into operations; (iv) risk appetite. The majority 63% (45/72) of the disclosures for this subcategory provided adequate and meaningful information for the entire twelve years studied. Only 4% (3/72) provided meaningful information and explanation detail that were regarded as excellent disclosure (score type 4) over the longitudinal period (Fig. 8.13b). Risk disclosure banking is generally regarded as complex and it is virtually impossible for a bank to prepare a flawless risk management narrative. However, this does not mean that clear guidance cannot be provided to aid senior directors in preparing and disclosing a risk management and internal control narrative that is both meaningful and useful to stakeholders.

8.2.4.2 Internal Audit Disclosure

Since 1997, there have been significant developments in corporate governance practices worldwide, mainly influenced by large organisation failures and growth in influence by stakeholders, including national

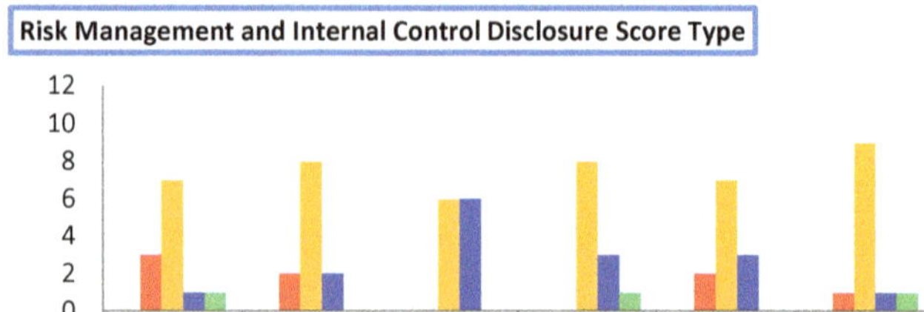

	HBOS	HSBC	Barclays	RBS	SCB	Lloyds TSB
0 - Not mentioned	0	0	0	0	0	0
1 - Inadequate	3	2	0	0	2	1
2 - Adequate	7	8	6	8	7	9
3 - Detailed	1	2	6	3	3	1
4 - Excellent	1	0	0	1	0	1

Fig. 8.13b Risk management and internal control distribution of disclosure information score type

governments, regulators, institutional investors and professional institutes. The value and need for good corporate governance practices has also moved into the public services and voluntary sectors, with promotion of governance principles that have grown out of Nolan (1995).

However, in the United Kingdom, the Hampel (1998) Report[2] reviewed governance developments since Cadbury (1992) and supported both the importance of measuring the effectiveness of control and the importance of reviewing annually the need for internal auditing in a company. Following its report, the Combined Code (1998) became part of the London Stock Exchange's listing requirements. Hampel's recommendation was included in the code and repeated in the 2003 code, which also followed the Higgs recommendations in 2003. At this time there was still no mandatory requirement for internal auditing in most companies and no Stock Exchange guidance on what internal auditing meant, or how its effectiveness could or should be measured.

[2]The Hampel Committee was established by the London Stock Exchange, the Institute of Directors, National Association of Pension Funds and Association of British Insurers. Its main aim was to update corporate governance debate and ensure the intentions of Cadbury were being implemented.

The internal audit function is increasingly seen to have an important role to play in corporate governance, particularly in banking institutions, in supporting the risk management functions. Internal Audit is an independent, objective assurance and consulting activity designed to add value and improve an organisation's operations. It helps an organisation accomplish its objectives by bringing a systematic, disciplined approach to evaluate and improve the effectiveness of risk management, control and governance processes. The corporate governance index used to determine this subcategory is mainly drawn from the UK code of best practice disclosure requirement. The findings of the assessment and evaluation of the sample annual reports disclosure narrative are represented in Figs. 8.14a and 8.14b.

An analysis of Figs. 8.14a and 8.14b show the total overall internal audit independence disclosure quality for each of the sample firms' data for the period 2001–2012. The overall quality for each bank represents the maximum quality of the disclosure checklist items achieved by each bank over the period. The level of disclosure relating to the provision of internal audit narrative reflects a mixed scenario among the sample firms. The assessment measure shows that RBS had the lowest information disclosure score over the twelve-year period with 48% (23/48) of the 100% maximum quality expected score. The highest scoring bank for internal audit independence disclosure index is Barclays with 60%

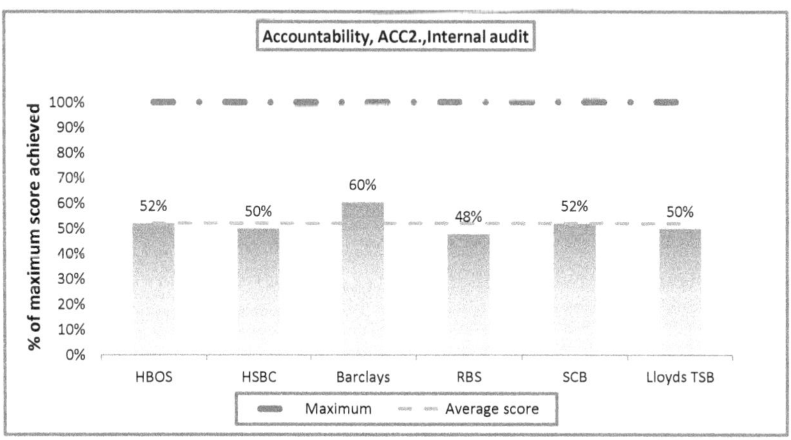

Fig. 8.14a Board accountability—Internal audit disclosure information

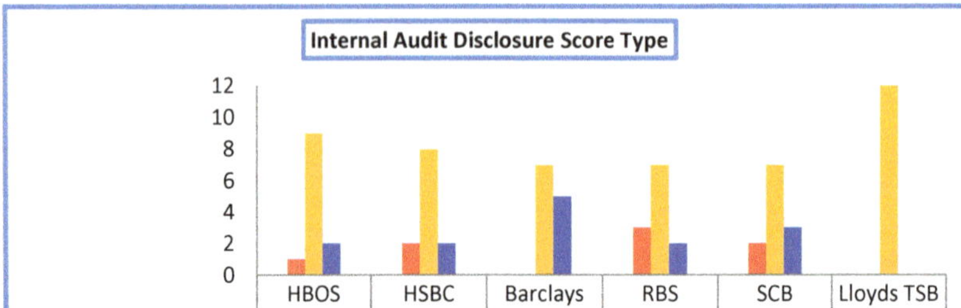

	HBOS	HSBC	Barclays	RBS	SCB	Lloyds TSB
0 - Not mentioned	0	0	0	0	0	0
1 - Inadequate	1	2	0	3	2	0
2 - Adequate	9	8	7	7	7	12
3 - Detailed	2	2	5	2	3	0
4 - Excellent	0	0	0	0	0	0

Fig. 8.14b Distribution of internal audit disclosure quality score type

score (29/48) achieved over the expected maximum score. Again, the result confirms that Barclays Bank provided more quality and meaningful information disclosures to its stakeholders.

Moreover, a further detailed analysis of the distribution of information quality scale shows that there were no type 0 (not mentioned) or type 4 (excellent) scores awarded over the sample period of twelve years overall. The overwhelming majority 69% (50/72) of the disclosures within this index were assessed and recorded as adequate disclosure in the annual report for the sample years, compared to 11% (8/72) and 19% (14/72) for inadequate disclosure and detailed disclosure of meaningful information, respectively.

8.2.4.3 External Audit Disclosures

Within a company's system of internal control, the external audit represents one of the most indispensable corporate governance mechanisms that help to monitor company management's activities, thereby increasing transparency. In addition to it being a statutory requirement under many jurisdictions including the United Kingdom, an external audit provides an independent and objective check on the way in which the financial statements have been prepared and presented by the directors. An annual audit is recognised as a vital component regarding "checks and

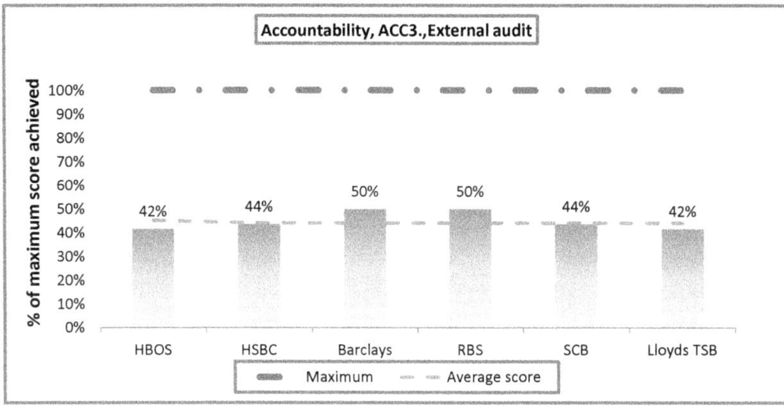

Fig. 8.15a Board accountability—External audit disclosure information

balances" required and is one of the cornerstones of corporate governance. However, from a stakeholder perspective, the audit function and its judgement disclosures represent another important governance accountability mechanism that helps stakeholders monitor and control company management and senior directors. This book wishes to stress that there was no question as to whether or not banks should have an external audit but rather how its effectiveness and objectivity could be enhanced in carrying out its functions without compromising its independence.

The findings from the longitudinal analysis regarding the quality of corporate governance disclosures of the external audit checklist for the sample banks over the twelve years are presented in Figs. 8.15a and 8.15b. The findings below can be attributed to the statutory duty of an external auditor which requires the external auditor to report to the members of a company that the annual financial statements of that company were audited and whether they fairly presented the financial position of the company and the results of its operations in the manner required by the Act. The majority of the disclosure commentary and discussions tend to be structured and standardised; a tick-box exercise that is repeated year-after-year in the annual reports.

8.2.4.4 Audit Committee Scrutiny Disclosures

The effectiveness of audit committees also depends on how independent the committees are in scrutinising the activities of senior management and

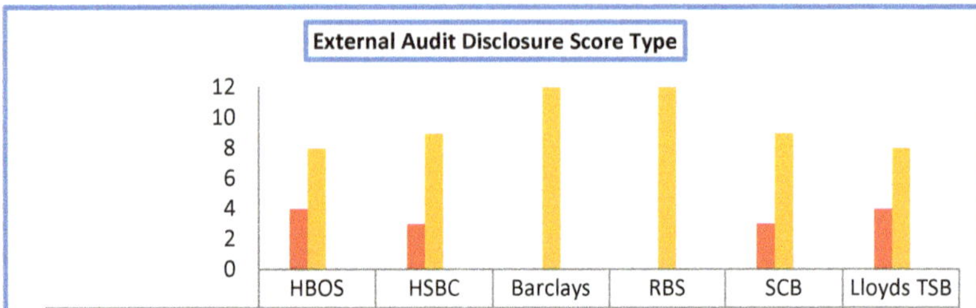

	HBOS	HSBC	Barclays	RBS	SCB	Lloyds TSB
0 - Not mentioned	0	0	0	0	0	0
1 - Inadequate	4	3	0	0	3	4
2 - Adequate	8	9	12	12	9	8
3 - Detailed	0	0	0	0	0	0
4 - Excellent	0	0	0	0	0	0

Fig. 8.15b Distribution of external audit disclosure quality score type

reporting its work to stakeholders. Thus, the task of the audit committee is objective and independent and ought to support the board of directors to fulfil its required legal or legislative accountabilities. Figures 8.16a and 8.16b displayed the result of the narrative disclosure findings for the work

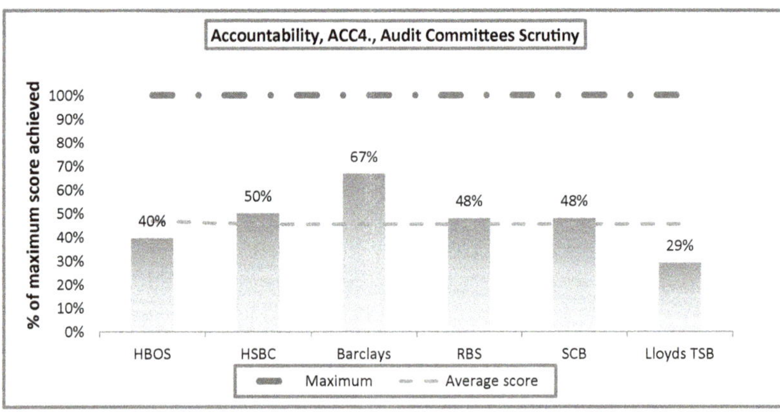

Fig. 8.16a Board accountability—Audit committees' scrutiny disclosure information

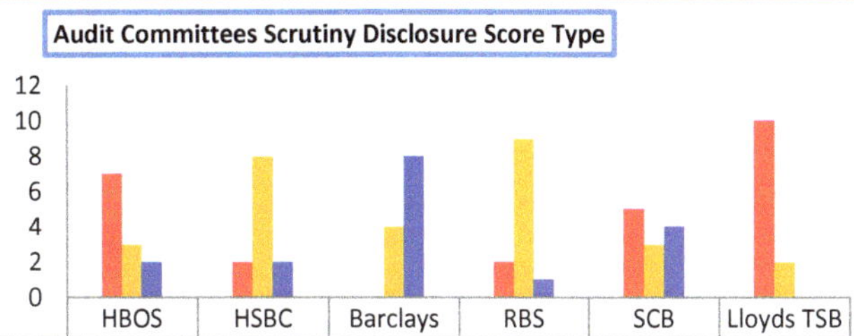

	HBOS	HSBC	Barclays	RBS	SCB	Lloyds TSB
0 - Not mentioned	0	0	0	0	0	0
1 - Inadequate	7	2	0	2	5	10
2 - Adequate	3	8	4	9	3	2
3 - Detailed	2	2	8	1	4	0
4 - Excellent	0	0	0	0	0	0

Fig. 8.16b Distribution of audit committees' scrutiny disclosure quality score type

of the Audit Committee Scrutiny in the annual report over the sample period for the sample banks.

As indicated in the results, Barclays had the highest information disclosure in this subcategory with an average overall score of 67% for the twelve-year longitudinal period. This result confirms that Barclays had been one of the best UK banks that has been consistently disclosing the most meaningful and detailed information to its stakeholders about the work of its audit committees' activities and actions. This is followed by HSBC disclosing the second highest average quality score of 50%. The sample bank with the worst performance disclosure score of 29% overall over the twelve-year period is Lloyds TSB; significantly well below the average score of 47% within this subcategory of corporate governance disclosure.

Figure 8.16b shows the results of the distribution of the disclosure quality level score over the twelve year period for all sample firms. Of the total quality disclosure scores for this subcategory regarding audit committee scrutiny disclosures, 40.3% (29/72) were evaluated and assessed as adequate quality disclosure of information to enable stakeholder's decision-making effectiveness. Detailed (type 3 score) disclosure for this subcategory overall was 24% (17/72) and the rest, 36% (26/72) of the quality distribution scores were recorded as inadequate. Also, findings observed a noticeable improvement over the sample period under this study. Despite this, it is recommended that the activities and evidence supporting the audit committees work that are reported to key stakeholders via annual reports ought to be strengthened and explicitly prescribed within the current governance framework.

8.2.5 Disclosure of Performance/Results Findings

This subsection of the corporate governance index findings deals with narratives and disclosures on four main subcategory criteria, namely: (1) Key performance indicator disclosures and explanation; (2) Detail explanation and reference to the bank code of conduct or ethics and disclosure of either the code or a summary of the code as to (a) the practices it includes to maintain confidence in the banks' integrity; (b) the responsibility and accountability of individuals for reporting and investigating reports of unethical practices; (c) bank monitoring of compliance with code of conduct and professional standards and (d) the practices it includes to take into account their legal obligations and the reasonable expectations of individual employees and other stakeholders; (3) Discloses bank "whistle blower" or confidential policy and practices; and (4) Disclosure reference and discussion on incidences breaching the code of conduct, and disciplinary procedures to deal with the incidences, sanctions and penalties for legal and compliance breaches, misconducts and fines by banking regulators.

As already discussed in Sect. 8.1, across all the five main categories of corporate governance disclosures, this was perhaps the least or the lowest scoring criteria for the entire sample banks over the twelve-year period with an average of 39% overall for combined 5 main categories index and compared to the 24% overall average disclosure score achieved within the performance category index for all the 72 annual reports. There are significant variations in the quality of disclosed information within this corporate governance subcategory constructed index. This result is perhaps not surprising given the fact that there is lack of specific standard descriptors and principles guidance from the UK Code of Corporate governance as well as lack of prior disclosure studies within the banking industry.

8.2.5.1 Key Performance Indicators Disclosures Information

Disclosure quality on key performance indicators in sample annual reports for the period had an overall average disclosure score of 48% and the top disclosure score of 69% for Barclays bank. The least disclosed bank over the period is Standard Chartered bank with a disclosure quality overall score of 40% (see Fig. 8.17a). This is perhaps one of the weaknesses found in a number of national and international Codes of Best Practices. The aim of this disclosure is to address the extent to which banking firms disclose specific key performance indicators (KPIs) which measure the performance of their business and provide narrative discussions that are clearly linked to their specific business objective or model. The requirement for disclosing key performance indicators in annual reports in the United Kingdom is underpinned by mandatory legal/law in the form of the company act. For example, as part of the disclosure guidance: "The [business] review must, to the extent necessary for an understanding of the development, performance or position of the company's business, include (a) analysis using financial key performance indicators, and

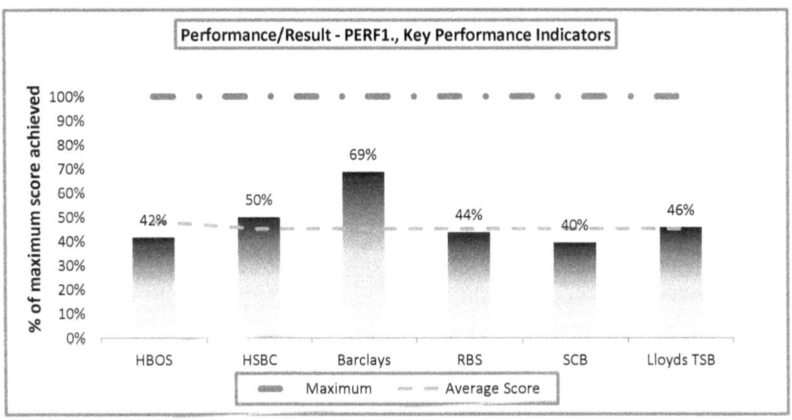

Fig. 8.17a Performance/result—Key performance indicators disclosure information

(b) where appropriate, analysis using other key performance indicators[3] (Companies Act 2006 s417; 6)" (Irish Stock Exchange 2012).

Encouragingly from the findings, there was evidence of a strong improvement in the quality of KPI disclosures since 2008, with 60% of the sample firms in 2012 providing detailed descriptions and narratives and 40% providing excellent quality disclosure in their annual reports. This result is, however, consistent with the findings from Grant Thornton report in 2012 which show that there was evidence of a strong improvement in the quality of KPI disclosures in their annual report, with nearly half of all FTSE companies, 49% in year 2012 (2011: 38%) now providing detailed descriptions. However, this study noted that during the pilot study that the best company KPIs go beyond financial data—such as Earnings Before Interest, Tax, Depreciation and Amortisation (EBITDA) and Return On Capital Employed (ROCE)—to embrace indicators that measure success against the business model. For example, retailers measure brand awareness, customer footfall and sales per square foot while pharmaceuticals look at new patent numbers and service companies and employee satisfaction. According to Grant Thornton 2012, the average number of KPIs reported in FTSE company annual reports was 9.6 (6.1 financial and 3.4 non-financial). This is similar to the results found in this study with average number of KPIs disclosures of 7.8 (6.1 financial and 1.7 non-financial).

Further investigation of Fig. 8.17b indicated that the overall total quality level of scores for all banks within the study timeframe shows that half of the sample banks disclosed adequate information with 50% score (36/72), compared with inadequate disclosure information score of 28% (20/72); detailed disclosed score was a mere 13% (9/72); and 7% (5/72) information disclosed was recorded for excellent disclosure score. Only 3% (2/72) of the disclosures provided type 0 score or no mention or did not disclose at all any of the required information items (Fig. 8.17b). It was observed that excellent disclosure information in the annual report demonstrated that the following key features, namely; (1) disclosures that link company KPIs to the company's objectives explaining why they have been selected and what they measure; (2) disclose quantifiable results that

[3] Key performance indicators means factors by reference to "which the development, performance or position of the company's business can be measured effectively" (Irish Stock Exchange 2012)

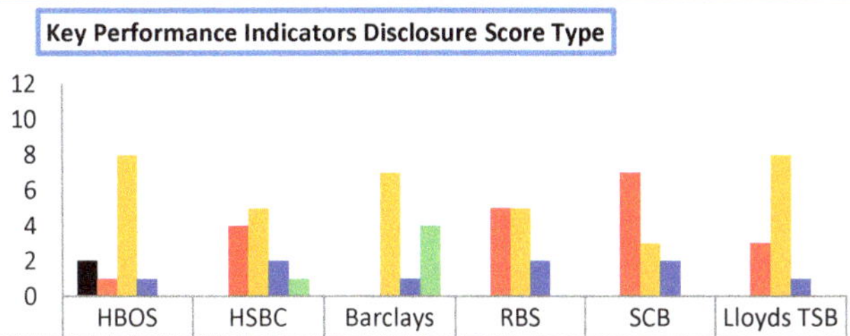

	HBOS	HSBC	Barclays	RBS	SCB	Lloyds TSB
0 - Not mentioned	2	0	0	0	0	0
1 - Inadequate	1	4	0	5	7	3
2 - Adequate	8	5	7	5	3	8
3 - Detailed	1	2	1	2	2	1
4 - Excellent	0	1	4	0	0	0

Fig. 8.17b Distribution of key performance indicators disclosure quality score type

are compared to prior years; (3) explain how they are calculated and the source of data; and (4) include future targets or expectations.

8.2.5.2 Code of Conduct or Ethics Disclosures Information

Conduct codes make expectations about legal and ethical behaviour clear, increase the likelihood of detection, assure the punishment of transgressions, reward desired behaviours and discipline those who engage in illogical behaviour. An organisation code heightens outside stakeholders or executive awareness of corporate policy and enlists their support in fighting and monitoring misconduct. A bank should demonstrate its commitment to organisational integrity by qualifying its professional standards in a code of ethics in annual reports. Codes may contain general precepts, mandate specific practices and provide clearly stated provisions to address legalities, deal with ethical concerns and detail sanctions, outline enforcement and stipulate methods of investigation. The diagram in Figs. 8.18a and 8.18b reflects the findings of the disclosure of the narratives of companies' codes of ethics in the annual reports over the sample period from 2001 to 2012. Disclosures on ethical or code of conduct had an average of 25% and top disclosure score of 38% for Standard Chartered Bank and least disclosure average score of 10% for Lloyds bank (see Fig. 8.18a). On average, while some of the annual report

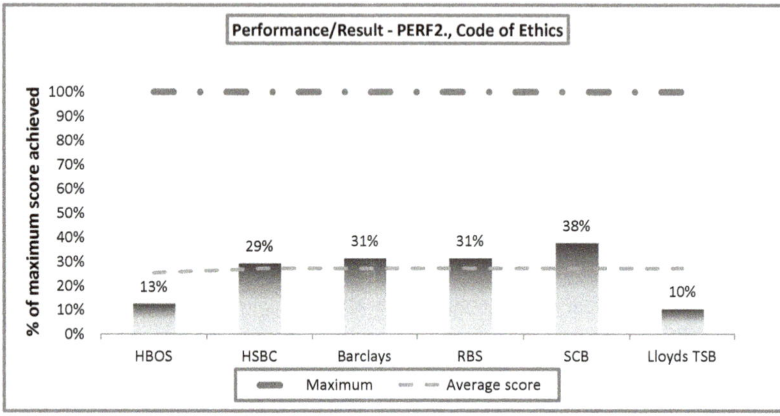

Fig. 8.18a Performance/result—Code of conduct/ethics disclosure quality

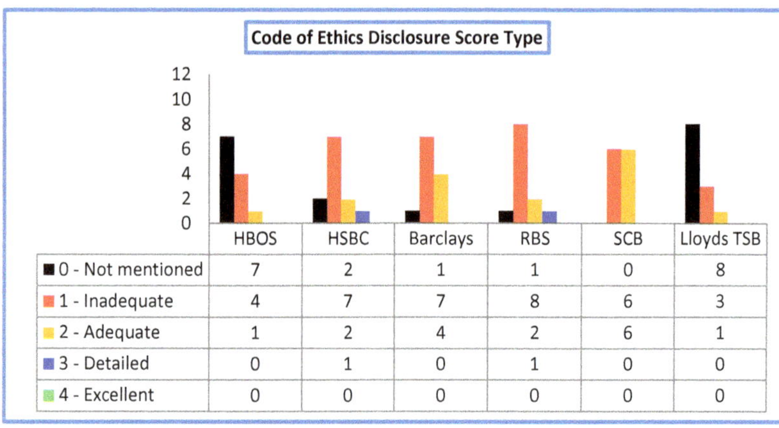

	HBOS	HSBC	Barclays	RBS	SCB	Lloyds TSB
0 - Not mentioned	7	2	1	1	0	8
1 - Inadequate	4	7	7	8	6	3
2 - Adequate	1	2	4	2	6	1
3 - Detailed	0	1	0	1	0	0
4 - Excellent	0	0	0	0	0	0

Fig. 8.18b Distribution of code of conduct/ethics disclosure quality score type

included information on a bank code of conduct or ethical business standard practice, evaluating how the bank had implemented these relied on disclosing any breaches of the code, which were barely discussed or were less consistently referred to in the assessed annual reports.

According to Fig. 8.18b, 49% (35/72) of the disclosure information relating to their code of ethics or conduct in their annual reports were regarded as inadequate. Further analysis indicates that 22% (16/72) disclosed adequate information score over the period, while only 3% (2/72) disclosed detailed information that were recorded. None of the entire disclosure information in the study period were regarded as excellent (score type 4 disclosure). Additionally, detailed analysis of the information reveals that 26% (19/72) provided no disclosure or did not mention any information items in the annual reports regarding code of ethics or conduct practices, policies and procedures.

8.2.5.3 Whistleblowing Disclosures Information

For a disclosure reporting mechanism to be effective, it should be accompanied by adequate guidance and policies on confidentiality and non-retaliation in order to foster open communication when ordinary channels fail. The UK Combined Code (2008) as part of its best practice code provision requires that "*the audit committees should review arrangements by which staff of the company may, in confidence, raise concerns about possible improprieties in matters of financial reporting or other matters. The audit committee's objective should be to ensure that arrangements are in place for the proportionate and independence investigation of such matters and for appropriate follow up actions*".

This book evaluates and assesses how the sample firms provide and communicate whistle- blowing policies, processes and practices in their annual reports to enable stakeholders to conduct effective accountability oversight and better monitoring. The performance of disclosure on whistle-blowing policies processes and practices had an average disclosure score of 7% over the study period from 2001 to 2012 among the companies. The top disclosure quality score of 17% was Barclays bank overall for the twelve-year period. Over this period, RBS had the least disclosure score for this category with 0%. This is also perhaps one of the most surprising and unexpected results in this book (Fig. 8.19a). The findings illustrate the extent to which there is clearly poor disclosure reporting practices among the banking institutions within the United Kingdom. It also points to the fact that there is currently no specific guidance from the banking supervisory regulators on how such details should be disclosed and reported in the annual reports.

Furthermore, Fig. 8.19b portrays the distribution of the quality score for whistle-blowing disclosure information for all the companies over the sample period. There were no information classifications recorded for both information score type 3 (detailed disclosure) and score type 4

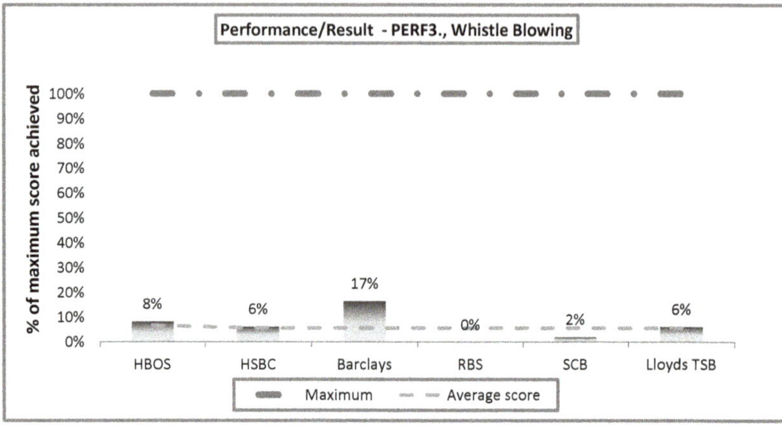

Fig. 8.19a Performance/result—Whistleblowing disclosure information

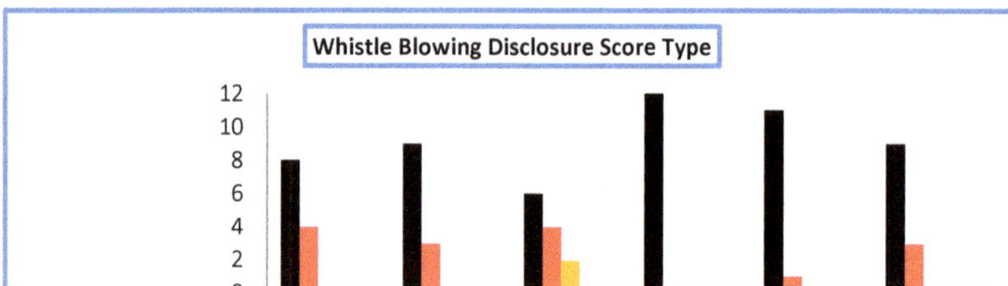

	HBOS	HSBC	Barclays	RBS	SCB	Lloyds TSB
0 - Not mentioned	8	9	6	12	11	9
1 - Inadequate	4	3	4	0	1	3
2 - Adequate	0	0	2	0	0	0
3 - Detailed	0	0	0	0	0	0
4 - Excellent	0	0	0	0	0	0

Fig. 8.19b Distribution of whistleblowing disclosure quality score type

(excellent disclosure). More than two-thirds, 76% (55/72) of the total reports reviewed and evaluated were recorded as type 0 information score classification, indicating that the majority of the report provided no disclosure or did not mention any information items in the annual reports regarding their whistle-blowing policies and responsibilities. This is followed by 21% (15/72) of the disclosure information relating to their whistle-blowing information in their annual reports which were regarded as type 1 score (inadequate disclosure). Further analysis indicated only 3% (2/72) disclosed adequate information scores over the period.

8.2.5.4 Breaches and Penalties Disclosures Information

As already discussed in the literature regarding bank corporate governance, the stakeholders theory states that governance mechanisms can help solve the problem of moral hazard and adverse selection only if effective enforcement creates credible deterrence. For example, the theory argues that the regulator (i.e. external stakeholder) can prevent adverse selection through rigorous rule enforcement. Indeed, the manner in which governance mechanisms, in particular rules and codes, are enforced will clearly affect incentives to comply. The effectiveness of the UK bank corporate governance framework is therefore due to substantive governance-related rules, codes and enforcement mechanisms (Armour 2008).

This section seeks to understand the role of boards in disclosing different governance enforcement mechanisms in mitigating the two-tier agency problems[4] in the UK banking sector between 2001 and 2012 annual reports. The disclosure narratives will focus upon public and private enforcement (formal or informal) described in the checklist criteria. Disclosure quality information on breaches and penalties had an overall average disclosure score of 15% over the study period from 2001–2012. The highest disclosure score of 21% was recorded jointly between Barclays, HSBC and SCB. The lowest disclosure score for this subcategory was HBOS with 4% disclosure quality score (Fig. 8.20a). Detailed analysis of the entire 72 annual reports revealed that 61% (44/72) of the reports provided no information or did not discuss breaches, sanctions and penalties in their disclosure report over the entire twelve-year

[4]Two-tier agency problem in banking can be categorised as debt governance and equity governance mechanisms. Debt governance mechanisms are designed to address the moral hazard of risk-shifting and the consequent systemic externalities of banks' excessive risk-taking. They may include bank regulation and supervision, monitoring of boards of directors and market discipline (i.e. monitoring by depositors, creditors and gatekeepers as well as information transparency). Equity governance mechanisms, on the contrary, are designed to deal with problems associated with managerial opportunism, misalignment of objectives between managers and shareholders as well as distortions of managerial incentives (i.e. board of directors, executive remuneration, information disclosure and transparency, legal rules and codes of corporate governance.

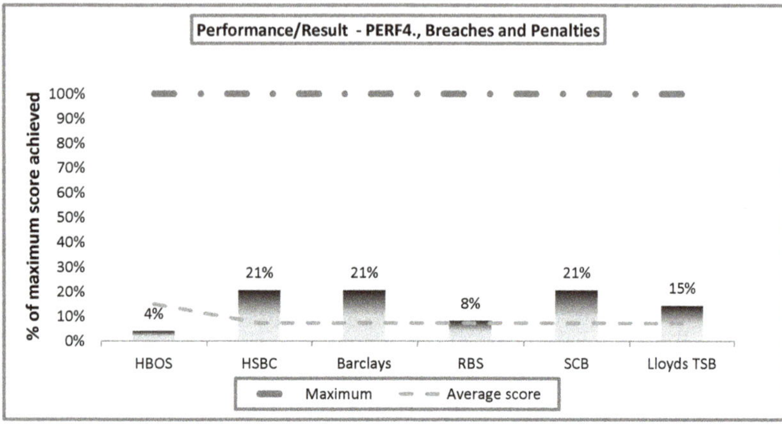

Fig. 8.20a Performance/result—Breaches and Penalties disclosure information

period. 24% (17/72) disclosure information was assessed as inadequate and provided little or no explanation. Detailed disclosure information over the period is only 7% (5/72), compared to 8% (6/72) disclosure score regarded as adequate score (Fig. 8.20b). From the empirical literature, there are a number of possible explanations that could be attributed

	HBOS	HSBC	Barclays	RBS	SCB	Lloyds TSB
0 - Not mentioned	10	7	5	10	5	7
1 - Inadequate	2	1	5	1	5	3
2 - Adequate	0	3	1	0	1	1
3 - Detailed	0	1	1	1	1	1
4 - Excellent	0	0	0	0	0	0

Fig. 8.20b Distribution of breaches and penalties disclosure quality score type

to such poor-quality disclosure reporting found in this area of the book. However, one possible explanation for the inadequate quality disclosure among the sample firms under this study may imply a lack of "credible" deterrence against banking firms and senior individuals therein, which engaged in unsound corporate governance and reporting practices.

The findings in this subcategory of corporate governance (i.e. lack of quality disclosure among the banks) support a number of prior empirical findings (Armour 2008; Hong 2011; Liebman and Milhaupt 2008; Walker 2009). Empirical analysis using FSA public enforcement disclosures by Armour concluded that the number of enforcement actions against UK banks is too low compared to the number of quoted banks in the United Kingdom (Hong 2011). It found that there are, on average, only 2.3 cases per annum enforcement actions against banks and less than one case per annum against individuals with no cases directed at non-executive directors. It also concluded by indicating that the low number of enforcement may be due to the lack of adequate deterrence by supervisory authorities. However, in terms of sanction type, it can be noted from the literature that the FSA in the United Kingdom had hitherto not used public censure against banks and its senior executive individuals in grappling with bank corporate governance weaknesses. For example, Liebman and Milhaupt report that public censure by a regulatory authority had a negative effect upon the censored party's share price (Liebman and Milhaupt 2008). This could affect the disclosure practices of these firms in providing such information to stakeholders publicly.

There are four major public enforcement agencies of UK banks. The FSA (now FCA) as both the UK prudential regulator and the UK Listing Authority, the Financial Reporting Review Panel (FRRP), the Department for Business Innovation & Skills (BIS), and the Takeover Panel. The enforcement activities of each of these agencies comprise a mixture of formal and informal actions. The FSA has established a regulatory framework for corporate governance of banks and other financial institutions under the FSMA 2000 (c.8), which is designed to safeguard the interests of stakeholders, such as consumers, depositors, policyholders and taxpayers. It has very wide enforcement powers regarding corporate governance breaches and compliances applicable to banking entity, practices and senior directors. Prior to the recent banking and financial crisis in 2007/2008, the FSA had a preference for informal enforcement, e.g. issuing a private warning (a non-statutory tool) (FSA 2007, pp. 23–36). Since the FSA only discloses cases of formal enforcement and the aggregated number of investigated cases (Armour 2008), it is impossible to know the figure of informal enforcement activities against banks for corporate governance failures. Furthermore, the then FSA as the UKLA has responsibility for drafting and enforcing all the rules "(the Listing Rules, the Disclosure and Transparency Rules, and the Prospectus Rules, applicable to banks quoted on the Official List)". Apart from enforcement powers conferred on the FSA as the UK prudential regulator, for quoted banks, UKLA has the power to require delisting of securities. Prior to September 2009, there appeared to be no formal enforcement activity pursued by the UKLA for breaches of the Listing Rules by a bank in the United Kingdom (Hong 2011). Additionally, prior to September 2009, there was an absence of formal private enforcement in the United Kingdom against bank directors. This may be partially attributed to financial disincentives, free-rider effects faced by bank shareholders and the fact that bank shareholders enjoyed high profits during the last economic boom.

8.3 Conclusion

This chapter has presented the second part of the findings and analysis from the empirical work on the assessment of the quality of corporate governance disclosure reporting in the annual reports of the top six UK-listed banking firms over the period 2001–2012. The approach adopted the form of longitudinal information design of the categories and subcategories constructed under the study. The primary objective of this chapter was to determine the impact of the long-term changes (i.e. longitudinal) and trends that have affected the quality of corporate governance disclosures inside the UK financial industry. The findings have shown that all the companies have increased their corporate governance disclosures over the period between 2001 and 2012, both in terms of the quality level of corporate governance categories and by the volume of disclosures. However, the study found that there were corporate governance categories that have experienced some degree of changeability and variability across the different years. Possible explanations that could be attributed to this variance in the level of disclosure are either the demand for stakeholder reporting requirements (the revised UK Code of Corporate Governance for example) or unexpected situation that has forced changes in approach (for example, the financial crisis of 2007/8).

To identify the overall corporate governance categories that have influenced UK banks in terms of quality of disclosure, a volumetric analysis was performed in this study. The total overall proportion of disclosure of corporate governance quality level score achieved as a percentage of maximum expected score over the twelve-year period of study was 39% (as a proportion of required maximum quality score expected) for all companies in all years of the disclosed checklist items. The average overall corporate governance disclosure quality over the period under investigation is considered to be low and relatively poor. Overall, the research findings confirm that prior research conclusions based on ordinary firms do not hold for banks. Also, existing studies within the accounting literature present unconvincing arguments in relation to the different dimensions of governance and the metrics used for bank accountability disclosures (Bayou et al. 2011; Beretta and Bozzolan 2004). The results from Fig. 8.21 confirm that the total occurrences of qualitative disclosure were mainly scored "Type 2" (Adequate) by all companies. It can be observed from the graph that Barclays provided the largest proportion of qualitative disclosure score "Type 2" (105) over the twelve-year period. However, it is also important to note that overall there has been an improvement in the quality of information disclosed in the annual reports for the corporate governance indicator categories used for this study. Additionally, although an improvement was observed in the disclosures, the inadequacy of "Type 3" (Detailed) and "Type 4" (Excellent) quality

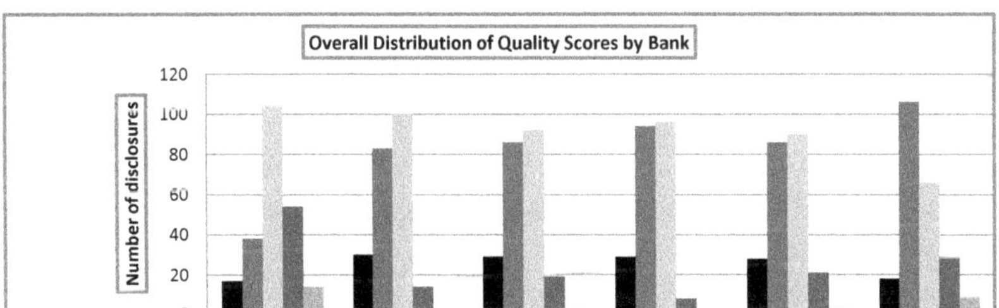

	Barclays	HBOS	HSBC	Lloyds TSB	RBS	SCB
0 - Not mentioned	17	30	29	29	28	18
1 - Inadequate	38	83	86	94	86	106
2 - Adequate	105	100	92	96	90	66
3 - Detailed	54	14	19	8	21	29
4 - Excellent	14	1	2	1	3	9

Fig. 8.21 Overall distribution of quality scores by banks in the study

scores disclosed by all the companies over the twelve-year period indicates that there is still a long way to go towards the level of quality disclosures and narratives for a number of the companies to achieve an international best practice or excellent level of quality disclosure in banking.

The findings show that the overall average percentage scores for criteria in the main category group ranged from 50% disclosure quality scores achieved to just 24% over the period. Narrative with accountability disclosure returned a 50% score achievement for all companies, which is the highest within the overall categories. Conversely, a total of 24% score was awarded for performance disclosure regarding the achievement of the corporate governance mechanisms over the twelve-year period.

The empirical results of previous studies cannot be directly compared with the results of the current study because of the time period and the different types and number of information items measured. As the above discussion attests, the results of the current study can be seen as primary evidence taking into account the development of disclosure practices by listed banks over a period of time. Also, very few previous empirical disclosure studies have focused on the extent of banking disclosure, since most of the prior earlier disclosure studies have excluded banks and other financial institutions from their samples.

Overall, the implication of the findings from this chapter has a number of managerial consequences for different stakeholders that use annual reports to demand accountability. The findings provide significant information for commercial banking management, banking regulators, the Central Banks, the accounting profession, potential local and foreign investors, researchers, international institutions and other government agencies to help them to assess the transparency level and the amount of information available from these UK banks. This is particularly important for the decision-making processes as there is no direct enforcement of accounting and auditing standards with respect to corporate governance disclosure in the United Kingdom.

The empirical findings from this chapter shows that there are relatively different and varied levels of corporate governance disclosure quality in the UK banking sector among the categories, which highlights that firms are fulfilling their responsibilities—meaning that they need to react to the demands of diverse stakeholders (i.e. to shareholders, depositors, supervisory regulators and the public). Furthermore, there has been an increasing trend in the quality of corporate governance responsibility by the listed banks over the study period, emphasising the increased awareness and compliance of corporate governance responsibility by UK-listed companies over time. This could be considered reasonable and attributed to the issuance of the Combined Code of corporate governance in 2003 and revised in 2010.

A further analysis of the different dimensions of quality score types of the corporate governance subcategory disclosure quality provided a deeper insight into the different quality dimensions of the company's disclosure strategy in the annual reports. The quality of disclosure depends on both the quantity of narrative information disclosed and on the quality or richness offered by additional information. In departing from existing literature (both in terms of study timeline and measurement), the quality disclosure is one of the indicators that are used to measure how well companies disclose in their annual report, in particular, the qualitative features of information. Overall, the study results of the disclosure content scale in a year-by-year basis shows that significant differences were found at some quality levels for the majority of the companies in the study. It shows the trend in the quality of such disclosure over time. For Type 1 disclosures (inadequate), there was a consistent decrease in disclosure in the overall sample from 2002 to 2012, indicating a trend towards more detailed and company-specific reporting on corporate governance-related themes. Type 2 (adequate) disclosures recorded a steep increase in the number of score information from 2003 to 2010. However, the level of these disclosure types decreased in 2011 and 2012. Type 4 (excellent) corporate governance disclosures were rare. Overall, one might be tempted to conclude from this data finding that the quality of reporting is improving over time but in actual fact, the very low level of Type 4 disclosures and the frequency of Type 4 disclosures across the sample banks suggest that there is ample room for major improvement.

References

Aburaya, R. K. (2012). *The relationship between corporate governance and environmental disclosure: UK evidence*. Durham thesis, Durham University.

Adams, R. B., & Mehran, H. (2003). Is corporate governance different for bank holding companies? Federal Reserve Bank of New York. *Economic Policy Review*, *9*(1), 127–141.

Armour, J. (2008). *Enforcement strategies in UK corporate governance: A roadmap and empirical assessment* (Law Working Paper No. 106/2008).

Basel Committee on Banking Supervision (BCBS). (1999). *Enhancing corporate governance for banking organisations*. Basel: Bank for International Settlements.

BCBS. (2010). *Principles for enhancing corporate governance*. Basel Committee on Banking Supervision.

Bayou, M. E., Reinstein, A., & Williams, P. F. (2011). To tell the truth: A discussion of issues concerning truth and ethics in accounting. *Accounting, Organization and Society, 36*(2), 109–124.

Baysinger, B., & Butler, H. (1985). Corporate governance and the board of directors: Performance effects of changes in board composition. *Journal of Law, Economics, & Organization, 1*(1), 101–124.

Belkhir, M. (2009). Board of directors' size and performance in banking industry. *International Journal of Managerial Finance, 5*(2), 201–221.

Beretta, S., & Bozzolan, S. (2004). A framework for the analysis of firm risk communication. *The International Journey of Accounting, 39*(3), 265–288.

Borokhovich, K. A., Parrino, R., & Trapani, T. (1996). Outside directors and CEO selection. *The Journal of Financial and Quantitative Analysis, 31*(3), 337–355.

Cadbury Report. (1992). *Report of the committee on the financial aspects of corporate governance*. London: Gee.

Ciancanelli, P., & Gonzalez, J. A. (2000). Corporate governance in banking: A conceptual framework. *Social Science Research Network*, European Financial Management Association Conference, pp. 2–24.

Combined Code. (1998). *The combined code on corporate governance: Principles of good governance and code of best practice*. Committee on Corporate Governance, London Stock Exchange Limited. London: Gee & Co.

Fama, E. F. (1980). Agency problems and the theory of the firm. *Journal of Political Economy, 88*(2), 288–307.

Fama, E. F., & Jensen, M. C. (1983). Separation of ownership and control. *Journal of Law and Economics, 26*(2), 301–325.

Financial Reporting Council (FRC). (2012). *The UK corporate governance code*. London: Financial Reporting Council.

Financial Service Authority (FSA). (2007). *Enforcement guide*. London: Financial Service Authority.

Financial Service Authority (FSA). (2009a, September). *Reforming remuneration practices in the financial services, Consultation Paper*. London.

Financial Service Authority (FSA). (2009b, March). *The Turner review: A regulatory response to the global banking crisis*. London.

Flannery, M. J., Kwan, S. H., & Nimalendran, M. (2004). Market evidence on the opaqueness of banking firms' assets. *Journal of Financial Economics, 71*(3), 416–460.

Group of 20 (G20). (2009a, September 5). *G20 banking statement*.

Group of 20 (G20). (2009b, April 2). *Declaration on strengthening the financial system.*

Group of 20 (G20). (2011, November). *Cannes summit final declaration: Building our common future: Renewed collective action for the benefit of all.* Cannes.

Hagendorff, J., & Keasey, K. (2012). The value of board diversity in banking: Evidence from the market for corporate control. *The European Journal of Finance, 18*(1), 41–58.

Hampel Report. (1998). *Final report: The committee of corporate governance.* Hampel Committee.

Hermalin, B. E., & Weisbach, M. S. (2003). Board of directors as an endogenously determined institution: A survey of the economic literature. *Federal Reserve Bank of New York Economic Policy Review*, 7–26.

Higgs Report. (2003). *Review of the role and effectiveness of non-executive directors.* London: Department of Trade and Industry.

Hong, W. (2011). *The UK bank corporate governance framework: A holistic and critical analysis with a focus upon banks risk and executive remuneration governance.* University of Manchester.

Hopt, K. J. (2013). Better governance of financial institutions. *ECGI Working Paper Series in Law* (Working Paper N°. 207/2013).

Irish Stock Exchange. (2012). *Report on compliance with the combined code on corporate governance by Irish Listed companies.* Dublin: Irish Stock Exchange.

Kirkpatrick, G. (2009). The corporate governance lessons from the financial crisis. *Financial Markets Trends, OECD: Financial Regulation and Compliance, 16*(1), 8–18.

Liebman, B. L., & Milhaupt, C. J. (2008). Reputational sanctions in China's securities market. *Columbia Law Review, 108*(4), 929.

London Stock Exchange (LSE). (2012, September). *Corporate governance for main market and AIM companies.* London: White Paige Ltd.

Macey, J. R., & O'Hara, M. (2003). The corporate governance of banks. *FRBNY Economic Policy Review, 9*, 91–107.

Mehran, H., Morrison, A. D., & Shapiro, J. D. (2011, June 1). *Corporate governance and banks: What have we learned from the financial crisis?* (FRB of New York Staff Report No. 502).

Mizruchi, M. S. (1983). Who Controls Whom? An examination of the relation between management and boards of directors in large American corporations. *Academy of Management Review, 8*(3).

Nolan, L. (1995). *First report of the committee on standards in public life. Committee on standards in public life* (Vol. 1). United Kingdom.

OECD. (1999). *OECD principles of corporate governance.* Paris: OECD Publishing.

OECD. (2009a). *The financial crisis, reforms and exit strategies*. France: Organisation for Economic Co-operation and Development.
OECD. (2009b). *Business ethics and OECD principles: What can be done to avoid another crisis*. France: Organisation for Economic Co-operation and Development.
Stiles, P., & Taylor, B. (2001). *Board at work*. Oxford: Oxford University Press.
Thornton, G. (2012). *Corporate governance review: The chemistry of governance, a catalyst for change*. London: Grant Thornton.
Turner Report. (2009). *A regulatory response to the global banking crisis*. London.
United Nations Conference on Trade And Development (UNCTAD). (2010, October). *Corporate governance in the wake of the financial crisis, selected international reviews*. New York and Geneva: United Nations.
Walker, S. D. (2009). *A review of corporate governance in UK banks and other financial industry entities*. Walker Review, Final recommendations.
Zahra, S. A., & Pearce, J. A. II. (1989). Board of directors and corporate financial performance: A review and integrative model. *Journal of Management, 15*(2), 291–334.

CHAPTER 9

The Inside Scoop—What Stakeholders' Think of Corporate Governance in Financial Institutions

9.1 Introduction

Financial institutions, particularly banking business operations, are mainly characterised and often viewed as driven by opacity and increased complexities both in terms of structure as well as business operations within an organisation. A key objective of reporting is to promote transparency and accountability by enhancing the quality of disclosure and by reducing information asymmetry. Good quality corporate governance and disclosures have a number of potential benefits for stakeholders. It must, however, be recognised that disclosure in itself would not enhance transparency if it appears to lack useful and meaningful information for shareholders, depositors, market analysts, regulators and other stakeholders that are backed by some form of relevant legal, regulatory or compliance requirements. This philosophical shift is a result of the post financial crisis of 2008 that reflect many legal systems changes from a mere supervisory shareholder centric to a more appropriate regulatory approach to stakeholder financial firm governance. This chapter examines from the perspective of the broader stakeholder the relevance of financial organisations' corporate governance and disclosure issues with regard to information richness on a longitudinal basis.

J. A. Akuffo, *Corporate Governance and Accountability of Financial Institutions*, Palgrave Studies in Accounting and Finance Practice, https://doi.org/10.1007/978-3-030-64046-0_9

9.2 The Notion of Financial Institution Stakeholders and Shareholders

The topic of corporate governance is a vast subject and it incorporates managerial accountability, board structure and shareholder rights. The issue of balance of power and decision-making between the board of directors, senior executives and shareholders has been evolving for centuries. This in effect has been a hot topic among academic scholars, executives, investors and regulatory bodies in particular, and they have been insisting on the implementation of adequate corporate governance policies and practices by the companies. It has therefore been established that there is no commonly acknowledged precise definition of corporate governance (Tricker 2009; Belcredi and Ferrarini 2013). What is the meaning of "governance" in the context of a financial institution (FI)?[1] Conventionally, corporate governance is defined as the system by which companies are directed and controlled. The *OECD Principles of Corporate Governance* (2004) defines corporate governance as involving: "*a set of relationships between a company's management, its board, its shareholders and other stakeholders. Corporate governance also provides the structure through which the objectives of the company are set, and the means of attaining those objectives and monitoring performance are determined*" (OECD 2004, p. 11). Particularly, in the context of financial institutions in this circumstance, primary among the "other stakeholders" as implied by the OECD definition are supervisors and regulators with responsibility for ensuring safety, soundness and ethical operation of the financial system for the public good. They have a major stake in and can make a significant contribution to the development and implementation of effective governance. While this definition is good at setting out the broad notion of governance, it only goes so far. It leaves some confusion and the illusion of ultimate accountability to whom in question.

With respect to the argument of stakeholder philosophy of corporate governance, the term stakeholder is used to describe any person or organisation with an interest in the company. On the one hand is the narrow view of stakeholder as embraced by agency theory (i.e. one principal) and on the other hand, the broader view espouses by stakeholder theory perspective (i.e. multiple principals). Nonetheless, it is important to note that having an undefined view of corporate stakeholders can be problematic in accountable corporate governance which may undoubtedly compound agency problems. In the United Kingdom, the Chartered

[1] In this chapter, "financial institutions" are defined to include large banks, insurance companies, and securities firms.

Institute of Management Accountant (CIMA) in its curriculum classified stakeholders into two main groups, namely; (a) "Financial stakeholders are those with a financial relationship with the organisation, in other words, should a financial problem occur to the organisation, then these stakeholders will suffer (e.g. shareholders and other investors, employees, customers, suppliers, government); and (b) Interest stakeholders who are interested in how the organisation behaves and are very often more powerful than the financial stakeholders due to the level of influence they have over it (e.g. media, non-governmental organisation, activist groups, depositors, competitors, regulators)" (CIMA 2008, p. 437). While this distinction is largely true for ordinary firms in general, when it comes to financial organisations specifically, the categorisation is very complex to define, or it is irrelevant to make explicit groupings given the legitimate interest and claims that both groups will have in these institutions whether directly or indirectly.

Figure 9.1 shows the various stakeholder groups whose interest the financial organisation may need to take into consideration in relation to accountability in corporate governance. For example, financial firms need to not only provide pay and pensions for its employees, but also must take into consideration the compliance with employee legislation such as equal pay and opportunity, diversity, health and safety at work and other aspects in its obligations and responsibility. Conversely, employees are also very interested in the long-term success of the company as so much of their own personal livelihood is directly dependent on this for example, their pension and other offered conditions of employment are inherently linked to the company output. We also know, that regulators and financial supervisors are interested too in how these institutions are well governed and managed[2] in the interest of financial market stability concerns (BCBS 2010; House of Commons Select Committee 2009a, b). They provide regulation and supervisory tools to ensure they are complying and disclosing on how they are achieving all that they say they are.

[2] Although, we can distinguish the regulatory function from the supervisory function in practice, sometimes there can be overlapping in overall corporate governance function. The regulator sets the rules and regulations within which financial institutions are compelled to operate, while the supervisor has oversight of the actions of the board and management to ensure compliance with those rules and regulations. Confusion arises because both functions are often performed within the same institution (e.g. the US Federal Reserve and the UK Financial Conduct Authority—previously known as FSA).

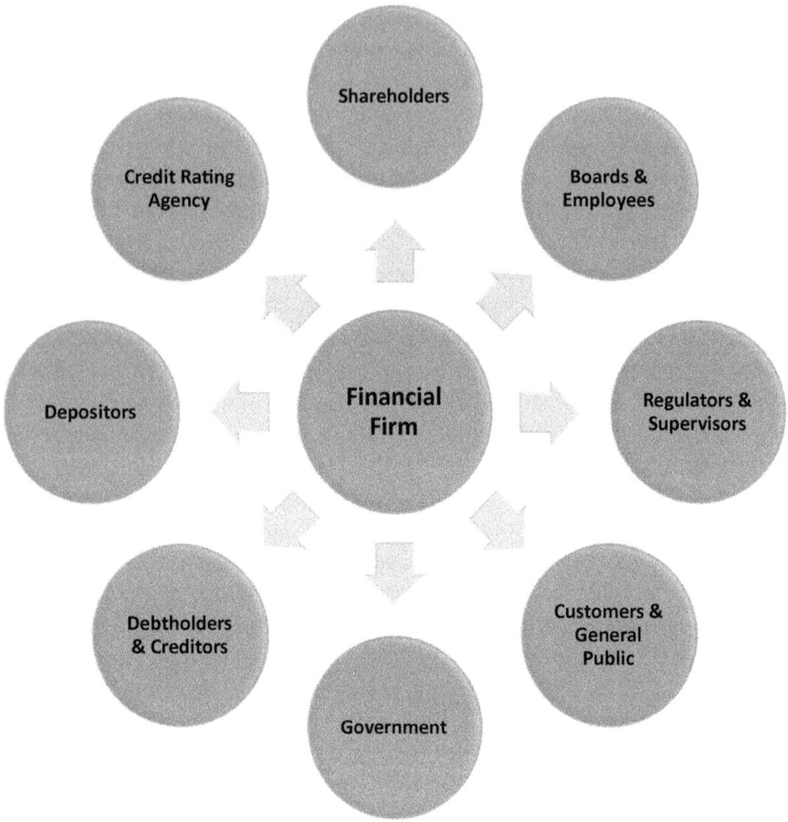

Fig. 9.1 Map of financial institutions stakeholder governance interest groups (*Source* Created by the author)

Furthermore, for the governance of financial institutions, it has been established that shareholder focused governance is inadequate (Turner 2009; Hopt 2013; UNCTAD 2010). The widest definitions cover that organisations are accountable to shareholders and other stakeholders. I am particularly interested in the description offered by Tricker (1984) "*the governance role is not concerned with the running of the business of the company* per se, *but with giving overall direction to the enterprise, with overseeing and controlling the executive actions of management and with satisfying legitimate expectations of accountability and regulation by interest beyond the corporate boundaries*". This broader definition is even more relevant and applicable to financial institutions as when it was originally proposed thirty-six years ago. It is also more in line with my own view as adopted in this book on corporate governance and accountability disclosure issues.

The development corporate governance code of ethics and best practice guidance over the years have mirrored the need to ensure accountability for the various stakeholders that are being affected by the company's core decisions. This development has largely been driven by the governments, financial regulators and supervisors around the world. In the United Kingdom, the 1992 Cadbury Report is a good example of a direct reaction to UK governance failures in companies such as Polly Peck, BCCI and Maxwell. The Committee in producing its reports investigated accountability of the Board of Directors to shareholders and society. The resultant outputs led to an introduction of codes of compliance and disclosures such as the separation of chairman and chief executive roles, the requirement for two independent NEDs and finally the requirement for an audit committee of NEDs with a clear aim of improving financial reporting, accountability and directors of board oversight.

Another government reaction would be the 2003 Higgs Report in the United Kingdom which resulted from US corporate failures from companies such as Enron, WorldCom, Adelphi and Tyco due to malfunction of corporate governance systems. It was established that within each of these firms, members of board of directors and senior executives "did not live up to the legal standard of duty of care that obligates top corporate officials to act carefully in fulfilling the important tasks of monitoring and directing the activities of corporate management" (Mintz 2006). These led to introductions of new laws and major code of compliance changes and revisions in the United Kingdom, United States and other jurisdictions. Examples of these changes included a requirement for half of the board at a minimum to be independent NED's, and the introduction of annual board and director evaluations. A final example that I would highlight would be the resultant output of both the 2009 Walker Report and the 2010 Stewardship Code to improve a number of key stakeholders' accountability. Both of these changes resulted from collapses of major financial institutions due to the financial crisis of 2008. A number of recommendations were enacted during this time and the newly titled 2010 UK Corporate Governance Code was launched. The 2010 Stewardship Code was intended to improve the level of engagement between institutional investors and companies. Each of the four participants in the governance system—boards of directors, management, supervisors and (to an extent) long-term shareholders—needs to reassess their approach to financial institution corporate governance and take meaningful steps to make governance stronger.

9.3 The Function of Financial Institution Stakeholders in Corporate Governance and Disclosure Accountability

Financial institutions are governed by several different key mechanisms, and there is a core framework of taxes, laws and social customs that companies have to adhere to—there is an added layer for financial institutions, however, with both supervisory actions and regulations that are specific to their context. Both internal governors (e.g. risk officers and board of directors) and external governors (e.g. regulators or legislators, etc.) have the power to influence all key decisions a company makes. The motivations of this group do not always match or have the same level of power. The reason for this is that they do not always share the same desire for the risk profile results for the financial companies.

For financial institutions, stakeholder corporate governance really matters enormously. Many governance experts frequently describe what good governance looks like in general but offer barely any thought to how to measure or achieve high-performance results in a practical world. Nonetheless (as shown in Fig. 9.1) in the eyes of the law, the four key direct participants in a corporate governance system—boards of directors, management, supervisors/regulators and long-term shareholders—still ought to re-evaluate their approach to financial institutions governance and take meaningful steps to make the mechanisms of accountability stronger. There have recently been a number of growing discussions within the academics, practitioners and developed communities about the different accountability typologies and its impact on corporate governance. The need for accountability implies relationships between people and raises the question of *to whom* accounts of oneself should be directed (Joannidès de Lautour 2019; Schweiker 1993; Shearer 2002). Accountability is one of the keystones of good corporate governance; however, it can be difficult for scholars and practitioners alike to navigate the myriad of different types of accountability within the norms of corporate governance in order to demonstrate the best fit for effective governance. An important theme of corporate governance is the nature and extent of accountability of particular individuals within the organisation, and mechanisms that try to reduce or eliminate the principal–agent problems.

Conventionally, investigation into corporate governance from accounting and finance literature has employed an agency theory approach, completely aimed at resolving conflict of interest between corporate management and accountability to the shareholder (Jensen and Meckling 1976; Fama and Jensen 1983a, b). The key argument made by the author of this book departs from those studies and strongly advocates the use of stakeholders' philosophy to hold financial organisations accountable. This viewpoint is thus supported by the nature and specificities of banking and other financial firms' activities in the literature as well as my own investigative findings. It is argued in this book that both the quality of information disclosed and mechanisms of corporate governance disclosures are firmly rooted in the concept of providing stakeholder's accountability (Ciancanelli and Gonzalez 2000; Solomon 2007; Brennan and Solomon 2008) and claim that this theory focuses on senior managerial decision-making to ensure that there is no lead stakeholders' controlling the process of generating value in a sustainable manner.

Indeed, my own empirical research in the United Kingdom has provided considerable support for the view that good quality corporate governance disclosures are important to effective corporate accountability to stakeholders. The research was specifically aimed at investigating the interrelationship of the quality of corporate governance mechanisms and accountability practices, and suggested opportunities for future research. Stakeholder theoretical framework was employed using content analysis to investigate corporate governance narrative disclosures in large banks annual reports to help to elucidate the demand of numerous stakeholders. Contrary to agency theory, "stakeholder theory views the corporation as a locus in relation to wider external stakeholder's interest rather than merely shareholders' wealth". This research focused on the disclosure of mechanisms of accountability within banking organisations' corporate governance to numerous stakeholders with diverse attention and influence. Thus, it could be debated that the disclosure of high-quality corporate governance information in the annual report of United Kingdom banks towards a number of stakeholders is improved when senior directors' behaviours are monitored by the nature of mechanisms of accountability within corporate governance. The increased scrutiny of those in leadership positions post financial crisis resulted in a significant increase in all accountability categories disclosed following the financial crisis which supports this theory.

Within the accounting studies, stakeholder philosophy is being broadly used to provide robust defence for disclosure studies in corporate governance. Accordingly, the viewpoint of stakeholder thesis encompasses the acknowledgement and the recognition of the association between the behaviour of the firm and the impact on its stakeholder. Corporate governance in this context becomes a problem of finding mechanisms that elicit firm-specific investments on the part of various stakeholders, and that encourages active co-operation among stakeholders in creating wealth, jobs and the sustainability of financially sound enterprises.

The critics of stakeholder theory (Letza et al. 2004; Sternberg 1997; Tse 2011) argued that putting shareholders first does do harm to other stakeholders. Making managers accountable to a group of stakeholders which are undefined will, in effect, make them accountable to none as there is no yard sticks by which to measure their performance. This stream of criticism from the accountability literature stems from the legal foundation of what is a corporation or an enterprise from an Anglo-Saxon model of corporate governance? On the contrary, traditional mechanisms of accountability from the finance and banking studies include governance regulations and supervision disclosures, boards of directors, financial reporting and disclosures, audit committees, external audits and institutional investors. In the finance discipline, research into board leadership accountability as a mechanism for improving corporate governance has adopted a more stakeholder-oriented approach. For example, there is a greater focus on financial services accountability to a broader range of stakeholders (EC 2014; FRC 2009a, b; G20 2009a, b, 2010; Solomon 2007; Tricker 2009) via the quality of explicit disclosure of codes of governance required in United Kingdom annual reports. This reorientation within the financial services industry, particularly banking, is paving the way for new research in corporate governance which examines the broader accountability of financial institutions to meet the needs of multiple stakeholders. This was proven to be the case for all companies examined by my empirical study with the visible improvement in disclosures seen post the 2010 publication of the UK Code of Corporate Governance revised edition.

Furthermore, a key stakeholder that has largely been ignored in the literature or their interest not taken directly by boards of directors is depositors. The issue here normally arises on whether and to what extent the board and stockholders' authority should be structured to reflect other stakeholders' interest. This is specifically important for deposit-taking financial intermediaries, where financial supervisors' primary concerns are more aligned with depositors rather than shareholders interest (Ferrarini 2017). Needless to say, in most jurisdictions financial supervisors and regulators intervene on behalf of depositors by providing deposit protection/insurance schemes in the interest of financial stability. Perhaps this is not surprising as disclosures in this area are ambiguous in the disclosure literature. Also, the financial crisis gave a new momentum to the discussion on the role of deposit insurance and bailout systems in corporate governance and accountability disclosure. Despite the shift towards broader stakeholder emphasis, there are still a number of fundamental unresolved concerns for financial institution's corporate governance mechanisms reporting. For example, UK legislation requirements enacted (updated listing rules and the stewardship code) following the Walker review remain shareholder-oriented focus.

There is a belief among some, including this author, that the use of stakeholder philosophy of corporate governance is seen to be somehow superior and fitting when ensuring that directors are fully accountable to stakeholders within banks and other financial institutions. Other authors of academic pieces of research who mirror this belief when encouraging the study of corporate governance theory include Turnbull (1997), Aburaya (2012), Blair (1995) and Tricker (2009). The theory, for the core purpose of this book, is more suited to the environment of banking and regulatory supervision in financial institutions in the United Kingdom and beyond. Thus, the quality of the mechanisms of corporate governance employed by the banking firms provide a signal with regard to the degree of emphasis on the stakeholders' importance that its board of directors reflect on their disclosure decisions and reporting practices.

One key merit in advocating the stakeholder concept of governance is its ability to explain and offer a mechanism for dealing with numerous stakeholders with various levels of concerns that are often contradictory. Proponents of this theory in social accounting argued that the demand of stockholders in fact cannot be met without simultaneously meeting the needs of other key interested parties for an organisation (Gray et al. 1995a).

Thus, this theory as advocated in this book, offers valuable structures for assessing disclosure requirements and accountability reporting for broader stakeholder's requirement. Two types of viewpoint (i.e. ethics and management responsibility) are generally used to support this (Gray et al. 1995b). The stakeholder theory adopted supports the empirical findings in this book. The results reinforce the study's general argument that corporate governance plays an important role in determining how financial firms mitigate agency problems and respond to the needs and interests of various stakeholders.

Nevertheless, corporate governance disclosures currently employ financial accounting statements or annual reports as a means to share information—these are key mediums that diverse stakeholders employ to hold corporate executives accountable for their actions and decisions. Companies, along with accounting and auditing professionals face problems when it comes to disclosures within the topic of comprehensive reporting by financial organisations to various users of such information. Some core challenges that fall in the corporate reporting category:

- Shortage of expertise—a set of agreed credible standards for both reporting and measuring nonfinancial information is still being developed
- Cost of producing information—the cost of collecting data, producing corporate reports and obtaining assurance opinions from auditors all stand to potentially rise
- Complexity of information—it has been voiced that the introduction of the International Financial Reporting Standards has made the process of accounting lengthier and increased its complexity

9.4 Corporate Governance Issues in Other Financial Institutions

A financial system in any economy essentially consists of financial markets and financial institutions. As discussed throughout this book, I am particularly interested in financial institutions and how its role interacts and affects the system with respect to governance. Financial organisations or institutions are companies that offer diverse financial services. Financial services make up one of the economy's most important and influential sectors (Bush et al. 2014). The institutions can thus be grouped into two—(1) banks and (2) non-bank firms. Overall, these firms particularly are in the business of taking risks and managing them. The conventional approach to corporate governance is very different to the way banks and other financial institutions function. The overwhelming evidence suggests that the extent of financial institutions' corporate governance exceed more than just the traditional shareholder model and includes other relevant stakeholders such as taxpayers, debtholders, insurance policy holders, regulators, supervisors and debt governance (other creditors). Each of these stakeholders has a different perspective and interest in terms of expected managerial accountability and control functions. The failures in the corporate governance of banking and other financial institutions (i.e. non-banking firms) contributed significantly to the financial crisis in 2008–2009. Following the crisis, a number of national regulators and supervisors across the OECD have acknowledged that other financial institution industry "should not be seen solely in terms of the risks that it poses; it is also essential to acknowledge the important role that it plays within the financial sector. It constitutes an alternative financing channel that is essential to the real economy, particularly at a time when traditional actors in the banking system are reducing financial support" (EC 2013a, p. 14). The use of the term "other financial institutions" in the following subsections denoted specifically as "Non-banking Financial Institutions" (NBFIs), Non-banking Financial Companies or other financial companies that are not officially classed as banks globally. Several regulators, international organisations or government agencies also refer to non-banking firms as shadow banking depending on the scope of definition whether broad or narrow by various international bodies and government regulatory agencies. However, since the terms "shadow banking" and "other financial institution" and "NBFIs" are equivalent, these terms are used interchangeably throughout the coming subsections to refer to as other financial institutions. The issue of corporate governance and its accountability framework does not just exclusively affect banking organisations, but is a wider reaching challenge faced by multiple institutions including other small or large non-banking enterprises across the wider financial market. It also seeks to highlight the similarities and differences in governance and accountability issues in other financial institutions (non-banking) across the United Kingdom, United States and the EU that are mainly listed on the Stock Exchanges. The aim is to see if there are any wider learnings that policymakers could adopt to improve best practices of corporate governance of other financial institutions overall.

9.5 The Importance of Other Financial Institutions in the Financial Market

A financial system in any economy can essentially consist of financial markets and financial institutions. Financial organisations or institutions are companies that offer diverse financial services.[3] Financial services make up one of the economy's most important and influential sectors. The institutions can thus be grouped as banks and other financial (i.e. non-bank) firms. In this chapter, we are particularly interested in the aspect of corporate governance concerns and its interaction of non-banking firms' function in the financial system (FSB 2013, 2014). According to the World Bank (2012) "A non-bank financial institution (NBFI) is a financial institution that does not have a full banking license and cannot accept deposits from the public". Figure 9.2 shows the illustration of the traditional distinction between banking and non-banking permitted functions.

While the classification highlighted in Fig. 9.2 indicates the appearance of a clear-cut distinction in theory, in the real world, the operations and activities of various financial institutions in relation to each of the index of classifications are still considered to be very complex in nature and scope, opaque and multifaceted making it very difficult to regulate or provide effective supervisory tools. In most advanced countries, existing definitions of financial institution is somehow confusing and not clear although the classification exists. According to ICB (2011) report in the United Kingdom—"The distinction between financial and non-financial companies is one which is important in existing and proposed regulation. For example, the Basel Committee on Banking Supervision (BCBS) proposals for liquidity regulation treat exposures to financial companies differently from exposures to non-financial companies".[4] The precise definition of financial companies is left for national regulators. The credit rating agency, Fitch, currently rates over 600 Non-Bank Financial Institutions globally, including finance and leasing companies, securities firms, asset managers, business development companies and traditional

[3] Financial services are a broad range of more specific activities such as banking, investing and insurance.

[4] For detailed discussion, see BCBS 2010, *Basel III: International Framework for Liquidity Risk Measurement, Standards and Monitoring*, and also European Commission, 2010, *Proposal for a Directive on Deposit Guarantee Schemes*.

Banking/Deposit Taking Financial Institutions	Index used for comparison	Other (Non-banking) Financial Institutions
Hold a license to offer banking services	*Official definition*	Offer financial services but does not hold an official bank license
Banking firms are connected institutionally through interbank market	*Financial interconnectedness*	This institution are stand-alone operators
There is the Companies Act / Banking Act or Regulation	*Incorporated under?*	The Companies Act
These are rooted in the fundamentals of banking	*Transformation of maturity & leverage*	Matching of liability and asset duration, partial acceptance of leverage
Deposits are permitted	*Demand deposits*	Not permitted to accept deposits
Inherent in banks: short-term	*Exposure to liquidity risk*	Inherent: long-term (e.g. insurance firms)
Highly regulated for both the market and the products	*Regulated activities*	Much non-regulated activity (country dependent) *
Permitted to create money	*Money creation*	Not permitted to create money (but offer some credit facilitation)
Critical to the constitution of the payment system in general	*Payment system*	Use parts of the payment system
Permitted	*Facility for deposit insurance*	Not permitted

**In the UK and the EU, investment firms and insurers are regulated both at an entity level as well as several of their activities also being regulated and supervised*

Fig. 9.2 Differences and similarities between banking and non-banking Financial Institutions (*Source* Compiled by the Author)

and alternative investment managers. In fact, some of these NBFIs are either subsidiaries or part of conglomerate that is owned by large banking firms.

In existing European law, the term "financial institution" is defined somewhat narrowly in that it excludes, for example, insurance companies. According to the ICB, the most suitable "starting point for those entities which should be considered 'financial' for the purposes of the ring-fence would be those whose deposits are proposed to be excluded from deposit insurance under the Deposit Guarantee Scheme Directive. As well as those which count directly as financial institutions, this includes investment firms, insurance undertakings, collective investment undertakings, pension and retirement funds" (ICB 2011, p. 58). Additionally, it is very important to make the distinction between banking, financial and non-banking financial institutions in order to define appropriate protected services to reduce the exposure of ring-fenced banks to failures elsewhere in the financial system. However, after much intense debate among the G20 and the EU, there is some agreement among regulators to use the term shadow banking with a definition aimed at eliminating all the "dark corners in the financial sector and extend" regulation and oversight to all systemically important financial institutions, instruments and markets (G20 2009a, b, 2011). According to the FSB (2011a) financial supervisors and regulators define other financial institutions or shadow banking as a system of credit intermediation that involves *entities* and *activities* outside the regular banking system. These comprised *entities* "which: raise funding with deposit-like characteristics; perform maturity and/or liquidity transformation; allow credit risk transfer; use direct or indirect leverage.[5] Shadow banking (i.e. Non-banks) activities, in particular securitisation, securities lending and repurchase transactions, constitute an important source of finance for financial entities" (EC 2013a, p. 3).

However, proponents and advocates for these institutions argue that these firms are in fact a key source of consumer credit (along with licensed banks) to households, businesses and the economy at large and hence, require effective corporate governance, supervision and regulation. The firms that are normally classified as "other financial institutions" include insurance firms, venture capitalists, hedge fund managers, currency exchanges, mutual funds and pension funds. These firms tend to offer a variety of financial services and products that are not necessarily suited to banking organisations, serve as a direct competition to banks, and on several occasions, specialise in sectors or groups that are unique. Figure 9.3 illustrates the financial market structure players using the United Kingdom as an example. It shows the value and the significance of these institutions in an advanced economy such as the United Kingdom.

Although the banking sector is the basis of the financial services group, other non-bank financial service sectors are also a key part of the primary drivers of a nation's economy and its development for providing prosperity (Burrows and Low 2015). It is critical in the provision and support of the free-flow of capital and liquidity in the financial marketplace. It is important to emphasise that when this part of the sector is performing

[5]The EC (2013a, p. 4) attempted to offer some sort of description in saying "these may include ad hoc entities such as securitisation vehicles or conduits, money market funds, investment funds that provide credit or are leveraged, such as certain hedge funds or private equity funds and financial entities that provide credit or credit guarantees, which are not regulated like banks or certain insurance or reinsurance undertakings that issue or guarantee credit products".

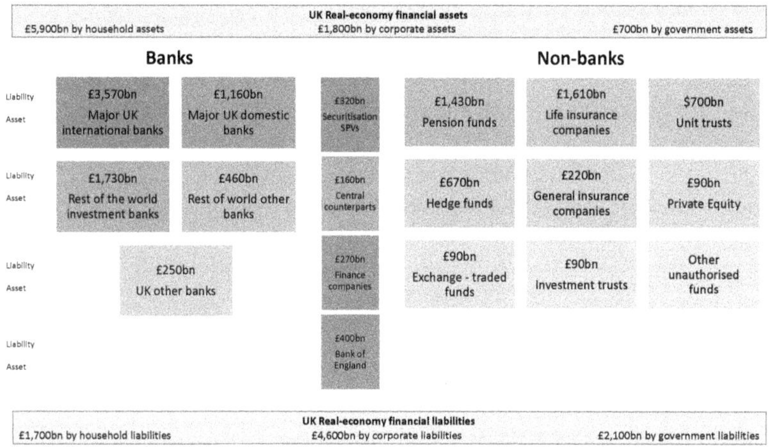

Fig. 9.3 The financial balance sheet of the UK economy in 2014 (*Source* Adapted from Bank of England Quarterly Bulletin 2015)

robustly, the economy keeps growing, and firms in this industry are better able to manage risk effectively. According to the IMF (2012), other financial institutions offer services to individuals and businesses that complement banking organisations. They can provide competition for banking firms in the provision of these services. While banks may offer a set of financial services as a package deal, other financial firms can either bundle (package) or unbundle and repackage these services, tailoring them to specific groups. Furthermore, some of these institutions can specialise in a particular sector and thereby gain an informational advantage that is unique (IMF 2012). It is further suggested that where an economy "having a multi-faceted financial system, which includes non-bank financial institutions, can protect economies from financial shocks and recover from those shocks". NBFIs provide multiple alternatives to transform an economy's savings into capital investment, which act as backup facilities should the primary form of intermediation fail. The causes of the global financial crisis of 2007/08 illustrate the seriousness of role played by non-bank financial institutions as many of these institutions' activities were implicated in the crisis (Turner 2009).

In fact, NBFIs is an interesting area to examine; it has connections to the regulated financial sector, must be observed due to its size, and presents the chance of systemic risk (along with the risk regarding potential evading of current rules and at times secretive accrual of large debt levels that these units can encourage). Reflecting on the size of non-banks in the financial system, both the complete size and also its portion of the whole financial sector internationally, allows you to see that elements of its make-up could be significant within the system. For example, the FSB (2012) research using the statistical proxied as "other financial intermediation" show that value of non-banks (shadow banking) assets is about half the size of the regulated banking system globally. Specifically, the overall value in 2011 was EUR 51,000 billion with a geographical distribution that is concentrated in the United States (around EUR 17,500 billion) and in the EU (Eurozone with EUR 16,800 billion and the United Kingdom with EUR 6800 billion).

Another area that could serve to heighten the level of risk is regarding the high rate of interconnectedness between the rest of the financial sector and the non-banks (previously called shadow banking system), where the regulated banking system being one of the most interconnected. The shadow banking system has the power to negatively impact sectors that are governed by the highest standards through the mismanagement of any areas of limitation or the weakening of a core element of the system. The overriding aim is to ensure the integrity of the market is maintained and improved through ensuring the chance of regulatory arbitrage is small. It also sets out the need for implementing effective management for any systemic risks that could negatively impact the financial sector. These actions will serve to reaffirm the trust of both consumers and savers. The instability of the financial system in countries that do not have efficient regulations can be magnified by non-bank financial institutions. The NFBIs that are part of the credit intermediation (i.e. shadow banking system) are all lightly regulated, this is in contradiction to some other NFBI's who are not. Regulators mostly disregarded structured investment vehicles, hedge funds and other such organisations, focusing their NBFI attention on the supervision of insurance organisations and pension funds in the run up to the financial crisis. Reflecting on the potential impact of this more widely, the stability of the whole financial system would be put at significant risk if a high percentage of it consists of NBFIs that are conducting business mostly without government supervision or regulation. The gaps that exist in the regulation and supervision (corporate governance included) of NBFIs can cause a number of negative outfalls including overpricing of assets, loan defaults and the collapse of asset prices.

9.6 Corporate Governance and Disclosures as it Applies to Non-banking Financial Institutions

9.6.1 *Legal Frameworks and Regulation of NBFIs*

How are Non-banking Financial Institutions Governed? Ever since the financial crisis in 2008, there has been numerous assertions made in relation to other financial organisations, some of these claims reflect either the state of reality, some are just a myth or illusions that are not based on facts and others reflect emotional thoughts from politicians based on public angers. As such, countless papers and policies have been proposed, discussed and published on nearly every aspect of banking and finance. The bulk of this attention almost certainly springs from the financial crisis as a powerful reminder of the importance of the financial system. The crisis in fact has altered into a grim reality the academic proclamation that economic health cannot exist without a well-functioning financial system. Yet in the face of all these investigations and assertions, other financial institutions continue annoyingly enigmatic. Notwithstanding, for almost a century of determined studies and intermittent financial crises, the connections between the corporate governance of banks and non-banks, their individual performance and the long-running stability of the financial system are still not well understood (Mehran and Mollineaux 2012). One key myth that some scholars, politicians and some other stakeholders have made is the notion that other financial institutions or NBFI are not regulated or governed. On the contrary, financial institutions (both banks and non-banks) are governed by several different key mechanisms, and there is a core framework of taxes, laws, stock exchange listing requirements and social customs that companies have to adhere to—there is an added layer for these institutions however, with both supervisory actions and regulations that are specific to their context. Both internal governors (e.g. risk officers and board of directors) and external governors (e.g. regulators or legislators etc.) have the power to influence all key decisions a company makes. In the United States, the United Kingdom and the EU, NBFIs are regulated at both the entity level as well as the activities they are authorised to undertake. Several of the sub-sector markets that the NBFIs operates are also regulated. For example, in the United Kingdom, NBFIs are subject to both prudential and financial conduct regulations and supervisions. Prudential Regulation Authority regulates around 1500 banks, building societies, credit unions, insurers and major investment firms. The Financial Conduct Authority is the conduct regulator for 59,000 financial services firms and financial markets in the United Kingdom and the prudential supervisor for 49,000 firms, setting specific standards for 19,000 firms.

In the United States, there are various laws and regulations in addition to state laws that are meant to be regulating the supposed unregulated NBFIs. For example, the Security Exchange Act of 1934 focuses on listed companies regarding establishing laws to provide governance of security transactions on secondary markets. It also sought to regulate the stock exchanges and broker-dealers so that the public who were investing were better protected. The act enabled the creation of the Security Exchange Commission with regulatory and disclosure enforcement powers. Also, the 1940 Investment Company Act and Investment Advisors Act legislations passed by the US congress that focuses on regulation and supervision of investment funds, trading in securities, reinvestment and companies whose own securities are presented to the investing public to minimise conflict of interest all affects not only banks but also NBFIs. NBFI industries are extremely diverse, ranging from large multi-national corporations to small, independent businesses that offer financial services only as an ancillary component to their primary business. The range of products and services offered, and the customer bases served by NBFIs, are equally diverse. As a result of this diversity, some NBFIs may be lower risk and some may be higher risk for money laundering. This make it very difficult and challenging to have effective governance laws and supervisory regimes. The challenges posed by NBFIs should not be construed as no regulation but rather how effective should both regulation and supervision be drawn without stymieing their growth and innovation in the financial market. As discussed in the previous section, the utmost significant difference between non-banking financial institution and banks is that these firms don't take demand deposits, and do not have a full banking license or are not supervised by a national or international banking regulatory agency (e.g. Insurance firms don't have an equivalent of EBA) and according to many, observation can be problematic. In Asia, according to the World Bank, approximately 30% total assets of South Korea's financial system was held in NBFIs as of 1997 (Carmichael and Pomerleano 2002) and it was suggested in a report that the lack of regulation in this area was claimed to be one reason for the 1997 Asian Financial Crisis. Within the EU, the Payment Services Directive (PSD) is a regulatory initiative from the European Commission to regulate payment services and payment service providers throughout the EU and European Economic Area (EEA). The PSD describes which type of organisations can provide payment services in Europe[6] (credit institutions (i.e. banks)) and certain authorities (e.g. Central Banks, government bodies), Electronic Money Institutions (EMI), and also creates the new category of Payment Institutions. Organisations that are not credit institutions or EMI, can apply for an authorisation as Payment Institution in any EU country of their URL choice (where they are established) and then passport their payment services into other Member States across the EU. The academic studies in banking and finance are besieged with various examples of banks and other financial institutions failures which can be attributed to regulation and some form of governance weaknesses in the last 40 or more years (see Hughes and MacDonald 2002; Goldstein and Turner 1996; Penrose 2004).

There are a number of requirements that NBSIs-D must adhere to—these include Exposure norms, Capital adequacy, ALM discipline, reporting rules and Liquid assets maintenance. NBFIs-ND had to adhere to minimal regulation in comparison until 2006. Non-deposit-taking NBFCs who have 1 billion or above worth of assets have been classified as Systemically Important Non-Deposit-taking NBFCs (NBFCs-ND-SI) since the 1st April 2007. Further to this, additional regulations have been applied to them (e.g. exposure norms, capital adequacy, etc.) and also, at times, asset liability management (ALM) reporting and disclosure norms too.

Banks have predominantly been the core focus of the empirical study in this book because of the depth, challenge and wide range of complicated problems of corporate governance in this particular industry. I fully recognise and acknowledge the corporate governance challenges faced by other financial institutions, which I aim to unpick in future studies, but the layers of intense regulation, the "too big to fail" belief among other things dictated the scope of this book. The financial crisis of 2007/8 highlighted the need for improved financial sector disclosures and its reporting information by not only banks but also non-bank financial institutions.

[6] In the United States and the EU, depending on the Liability Structure, OFIS or NBFIs have been divided into two categories. 1. Category "A" companies (NBFIs accepting public deposits or NBFIs-D), and 2. Category "B" companies (NBFIs not raising public deposits or NBFIs-ND).

Effective policies and conventions including rules are essentially important in running businesses sustainably. Corporate scandals like Barings, Enron, Northern Rock and WorldCom show just what can happen when a business goes too far in pursuing its "self-interest and breaks its own internal guidelines". Corporate governance, encompassing all the principles of open and responsible management, is a way of ensuring that a company keeps within clear ethical lines. Although, it has been top of the policymaker's agenda for some time now, nevertheless can be a challenge for businesses on several levels especially in the areas of NBFIs supervisions. As mentioned above, non-bank financial institutions provide a valuable alternative to bank financing and helps to support real economic activity. Nonetheless, it is now acknowledged that "if such financial intermediation roles involve services and activities that are typically performed by banks, such as maturity/liquidity transformation and/or the creation of leverage, it can become a source of systemic risk for the entire financial system" (FSB 2019a, b). This risk can be compounded where non-bank activities have links to the banking system posing a fundamental issue around effective corporate governance and accountability framework with respect to the safety and soundness of the financial market. In addition, Mehran and Mollineaux (2012, p. 221) opined that "for an entity to govern financial institutions, it must possess both the ability and the will to do so. Much work has examined the influence of boards of directors and market forces upon financial and nonfinancial firms. A related line of literature examines the incentives that regulators face when choosing both when and how to intervene in markets. Just as principal-agent problems exist between the owners and management of firms, there may also be a disconnect between the interests of society and of regulators as the designated protectors of public interest (Levine 2011)". The implication of their assertion is the confirmation that regulators or financial have a key role to play in the affairs of NBFIs. It is interesting to note that irrespective of their assertion, NBFIs are also subject to internal corporate governance through boards of directors and external governance through market forces (Turner 2009; Walker 2009; G20 2009a, b, 2011).

Several NBFIs undertake credit intermediation that involves entities and activities outside the regular banking system. Although this sub-sector plays an important role in financing the economy, its operation outside of traditional banking regulations raises concerns over the risks it poses to the financial system, and requires regulation because of its size, its close links to the regulated financial sector and the systemic risks that it poses. There is also a need to prevent them being used for regulatory arbitrage. Since 2008 and when the recent financial crisis began, the EC (2013b) has undertaken a comprehensive reform of the financial services sector in Europe. However, the benefits achieved by the new rules could be diminished by risks moving to less regulated sectors. According to Bank of England (2018), around 50% of the global financial sector is made up of non-bank financial intermediation; in the United Kingdom, private non-financial organisations have exchanged funding from banks for tradable securities. There has also been a sizeable rise in the share of electronic trading over the last several years within financial markets. The non-bank financial sector along with the developing market infrastructure has required real robustness to be able to deliver funding to the real economy. This strength has the additional benefit of making sure that the resultant stresses are absorbed as opposed to intensifying. The importance of truly understanding risks that result from non-bank financial institution activity and the market infrastructure that supports it will be crucial for both policymakers and researchers to be able to adequately assess the impact of these changes on financial stability and provide effective corporate governance and accountability disclosures.

9.6.2 *Accountability Governance and Supervision of NBFIs*

The role of boards of directors whether in a unitary or a two-tier corporate governance model cannot be underestimated for all financial institutions. There are three core roles conducted by the boards of directors that underpin the crucial role they play in governance of financial institutions; these are the assessment of risk-taking, the choice of strategy and finally the monitoring to ensure the most important positions, such as the CEO are filled by individuals with the skills and abilities to take the strategy forward. These elements have the power to impact the level of success an organisation reaches. Many financial conduct supervisors and regulatory authorities promote safety and soundness in financial institutions including NBFIs. For example, US regulators have looked to boards of directors to play an important role in guiding these institutions towards prudent behaviour. Although the institutions management is normally called upon to exercise day-to-day responsibility over their affairs, the board has traditionally been seen by supervisors as a source of independent oversight of management decision-making. The vital corporate management decisions such as strategy, risk appetite, organisation and internal controls are all regarded as suitable matters for directors of board to review. Regulators also expect boards to actively monitor progress in addressing control weaknesses cited by the regulators or other control groups, such as internal and external auditors (Mehran and Mollineaux (2012). Table 9.1 shows the current corporate governance laws and applicable requirements governing non-banking financial institutions.

In the financial services industry probably more than in other industries, risk governance is of supreme significance to the stability and profitability of the firm. Without an ability to properly understand,

Table 9.1 Corporate governance requirement and issues affecting NBFIs in selected Jurisdictions

Corporate governance policy issues			*US*	*UK*	*EU*	*Japan*
Board roles and responsibility						
1	a	Audit committee	R, LR, PLI	R, CGC, O, PLI	R	R
	b	Risk management committee	NR	R, CGC, O, PLI	R	NR
	c	Remuneration committee	R, LR	R, CGC, O, PLI	R, O	R
	d	Nomination committee	L, PLI	R, CGC, O, PLI	R, O	R
Disclosures and transparency						
2	a	Disclosure of financial market risk	R	R	R	R
	b	Disclosure of risk relating to off-balance sheet transactions and derivatives	R	R	R	R
	c	Disclosure of business conduct and risk	R	R	R	R
	d	Disclosure policies relating to how RPTs are identified and managed	R	R	PLI	PLI
Accountability to stakeholders						
3	a	Disclosure to shareholders	LR, R	R, CGC	R, O	CGC
	b	Disclosure to other stakeholders	NR	O	O	O

Key: R = Law/Regulation; LR = Listing Rules; CGC = Corporate Governance Code; O = Other; NR = Not required ID = Independent Director NED = Non-Executive director PLI = Publicly listed institutions

Source Created by the author

measure, manage, price and mitigate risk, FIs are destined to underperform or be unsuccessful. Effective risk governance requires a dedicated set of risk leaders in the boardroom and executive suite, as well as robust and appropriate risk frameworks, systems and processes. Since 2007, numerous expectations have been placed on the boards of other financial institutions in regard to both publicly listed firms and non-listed firms, signalling the significant role they have in our economy. As it can be noted, a number of these requirements comes from federal law and/or regulations in the United States, financial supervisory regulators from national government within the EU including the United Kingdom, and international agencies such as the World Bank, FSB and OECD). Others are included in guidance provided to boards by the bank regulatory agencies (see, for example, The Clearing House 2012). In the United States, boards of directors of other financial institutions (same as banks) can be held accountable for exercising the same duties that are assigned to all corporate boards by state corporate law. Chief among these are the duty of loyalty (putting the company's interests ahead of self-interest) and the duty of care (using the care ordinary and prudent persons would in similar circumstances). Interestingly directors are not expected to consider the interests of other stakeholders (e.g. creditors and taxpayers) when making decisions. Although successful corporate prosecutions are often rare (Valukas 2010),[7] yet directors may be legally liable for failing to fulfil their fiduciary duty, but in practice, proving this negligence is unbelievably problematic. In the United Kingdom, applicable to NBFIs is the statutory corporate governance responsibility under the Companies Act 2006 (CA 2006), which is also supplemented by the "comply or explain" principles of the Combined Code which is overseen and maintained by the regulator, FRC and by financial regulation under the Financial Services and Markets Act 2000 (FSMA). In fact, the applicability of the UK corporate governance laws and regulation to other financial institutions or NBFIs was established by the final Walker Report in 2009.

[7] According to Mehran and Mollineaux (2012, p. 222), "under Delaware corporation law, directors can be found liable only if their lack of monitoring is "egregious ... The Delaware courts have called this type of claim—referred to as a Caremark claim—'possibly the most difficult theory in corporation law upon which a plaintiff might hope to win a judgment'" (see Valukas 2010, p. 55, and references therein). As of January 2012, the FDIC has filed claims against 161 former directors and officers of banks that failed during the financial crisis period (Fed. Depos. Ins. Comm. 2012)".

Although, the original scope of Walker Review was based on UK banks, the terms of reference were subsequently extended so that the Review should also identify where its recommendations are applicable to other financial institutions to reflect the significant role these institutions contribute to the economy. As Walker stated "*The principal focus of this Review throughout has been on banks, but many of the issues arising, and associated conclusions and recommendations, are relevant if in lesser degree for other major financial institutions such as life assurance companies. The recommendations in relation to institutional investors and fund managers were prepared with particular regard to their shareholdings in banks and other financial institutions but have wider relevance for their holdings in other UK companies*" (Walker 2009, p. 5). Several of Walker's recommendations were reflected in the updated 2010 and 2012 UK code of corporate governance. Walker made 39 specific recommendations and a number of these particularly affect other financial institutions and not just only banks. For example, "fund managers and other institutions authorised by the FSA to undertake investment business should signify on their websites their commitment to the Principles of Stewardship. Such reporting should confirm that their mandates from life assurance, pension fund and other major clients normally include provisions in support of engagement activity and should describe their policies on engagement and how they seek to discharge the responsibilities that commitment to the Principles entails. Where a fund manager or institutional investor is not ready to commit and to report in this sense, it should provide, similarly on the website, a clear explanation of the reasons for the position it is taking" (Walker 2009, p. 14).

Several of the policies and directives that the EU has provided seek to address specific issues also affecting other financial institutions, including items such as enhancing board effectiveness, shareholder protection rights, enhancing corporate transparency and disclosure and building engagement with shareholders and stewardship. The corporate governance issues were also identified as an important area to focus on in the context of implementation of the EU Commission Action Plan on financing a sustainable growth, and in particular its Action 10. EU company law rules also address corporate governance issues, focusing on relationships between a company's management, board, shareholders and other stakeholders, and therefore, on the ways the company is managed and controlled. These include Shareholders rights—Directive 2007/36/EC, which sets out certain rights for shareholders in listed companies and this Directive was amended by Directive (EU) 2017/828, with the objective of encouraging more long-term engagement of shareholders. Additionally, the 2018 Commission Implementing Regulation (EU) 2018/1212 lays down minimum requirements as regards shareholder identification, the transmission of information and the facilitation of the exercise of shareholders rights all affecting large systemic important other financial institutions. Furthermore, there are specific rules on corporate governance and remuneration applicable to banks and insurance and investment firms. The aim of these rules is to curb excessive risk-taking and thereby help ensure financial stability. Guidelines on corporate governance and compensation in banks and systemic investment firms can be found in the Capital Requirements Directive (Directive 2013/36/EU as amended by Directive 2019/878/EU) and the Capital Requirements Regulation (Regulation No 575/2013 as amended by Regulation No 2019/876). Rules on corporate governance and remuneration in non-systemic investment firms can be found in the Investment Firms Directive (Directive 2019/2034) and the Investment Firms Regulation (Regulation 2019/2033). Overall, the EC maintain that, while systemic investment firms (including large NBFIs) stay under the banking rules (i.e. there currently no NBFI specific regulator akin to bank), non-systemic investment firms are subject to a separate regime. This according to the EC where it has established that the prudential structure for banks was not well adapted to the business model of these investment firms and other significant non-banking firms.

9.7 Governance Policy Issues Affecting Non-banking Financial Institutions

The aim of this subsection is to see if there are any wider learnings that policymakers could adopt to improve best practices of corporate governance of other financial institutions overall. The financial crisis did establish that the following themes may have significantly contributed to the causes of the crunch, namely: (1) Risk management and internal control requirements; (2) Compensation and misalignment of enticement arrangement in financial institutions; (3) Board behaviour and competence; (4) The ineffectiveness of supervision and regulatory oversight; (5) Misleading information provided by rating agencies and (6) Shareholder engagement in scrutinising boards of directors (Acharya 2009; Ashby

2008; UNCTAD 2010; Walker 2009). Although, many of the post-crisis research and investigations have largely focused on banks, several non-banking institutions were also directly responsible for causing and exacerbating the crisis even further. It is interesting to note that, on the publication of its Global Monitoring Report on Non-Bank Financial Intermediation 2019, Klaas Knot, Chair of the FSB Standing Committee on Assessment of Vulnerabilities, said: "*Non-banks play an increasingly important role in the global financial system. The FSB's monitoring report provides a significant resource for authorities to assess trends and risks from NBFI. Such information is essential for a forward-looking, system-wide oversight framework*" (FSB 2020). The report encompasses data up to the end of 2018 and comes from 29 jurisdictions (80% of global GDP). It showcases the FSB's annual monitoring results focusing both on global trends and also risks from non-bank financial intermediation (NBFI). This forms a core part of the policy framework of the FSB and pays particularly close attention to areas of NBFIs that are most likely to cause any bank-like financial stability risks and/or regulatory arbitrage.

In addition, the important suggestions for improving banks corporate governance issues also affect NBFIs governance including clearer separation of the management and control function; the need for the establishment of a separate risk committee of the board or an independent chief risk officer; dealing with the problem of complex or opaque structure and organisation and group-wide corporate governance in single entities as well as in the group in the area of financial reporting and disclosures. Suitable supervisory law conditions are needed for the internal procedures of other financial institutions, specifically for risk management, internal control and compliance, and internal and external auditing. Establishing supervisory fit and proper tests for senior executives, the management and major shareholders is beneficial. Qualifications and experience of board members of non-bank financial institutions are more important than independence. These and other requirements of the regulation and supervision of banks and other financial institutions concerning good governance are challenging but are mandatory for regulated industries such as financial institutions (for example, insurers, investment firms and asset managers). Since the crisis, NBFIs face several key potential challenges that affect their corporate governance and disclosure practices in the financial market. Although there are many challenges in this area, a few have been selected that I would like to touch upon:

Firstly, disclosure of accurate accounting information matters greatly to stakeholders. Financial and regulatory reporting are essential for effective banking supervision and financial stability. It is vital for providing and ensuring corporate governance and its mechanisms of accountability are efficient and accurate to its stakeholders. Financial reporting information can be said to be transparent if it delivers accurate insights into the financial position and performance of a company, and if it reveals any risks the company is facing. Therefore, the information provided by non-bank companies must be relevant and understandable, should be comparable across jurisdictions and that the important role of NBFIs, especially those that are regarded as credit institutions for the public at large, needs to be explicitly acknowledged in the reporting framework. Reporting requirements should therefore be designed in such a way that they do not endanger financial stability.

For the purpose of transparency in corporate governance, it is vital to differentiate between *financial* reporting and *regulatory* reporting. Financial reporting information, on the one hand, is derived from accounting data and published via audited financial statements. It primarily targets market participants, in particular equity investors and other providers of risk capital. In the EU, listed firms are required to prepare their financial statements in accordance with International Financial Reporting Standards (IFRSs), as adopted by the European Commission (on the other hand, the United States, still using the US Generally Accepted Accounting Principles (US GAAP) making global harmonisation challenging. By contrast, regulatory reporting comprises, among other things, the IFRS-based financial reporting templates for supervisory purposes (known as "FINREP"), and the capital requirements and own funds reporting templates (known as "COREP"), based on the new EU framework for banking regulation under the Capital Requirements Regulation and Capital Requirements Directive (CRR/CRD IV). The aim is to provide supervisors with all relevant information on the financial institutions' risk exposures, as well as their capital and liquidity positions. Financial reporting forms the basis for regulatory reporting. The main difference between financial reporting and regulatory reporting is the audience: whereas financial reporting is mainly targeted towards investors and creditors, the main addressees of regulatory reporting are banking supervisors. For this reason, financial reporting and regulatory reporting also differ in their "scope of application": unlike financial reporting, regulatory reporting has a "narrower" focus, meaning that only "credit institutions" and "investment firms" are required to follow these rules. This explains why most of conduct and governance reporting has largely been slow to evolve to much broader stakeholders beyond regulators.

During the financial crisis, at least three accounting practices as part of the weaknesses in governance were cited as potentially obscuring the actual risks of banks and other financial institutions and providing adverse incentives to banks: (a) the excessive use of fair value accounting; (b) the delayed recognition of credit losses or "impairment charges"; (c) the inadequate treatment for exposures to "special purpose entities (SPEs)". Prior to the crisis, these exposures were often not properly accounted for. However, these lessons led the G20 to demand various revisions to the current accounting practices in 2009. In summary, the G20 called for changes related to a reform of fair value measurement, the introduction of a more forward-looking approach to the recognition of credit losses and a review of off-balance sheet financing. Also, the G20 made the case for more comparability in the area of financial reporting, by requesting the development of a single set of high-quality financial reporting standards. Effective communication between banks and non-banks and stakeholders, including both conduct and prudential regulators, requires more fundamental reconsiderations than just "piecemeal" revisions to individual financial reporting standards. In addition to transparency, comparability of reporting is essential if the European Commission Bank are to achieve the goal of effective communication.

Second, policy challenge regarding the designing of effective corporate governance that addresses ethical and behavioural aspects of directors (i.e. not specifically creating more rules or codes). Boards behaviour and practices in a number of large other financial institutions, in addition to banks, were implicated in the financial crisis. In fact, this is not new to in the academic literature about financial institutions failures over the last several decades. Values and culture may be the keystone of financial institutions governance because they drive behaviours of people throughout the organisation and the ultimate effectiveness of its governance arrangements. Eventually, any effective supervisory policy response to future financial crises necessitates mechanisms that help to prevent them from occurring in the first place. We believe that these mechanisms should be emphasising behavioural and ethical changes, identifying and addressing the underlying preconditions that are likely to form the basis for future crises from the underlying behaviours. Suitable structures and processes are a necessary but not a sufficient condition for good governance, which essentially depends also on patterns of behaviour. The pattern of corporate management behavioural aspects depends in turn on the extent to which values such as integrity, independence of thought and respect for the views of others are embedded in the institutional culture. In so doing, the ideal solution should not just be based on more prescription requirement, but the attention ought to be on raising risk management standards and creating the right sort of incentives for senior executive and stakeholders so that financial services firms are not only better prepared for the next crisis, but may also be able to stop it from happening in the first place (Ashby and Waite 2008).

A third challenge to policymakers is around appropriate regulatory and supervision changes for monitoring NBFIs (NBFI entities are diverse and have multiple products and services—most of them are very complex, innovative and opaque in the financial market). Following the financial crisis in 2008, in response to a G20 Leaders' demand in 2010, the FSB implemented a two-pronged strategy in an attempt to remedy the financial stability risks posed by non-bank financial intermediation (previously called shadow banking) namely: "(a) Monitoring – an annual system-wide monitoring exercise to assess global trends and risks from non-bank financial intermediation; and (b) Policymaking – developing a range of policies to address financial stability risks from non-bank financial intermediation" (FSB 2011b). The purpose of the FSB's implementation strategy is to ensure that non-bank financial intermediation is subject to appropriate oversight and regulation to address bank-like risks to financial stability emerging outside of the regular banking system, while not inhibiting sustainable non-bank financing models that do not pose such risks. The approach is designed to be proportionate to financial stability risks, focusing on those activities that are material to the system, using as a starting point those that were a source of problems during the crisis.

Since 2011, although a few challenges remain, the FSB has made great progress in both strategies. For example, FSB has been conducting an annual monitoring exercise since 2011 to assess global trends and risks in non-bank financial intermediation (NBFI). The monitoring exercise starts by casting the net wide to take a view of assets across all financial sectors and then focuses on the subset of non-bank financial intermediation with increased potential for systemic risks, and/or regulatory arbitrage. Non-bank financial entities are classified into five economic functions (or activities), each of which involves bank-like financial stability risks (i.e. credit intermediation that involves maturity/liquidity transformation, leverage or imperfect credit risk transfer). It is important to note that the classification allows national and international authorities to separately assess existing policy tools to address financial stability risks from non-bank financial intermediation and identify any residual risks or activities that may warrant policy responses. In addition, The FSB since 2011 has also been coordinating and adding to the advancement of policies in five areas where oversight and regulation need to be strengthened to mitigate the potential systemic risks associated with non-bank financial intermediation, namely; "(1) mitigating spillover risks between the banking system and the system of non-bank financial intermediation; (2) reducing the susceptibility of money market funds to 'runs'; (3) improving transparency and aligning incentives associated with securitisation; (4) dampening procyclicality and other financial stability risks associated with securities financing transactions such as repos and securities lending; and (5) assessing and mitigating systemic risks posed by other non-bank financial entities and activities". The FSB believed that if it can overcome the challenges in regard to the above policy issues and is able to encourage national government to implement a set of policies, they should be able to mitigate bank-like financial stability risks from non-bank financial institutions and enhance its resilience so that it can support economic growth sustainably (FSB 2017a, b).

Furthermore, technological and globalisation changes have also opened the door to new challenges in non-bank financial institutions' services in the market. Countries and companies in a globalised world have been dependent on international capital markets and funds for credit and the speed in which technological advancement facilitates such transactions (Carney 2013). On the one hand, and in good times, this means a ready pool of capital available for development (i.e. free flowing of liquidity in the financial market), which helps improve standards of living nationally, infrastructure upgrade and productivity enhancement. On the other hand, and in bad times, it means a drying up of the global capital pool leading to a credit crunch. In fact, such a crunch can be devastating to both national and global goals leading up to corporate failures and bankruptcies and rising unemployment. Examples of such impact are what we observed in the 2007/8 global financial crisis, the Latin American debt crisis in the 1980s and the Asian Contagion of 1997–1998 which exemplifies this negative view of globalisation and interconnectedness of banks and non-banks (Hughes and MacDonald 2003). Another challenge area that relates to globalisation and technological innovation is the spread of financial fraud and especially money laundering. The more rapid the ability to transmit and receive credit, the more difficult it is for supervisors, regulators and law enforcement to deal with the illicit flow of capital and practices by corporate management. Also, the nature of the definition of non-banking activities further complicates the financial system in the area of cross-border lending, supplemented by other form financing facilitation such as bonds (debt), equity, foreign exchange trading, exotic products and derivatives.

9.8 Conclusion

The financial services sector provides financial services to people and corporations. This segment of the economy is made up of a variety of financial firms including banks, investment houses, lenders, finance companies, real estate brokers and insurance companies. The financial services industry is probably the most important sector of the economy, leading the world in terms of earnings and equity market capitalisation. As mentioned above, non-bank financial intermediation provides a valuable alternative to bank financing and helps to support real economic activity. We now know that the nature of corporate governance of banking and other financial institutions varies substantially from conventional corporate governance of firms. More importantly, for financial organisations, the scope of corporate governance extends further than the traditional stockholders or shareholders to include other key interested stakeholders such as regulators, supervisors, debtholders, insurance policy holders and other creditors. The reality and the practical world in which these institutions operate means that the involvement of stakeholders and shareholders will depend on national and international rules, laws and practices as well as the individual organisation's approach.

Firms must disclose information accurately if they wish for mechanisms of governance to work effectively. As discussed in this book, the levels of quality differ when it comes to disclosure about stakeholder issues, and companies have been working to respond to changes in expectations. With the introduction of the 2018 Code and updated Guidance on the Strategic Report in the United Kingdom, the level of expectation around sharing exactly who are their stakeholders, the methods of engagement utilised, the impact this has on their strategy etc. has risen. Therefore, financial firms must take into consideration the views and requirements from various stakeholders including shareholders in the smooth running of their firms to achieve long-term sustainability. This means that stakeholders' interest cannot and must not be ignored within the context of effective corporate governance in ensuring broader management accountability by financial institutions. Malfunctions in the corporate governance of banking and other financial institutions contributed to the 2008–2009 financial crisis which impacted significantly on a variety of stakeholders nationally and internationally.

Thinking about the financial system as a series of interconnected balance sheets is a useful framework for macroeconomic analysis. Just as every transaction has a buyer and a seller, so every financial contract is an asset for one party and a liability for another. These stocks of wealth and debt create connections between individuals and different sectors of the economy. Macroeconomic policymakers need to consider both sides of these connections. Within the United Kingdom, building on the work in the National Accounts (of the United Kingdom), the Bank of England needs to be able to interpret the interconnections associated with this financial wealth and debt. Three core areas make up this analysis: (a) The need to fully digest the intricate structures of non-bank financial companies (for example, in 1968, sectoral balance sheets were incorporated into international standards for National Accounts. Developments in financial systems have moved on since this time, but as the United Kingdom has a substantial non-bank financial sector, the United Kingdom has a need to work out a way to best include this within standard reporting); (b) It is vitally important to fully comprehend the connection of these subsectors of the financial system link to wider areas of the economy and (c) Unpicking the differences between these groups to allow fully rounded and comprehensive policy analysis in order to enable effective implementation of corporate governance and improve disclosure of NBBFI activities in a transparent manner. The corporate governance of Non-Banking Financial Corporation (NBFIs) is different and unique as compared to other organisations but similar to banking institutions in a number of ways. This is because the activities of the NBFIs are less transparent. Thus, it becomes difficult for regulators, shareholders and creditors to monitor the activities of the NBFIs. Additionally, these financial institutions also differ from most other companies in terms of the complexity and range of their business risks, and the consequences if these risks are poorly managed. Furthermore, and insofar as directors of these institutions continue to use stock prices and value maximisation as a benchmark against which management is judged, financial institutions may continue to engage in systemically risky activities.

References

Aburaya, R. K. (2012). *The relationship between corporate governance and environmental disclosure: UK evidence*. Durham thesis, Durham University.

Acharya, V. (2009). A theory of systemic risk and design of prudential bank regulation. *Journal of Financial Stability, 5*(3), 224–255.

Ashby, S. (2008). Operational risk: Learning lessons from non-financial organisations. *Journal of Risk Management in Financial Institutions, 1*(4).

Ashby, S., & Waite, N. (2008). *The turner review on the global banking crisis: A response from the financial services forum*.

Bank of England (BOE). (2018, November). *Financial stability report* (Issue No 44).

BCBS. (2010). *Principles for enhancing corporate governance*. Basel: Basel Committee on Banking Supervision.

Belcredi, M., & Ferrarini, G. (2013). Corporate boards, incentive pay and shareholder activism in Europe: Main issues and policy perspectives. In M. Belcredi & G. Ferrarini (Eds.), *Boards and shareholders in European listed companies. Facts, context and post-crisis reforms*. Cambridge University Press.

Blair, M. (1995). *Ownership and control: Rethinking corporate governance for the twenty-first century*. Washington: Brookings Institution.

Brennan, N. M., & Solomon, J. (2008). Corporate governance, accountability and mechanisms of accountability: An overview. *Accounting, Auditing & Accountability Journal, 21*(7), 885–906.

Burrows, O., & Low, K. (2015). *Mapping the UK Financial System*. Bank of England Quarterly Bulletin.

Bush, O., Knott, S., & Peacock, C. (2014). Why is the UK banking system so big and is that a problem? *Bank of England Quarterly Bulletin, 54*(4), 385–395.

Carmichael, J., & Pomerleano, M. (2002). *The development and regulation of non-bank financial institutions*. Washington, DC: World Bank.

Carney, M. (2013). *The UK at the heart of a renewed globalisation*. Bank of England, London. Available at www.bankofengland.co.uk/publications/Documents/speeches/2013/speech690.pdf.

Chartered Institute of Management Accountants (CIMA). (2008). *Fundamentals of ethics, corporate governance and business law* (2nd ed.). BPP Learning Media Ltd.

Ciancanelli, P., & Gonzalez, J. A. (2000). Corporate governance in banking: A conceptual Framework. *Social Science Research Network*, European Financial Management Association Conference, pp. 2–24.

European Commission (EC). (2013a). *Communication from the commission to the council and the parliament. Shadow banking—Addressing new sources of risk in the financial sector*. Brussels: European Commission.

European Commission (EC). (2013b). *Strengthening oversight and regulation of shadow banking: Policy framework for strengthening oversight and regulation of shadow banking entities*. Brussels: European Commission.

European Commission (EC). (2014). *Directive of the European parliament and of the council: Amending directive 2007/36/EC*. Proposal. Brussels: European Commission.

Fama, E. F., & Jensen, M. C. (1983a). Separation of ownership and control. *Journal of Law and Economics, 26*(2), 301–325.

Fama, E. F., & Jensen, M. C. (1983b). Agency problems and residual claims. *Journal of Law and Economics, 26*(2), 327–349.

Ferrarini, G. (2017). *Understanding the role of corporate governance in financial institutions: A Research Agenda* (ECGI Working Paper Series in Law).

Financial Reporting Council (FRC). (2009a, December 1). *FRC launches proposed reforms to the UK corporate governance code* (Press Notice FRC PN 287).

Financial Reporting Council (FRC). (2009b, July). *Review of the effectiveness of the combined code—Progress report and second consultation*. London: FRC.

Financial Stability Board (FSB). (2011a). *Intensity and effectiveness of SIFI supervision: Progress report on implementing the recommendations on enhanced supervision*. Basel: Financial Stability Board.

Financial Stability Board. (2011b, October). *Shadow banking: Strengthening oversight and regulation*.

FSB. (2012, November). *Global shadow banking monitoring report 2012*.

FSB. (2013, August). *Strengthening oversight and regulation of shadow banking: Policy framework for strengthening oversight and regulation of shadow banking entities*.

FSB. (2014, October). *Global shadow banking monitoring report 2014*.

FSB. (2017a, May). *Global shadow banking monitoring report 2016*.

FSB. (2017b). *Assessment of shadow banking activities, risks, and the adequacy*.

FSB. (2019a, February). *Global shadow banking monitoring report 2018*.

FSB. (2019b, February). *Global monitoring report of non-bank financial intermediation 2019*.

Financial Stability Board (FSB). (2020, January). *Global monitoring report on non-bank financial intermediation 2019*.

Goldstein, M., & Turner, P. (1996). *Banking crises in emerging economies: Origins and policy options*. Basel: Bank for International Settlements.

Gray, R., Kouhy, R., & Lavers, S. (1995a). Constructing a research database of social and environmental reporting by UK companies. *Accounting, Auditing & Accountability Journal, 8*(2), 78–101.

Gray, R., Kouhy, R., & Lavers, S. (1995b). Corporate social and environmental reporting: A review of the literature and a longitudinal study of UK disclosure. *Accounting, Auditing & Accountability Journal, 8*(2), 47–77.

Group of 20 (G20). (2009a, September 5). *G20 banking statement*.

Group of 20 (G20). (2009b, April 2). *Declaration on strengthening the financial system*.

Group of 20 (G20). (2011, November). *Cannes summit final declaration: Building our common future: Renewed collective action for the benefit of all*. Cannes.

Hopt, K. J. (2013). Better governance of financial institutions. *ECGI Working Paper Series in Law* (Working Paper N°. 207/2013).

House of Commons Select Committee. (2009a). *Banking crisis: Dealing with the failure of the UK banks*. London: House of Commons.

House of Commons Select Committee. (2009b). *Banking crisis: Reforming corporate governance and pay in the city*. London: House of Commons.

Hughes, J. E., & MacDonald, S. B. (2002). *International banking text and cases*. Addison Wesley.

Hughes, J. E., & MacDonald, S. C. (2003). *International banking: Text and cases*. Addison Wesley.

Independent Commission on Banking (ICB). (2011, September). *Final report recommendations*.

International Monetary Fund (IMF). (2012). *Shadow banking: Economics and policy. IMF staff discussion note*. Washington, DC: International Monetary Fund.

Jensen, M. C., & Meckling, W. H. (1976). Theory of the firm: Managerial behavior, agency costs and ownership structure. *Journal of Financial Economics, 3*(4), 305–360.

Joannidès de Lautour, V. (2019). *Strategic management accounting—Volume III: Aligning ethics, social performance and governance*. London: Palgrave Macmillan.

Letza, S., Sun, X., & Kirkbride, J. (2004). Shareholding versus Stakeholding: A critical review of corporate governance. *Corporate Governance: An International Review, 12*(3), 242–262.

Levine, R. (2011). *Regulating finance and regulators to promote growth*. Presented at Fed. Reserve Bank The Company Act (CA) 2006 (c46), Section 172, United Kingdom.

Mehran, H., & Mollineaux, L. (2012). *Corporate governance of financial institutions* (Federal Reserve Bank of New York Staff Reports No. 539).

Mintz, S. M. (2006). A comparison of corporate governance systems in the US, UK and Germany. *Corporate Ownership & Control, 3*(4), 24–34.

Organisation for Economic Co-operation and Development. (2004). *OECD principles of corporate governance*. Paris: Organisation for Economic Co-operation and Development.

Penrose, R. H. L. (2004). *Report of the equitable life enquiry*. HMSO.

Schweiker, W. (1993). Accounting for ourselves: Accounting practices and the disclosure of ethics. *Accounting, Organizations and Society, 18*(2–3), 231–252.

Shearer, T. (2002). Ethics and accountability: From the for-itself to the for-the-other. *Accounting, Organizations and Society, 27*(6), 541–573.

Solomon, J. (2007). *Corporate governance and accountability* (3rd ed.). London: John Wiley and Sons Ltd.

Sternberg, E. (1997). The defects of stakeholder theory. *Corporate Governance: An International Review, 5*(1), 3–10.

The Clearing House. (2012). Matters to be addressed by Board of Directors pursuant to statute or regulation. *The Clearing House, 28,* 1–35.

The Company Act (CA). (2006). (c46), Section 172. United Kingdom.

Tricker, B. (2009). *Corporate governance: Principles, policies and practices* (1st ed.). New York: Oxford University Press Inc.

Tricker, R. I. (1984). *Corporate governance: Practices, procedures and powers in British companies and their boards of directors.* Aldershot: Gower Press.

Tse, T. (2011). Shareholder and stakeholder theory: After the financial crisis. *Qualitative Research in Financial Markets, 3*(1), 51–63.

Turnbull, S. (1997). Corporate governance: Its scope, concerns and theories. *Corporate Governance: An International Review, 5*(4), 180–205.

Turner Report. (2009). *A regulatory response to the global banking crisis.* London.

United Nations Conference on Trade And Development (UNCTAD). (2010, October). *Corporate governance in the wake of the financial crisis, selected international reviews.* New York and Geneva: United Nations.

Valukas, A. (2010). *Lehman brothers holdings Inc. Chapter 11 proceedings examiner's report.* New York: Jenner & Block.

Walker, S. D. (2009). *A review of corporate governance in UK banks and other financial industry entities.* Walker Review, Final recommendations.

World Bank. (2012). *Global financial development report 2013: Rethinking the role of the state in finance.* Washington, DC: World Bank.

CHAPTER 10

A New Dawn: Accountable, Transparent Governance…What the Practitioners Want?

10.1 Introduction

The need for effective corporate governance one might argue is a necessary complement to rules-based prescriptive regulation. A wisely produced rules-based regulation concerning capital, liquidity, permitted business activities and so forth are essential safeguards for the financial system, while effective financial supervision of governance shapes, monitors and controls what actually happens in financial firms. Ineffective governance within financial institutions was not the sole contributor to the global financial crisis, but it was often regarded as an accomplice in the context of massive macroeconomic vulnerability. Effective corporate governance can make a significant positive difference by helping to prevent future crises or by mitigating their damaging impact.

There is a real need within the financial sector to develop more effective, improved tools to discern the key aspects of measuring accountable governance, or, how I might put it, the secret ingredients to make a perfect system of governance. Finding these illusive secrets is just the start, there is then the need to find ways to make sure those activities are maintained and carried through into new areas. Being brave enough to allow outside experts to take your board through a self-review can yield very powerful insights into true feelings and workings. These sentiments were reflected in the recent G30 report (2018) and went on to say

J. A. Akuffo, *Corporate Governance and Accountability of Financial Institutions*, Palgrave Studies in Accounting and Finance Practice, https://doi.org/10.1007/978-3-030-64046-0_10

"it is sobering to consider that in 2007, most boards would likely have given themselves passing grades" showing the importance of this level of reflection.

Given the role that corporate governance inadequacy played in the massive failure of the financial industry's decision-making that led to the global financial crisis, it is natural that a number of supervisors and stock exchanges are now paying great attention to governance arrangements. The way this is being delivered is through very particular focus on the learnings being garnered from the best practice in play across the industry. Experts in the field will focus on the systems and practices that are proving to deliver the best corporate governance results. Boards and others with roles supervising and enforcing high expectations with governance practice in their respective companies have become increasingly more focused on compliance with known best practice guidelines. I hope that this book provides meaningful insights to governance practitioners on how to strategise for effective accountability in corporate governance and will be a useful tool for those tasked with shaping governance structures and its associated disclosure mechanisms. Therefore, this chapter addresses the managerial implications and conclusions based on the investigation evidence found in corporate governance disclosures by the financial institutions without pretending to be exhaustive. The purpose is not to go too far within the confines of the research but to give an overview of how governance and its accountability mechanisms have been disclosed over time and how it could be improved in the future.

10.2 Qualitative Disclosures: Drawing Managerial Implications for Key Stakeholders

This book set out to discuss corporate governance issues surrounding accounting and finance for financial institutions. Findings from this investigation showed that the amount of corporate governance quality information disclosed in the annual reports of the selected banks was very low—specifically in some categories of accountability information provided (Akuffo 2018). This may offer suggestions for improving the extent of corporate governance information provided in the financial institutions (i.e. banking firms) annual reports for their external users (i.e. shareholders, depositors, investors, stockbrokers, government bodies, academics and other users) in order to be able to make wise economic decisions and as well as improve effective governance supervision. Disclosure on corporate governance issues has been ascending since the early 1990s when these issues first became a major concern in the light of the Cadbury Report (1992) in the United Kingdom. However, the manner in which corporate governance content has been presented has indeed become increasingly complex and organised in recent years as companies have sought to comply with the range of mandatory and/or voluntary codes and increased market expectations. In the United Kingdom, corporate governance code compliance and disclosure is voluntary in law but effectively mandatory under the stock market listing rules (i.e. the nature of control in a principles-based jurisdiction). The Codes of Best Practice in governance reporting provide for information pertaining to a number of areas in the annual report. The overriding goal is to enhance the quality of practices within the area of corporate governance. This standard could be met if firms opted to fully incorporate, recognise and follow the guidelines as specified or provide explanation from its departure.

10.2.1 Is the Governance Reporting Structure Still Fit for Boards and Management in the United Kingdom?

A key managerial implication that could be drawn from the analysis in this book is that over the twelve-year period, the average quality level of corporate governance disclosure was significantly lower for all financial institutions combined (Akuffo 2018). This was much lower than expected and highlights the need for advancement in the area of provision of relevant qualitative information to stakeholders through the use of the annual report. As a practitioner of corporate governance, I was unsure as to whether the UK's system of corporate governance reporting is working well with regard to both in practice as well as meeting the spirit of best practice Codes at the time of my assessment. We can also imply from the low quality evidence that it may be that there are too many conflicting pressures and influences on boards and executive management for the system to work fully, as well as unrealistic expectations to what boards can actually achieve with very limited time—or as observed especially in the United Kingdom, the system seems to be in constant change with little time to evaluate the impact of change prior to the next move year-on-year. However, if you consider the results alongside other governance research (Ferdous 2012, who examined disclosure in different contexts), although this particular conclusion is not in line with their findings when looking at overall disclosure, the apparent trend of levels of disclosure improving over time is consistent with their work. Similarly, Ferdous (2012) study, when looking at sample companies in Bangladesh, discovered that the amount of quality level disclosures were of a moderate level at 67%—in contrast, the current study returned results of firms evidencing a high level of reporting, with 89% disclosing at least some form of explanation of corporate governance indicators in their annual reports, irrespective of the level of distribution of quality classification disclosed. One can pose the question—does the UK corporate governance disclosure framework still fit from when it was originally proposed? We can only try to address this by unpicking the reasons why the framework was brought in, in the first place. It is important to note that among others there were specifically three key underlying assumptions that the UK Cadbury Committee based its recommended approach on: First, the Committee had the aim to promote the betterment of conduct within organisations. It is important to recognise that it was only strongly suggested and this is why it was not delivered as new law, but rather a voluntary code aiming to encourage reporting. Second, they recognised that while not a lawful requirement, there would be some firms that needed a stronger steer to follow protocol. This is why there was a "comply or explain" element within the requirements for reports. Third, power of "enforcement" was given to shareholders to assess whether the board truly was always acting with the company members at the forefront of their minds.

Furthermore, in the period when this was introduced, the UK market had a range of facets that prevented the need for "hard law" enforcement tactics. These were the fact that "(1) relatively strong shareholder rights, which gave shareholders the ability to hold the board to account if they felt it necessary; (2) the majority of companies had dispersed ownership, with few controlling shareholders. 'Comply or explain' would not have been seen as an effective mechanism where the controlling shareholders were essentially explaining to themselves and (3) a critical mass of shareholders who would be willing to carry out the enforcement role based on the belief that they would therefore see it as being in the interest of clients (mainly UK-based investors such as pension funds and insurance companies) and beneficiaries to invest in well-governed companies, and to put resource into monitoring and engagement" (ICSA 2016, p. 6). Can we reasonably say that these previous conditions and assumptions remain valid in the current practical business and market environment? Many practitioners in the OECDs believe that best practice codes are more effective than regulation as a way of raising general governance standards. The underlying premise of this belief is that they can set those standards higher than is usually possible in law or enactment of legislations, which in accord tends to be used to set the lowest acceptable rather than highest desirable expectations. However, some form of requirement to report on the extent to which those standards have been adopted is useful, so that companies cannot choose simply to ignore them. From the perspective of corporate governance practices, it is easy to see why the shareholders should be chosen to perform both the enforcement and judgement of the results delivered by their own board. The only question is whether they truly have the power to change anything if they find a particular area of conduct is lacking. Having said that, taking the perspective of financial institutions, I do not find myself advocating for shareholder primacy as a fully effective governance model. The other side of this discussion is that there is a need to amend some of Section 172 of the Companies Act 2006 in the United Kingdom which outlines the duties of directors. Nevertheless, it is fitting for shareholders to maintain this enforcement role, but this only stands if the foremost focus of duty by directors is geared towards their shareholders only. For these reasons, I believe that the governance framework remains, in principle, the right approach for those aspects of corporate governance that it was originally designed to address. On the other hand, where directors are not primarily responsible to members of a firm with regard to financial institutions and judgement of its control, monitoring and oversight functions rest with wider stakeholders such as shareholders, regulators/supervisors and government. In this regard, I believe the corporate governance structure, in particular the monitoring and enforcement, needs to be revisited from how it was originally designed to address the issue. This is well supported by the type of corporate governance issues discussed and the conclusive evidence provided in this book.

Additionally, one implication that can be drawn from the overall findings in this book using the volumetric analysis presented in the empirical chapters confirm the findings of a number of previous disclosure studies (for example, Lajili and Zeghal 2005; Helbok and Wagner 2006; Bischof 2009; Smith and Perignon 2010; Hughes et al. 2011) as well as similar recent discussion papers that have focused upon the issues of how to reduce the complexity of corporate reports while also improving their usefulness and disclosure of quality information for the reader (see for example, ASB 2009a, b; FRC 2009a, b, 2010; GAA 2008, IFAC 2008,

Walker 2009). The evaluation and analysis as presented in chapters 8 and 9 showed that the volume of corporate governance disclosures (in all accountability categories and for all the banking firms investigated) increased over time despite the level of quality explanations. The findings particularly confirmed some of the conclusions of both Perignon and Smith 2010 and Hughes et al. 2011 with regard to disclosure practices. In this respect, we can safely imply that the current disclosure reporting framework in the United Kingdom remains the correct approach to governance disclosures by the board's practices point of view. The structure has been improved over the past 28 years with virtually year-on-year enhancement in different governance areas—for example, some issues such as executive remuneration are now dealt with primarily in law rather than through the UK Corporate Governance Code (the Code), and the Stewardship Code has been introduced to strengthen the enforcement mechanism. It has not, however, fundamentally changed (ISCA 2016).

The result of the disclosure content scale in a year-by-year basis has confirmed that significant differences were found at some quality levels over time. With regard to disclosure of information content score type 1 (inadequate), there was a consistent decrease in disclosure in the overall sample from 2002 to 2012, indicating a trend towards more detailed and company-specific reporting on corporate governance-related themes. Type 2 (adequate) disclosures recorded a steep increase in the number of score information from 2003 to 2010. These findings could reflect a trend towards more improved accountability and the quality of disclosure reporting. However, the level of these disclosure types decreased in 2011 and 2012. Type 4 (excellent) corporate governance disclosures were rare. However, over the twelve years of study, their increased appearance in the annual report proved to be significant between 2009 and 2012. Overall, one might be tempted to conclude from this data that the quality of reporting is improving over time but in actual fact, the very low level of type 4 disclosures and the frequency of type 4 disclosures across the sample banks suggest that there is ample room for major improvement showing another slightly misleading illusion within reports. Additionally, the result confirms that the number of quality disclosures in the bank's annual reports has been increasingly steady over time for all banks until 2007 with a slight fall in 2008. However, the rate of increase from 2009 to 2012 has been significant. The visible incline appears to confirm the growth of consciousness regarding the expectations of governance and accountability disclosure standards within banking firms in the United Kingdom that are also registered on the London Stock Exchange.

Moreover, the discussion and findings include the observation that information diversity reported by the banking firms has been broadened over time. This is particularly useful for regulators and supervisors who are responsible for maintaining the integrity of the stock exchange and financial market. The study also notes the dominance of repetitive narratives or (boilerplate) with little disclosure containing comparative or detailed specific contextual information relating to the individual financial organisations. However, the study results highlight that more could be done by policymakers, company board of directors and regulators to ensure that information that stakeholders rely on from the annual report is of a high enough level to be of use. Disclosures from among the financial institutions investigated across all 19 subcategories of accountability measures provided evidence ranging from 51% quality disclosure score down to a relatively poorly 34% overall disclosure quality score. The findings confirm that there is a significant degree of variability among the individual UK-listed banks regarding the disclosure quality level and explanations provided in their annual reports to stakeholders. Again, the findings here confirm that there are examples of both inadequate quality disclosures and excellent or best practice disclosures among the sample companies. This illustrates the current observation that one size fits all with governance disclosures is practically impossible to achieve, the practical implication of this variability shows that individual financial company's must either adapt or learn from others showcasing best practice disclosures. In addition, we could also draw a key lesson for boards of financial institutions, especially for those investigated, which is that honest introspective reflection is needed to see how they could improve on providing detailed and best practice high-quality information.

The findings drawn from this book's analysis confirm an increasing trend in the quality of each category disclosure over the years. Using ranking analysis confirms that the highest disclosure category across all the studied banking firms was "Accountability" governance mechanism and the least disclosure quality category was "Performance" mechanism, which is conceivably linked to the requirement for provision of certain information for shareholders by law and Codes. However, the performance category shows the most improvement in disclosure scores over the sample period, while the least improved disclosure category was accountability. It could be said that there is a recognition among boards and supervisors that work needs to be done which could explain the upward trend in these governance concern areas. This apparent recognition is reassuring to see. The findings confirm that there is still significant progress to be made on the overall quality narrative of corporate governance disclosures in annual reports for the sample banks, as well as the individual category groups in the UK banking sector. There is not a need for more codes or disclosure requirements in this area as the level of detail should be completely sufficient if delivered well. What we do need in this area, however, is to actually enforce what is being demanded in order to ensure effective accountable governance. Perhaps this is an area where there could be an intrusive and effective supervision by regulators.

10.2.2 Providing and Improving Information Transparency to Shareholders, Supervisory Regulators and the Government

The concerns and the information in this book with regard to corporate governance and its mechanisms of accountability for banking and other financial institutions offer profound implications for key stakeholders. The evaluations from the empirical chapters in the book revealed that the overall level of the qualitative corporate governance disclosed in the annual reports for the financial institutions listed on the stock exchange was very minimal for a number of accountability mechanisms. This may offer suggestions for improving the extent of corporate governance information provided in the financial institutions (i.e. banking firms) annual reports for their external users (i.e. shareholders, depositors, investors, stockbrokers, government bodies, academics and other users) in order to be able to make wise economic decisions. It also enables them to evaluate the institutions' activities and corporate governance practices, since the annual report published by a bank or other financial organisation is considered an important means of communicating corporate information between the institutions' executive management and outsiders. For financial intermediation, the presence of leverage and the practice of limited liability offers a vindication of both public monitoring and prudential regulation for these institutions (Akuffo 2018: Ferrarini 2017). The creditors for financial firms need to be protected from failure. This is predominantly factual with regard to financial institutions for whom many of their creditors (such as depositors and policy holders) are unable to protect themselves adequately due to poor disclosure of information and opaqueness of governance decisions. Boards and management will need to pay more attention to the key demands of their stakeholders by ensuring that accountable and honest information is provided to support the protection of these more vulnerable stakeholders who do not have direct say in the management of the companies they seek to invest in.

Overall, the research findings of this book have implications to various stakeholders of the banking firms; especially shareholders, supervisory regulators and the government. More importantly, this knowledge provides a significant benefit both to the Financial Conduct Authority (as the supervisory authority responsible for all banks supervision and regulation) and the UK Financial Reporting Council. The outcome of this would be for them to adopt more proactive regulations to increase the extent of information disclosure in the commercial banks' annual reports, and to improve disclosure transparency in the banking sector. A bank that has poor transparency is not likely to voluntarily disclose additional information about their management performances. It is widely recognised that increased transparency leads to a reduction in the frequency and magnitude of bank difficulties. In addition, the empirical chapters presented also give a better understanding and more insight into corporate disclosure practices in the banking sector in a developed country. It also provides beneficial insight into international institutions, especially those that are more interested in enhancing the regulatory framework for financial reporting and corporate governance in the advanced economies (such the BCBS, FSB, the IASB, WB and the IMF). Generally, the author in researching this book has found that more efforts from regulatory authorities must be undertaken to improve qualitative and quantitative disclosures in the commercial banks' annual reports in a way that better enables various stakeholders to assess management performance and risks. Undoubtedly, disclosing sufficient information in the annual reports may be advantageous to the management of banks, in building customer confidence and profitable customer relationships. Achieving effective disclosure and transparency is an overall objective in practice, but it is rarely achieved in a fully satisfactory manner unless enforced by law or effective monitoring by supervisors. Principally if the financial institutions disclosure activities and structures are complex in disguise or opaque, then market discipline does not function properly. Additionally, if new risks are not even adequately established and understood by the bank board itself and let alone disclosed properly in the annual report, it is difficult for the supervisory agency to grasp them and practically impossible for the shareholders and the debtholders to react to them. In a nutshell, the categories of accountability in governance offered by the empirical chapters, if taken note of by both board members and financial supervisors, could shed some light and serve to help improve the process going forward. A key example would have been to use the categories in devising stakeholder accountability mechanisms that could be developed to support legislation improvement that goes beyond the shareholder focused accountability. This could address the needs of more diverse stakeholder groups.

Furthermore, findings from the different levels of qualitative score levels in this book revealed that the current financial reporting and mandatory disclosure practices by UK banks compared to other international practices are still not robust enough, regulated enough and display a lack of accounting regulation on the disclosure requirements to satisfy the information needs of external stakeholders. Therefore, bank regulators should consider issuing a set of accounting and financial reporting standards or guidelines for the preparation of annual reports, which seem to be demanded from the viewpoint of those who prepare banks annual reports. It is important to distinguish the regulatory function from the supervisory function. The regulator sets the rules and regulations within which financial institutions are obliged to operate, while the supervisor oversees the actions of the board and management to ensure compliance with those rules and regulations. Sometimes confusion may arise because both functions are often performed within the same institution (for example, UK Financial Services Authority (now Financial Conduct Authority) and the US Federal Reserve). The implication here is that supervisors that more fully comprehend banks and other financial firms' disclosures regarding strategies, risk appetite, profile and controls, culture, and corporate governance effectiveness will be better able to make the key judgements their mandate requires. Financial supervisors have legally defined responsibilities relating to risk control disclosures; fraud control; and conformance to laws, regulations and standards of conduct. Following the recent crisis, supervisors are now seeking a much deeper and more nuanced understanding of how the board works, how key decisions are reached, and the nature of the debate around them, all of which reveal much about the firm's corporate governance. Regrettably, as it stands, it is the quantitative rules-based regulatory necessities that take the attention within policymaking debates as opposed to the more qualitative strands of supervision disclosure that could also deliver some interesting results. To move towards a global financial structure with enhanced stability, liquidity, new capital, related standards will be needed along with much improved understanding of both decision-making protocols (the G30) and performance of major banking and other significant financial firms will be essential.

Among other findings useful for financial boards and supervisors, the book provides empirical evidence supporting the applicability of stakeholder theory in financial institutions which was selected as the underlying theoretical framework in this research to explain corporate governance disclosure in annual reports of banks. Application of this theory in explaining the variability of the nature of disclosure practices observed and as a factor influencing both mandatory and voluntary disclosure in the banks' annual reports was supported by the empirical results as set out in the empirical chapters. There is no singular straightforward by and large accepted definition of corporate governance (Akuffo 2018; Belcredi and Ferrarini 2013; Tricker 2009). Finance scholars predominantly focus on the relationship between firms and suppliers of funds (i.e. shareholder supremacy protected by law) and under a narrow viewpoint argue that corporate governance deals with the ways in which suppliers of finance to corporations assure themselves of getting a return to their investment (Shleifer and Vishny 1997).

On the other hand, and under a broader definition, corporate governance is concerned with the resolution of collective action problems among dispersed investors and the reconciliation of conflicts of interest between various corporate claimholders (Becht et al. 2002) although limited in applicability of stakeholders' protection by law. However, Ferrarini asserts that "the presence of multiple principals' blurs corporate objectives and may ultimately compound agency problems, providing the management with an ad hoc rationale to explain any decision whatsoever" (Ferrarini 2017). Nonetheless, as I have argued in the book, financial institutions present a special case where stakeholders legitimacy and interest matter a lot. Finally, there are a number of key managerial implications from the findings that highlight the need for consideration by directors of financial institutions, policymakers and regulators to improve best practice governance disclosures to stakeholders. These includes the following: (a) Companies should disclose or report more openly on the key outcomes of their evaluations and the steps they intend to take to address the issues that have been highlighted; (b) Policymakers should strengthen guidelines for compulsory reporting of serious facts by external auditors to the board and supervisors and how this is to be disclosed as part of annual report; (c) Disclosure of alerts by external auditors on banks' situations reported to regulators and an explanation of a summary report should be part of governance reporting; (d) Company boards should provide a detailed description of the organisational code of conduct, including policy on areas such as disclosing ethical behaviour by senior employees, anti-bribery and facilitation payments; (e) The report should also explain how compliance with this code is monitored and any performance data (on breaches and non-compliance related to dismissals) and (f) Policymakers or regulators should consider developing specific guidance provisions relating to mechanisms of disclosing whistle-blowing practices in annual reports. Regulatory support is necessary in communicating the relevant Code successfully. These specific areas were found to be seriously lacking, and hence an improvement across all facets would go a long way to enhance the quality of disclosures and meet the demands of broader stakeholder accountability. The breadth of the scope of this work could serve to disband some of the illusion created where less specific disclosures are currently delivered by board of directors of these firms.

10.3 Where Do Corporate Governance Go from Here; Agenda for Further Research

This book has sought to offer knowledge and insight on corporate governance disclosure reporting in annual reports for financial institutions. I have attempted to show how this important subject has evolved in recent times with regard to industry practice and within the academic sphere of influence for financial institutions. It is believed that the results provide a useful insight into the disclosure practices by large banking firms and give a starting point for future academic and empirical research. Thus, a number of suggestions for possible further research are highlighted. There is a potential further research opportunity suggested by the method aspect of this empirical work. Also, a clear opportunity is presented for the application of mixed content analysis instruments to compliment the method employed by the author in this book in other areas of disclosure research in accounting, such as the extent of regulatory compliance disclosure reporting and stakeholder reporting. The investigation relied on annual reports on a qualitative basis for the empirical chapters, additional studies on corporate governance disclosure could complement these findings by incorporating the use of corporate websites and internal minutes of board meeting deliberations. In addition, this research was limited to one country (i.e. United Kingdom). Further investigation could be conducted to evaluate corporate governance quality disclosure in the financial sector in other countries on a long-term cycle, especially major EU nations who were severely affected by the recent financial crisis of 2007/08. Also, the empirical chapters research sample size covered the largest UK financial listed firms on the London Stock Exchange; which were carefully and purposefully selected, this could be broadened to cover all listed financial institutions including insurance and others within the United Kingdom. This would serve to provide a fuller reflection of the performance of organisations within the United Kingdom.

Furthermore, the apparent lack of detailed and excellent disclosures in corporate governance disclosure reporting suggests a relative paucity of agreed definitions and technical details in the disclosures. It offers policymakers and regulatory standard setters the opportunity to develop detailed and specific guidelines regarding corporate governance disclosure requirements that go beyond the traditional minimum requirements for compliance and disclosures by firms. Accountable corporate governance is really not about box-ticking and boilerplate disclosures. It needs to be about meaningful, quality reporting and superior transparency especially for financial firms. Effective disclosure of corporate governance is about complying to the spirit of any governance requirements or Codes of best practice.

10.3.1 Broadening the Scope and Use of Annual Reports for Qualitative Corporate Governance

Throughout this book there has been a deliberate emphasis on the widening outline for accountability and corporate governance. The text has offered enough evidence that firms and regulators are embracing a broader approach to corporate governance in a manner of discharging accountability to a wider range of stakeholders. The annual report is still an important tool for companies to communicate information about their business to investors. It is also how companies deliver their message to other key stakeholders and a great opportunity to improve trust in the business. Traditionally, financial accounting information as reported in annual reports is the product of corporate accounting and external reporting systems that measure and routinely disclose audited, quantitative data concerning the financial position and performance of the publicly held firms. There is a set of information that is specifically about the firm that is available to both regulators and investors. Details included are income statements, cash flow statements, audited balance sheets and are accompanied by supporting disclosures. The mere expectation of degrees of disclosure has had a positive impact on the practices of some managers. It has served to begin to create a somewhat fairer and more resourceful capital market—however, for some, it is still not enough to assume expectations are going to be followed and more must be done.

The information disclosed enables the shareholders, investors, creditors and other persons who are interested in the affairs of the company to have better understanding of the affairs of the company. Investors, employees, customers, suppliers and other stakeholders are interested to see: (a) Information that is specific to the company and how value is created and protected; (b) Key markets and market segments, key revenue and profit drivers; (c) A clear and comprehensive overview of the company, business model, key performance indicators, principal risks and board matters. Showing how the strategy is integrated with the business model, the company can better explain how its strategy has been specifically devised to optimise its resources and relationships to achieve its objectives; (d) Your company's competitive advantage—what differentiates you, not the secret recipe and (e) Plain, clear, concise and factual language. There is therefore, the need to study the impact of these specific information contents in relation to corporate governance and how they offer accountability to stakeholders. Following the recent financial crisis, the UK Government in 2013, published new regulations resulting in an amendment to company law requirements. The changes entail the requirement for large and medium sized businesses to provide a "Strategic Report" as part of their annual report. This in effect is an opportunity for the business to communicate messages about the company's priorities and achievements—past, present and in the future. It will also be a wonderful opportunity to study and evaluate how these changes are being reported by organisations about what they have done and need to improve their disclosures in the future. This was an area which was barely discussed and reported meaningfully by most listed firms. There are other crucial corporate governance reporting trends that require careful and considerable research agenda to improve corporate accountability using annual reports. This includes culture, diversity beyond gender in the boardroom and business models of companies. For example, the UK governance regulator, the Financial Reporting Council, has recently stressed that the reporting of an organisation's culture[1] is a key focus because it can help to determine the likelihood of corporate success or failure. Are your values well defined by the board and are your employees' behaviours aligned with these values? Also, the relevancy of diversity beyond gender is becoming more significant to the FTSE 350[2] organisations listed on the London Stock Exchanges. In 2016, according Grant Thornton, 76% of companies identified diversity, in its broadest sense, as a priority. This is no longer just a challenge for board level, especially with the review by Parker[3] (2017, 2020) into ethnic diversity recommending FTSE boards to have at least one director of colour and the EU focus on diversity within the non-financial reporting. Certainly, these developments call for further academic and empirical work to improve our understanding around the effectiveness of this as a governance accountability mechanism. Finally, it is crucial to clearly articulate what the company does, how and why; and identify the organisation's competitive advantage. This is an emerging area where most organisations listed or unlisted are focusing their corporate governance efforts and would benefit from detailed qualitative assessment using disclosure on this in annual reports, especially explanation about their business model and how they are connecting it to KPIs and strategic risks.

10.3.2 *Broader Stakeholder Governance Reform—Impossible or Unwillingness for Legal Changes?*

There is a need for a much larger amount of research into this area for financial institutions to fully discern the need and interest of stakeholders and how to hold company directors accountable. A new methodology

[1] According to the 2016 review by Grant Thornton, in its annual review of UK corporate governance found that only twenty per cent of the FTSE 350 provide good discussion on culture yet this will continue to be an area of importance.

[2] The FTSE 350 Index is a market capitalisation weighted stock market index made up of the constituents of the FTSE 100 and FTSE 250 index companies by capitalisation which have their primary listing on the London Stock Exchange. It is a combination of the FTSE 100 Index of the largest 100 companies and the FTSE 250 Index of the next largest 250.

[3] This independent review considers how to improve the ethnic and cultural diversity of UK boards to better reflect their employee base and the communities they serve. The report sets out objectives and timescales to encourage greater diversity and provides practical tools to help business leaders to address the issue.

that goes beyond the traditional finance valuation techniques or efficient market quantitative indicators, which solely focused on shareholders, in finance is required to achieve this. The governance framework as it is currently designed in the United Kingdom and many OECDs jurisdictions does not include sanctions by stakeholders that are adequate for the purposes of punishing bad behaviour by senior managers or directors. The other related reason for my reservations about the legal adequacy of the current corporate governance framework, as a way of achieving wider stakeholder accountability aims, is that it depends profoundly on corporate reporting for its effectiveness. In fact, as many practitioners believe, reporting can be a very effective way of bringing about change, but only when there are legal consequences. If organisations believe that regulators or stockholders might take action against them (for example, imposing severe sanctions or voting against a resolution or selling their shares) they then will act in order to protect themselves from such consequences. However, if there are no severe consequences, reporting in itself achieves nothing. If investors in listed companies do not see it as their duty to look after the public interest, or do not use the disclosures to inform their investment decisions, then making companies report to them on a particular issue is unlikely to achieve much. In addition, reporting alone has little value as a means of identifying and dealing with breaches of law or truly egregious behaviour, as companies have no incentive to disclose such events. A key example of this predicament, was acknowledged by the Financial Reporting Council in the United Kingdom, stating when providing "its evidence to the House of Commons BEIS Select Committee Inquiry on corporate governance, legal sanctions are at best incomplete" (ICSA 2016, p.11).

This book takes the view of discussion and research from the finance and accounting perspective, rather than a legal perspective on the important topic of corporate governance and disclosure. The mechanisms of governance accountability discussed in this book could benefit from further detailed and long-term academic research using legal scholarly investigation and an extensive body of professional practice evidence. For example, the performance category of accountability found in its discussions that there has rarely been any professional scholarly work completed looking at financial institutions in particular. This is in contrast to a plethora of political rhetoric and emotion being more readily available regarding the topic of effective corporate governance. This sort of research will provide a framework that empowers and enables both management scholars and legal practitioners to make sound decisions that are supported by careful and well researched evidence.

At last, we need robust evidence to address the issue of sanctions to improve the effectiveness of the mechanisms by which companies are held accountable to stakeholders. Legal duties, good corporate governance standards and scrutiny by shareholders and other stakeholders can all diminish the risk of bad behaviour or poor decisions by senior executives, but they cannot eradicate the human failings that cause them in the first place. Currently, there is no means of effectively and appropriately punishing actions by directors that have a significant adverse impact on their shareholders, stakeholders or on society in general. This is an example of where monitoring by shareholders and reporting to them does not suit the needs. There is a need for sanctions brought in (and needed) to be appropriate and able to identify wrongful conduct as opposed to well-intended bad judgement. The emphasis of the call for this further research is not for development of more code but for more on the sanction regimes and how effectively it could improve how companies are held accountable by stakeholders.

10.3.3 Disclosure of Code of Best Practice: Enforcement Still Remains Insufficient

The lack of excellent disclosure measures found in this book suggests that the majority of best practices that are recommended (for example by the Financial Reporting Council in the United Kingdom) or those that are mandated by regulators and financial supervisors are highly likely to have not been verified or systematically been tested before implementation expectation set-up by the reform process. This is an illusion that could be said to be impossible to achieve in practice. This implies that most of these best practice recommendations have not been properly understood or supported by considerable evidence to prevent future disastrous events in relation to governance. For example, the SOX act of 2002, and the 2010 Dodd–Frank act, both in the United States, and the 2002–2006 code of best practices reforms enacted in the United Kingdom all failed to prevent the 2008 financial crisis from occurring. In the United Kingdom, prior to 2009, there were four key major public enforcement agencies of UK banking and other financial institutions. These are—the FSA as both the UK prudential and conduct regulator and the UK Listing Authority

(UKLA)[4]; the Financial Reporting Review Panel (FRRP), the Department for Business Innovation & Skills (BIS) and the Takeover Panel. The enforcement activities of each of these agencies comprise of a mixture of formal and informal actions. It can be noted that, until the recent financial crisis, the FSA had preference for informal enforcement, e.g. issuing a private warning (a non-statutory tool) and only discloses aggregated total cases of formal enforcement making it is virtually impossible to know the figure of informal enforcement activities against banks for corporate governance failures (Wu 2011). As we discussed in the empirical chapters of this book, the disclosure in the annual report for the banks investigated were inadequate and in a number of cases no disclosure at all although banks are required to disclose information as required by the governance Code or the law. In addition, The Financial Reporting Review Panel (FRRP) under the structure of the Financial Reporting Council, is a public enforcement agency with responsibilities for investigating, and persuading companies to rectify breaches of accounting standards, own public record over the period of 2002 to 2009, show that no court order was sought and only one public notice was issued, indicating that the FRRP's enforcement activity against banks is, to a significant extent non-existence or informal at best (Wu 2011).

Any new best practice reform recommendation implies that something better compared to what we have in place is needed. So, the question is, has this best practice been proven, established testing completed, universal applicability and consensus of acceptability been agreed by everyone? These core questions should be given the time needed to be adequately answered before any changes have been implemented, backed-up by either legislation or voluntary adoption. Most practitioners believe that corporate governance is very costly to implement by corporate management, but what is more significant, is that failure of corporate governance can be even more consequential to all of us (as we saw in the 2008 financial crisis). Therefore, I do believe that careful insights and more research is needed—both empirically and theoretically. This would go a long way

[4] UKLA has power to require de-listing of securities. Prior to September 2009, there appeared to be no formal enforcement activity pursued by the UKLA for breaches of the Listing Rules by a bank. This is despite that fact that it has responsibility for drafting and enforcing the Listing Rules, the Disclosure and Transparency Rules, and the Prospectus Rules, applicable to banks quoted on the Official List.

to better understand the impact of any recommended changes to the code of best practice, especially in financial institutions.

10.3.4 Focus Should Move from Physical Structures to Behavioural in Governance Decision-Making

The need for suitable structures and processes are a necessary but not a sufficient condition for good corporate governance, which critically depends also on patterns of behaviour directors and management corporations. Academy, society and the accounting profession all call for greater business ethics and accountability (Joannidès de Lautour 2019). Behavioural patterns depend in turn on the extent to which values such as integrity, independence of thought and respect for the views of others are embedded in the institutional culture. Cultural, ethics and human behaviour issues form a basis for a piece of much needed research that it would be timely to complete. Issues that are difficult to measure, regulate or control but have significant effects on accountable governance decisions require in-depth evaluation. Following the financial crisis in 2008, financial institution leaders globally, across countries and cultures, continue to cite a remarkably consistent set of values that they considered to be essential to a culture in which effective governance could thrive (G30 Report). This is perhaps not surprising and could offer one explanation of the importance put on culture in post-crisis corporate governance discussion, which underlines the roles that ethics and the relevant monitoring play in the financial services sector (Ferrarini 2017, Takor 2016). According to Takor (2016, p. 22) *"with over $100 billion in fines imposed on the largest financial institutions since the financial crisis, there is now a growing suspicion that ethical lapses in banking are not just the outcome of a few bad apples – deviant rogue traders – but rather a reflection of systematic weaknesses in governance"*. Examples of such categories could include trust and mutual respect, risk culture, performance culture and societal responsibility culture (i.e. behaviour such as personal values, values concerning respect for ideas and dialogue and values that shape personal interaction both within and outside these institutions). These areas are current and future accountable governance agenda items that require exploration. Accountability implies relationships between people and raises the question of *to whom* accounts of oneself should be directed (Joannidès de Lautour 2019; Schweiker 1993; Shearer 2002). How these issues are accounted, reported and discussed both internally and externally to a firm remain relatively unexplained or still in the black box in the annals of corporate accountability and governance. While it is important that we have frameworks and structures as set up by corporate governance currently, the impact of human behaviour cannot be underestimated or regulated, let alone translated into a format for disclosure. It calls for new research and new thinking to address this underlying corporate governance issue.

Moreover, disclosure discussions generally bring about additional disclosures. As disclosure becomes better-off, regulators, boards of directors, senior managers, stockholders or shareholders and stakeholders will want a more holistic understanding of the business they are involved with. This is normally forced by failure and crises, the knowledge and understanding of the "culture" of the individual firms is increasingly coming within the sights of boards and stakeholders. Starting with the financial sector, understanding the culture of a company is becoming increasingly a best practice requirement for company boards. I am convinced that in the coming decade, a significant number of cultural "audits" will become the norm for large firms. The UK regulators have begun the process of delving into the cultural issues of governance and how disclosure in this area can be improved. According to the 2016 review conducted by Grant Thornton, only 20% of the FTSE 350 provide good discussion on culture, yet this will continue to be an area of importance for the next 10 years. The UK corporate governance regulator, Financial Reporting Council, have said that the reporting of an organisation's culture is a key focus because it can help to determine the likelihood of corporate success or failure. Are your values well defined by the board and are your employees' behaviour's aligned with these values?

Interaction with multiple layers and levels of stakeholders would be needed to establish their level of confidence in their more senior leaders (in making core company decisions) and their opinions of management persona. Getting absolute honesty in these reflections would be crucial to gain a true insight. There is no doubt, therefore, that future research on the governance and accountability of financial institutions should not be restrained to legal and economic analysis but extended to the role and impact of culture and ethics in financial firms from a broad social sciences perspective. Perhaps utilisation of other disciplines such as sociology, psychology and anthropology will help in understanding the "informal constraints" which determine financial institutions' behaviour and complement their regulation and supervision (Morrison and Shapiro 2016).

10.3.5 Broadening the Scope of Disclosure Research Datasets

The evaluation and empirical evidence within this book focuses only on the corporate governance disclosure practices in corporate annual reports data information. Corporate governance disclosure can be done through other forms of communication or media, such as corporate websites, surveys, questionnaires and press releases. The extent and trend of disclosure in this book does not represent the overall totality of corporate disclosure practices. This presents an opportunity for further extended research which could give a broader review of the topic. The criteria adopted could also be widened to support this potential study.

Cultural audits are being utilised more often by financial organisations (particularly banks) both in the United Kingdom and further afield. In order to adequately review a firm's performance and behaviour, the accuracy of the audit relies on the availability of resources such as employee/customer surveys and information on corporate governance processes adopted—these make up the internal and external "disclosure" systems. The use of cultural audits don't only help larger organisations, they are also being developed to identify "red flags" for investors, clients and other key stakeholders. Developments in this area will be encouraged by data and the widespread availability of it. In several sectors, it is the ability to access the "big" data that is playing a core part in disruption that is incited by technology. Development of data will not only help to recognise risks, find niches and price products; it will enable firms to do this with heightened precision and clarity that was previously not possible for such debt and equity providers.

Third party providers are already working towards improving this within corporate governance as currently the focus of data provision is on governance of banks or big financial institutions (e.g. Sustainalytics or Institutional Shareholder Services). There is a movement among existing data providers to find new ways to gain, combine and anonymise and share corporate governance information among firms, with the aim of offering benchmarks along with quantifiable "rankings" to institutional investors. The increased and improved usage of data will lead to a shift to allow audit committees to have automated methods of analysing compliance data, thus impacting the whole way that boards work. The board directors also benefit from this change, having somewhat easier access to detailed data (e.g. via board portals that are increasingly used in OECD markets) to allow improved scrutiny into all aspects of a company's performance.

10.3.6 *Call for Further Studies on Financial Supervision Effectiveness: Investigate the Investigators?*

We need research about the effectiveness of regulators oversight as a governance accountability mechanism of financial firms. It is often cited that organisations perform better when under the scrutiny of regulators but how do we know that the people regulating are looking for the right things? I propose that a review of the reviewers could be interesting to gain insight into how governance is being checked, enforced and reported. Furthermore, a deep dive to see if they are practicing what they preach would provide a fascinating insight as they are the ones setting the industry standard. Following the financial crisis, for example, the UK government abolished the Financial Service Authority (FSA) and replaced it with a new regulatory body (Financial Conduct Authority and the Prudential Regulatory Authority) due to their failure as observed by the then FSA to effectively regulate and supervise the conduct of the financial institutions.

I believe supervisors that are more able to fully comprehend financial organisation strategies, risk appetite and profile, culture, and governance effectiveness will be better able to make the key judgements their mandate requires. Many supervisors realise this and have begun to enhance their effectiveness in this area. It is not surprising to note that according to FSB (2011, p. 17) group report "More intense supervisory oversight is needed to evaluate the effectiveness of improved corporate governance, particularly risk governance, in affecting behaviour and improvements in this area will be" (FSB 2011, p. 17). Therefore, higher-quality supervision research evidence, conducted on the basis of a solid foundation of mutual respect and trust between supervisor and supervised, is also needed. Trust-based reform agenda relationships will also be very valuable in addressing the next potential crisis, whatever it may be. Most governance practitioners believe that supervisors are uniquely positioned to perceive emerging trends across institutions and potential systemic risks and should share concerns with the institutions they oversee from any observation they may uncovered in their investigation.

Recently, regulation of financial institutions in a number of jurisdictions including the United Kingdom is undergoing a fundamental transformation. There are many changes developing in the world of corporate governance, for example, regulation, systems based solely around rules, enforcement and also supervision. When reviewing the practices that preceded the financial crash of 2008–2009, it was ineffective supervision and regulation that resulted in the catastrophic failures in the banking sector. There has been evident refocusing of financial firm regulation and supervision in the years after the crisis.

10.4 Conclusion

If there is one major lesson learnt that I can draw from the past twelve years following the financial crisis, it is that corporate governance does matter significantly. Directors, regulators and shareholders, but also policymakers and the general public, must pay far more attention to corporate governance issues. It tells us how firms operate, what are their motives and principles, their reporting lines and quality types, who they are accountable to, and how they manage profit, remuneration and, in the case of many financial institutions, other people's money.

In a nutshell, the implication of the findings from this book has a number of managerial consequences for different stakeholders that use annual reports to demand accountability. The findings provide significant information for commercial banking management, banking regulators, the Central Banks, the accounting profession, potential local and foreign investors, researchers, international institutions and other government agencies to help them to assess the transparency level and the amount of information available from these UK banks.

The question of whether it is laws, guidelines, rules or market behaviour that could have the best impact on the standard of corporate governance practices has been discussed for a long time. For the majority, the regulation and legislation set out to ensure core principles are followed presents a fair opportunity for all to conform and can be useful for any companies finding it hard to start their disclosure journey. As we have seen through the evaluation completed for this book, sadly the presence of these firm guidelines is still not enough for many to deliver high-quality disclosures or practices. Therefore, as mentioned earlier in this chapter, I believe that improving the day-to-day scrutiny of delivery is vital to hold companies even more accountable, especially in the financial industry.

References

Akuffo, J. A. (2018). *Corporate Governance and bank accountability: The role of accountability in improving the quality of corporate governance disclosures in bank annual report*. A UK perspective. DBA thesis, Grenoble Ecole De Management.

Accounting Standards Board (ASB). (2009a). *Improvement to financial reporting standards*. London: ASB.

ASB. (2009b). *Rising to the challenge—A review of narrative reporting by UK listed companies*. London: Financial Reporting Council.

Becht, M., Bolton, P., & Roell, A. (2002). Corporate governance and control. *NBER Working Paper Series* (Working Paper 9371).

Belcredi, M., & Ferrarini, G. (2013). Corporate boards, incentive pay and shareholder activism in Europe: Main issues and policy perspectives. In M. Belcredi & G. Ferrarini (Eds.), *Boards and shareholders in European listed companies. Facts, context and post-crisis reforms*. Cambridge University Press.

Bischof, J. (2009). The effects of IFRS 7 adoption on bank disclosure in Europe. *Accounting in Europe, 6*(2), 164–193.

Cadbury Report. (1992). *Report of the committee on the financial aspect of Corporate Governance: The code of best practice*. London: Gee Professional Publishing.

Ferdous, C. S. (2012). *Compliance with code of Corporate Governance in developing economy: The case of Bangladesh*. Student thesis, University of Birmingham.

Ferrarini, G. (2017). *Understanding the role of Corporate Governance in financial institutions: A research agenda* (ECGI Working Paper Series in Law).

Financial Service Authority (FSA). (2009a, September). *Reforming remuneration practices in the financial services, Consultation Paper.* London: Financial Services Authority.

Financial Service Authority (FSA). (2009b, March). *The Turner review: A regulatory response to the global banking crisis*. London: Financial Service Authority.

Financial Reporting Council (FRC). (2005). *Internal control: Revised guidance for directors on the combined code*. London: FRC.

Financial Reporting Council (FRC). (2008). *Consultation on proposed changes on audit committee (The Smith guidance)*. London: FRC.

Financial Reporting Council (FRC). (2010). *The UK corporate governance code*. London: Financial Reporting Council.

Financial Reporting Council (FRC). (2016). *Corporate culture and the role of boards*. London: FRC.

Financial Reporting Council (FRC). (2017). *Developments in Corporate Governance and Stewardship 2016*. London: Financial Reporting Council.

Financial Stability Board (FSB). (2011). *Intensity and effectiveness of SIFI supervision: Progress report on implementing the recommendations on enhanced supervision*. Basel: Financial Stability Board.

GAA. (2008). *Can financial reporting be made simpler and more useful?* London: Global Accountancy Alliance.

Helbok, G., & Wagner, C. (2006). Determinants of operational risk reporting in the banking industry. *Journal of Risk, 9*(1), 49–74.

Hughes, S. B., Wood, A. L., & Hodgdon, C. (2011). Bank response to SEC disclosure guidance issued during the 2007–2008 US financial crisis. *Research in Accounting Regulation, 23*(2), 149–159.

International Federation of Accountants (IFAC). (2008). *Financial reporting supply chain: Current perspectives and directions*. New York.

Institute of Chartered Secretaries and Administrators (ICSA). (2016). *The future of governance: Untangling corporate governance*. London: Institute of Chartered Secretaries and Administrators.

Joannidès de Lautour, V. (2019). *Strategic management accounting—Volume III: Aligning ethics, social performance and governance*. London: Palgrave Macmillan.

Lajili, K., & Zeghal, D. (2005). A content analysis of risk management disclosures in Canadian annual reports. *Canadian Journal of Administrative Sciences, 22*(2), 126–141.

Morrison, A., & Shapiro, J. (2016, February). *Governance and culture in the Banking sector* (Working Paper).

Parker Review Committee. (2017). *A report into the Ethnic Diversity of UK Boards*. Final Report in Association with EY and Linklater.

Parker, Sir J. (2020). *Ethnic diversity enriching business leadership*. The Parker Review Committee Report in Association with EY and Linklater.

Schweiker, W. (1993). Accounting for ourselves: Accounting practices and the disclosure of ethics. *Accounting, Organizations and Society, 18*(2–3), 231–252.

Shearer, T. (2002). Ethics and accountability: From the for-itself to the for-the-other. *Accounting, Organizations and Society, 27*(6), 541–573.

Shleifer, A., & Vishny, R. W. (1997). A survey of corporate governance. *Journal of Finance, 52*(2), 735–782.

Smith, D. R., & Perignon, C. (2010). The level and quality of value at risk disclosure by commercial banks. *Journal of Banking and Finance, 34*(2), 360–375.

Takor, A. (2016). *Corporate culture in banking*. Economic Policy Review, Federal Reserve Bank of New York.

The Group of Thirty (2018). *Towards effective governance of financial institutions*. Washington, DC: G30.

Tricker, B. (2009). *Corporate governance: Principles, policies and practices* (1st ed.). New York: Oxford University Press Inc.
Walker, D. (2009). *A review of corporate governance in UK banks and other financial industry entities.* Final recommendations.
Wu, H. (2011). *The UK Bank corporate governance framework: A holistic and critical analysis with a focus upon banks risk and executive remuneration governance.* Manchester: University of Manchester.

CHAPTER 11

Conclusion

The relationship between corporate governance and accountability are mutually facilitative, inclusive and interdependent. Corporate governance involves corporate fairness, transparency disclosure and accountability. Corporate accountability is the extent to which a company is transparent in its corporate activities and responsive to those it serves. Hence, accountability is both a key element as well as requirement for corporate governance, fortifying it by providing a transparent template governing the critical decision-making, procedures and activities. In fact, because corporate directors and executives are often perceived as being accountable for corporate performance and firms' legal and ethical behaviours, their accountability is also an integral part of corporate governance. Moreover, board of directors in the traditional sense, represents shareholders' interests and as such, monitor and control the opportunistic behaviour of managers; thus, in the presence of effective accountability, agency cost can be reduced. Financial institutions' corporate governance has been recognised as multidimensional, very complex in character and can be embodied in a variety of systems. For example, this can take the form of firm legislation, supervisory structures, stock exchange admission requirements, standards and best practice guidelines as well as individual firm policies. Following the banking crash in 2007/2008, a number of

J. A. Akuffo, *Corporate Governance and Accountability of Financial Institutions*, Palgrave Studies in Accounting and Finance Practice, https://doi.org/10.1007/978-3-030-64046-0_11

findings have demonstrated that serious lapses in governance and banking supervision were critical aspects of the causes of the crisis.

The research discussed in this book is about financial institution boards of directors, corporate governance disclosure and the mechanisms it uses to offer accountability to stakeholders. The motivation stemmed from the backdrop of the 2007/2008 financial crisis, the Walker Review (2009) and the publication of the new UK Corporate Governance Code and continued to reflect on significant events to date. The significant events saw bank boards of directors and senior executives being subject to some blame, and emphasis was being placed on the important role of boards in corporate governance and in managing risk. The analysis and the findings provided in this book are therefore pertinent to recent corporate governance regulation regarding the effectiveness of internal corporate governance mechanisms in mitigating financial crisis. The overall contribution of this study lies in both its methodology and its findings that are applicable to the UK in particular, and elsewhere in general.

The power that corporate governance holds over the success of some of the largest financial institutions in the world is not to be downplayed. Governance underpins the fundamental structure needed to create wealth in a sustainable way. It holds all the crucial ingredients to make a prosperous company, essentially, it is how a company is run in the best interest of its stakeholders. The power of each individual element and mechanism within an institution and the destruction that can be caused by the fallout of any element not delivering on their requirements, has the ability to be devastating (as the financial crisis has demonstrated).

The illusion that can be swept over shareholders and wider stakeholders if something is misrepresented in disclosures, has the potential to increase risk in other areas and breakdown trust between an organisation and its core stakeholders (which could be challenging to recover from). Illusion also touches on the other end of the scale, regarding misleading's around levels of success, especially where the governance components are also based on ethics and human interactions that are not captured in any disclosure mechanism (i.e. the assumption of using a market-based indicator to represent the pursuit of individual human interest within an organisation cannot be underestimated). As we have said previously, you can incentivise, but you cannot regulate human behaviour and this is what gives the space needed to start to cultivate potential illusions within governance. After all, the financial crisis was triggered and caused by some of the most admired financial companies and institutions, with corporate executives that for years were perceived as exemplary in the financial market.

This book set out to discuss corporate governance issues surrounding accounting and finance. The first chapter of this book introduced the corporate governance industry and the concept of accountability to the reader. Chapter 2 looked at the history of the key developments over the past three decades. It focused on the United Kingdom as a key starting premise on the basis that it has led the way towards good corporate governance guides for listed firms since the 1990s, but it goes on to explore wider influences across the globe. Chapter 3 reviewed the relevant prior literature in the field of corporate governance, mechanisms of accountability and disclosure research. It aimed to provide a clear idea about the prior studies and to link the empirical study with disclosure literature. Chapter 4 outlined a number of growing studies and debates within the academics, practitioners and developed communities about the different accountability typologies and its impact on corporate governance. It has specifically reviewed the related empirical literature regarding the relationship between corporate governance and the nature of accountability mechanisms within accounting and finance studies. Chapter 5 explored and examined the implication of ineffective corporate governance and the various mechanisms of accountability, which contributed to the collapse of a variety of banking and other financial institutions, specifically linked to the financial crash of 2007–2008. Many banking and financial institutions did not pay due attention to corporate governance before and during the crisis. Chapter 6 has outlined and discussed the structure of the UK financial sector and its regulatory framework for corporate governance. Chapter 7 focused on the evaluation of corporate governance and accountability mechanisms in financial institutions in the United Kingdom. The chapter presented and discussed the results of the empirical data employed in the empirical study for the book. Chapter 8 focused on the role of disclosure and the quality of corporate governance reporting as discovered from the empirical study conducted. Chapter 9 looked at a stakeholder's perspective on financial institution corporate governance. The chapter examined from the perspective of broader stakeholders relevant to financial organisations' corporate governance and disclosure issues with regard to information richness on a longitudinal basis. It also examined corporate governance issues in other financial institutions. Chapter 10 looks forward to the future of corporate governance, addressing what practitioners need as well as the need for broader research to increase the scope of stakeholder accountability.

References

BCBS. (2010). *Principles for enhancing corporate governance*. Basel Committee on Banking Supervision.

Financial Stability Board (FSB). (2009, September). *FSB principles for sound compensation practices—Implementation standards*. New York.

Walker, S. D. (2009). *A review of corporate governance in UK banks and other financial industry entities*. Final recommendations.

Appendices

Appendix 1: Corporate Governance Measuring Criteria of Scoring Method Used

Description	*Quality score type*	*Definitions of scoring criteria*
Not mentioned	0	• The annual report made no mention or no disclosure of the selected indicator or category at all • Normally reserved for instances where there is a clear omission of required information
Inadequate	1	• The annual report discloses indicator or category only, or mention only with little or no discussion of the category • 'Vague undetailed mentions of the categories providing little or no productive content/description

(continued)

J. A. Akuffo, *Corporate Governance and Accountability of Financial Institutions*, Palgrave Studies in Accounting and Finance Practice, https://doi.org/10.1007/978-3-030-64046-0

(continued)

Description	*Quality score type*	*Definitions of scoring criteria*
Adequate	2	• Disclosure with contextualised or general explanation or either pure narrative or numerical description that meet the minimum required information • Content makes use of predictable descriptions/definitions (Boilerplate[a]) from a direct source or code of principle/provision, but fails to elaborate to provide particular justifications which are relevant to the circumstances of the firm to aid stakeholders in understanding how the provision of the category has been fulfilled
Detailed	3	• Stipulate **(specific)** detailed disclosure matters in relation to the category, including quantitative explanations, providing a detailed description and qualitative disclosure • Adequate detailed provision of descriptions/definitions that are relevant and goes on to elaborate to provide appropriate justifications specific to the context of the company that aid stakeholders in how the provision of the category has been fulfilled
Excellent	4	• In addition to type 3, disclosures provide (specific) issues regarding the category in comparison to accepted peer benchmark plus information that is quantified along with qualitative explanation • Very detailed provision of descriptions/definitions that are comprehensive, relevant and elaborate to a significant extent providing good justifications specific to the context of the company that aid stakeholders in fully understanding how the category has been fulfilled. The company goes beyond the required disclosure to provide the type of best practice reporting that is superior in comparison to its peers

Source Compiled by Akuffo (2018)

[a]The lack of any elucidation and often used boilerplate descriptions in annual financial statement reports have also been recognised by the financial regulator in the United Kingdom Financial Reporting Council) in its 2009 Review of the Effectiveness of the Combined Code

Appendix 2—Constructed Corporate Governance Checklist Index Used for the Assessment in Chapters 7 and 8

Code reference	*Main theme*	*Sub-theme*	*Disclosure required and explanation*	*Source of the disclosure*	*Annual report data location*
COC	Governance in Context	Statement of Compliance	1. A statement in the annual report of how the listed bank has applied the Principles set out in the UK Corporate Governance Code, in a manner that would enable shareholders to evaluate how the principles have been applied 2. A statement as to whether the listed company has: (a) Complied throughout the accounting period with all the relevant provisions set out in the UK Corporate Governance Code and set out in the Annex	LR 9.8.3 (6) & 9; Code, DTR	Chairman Statement/ Governance Report
CONC		Statement of Non-compliance explanation	1. Where a company has not complied with all relevant provisions of the UK Corporate Governance Code has it set out the nature, extent and reasons for non-compliance? 2. Not complied throughout the accounting period with all relevant provisions set out in the UK Corporate Governance Code and set out in the Annex and if so, setting out: (i) Those provisions, if any, it has not complied with; (ii) In the case of provisions whose requirements are of a continuing nature, the period within which, if any, it did not comply with some or all of those provisions and (iii) The company's reasons for non-compliance. (iv) Detail or more disclosure is achieved where a bank provides a detailed explanation to support each area of disclosure Code with which they choose not to comply. (v) Code or the LSE Annex but actively intends to do so in the future, does the explanation indicate how and when it will comply? (vi) Where a company has decided not to implement a particular provision, has an outline of its rationale been detailed? Has the company provided meaningful descriptions of how they apply the provisions of the UK Code?	LR 9.8.6 (6b, iii) & 9; Code, DTR	Chairman Statement/ Governance Report

(continued)

(continued)

Code reference	*Main theme*	*Sub-theme*	*Disclosure required and explanation*	*Source of the disclosure*	*Annual report data location*
LE1.1	Board Leadership	Board Responsibilities/Role of the Board	1. A statement of how the board operates, including a high-level statement of which types of decisions are to be taken by the board and which are to be delegated to management should be included in the annual report 2. The annual report describes the actual activities undertaken by the board as well as matters reserved for it 3. The annual report should provide the names of the chairman, the deputy chairman (where there is one), the chief executive, the senior independent director and the chairmen and members of the board committees	Code, TLR, L, UKLR	Chairman Statement/ Governance Report
LE1.2		Responsibilities/Role of board chairman	1. Disclose explanation If the same person is occupying the CEO and Board Chairman position 2. The chairman is responsible for leadership of the board and ensuring its effectiveness on all aspects of its role 3. The chairman is responsible for setting the board's agenda and ensuring that adequate time is available for discussion of all agenda items, in particular strategic issues. The chairman should also promote a culture of openness and debate by facilitating the effective contribution of non-executive directors in particular and ensuring constructive relations between executive and non-executive directors 4. The chairman is responsible for ensuring that the directors receive accurate, timely and clear information. The chairman should set out how it has ensured effective communication with shareholders Detail disclosure in the annual report includes: a. Disclosure of the extent to which the features of governance discussed in the chairman's statement in the annual report? Disclosure of how the Chairman describes the key features of the governance in the governance reports	Code, TLR, L, UKLR	Chairman Statement/ Governance Report

(continued)

(continued)

Code reference	*Main theme*	*Sub-theme*	*Disclosure required and explanation*	*Source of the disclosure*	*Annual report data location*
BE1	Board Effectiveness	Board Size	1. Every board of directors should examine its size, with a view to determining the impact of the number upon effectiveness, undertake where appropriate programme to reduce the number of directors to a number which facilitates more effective decision-making. Detail disclosure in the annual reports should: (1a) Describe the evaluation process of the board size; (1b) Disclose the person or committee responsible for this evaluation (1c) Disclose how often the size of the board is reviewed (1d) Outline the rationale for the current board size and structure, explaining why the company believes it to be appropriate and provide details of any planned or anticipated changes to the board size or structure	Code, TLR, L, UKLR	Governance reports
BE2		Meetings	1. The annual report should set out the number of meetings of the board and its committees and individual attendance by directors 2. The annual report should disclose attendance records of individual directors at board meetings during the year 3. The annual report section should disclose the topic and outline key issues discussed at the meeting 4. The annual report should disclose the summary outcomes of the meeting discussions	Code, TLR, L, UKLR	Governance reports
BE3		Board Balance or board composition	1. Explain why the company regards the number of non-executive directors appointed to the board as sufficient and robust; 2. Set out how the specific skills, expertise and experience of the board are harnessed to best effect in addressing the major challenges for the company; 3. Where a company has diverged from the requirements of provision of the UK Code, give a reasoned explanation for the departure. 4. The section of the Annual Report including the Directors' biographies should include the following: 5. The date of appointment of each director, the length of service of each director as a director and, where applicable, the length of service of each director on a board committee; A detailed description of the skills, expertise and experience that each of the directors brings to the board;	Code, TLR	Governance reports

(continued)

(continued)

Code reference	*Main theme*	*Sub-theme*	*Disclosure required and explanation*	*Source of the disclosure*	*Annual report data location*
BE4		Non-Executive Directors Independence	1. The annual report should state the names of the non-executive directors whom the board determines to be independent, with reason where necessary 2. A statement in the annual on how the non-executive directors have constructively challenged and help develop proposals on strategy 3. A statement in the annual report that identifies how the board considers each of the non-executive directors to be independent 4. The board should state in the annual on how it scrutinise the performance of management and monitor the reporting of performance 5. They should satisfy themselves on the integrity of financial information and that financial controls and systems of risk management are robust and defensible	UKLR, Code, TLR	Governance reports
BE5		Board Evaluation	1. A statement of how performance evaluation of the board, its committees, and its individual directors has been conducted should be provided 2. A statement should be made available of whether an external facilitator has any other connection with the company 3. Has the objective and scope of the evaluation review, the methodology applied and the rationale for this methodology been provided? 4. Within the statement made under the annex requirement has a distinction between the evaluation of the board process, of individual directors and of the collective board strength been made? 5. Does the statement specify when the most recent externally facilitated performance evaluation was undertaken, if applicable, or when the board expects to engage an external facilitator? In circumstances where the process is one of self-evaluation, has the board included an explanation of the steps that were included in the methodology to achieve as robust and objective an approach as possible?	Code, TLR, L, UKLR	Governance reports

(continued)

(continued)

Code reference	*Main theme*	*Sub-theme*	*Disclosure required and explanation*	*Source of the disclosure*	*Annual report data location*
BE6		Committees working activities	The annual report should disclose details on: 1. Use of committee structures (at least three committees) and associated committee terms of reference for audit, remuneration and nomination committees' and explaining their role and the authority delegated to them by the board disclosed; specifically the rationale for use of audit, nomination and remuneration committees in the annual report should be disclosed 2. Disclosure on the use of external search agencies and advertising, with a reasonable justification provided when neither is used 3. A report of the process followed by Nomination Committees in identifying a pool of candidates and selecting and appointing the right candidate for each new appointee 4. Remuneration policy discussion disclosed: (1) A clear and concise disclosure on remuneration policy in line with the disclosure provisions contained in paragraph 5 of Section II (Remuneration Policy) of the EU Guidance on Remuneration; (2) Where there are particular challenges facing a company in attracting, retaining and motivating key personnel, the specific contextual facts leading to these challenges should be described, as well as the overall strategy for dealing with these challenges	Code, LR, M	Governance reports
BE7		Board Refreshment	1. An explanation of the process followed by the nomination committee in identifying a pool of candidates 2. An explanation of the process followed by the nomination committee in selecting and recommending the candidate 3. A clear statement that the company has used external search agencies and advertising to identify a candidate, or an appropriate negative statement 4. The section describing the work of the nomination committee should include a description of the board's policy on diversity, including gender, any measureable objectives that it has set for implementing the policy, and progress on achieving the objectives 5. State and explain the board's general policy for board renewal	Code, TLR, L, UKLR	Governance reports

(continued)

(continued)

Code reference	*Main theme*	*Sub-theme*	*Disclosure required and explanation*	*Source of the disclosure*	*Annual report data location*
ACC1.	Accountability	Risk management and internal control	1. Has the annual report disclosed a report to shareholders that the board has conducted a review of the effectiveness of the company's risk management and internal control systems should be provided 2. Has the annual report disclosed a summary of the process which the board (where applicable, through its committees) has applied in reviewing the effectiveness of the system of internal control (e.g. reports from management, the role of the audit committee and other relevant committee(s), the role of the internal audit function and the annual assessment of the system) and confirm that necessary action has been or, is being taken to remedy any significant failings or weaknesses identified from their review 3. Has the annual report disclosed a narrative statement of how the company has applied UK Code Principle C.2 disclosing at a minimum that: • There is an ongoing process for identifying, evaluating and managing the significant risks faced by the company; • It has been in place for the year under review and up to the date of approval of the annual report and accounts; • It is regularly reviewed by the board and It accords with the Revised Guidance	Code, TLR, L, UKLR	Governance reports

(continued)

(continued)

Code reference	*Main theme*	*Sub-theme*	*Disclosure required and explanation*	*Source of the disclosure*	*Annual report data location*
ACC2.		Internal audit	Disclosure detail of the scope of the internal audit functions: 1. The audit committee should set the principles for recommending use of the accounting firm of the external auditors for non-audit services, such as management consultancy and corporate finance services 2. Audit committees should have the necessary business acumen to address external auditor independence on a case-by-case basis thereby preserving the company's ability to select its external auditor for non-audit services if that is in the best interests of the company and its investors 3. In addition to the Companies Act requirements, there should be separate disclosure of the amount paid for non-audit services with a detailed description in the notes to the annual financial statements of the nature thereof, together with the amounts paid for each of the services described and or 4. A statement of disclosure of the internal control adequacy and details of any weaknesses of its internal control systems	Code, TLR, L, UKLR	Governance reports
ACC3.		External audit	1. Has the annual report disclosed an explanation of how, if the auditor provides non-audit services, auditor objectivity and independence are safeguarded should be provided? 2. Has the annual report disclosed an explanation of how it has assessed the effectiveness of the external audit process and the approach taken to the appointment or reappointment of the external auditor, and information on the length of tenure of the current audit firm and when a tender was last conducted 3. And if the external auditor provides non-audit services, has the report disclosed an explanation of how auditor objectivity and independence is safeguarded	Code, TLR, L, UKLR	Directors report, corporate governance statement/report section

(continued)

(continued)

Code reference	*Main theme*	*Sub-theme*	*Disclosure required and explanation*	*Source of the disclosure*	*Annual report data location*
ACC4.		Audit committees scrutiny	1. Disclosure of the terms of reference of the audit committee, including its role and the authority delegated to it by the board, should be made available and disclose 2. The code states that this requirement may be met by making the information available on request and placing it on the company's website. Companies may wish to include this information in the annual report. Has the annual report disclose this information? 3. A separate section of the annual report should disclose and describe the work of the audit committee in discharging its responsibilities 4. The reference to a "separate section" of the annual report helps to ensure that the description is clearly identifiable. A subsection within a larger corporate governance statement would generally be acceptable 5. Has the company included a meaningful description of the work carried out by the audit committee during the financial year? 6. Does the description explain the work done by the committee relating to the oversight of risk management on behalf of the board? 7. Where the board has assigned work on risk management to a specific risk committee, has a meaningful description of the work carried out by that committee been disclosed? 8. Disclosure of a summary of the role of the audit committee and the names and qualifications of all members of the audit committee during the period and the number of audit committee meetings An explanation of how the audit committee reached its recommendation to the board on the appointment, reappointment or removal of the external auditors.	Code, TLR, L, UKLR	Directors report, corporate governance statement/report section
PERF1.	Performance/ Result	Key performance Indicators	The annual report should disclose the following categories: 1. Statements that link its KPIs to the company's objectives explaining why they have been selected and what they measure 2. Disclose quantifiable results that are compared to prior years 3. An explanation of how they are calculated and the source of data 4. Disclosure to include future targets or expectations	Codes, UKLR, LR, Law	Business review section

(continued)

(continued)

Code reference	*Main theme*	*Sub-theme*	*Disclosure required and explanation*	*Source of the disclosure*	*Annual report data location*
PERF2.		Code of ethics	1. Disclosure of external complaints policy (the organisation has a policy(s) on receiving and handling complaints from several external stakeholder groups) 2. Process and procedure and specific policies for dealing and handling of code of conduct 3. Disclosure of independent investigations and recommendation for improvement of breaches of ethical standards/company misbehaviour 4. A company should implement its code of ethics as part of corporate governance	LR	Directors report, corporate governance statement/report section
PERF3.		Whistle-blowing	1. The annual report should disclose details of whistle-blowing policies and procedures that have been put in place in the annual report 2. The annual report makes a commitment statement to discuss the following in the annual report:(a) Ensuring the confidentiality of the complainant and identifying clear exception rules for a confidentiality breach; (b) Guaranteeing non-retaliation towards complainants and (c) Sanctioning those that retaliate against companies	LR, L, M	Directors report, corporate governance statement/report section
PERF4.		Breaches and penalties	1. Detailed disclosure of breaches and penalties and sanctions applicable to individuals—i.e. the number, the type of breach/sanction, and the remedies for addressing it 2. The annual report should disclose and discuss or outline how they are dealing with public or private (formal and informal) enforcement mechanisms regarding; (a) Inappropriate behaviour; (b) Operational failure; (c) Treatment of customers and (d) Regulatory penalties for conduct failures	LRS, Law, Company Act, TLR	Directors report, corporate governance statement/report section

Key UK Listing Rules—UKLR; Requirement from compliance codes provisions (UK)—Code; Thesis Literature Review—TLR; Law or Legislation—L; Mandated by Regulations—M

Appendix 3—Table 6.4 UK Largest Banks and Transaction Networks

Largest United Kingdom Banking Firms

$bn, end-2010

		Tier one capital	Assets
1	HSBC Holdings	133.2	2,455
2	Royal Bank of Scotland	94.1	2,275
3	Barclays	83.8	2,331
4	Lloyds Banking Group	73.8	1,552
5	Standard Chartered	34.3	517
6	Santander UK	17	474
7	Nationwide Building Society *(as at 4/2010)*	11.7	294
8	Clydesdale Bank *(as at 9/2010)*	4.1	70
9	FCE Bank	3.7	22
10	The Co-operative Bank	3.2	71
11	Yorkshire Building Society	2.4	47
12	Investec Bank *(as at 3/2011)*	2	30
13	Schroders	2	21
14	Standard Bank	1.5	31
15	Coventry Building Society	1.3	35

Source: The Banker

Online Banking

	Online banking adoption, % of all individuals (2010)
Norway	83
Netherlands	77
Iceland	77
Finland	76
Sweden	75
UK US	45
Germany	45
Ireland	43
Spain	34
Poland	27
Italy	18
Greece	6

Source: DB Research, Eurostat, Forrester Research, Pew 2011

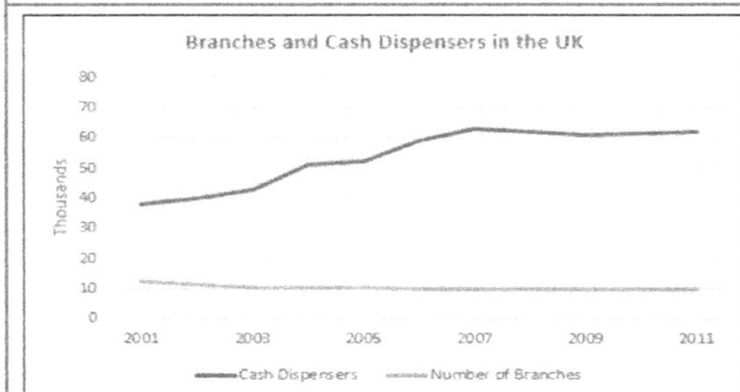

Source: Payments Council, British Bankers' Association

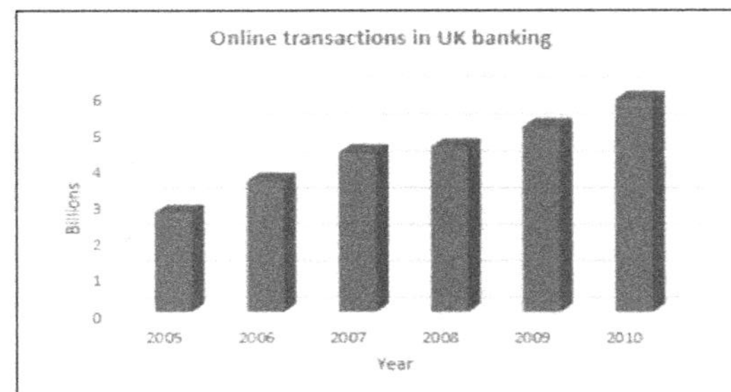

Source: British Bankers' Association

Appendix 4—Table 6.5a: Global Financial Markets: UK Market Share (April 2013)

Products	*UK market share (in per cent unless stated otherwise)*	*Global rank*
International banking		
Lending	19	1
Borrowing	21	1
European Activities	50	1
Insurance market		
Global Insurance Premia	$320 billion	3 (Global) and 1 (Europe)
Pension Fund Assets	10	1 (Europe)
Equities		
Global Foreign Enquiry Trading	19	2
Number of International Public Offerings (IPOs)	6 IPOs with 12% market share	17 IPOs in Hong Kong; 12 in the United States
Turnover on the London Stock Exchange (LSE)		5 of global turnover/7 global equity market capitalisation
Bonds		
Euro-bonds secondary market		70% of trading by bookrunners in London
Securitisation issuance	6	2 (behind the United States, 75)
Fund management (source of hedge funds)	8	2 (behind the United States, 50)
Hedge fund assets	18	2 (behind the United States, 68)
Private equity investment value	12	2 (behind the United States, 45)
Derivatives		
OTC interest rate derivatives	46 (turnover)	1
Exchange traded derivatives		Three derivative exchanges: New York Stock Exchange Liffe is #2 for interest rate derivatives in Europe (by volume). London Metals Exchange is #1 for non-ferrous metals. ICE Futures Europe is #1 in Europe and #2 worldwide for energy products.
Foreign exchange		
Turnover	38	1
Commodities		

(continued)

(continued)

Products	*UK market share (in per cent unless stated otherwise)*	*Global rank*
Commodity derivatives trading		London and New York are main international players (Chicago is the biggest domestic player).
Bullion markets (gold/silver)		The London Bullion Market Association (LBMA) is the largest OTC market ahead of New York and Zurich and clears most of the wholesale OTC trades.
Islamic finance		
	Largest number of 'sharia complaint' banks (22), exchange-traded funds (7), law firms (25) among Western countries; issued 37 sukuk on LSE.	

Sources TheCityUK, Bank of England

Appendix 5—Table 6.5b

Financial markets share by country (%)

	UK	*US*	*Japan*	*France*	*Germany*	*Singapore*	*Hong Kong*	*Others*
Cross-border bank lending (Sep 2012)	**19**	11	11	8	8	3	3	37
Foreign exchange turnover (Oct 2012)	**37**	17	6	3	2	6	5	24
Exchange-traded derivatives, number of contracts traded (2012)	7	**34**	2	–	8	–	1	48
Interest rates OTC derivatives turnover (Apr 2010)	**46**	24	3	3	2	3	1	14
Marine insurance net premium income (2011)	**19**	6	9	1	4	1	1	56

(continued)

(continued)

Financial markets share by country (%)

	UK	*US*	*Japan*	*France*	*Germany*	*Singapore*	*Hong Kong*	*Others*
Fund management (as a source of funds, end-2011)	8	**46**	8	–	2	–	1	32
Hedge funds assets (end-2012)	18	**65**	2	1	–	1	1	12
Private equity - investment value (2011)	12	**46**	1	1	2	1	–	33
Securitisation - issuance (2011)	6	**73**	2	–	1	–	–	17

Bold*= Market Leader*

UK share of financial markets (%)

	1992	*1995*	*1998*	*2001*	*2004*	*2007*	*2010*	*2012**
Cross-border bank lending	16	17	20	19	20	18	18	19
Foreign exchange turnover	27	30	33	31	32	37	37	37
Exchange-traded derivatives	12	12	11	7	7	6	6	7
Interest rates OTC derivatives turnover	–	27	36	35	42	44	46	–
Marine insurance net premium income	24	21	14	18	19	17	20	–
Fund management (as a source of funds)	–	–	8	8	8	9	8	–
Hedge funds assets	–	–	–	9	22	22	19	18
Private equity	–	–	–	6	24	17	21	–
Securitisation - issuance	–	–	–	–	4	14	6	–

Source
*Latest available data for 2012 (corresponds with dates in the first part of the table)
(1) International Monetary Fund-Spillover Report 2011
(2) TheCityUK calculations and estimates based on various sources

Appendix 6—Categories of Financial Sector Contribution to the UK Economy

Contribution to Gross Domestic Product and Employment

The prominence of financial services in the UK economy has developed and remains a growing area. In 2011, the sector made up 9.6% of the United Kingdom's Gross Domestic Product as opposed to only 5.2% in the year 2000 (BOE 2011; TheCityUK 2012). The UK financial services is a leading employer with over 2.1 million people working across the United Kingdom in financial and related professional services—including legal services, accounting services and management consultancy—accounting for over 7% of total UK employment. More than two-thirds are employed outside London, including over 200,000 in the North West and South East; around 150,000 in the East of England, Scotland and the South West and around 130,000 in West Midlands and Yorkshire and The Humber. Out of all 650 Parliamentary constituencies in the United Kingdom there are 150 (23%) where 3000 or more people are employed in financial and related professional services and a total of 486 (77%) with more than 1000 such employees. Over 20 towns and cities in the United Kingdom each have over 10,000 people employed in financial and related professional services. A vast number of people work within roles in the finance industry (over one million) with a huge number also taking roles that are associated such as accountancy, actuarial services and law.

However, out of the total financial services employment of 1 million that works directly in the sector, the majority was in banking (427,900 employees) and insurance (313,700 employees). Securities dealing (55,800) and fund management (33,400) were the other main categories, with other financial services accounting for 209,100 employees. Professional services employment of 1.1 m people is divided between management consultancy (411,200), legal services (314,200) and accounting services (336,800).

Appendix 7

Breakdown of UK Financial service sector employment (end of 2013)

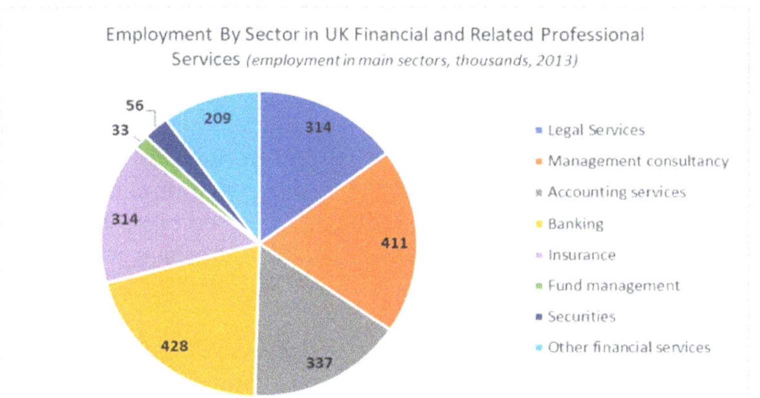

Total UK employment in financial and professional services 2.1m

Source: Adopted from ONS Business Register and Employment Survey

Additionally, financial and related professional services on average employ a younger workforce than other sectors. Just over 50% of industry workers are under 40 years old, compared to 47% in other sectors. Around 36% of those employed are between 40 and 54 years old (the same as in other sectors), and 12% are over 54 (17% for other sectors). The industry therefore has a positive effect in helping to offset the higher jobless rate amongst the younger population in the United Kingdom.

Furthermore, the banking industry contributed around £56bn to UK national output in 2010, or 4.8% of Gross Domestic Product (GDP), over half of the 8.9% accounted for by the financial sector as a whole. Activity in the banking sector has been more volatile than other sectors over the past decade, mainly due to the sensitivity of banking profits to the business cycle. During the past decade, banks have made considerable efforts to reduce costs including staffing which typically accounts for over half of operating expenses. Additionally, the regional breakdown shows that London accounted for 31% of UK employment in banking or some 141,000. It was followed by North West 10%, Yorkshire 10%, Scotland 9%, South West 8% and the South East 8%.

Contribution to Business and Household

According to the Financial Stability Board, "There are 64 million personal current accounts in the UK, with the vast majority of households having a current account and 90% of adult consumers having at least one current account, giving the UK one of the highest levels of banking penetration among advanced economies" (Financial Stability Board 2013, p. 45). More recently, the Government employed initiatives such as the basic bank account with the aim to increase dissemination of banking service use. In the United Kingdom in 2011, around 9.1 million people held basic bank accounts. This was a large increase from only 2.7 million six years earlier. "UK fund managers – representing saving through pensions, life assurance policies and other investments – helped protect and grow over GBP 3.2 trillion in financial assets, a significant proportion of which is on behalf of UK households and families" (Financial Stability Board 2013, p. 45).

The UK financial industry (for example banks) still remains an essential source of finance to UK businesses (providing about 80% of their finance) in key areas such as loans, stocks, pensions, insurance and equities. This contributes materially to the components of the UK gross domestic output.

Contribution to Current and Capital Accounts

UK financial and professional services generated a trade surplus of £67bn in 2013 (£47.2 billion in 2011), which represents around 4% of GDP in its own right: the trade surplus was up 10% in the first nine months of 2014 compared to the same period in 2013, pointing to a full year total of around £74bn. UK financial and professional services firms are the face of British businesses across the globe. The trade surplus of financial and professional services is larger than other UK firms' overall net export excess (FSB 2013). This helps to offset UK's large trade in goods deficit of over £100bn.

The United Kingdom is the leading exporter of financial services across the world. The United Kingdom's financial services trade surplus of $71bn in 2013 was more than twice that of the next largest trade surpluses recorded by the United States and Luxembourg. The United Kingdom's major trading partners include the United States, EU Member States and other advanced economies, such as Switzerland, Japan, Australia and Canada. These are followed by emerging economies such as Russia, Taiwan and Saudi Arabia, as well as trade with other international financial markets in Asia. The volume of trade with emerging economies has great potential for growth.

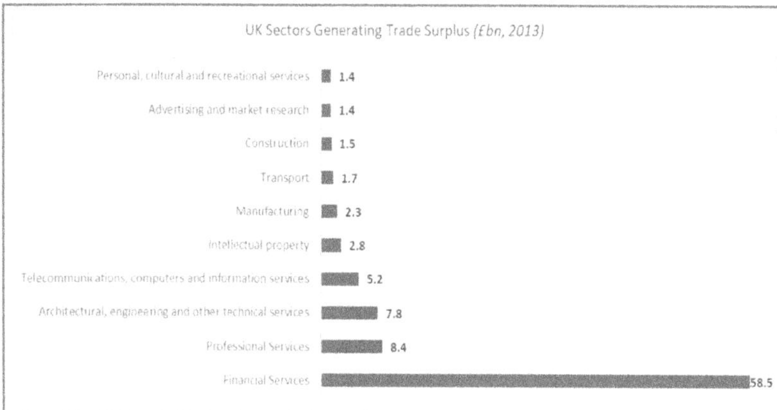

Source: Adapted from ONS Balance of Payments Yearbook

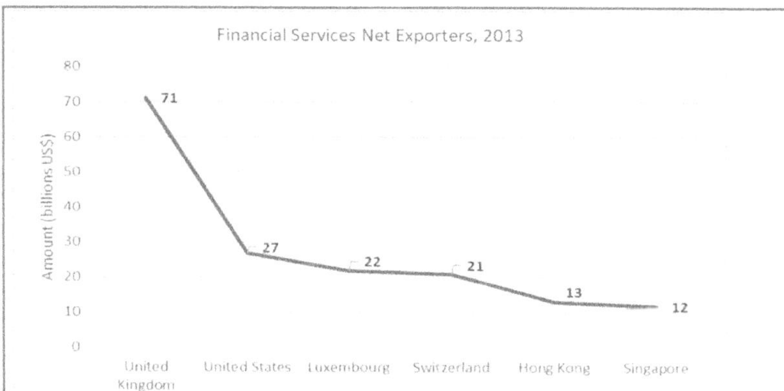

Source: Adapted from UNCTAD and TheCityUK

Contribution to general Tax Receipts

The tax paid by financial services in the United Kingdom that can be readily identified includes HMRC statistics for corporation tax paid by firms and income tax paid by employees. However, the tax contribution of the UK financial sector is much broader also including, for example, VAT, national insurance contribution and business rates. In recent years, an annual study by PricewaterhouseCoopers (PwC) has been commissioned by City of London Corporation to estimate the full tax contribution of the financial sector. Total tax intake of UK financial services is estimated to have been stable at £63.0bn in 2011/12 compared with the previous year, which was up from £53.4bn in 2009/10. Tax revenues previously had dropped from £67.8bn in 2007/08. The total tax take represented 11.6% of total UK government receipts down from 12.1% in 2010/11. Financial services' tax revenues were based on:

1. Taxes borne by employers totalling £23.8bn, including corporation tax, bank levy, employers' national insurance contributions, business rates, irrecoverable VAT and stamp duties.
2. Taxes collected by employers totalling £39.2bn, including employees income tax and national insurance contribution, insurance premium tax and net VAT.

Banks constitute the largest taxpayers in the financial services sector. By number, banks were 37% of the financial companies taking part in the 2011 City of London Corporation Total Tax Contribution study; they paid 72.8% of the total taxes borne and 66.5% of the total taxes collected. The banks are also the largest employers and generate the largest employment taxes. Corporation tax paid in the year ending April 2012 fell to £5.4bn from £7.2bn in 2010/11 and the peak of £12.9bn in 2007/08. In addition, £1.6bn was raised through the Bank Levy. UK Government tax receipts have been heavily impacted by the financial crisis and the challenging economic climate in recent years. The 13% share of corporation tax paid by financial services in 2011/12 remained well below the share of over a quarter in the years up to 2007/08. Contribution of financial services to corporation tax receipts remains just ahead of manufacturing and distribution but behind North Sea oil and gas companies, which raised £9.2bn. Income tax payments of those employed in financial services were estimated by PwC at £21.4bn in 2011/12, unchanged from 2010/11. These tax payments made up 15% of all income tax revenue in 2011/12, nearly four times the 4% share of financial services in total UK employment.

Tax contribution of UK financial sector

£bn, 2011/12

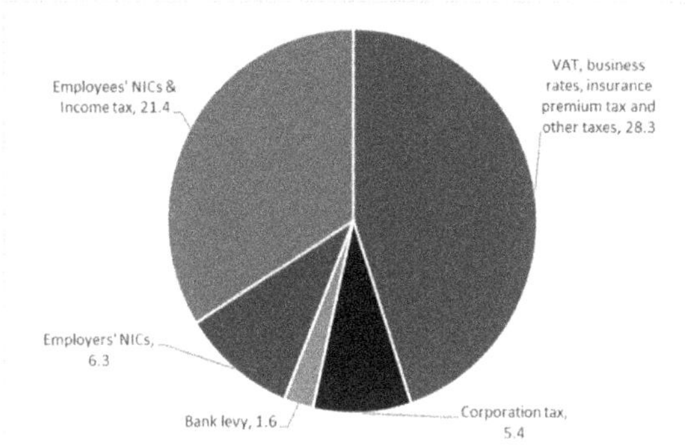

Total tax contribution of UK financial sector £63.0bn

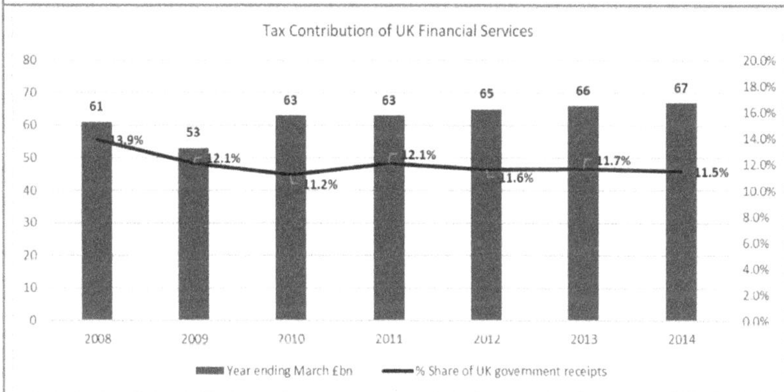

Source: Adapted by the author using a report from PricewaterhouseCoopers/City of London Corporation

References

Abbott, L. J., Parker, S., & Peters, G. F. (2004). Audit committee characteristics and restatements. *Auditing: A Journal of Practice and Theory, 23*(1), 72–86.

Abdelghany, K. E. (2005). Disclosure of market risk or accounting measures of risk: An empirical study. *Managerial Auditing Journal, 20*(8), 867–875.

Abdel-Fattah, T. M. H. (2008). *Voluntary disclosure practices in emerging capital markets: The case of Egypt*. Durham thesis, Durham University.

Abraham, S., & Cox, P. (2007). Analysing the determination of narrative risk information in UK FTSE 100 annual reports. *British Accounting Review, 39*(3), 221–240.

Aburaya, R. K. (2012). *The relationship between corporate governance and environmental disclosure: UK evidence*. Durham thesis, Durham University.

Accounting Standards Board (ASB). (1995). *Statement of principles for financial reporting*. London: ASB.

Accounting Standards Board (ASB). (2005). *Reporting standard 1—Operating and financial review*. London: ASB.

Accounting Standards Board (ASB). (2009a). *Improvement to financial reporting standards*. London: ASB.

ASB. (2009b). *Rising to the challenge—A review of narrative reporting by UK listed companies*. London: Financial Reporting Council.

Acharya, V. (2009). A theory of systemic risk and design of prudential bank regulation. *Journal of Financial Stability, 5*(3), 224–255.

Adams, C. A. (2002). Internal organisational factors influencing corporate social and ethical reporting: Beyond current theorising. *Accounting, Auditing and Accountability Journal, 15*(2), 223–250.

J. A. Akuffo, *Corporate Governance and Accountability of Financial Institutions*, Palgrave Studies in Accounting and Finance Practice, https://doi.org/10.1007/978-3-030-64046-0

Adams, C. A., Hill, W., & Roberts, C. B. (1998). Corporate social reporting practices in Western Europe: Legitimating corporate behaviour? *British Accounting Review, 30*(1), 1–21.

Adams, R. B. (2010). Governance at banking institutions. In H. K. Baker & R. Anderson (Eds.), *Corporate governance*. Hoboken, NJ: Wiley & Sons.

Adams, R. B. (2012). Governance and the financial crisis. *International Review of Finance, 12*(1), 5–329.

Adams, R. B., Benjamin, E. H., & Weisbach, M. S. (2010). The role of boards of directors in corporate governance: A conceptual framework and survey. *Journal of Economic Literature, 48*(1), 56–103.

Adams, R. B., & Daniel, F. (2009). Women in the boardroom and their impact on governance and performance. *Journal of Financial Economics, 94*(2), 290–303.

Adams, R. B., & Daniel, F. (2012). Regulatory pressure and bank directors' incentives to attend board meetings. *International Review of Finance, 12*(1), 227–248.

Adams, R. B., & Mehran, H. (2003). Is corporate governance different for bank holding companies? Federal Reserve Bank of New York. *Economic Policy Review, 9*(1), 127–141.

Adams, R. B., & Mehran, H. (2005). *Corporate performance, board structure and its determinants in the banking industry* (Working Paper), SSRN.

Adams, R. B., & Mehran, H. (2012). Bank board structure and performance: Evidence for large bank holding companies. *Journal of Financial Intermediation, 21*, 241–256.

Aerts, W., & Cormier, D. (2009). Media legitimacy and corporate environmental communication. *Accounting, Organizations and Society, 34*(1), 3–21.

Aggarwal, R., Isil, E., Miguel, F., & Pedro, M. (2011). 'Does governance travel around the world? Evidence from institutional investors. *Journal of Financial Economics, 100*, 155–180.

Aguilera, R. V., & Cuervo-Cazurra, A. (2004). Codes of good governance worldwide: What is the trigger? *Organization Studies, 25*(3), 413–440.

Aguilera, R. V., & Cuervo-Cazurra, A. (2009). Codes of corporate governance: Corporate governance. *An International Review, 17*(3), 372–383.

Aguilera, R. V., Williams, C. A., Conley, J. M., & Rupp, D. E. (2006). Corporate governance and social responsibility: A comparative analysis of the UK and the US. *Corporate Governance: An International Review, 14*(3), 142–151.

Ajinkya, B., Bhojraj, S., & Sengupta, P. (2005). The association between outside directors, institutional investors, and the properties of management earnings forecasts. *Journal of Accounting Research, 43*(3), 344–370.

Akhigbe, A., & Madura, J. (1996). Impact of anti-takeover amendments on corporate performance. *Applied Financial Economics, 6*, 519–529.

Akhigbe, A., & Martin, A. D. (2008). Influence of disclosure and governance on risk of US financial services firms following Sarbanes-Oxley. *Journal of Banking & Finance, 32*(10), 2124–2135.

Aljifri, K., & Hussainey, K. (2007). The determinants of forward-looking information in annual reports of UAE companies. *Managerial Auditing Journal, 22*(9), 883–894.

Alexander, K. (2004). *Corporate governance and banking regulation* (Vol. 17, pp. 2–38) (Working Paper), CERF Research Programme in International Financial Regulation, Cambridge.

Alexander, K. (2006). Corporate governance and banks: The role of regulation in reducing the principal-agency problem. *Journal of Banking Regulation, 7*(1), 17–40.

Allen, F., & Carletti, E. (2010). An overview of the crisis: Causes, consequences, and solutions. *International Review of Finance, 10*(1), 1–26.

Al-Tamimi, H. A. H., & Al-Mazrooei, F. M. (2007). Banks' risk management: A comparison study of UAE national and foreign banks. *Journal of Risk Finance, 8*(4), 394–409.

Al-Tuwaijri, S. A., Christensen, T. E., & Hughes, K. E., II. (2004). The relations among environmental disclosure, environmental performance, and economic performance: A simultaneous equations approach. *Accounting, Organizations and Society, 29*(5/6), 448–470.

Amran, A., Bin, A. M. R., & Hassan, B. C. H. M. (2009). Risk reporting: An exploratory study on risk management disclosure in Malaysian annual reports. *Managerial Auditing Journal, 24*(1), 39–57.

Anderson, L. B., Hager, D., Maberg, S., Naess, M. B., & Tungland, M. (2012). The financial crisis in an operational risk management context: A review of causes and influencing factors. *Reliability Engineering and System Safety, 105*, 3–12.

Antonacopoulou, E. P., & Meric, J. (2005). A critic of stakeholder theory: management science or a sophisticated ideology of control. *Corporate Governance: An International Review, 5*(2), 27–31.

Armour, J. (2008). *Enforcement strategies in UK corporate governance: A roadmap and empirical assessment* (Law Working Paper No. 106/2008).

Armstrong, C. S., Guay, W. R., & Weber, J. P. (2010). The role of information and financial reporting: In corporate governance and debt contracting. *Journal of Accounting and Economics, 50*(2/3), 182–229.

Arnold, V., Bedard, J. C., Phillips, J. R., & Sutton, S. G. (2011). Do section 404 disclosures affect investors' perceptions of information systems reliability and stock price predictions? *International Journal of Accounting Information Systems, 12*(4), 243–258.

Arsalidou, D., & Wang, M. (2005). Difficulties with enforcing western standards of corporate governance in Asia. *European Business Law Review, 16*(2), 329–340.

Arun, T. G., & Turner, J. D. (2003). *Corporate governance of banks in developing economies-concepts and issues* (Policy Working Paper No. 2/2003). University of Manchester, School of Environment and Development.

Ashby, S. (2008). Operational risk: Learning lessons from non-financial organisations. *Journal of Risk Management in Financial Institutions, 1*(4).

Ashby, S., & Waite, N. (2008). *The turner review on the global banking crisis: A response from the financial services forum.*

Association of Chartered Certified Accountant. (2014a, February). *Creating value through governance—Towards a new accountability: A consultation.* London.

Association of Chartered Certified Accountant (ACCA). (2014b, December). *Culture vs regulation: What is needed to improve ethics in finance.*

Association of Chartered Certified Accountants (ACCA). (1999). *ACCA social reporting award scheme.* London: ACCA Publishing.

Association of Supervisors of Banks of the Americas (ASBA). (2009). *Corporate governance in banking institutions.* Mexico, D.F.

Ayuso, S., & Argandoña, A. (2007). *Responsible corporate governance: Towards a stakeholder board of directors?* (Working Paper No. 701). IESE Business School—University of Navarra, Spain.

Balata, P., & Breton, G. (2005). Narratives vs numbers in the annual report: Are they giving the same message to the investors? *Review of Accounting and Finance, 4*(2), 5–14.

Ballestor, L., Ferrer, R., & Gonzalez, C. (2011). Linear and nonlinear interest rate sensitivity of Spanish banks. *The Spanish Review of Financial Economics, 9*(2), 30–44.

Bank of England (BOE). (2010). *The financial stability report* (Issue No. 28). Bank of England.

Bank of England (BOE). (2011). *The financial stability report* (Issue No. 30). Bank of England.

Bank of England (BOE). (2012a). *The financial stability report* (Issue No. 32). Bank of England.

Bank of England (BOE). (2012b). *Monetary financial institutions (MFIs) in the UK that feed into the national accounts. Bankstats table: Monetary financial institutions' balance sheets, income and expenditure.* Bank of England.

Bank of England (BOE). (2013a). *The financial stability report* (Issue No. 33). Bank of England.

Bank of England (BOE). (2013b). *The financial stability report* (Issue No. 34). Bank of England.

Bank of England (BOE). (2018, November). *Financial stability report* (Issue No. 44).

Bank for International Settlements (BIS). (1999). *Enhancing corporate governance for banking organisations*. Basel: Basel Committee on Banking Supervision.

Bank for International Settlements (BIS). (2006a). *Enhancing corporate governance for banking organisations*. Basel Committee on Banking Supervision, Basel.

Bank for International Settlements (BIS). (2006b). *International convergence of capital measurement standards*. Basel Committee on Banking Supervision, Basel.

Bank for International Settlements (BIS). (2008). *Principles for sound liquidity risk management and supervision*. Basel: Basel Committee on Banking Supervision.

Bank for International Settlements (BIS). (2009). *History of the Basel committee on banking supervision*. Basel: Basel Committee on Banking Supervision.

Banks, E. (2004). *The credit risk of complex derivatives* (3rd ed.). London, UK: Palgrave Macmillan.

Barkmeyer, R., Holt, D., Figge, F., & Napolitano, G. (2010). A longitudinal and contextual analysis of media representation of business ethics. *European Business Review, 22*(4), 377–396.

Barnhill, T. M., Papapanagiotou, P., & Schumacher, L. (2002). Measuring integrated market and credit risk in bank portfolios: An application to a set of hypothetical banks operating in South Africa. *Financial Markets, Institutions & Instruments, 11*(5), 401–443.

Barrell, R., Davis, E. P., Karim, D., & Liadze, I. (2010). Bank regulation, property prices and early warning systems for banking crisis in OECD countries. *Journal of Banking & Finance, 34*(9), 2255–2264.

Barry, T. A., Lepetit, L., & Tarazi, A. (2011). Ownership structure and risk in publicly held and privately owned banks. *Journal of Banking and Finance, 35*, 1327–1340.

Bayou, M. E., Reinstein, A., & Williams, P. F. (2011). To tell the truth: A discussion of issues concerning truth and ethics in accounting. *Accounting, Organization and Society, 36*(2), 109–124.

Baysinger, B., & Butler, H. (1985). Corporate governance and the board of directors: Performance effects of changes in board composition. *Journal of Law, Economics, & Organization, 1*(1), 101–124.

Baysinger, B. D., & Hoskisson, R. E. (1990). The composition of boards of directors and strategic control: Effects on corporate strategy. *The Academy of Management Review, 15*(1), 72–87.

Baysinger, B. D., & Zardkoohi, A. (1986). Technology, residual claimants and corporate control. *Journal of Law, Economics, and Organization, 2*(2), 331–342.

BCBS. (1998). *Enhancing bank transparency.* Basel Committee on Banking Supervision.

Basel Committee on Banking Supervision (BCBS). (1999). *Enhancing corporate governance for banking organisations.* Basel: Bank for International Settlements.

BCBS. (2001). *Public disclosures by banks: Results of the 1999 disclosure survey.* Basel Committee on Banking Supervision.

BCBS. (2003). *Public disclosures by banks: Results of the 2001 disclosure survey.* Basel Committee on Banking Supervision.

BCBS. (2009). *Enhancements to the Basel II framework.* Basel Committee on Banking Supervision.

BCBS. (2010a). *Principles for enhancing corporate governance.* Basel: Basel Committee on Banking Supervision.

BCBS. (2010b). *Basel III: International framework for liquidity risk measurement, standards and monitoring.* Basel: Basel Committee on Banking Supervision.

BCBS. (2011a). *Basel III: A global regulatory framework for more resilient banks and banking systems.* Basel Committee on Banking Supervision.

BCBS. (2011b). *Core principles for effective banking supervision.* Basel Committee on Banking Supervision.

Beattie, V., & Jones, M. J. (1992). The use and abuse of graphs in annual reports: Theoretical framework and empirical study. *Accounting and Business Research, 22*(88), 290–301.

Beattie, V., McInnes, W., & Fearnley, S. (2004). A methodology for analysing and evaluating narratives in annual reports: A comprehensive descriptive profile and metrics for disclosure quality attributes. *Accounting Forum, 28*(3), 202–231.

Beattie, V., & Pratt, K. (2002). *Voluntary annual report disclosures: What users want*. Edinburgh: Institute of Chartered Accountants of Scotland. Research Report.

Beattie, V., & Thomson, S. J. (2007). Lifting the lid on the use of content analysis to investigate intellectual capital disclosures. *Accounting Forum, 31*(2), 129–163.

Bebbington, J. (1997). Engagement, education and sustainability: A review essay on environmental accounting. *Accounting, Auditing and Accountability Journal, 10*(3), 365–381.

Bebbington, J. (2001). Sustainable development: A review of the international development, business and accounting literature. *Accounting Forum, 25*(2), 128–157.

Bebbington, J., Larrinage, C., & Moneva, J. M. (2008). Corporate social reporting and reputation risk management. *Accounting, Auditing and Accountability Journal, 21*(3), 337–361.

Bebchuck, L. A., & Fried, J. (2003). Executive compensation as an agency problem. *Journal of Economic Perspectives, 17*(3), 71–92.

Bebchuck, L. A., & Fried, J. (2004). *Pay without performance: The unfulfilled promise of executive compensation*. Harvard University Press.

Bebchuck, L. A., & Fried, J. (2005). Pay without performance: Overview of the issues. *Journal of Applied Corporate Finance, 17*(4), 8–22.

Bebchuck, L. A., & Fried, J. (2009). Paying for long-term performance. *University of Pennsylvania Law Review, 158*, 1915–1959.

Bebchuck, L. A., & Spamann, H. (2010). Regulating bankers' pay. *Georgetown Law Journal, 98*(2), 247–287.

Becht, M., Bolton, P., & Roell, A. (2002). Corporate governance and control. *NBER Working Paper Series* (Working Paper 9371).

Becht, M., & Roëll, A. (1999). Blockholdings in Europe: An international comparison. *European Economic Review, 43*(4–6), 1049–1056.

Beck, A. C., Campbell, D., & Shrives, P. J. (2010). Content analysis in environmental reporting research: Enrichment and rehearsal of the method in a British-German context. *The British Accounting Review, 42*(3), 207–222.

Beck, T., Demirguc-Kunt, A., & Maksimovic, V. (2004). Bank competition and access to finance: International evidence. *Journal of Money, Credit and Banking, 36*, 627–648.

Beck, T., Demirguc-Kunt, A., & Levine, R. (2006). Bank concentration, competition, and crisis: First results. *Journal of Banking & Finance, 30*(5), 1581–1603.

Behn, R. D. (2001). *Rethinking democratic accountability*. Washington, D.C.: Brookings Institution Press.

Belcredi, M., & Ferrarini, G. (2013). Corporate boards, incentive pay and shareholder activism in Europe: Main issues and policy perspectives. In M. Belcredi & G. Ferrarini (Eds.), *Boards and shareholders in European listed companies. Facts, context and post-crisis reforms*. Cambridge University Press.

Belkhir, M. (2009). Board of directors' size and performance in banking industry. *International Journal of Managerial Finance, 5*(2), 201–221.

Beltratti, A., & René, M. S. (2012). The credit crisis around the globe: Why did some banks perform better during the credit crisis? *Journal of Financial Economics, 105*(1), 1–12.

Beltratti, A., & Stulz, R. M. (2012). The credit crisis around the globe: Why did some banks perform better during the credit crisis? *Journal of Financial Economics, 105*(1), 1–12.

Belkaoui, A. (1983). Economic, political and civil indicators and reporting and disclosure adequacy: Empirical investigation. *Journal of Accounting and Public Policy, 2*(3), 207–219.

Belkaoui, A. (2004). *Accounting theory* (5th ed.). London: Thomson.

Belkaoui, A., & Karpik, P. (1989). Determinants of the corporate decision to disclose social information. *Accounting, Auditing and Accountability Journal, 2*(1), 36–51.

Benmelech, E., & Dlugosz, J. (2010). The credit rating crisis. *NBER Macroeconomic Annual, 24*, 161–207.

Berelson, B. (1952). *Content analysis in communication research.* New York: Hafner.

Beretta, S., & Bozzolan, S. (2004). A framework for the analysis of firm risk communication. *The International Journey of Accounting, 39*(3), 265–288.

Beretta, S., & Bozzolan, S. (2008). Quality versus quantity: The case of forward-looking disclosure. *Journal of Accounting, Auditing and Finance, 23*(3), 333–375.

Berger, A. N., Kick, T., & Schaeck, K. (2012). *Executive board composition and bank risk taking*. Deutsche Bundesbank Working Paper No. 3.

Berle, A., & Means, G. (1932). *The modern corporation and private property.* New York: McMillan.

Berle, A. A. Jr., & Means, G. C. (1967). *The modern corporation and private property* (Rev. Ed.). New York: Harcourt, Brace and World.

Bhagat, S., & Bolton, B. J. (2008). Corporate governance and firm performance. *Journal of Corporate Finance, 14*(3), 257–273.

Bhattacharya, S., Boot, A. W., & Thakor, A. V. (1998). The economics of bank regulation. *Journal of Money, Credit and Banking, 30*(4), 745–770.

Bhojraj, S., & Sengupta, P. (2003). Effect of corporate governance on bond ratings and yields: The role of institutional investors and outside directors. *The Journal of Business, 76*(3), 455–475.

Bischof, J. (2009). The effects of IFRS 7 adoption on bank disclosure in Europe. *Accounting in Europe, 6*(2), 164–193.

Bjorn, K., & Nordblom, T. (2013). *Corporate governance in banks following the financial crisis: An institutional perspective on changes in the banking sector*. Master's thesis, Copenhagen Business School.

Black, B. S., Jang, H., & Kim, W. (2006). Predicting firm's corporate governance choices, evidence from South Korea. *Journal of Corporate Finance, 12*, 660–691.

Blacconiere, W. G., & Patten, D. M. (1994). Environmental disclosures, regulatory costs and changes in firm value. *Journal of Accounting and Economics, 18*(3), 357–377.

Blair, M. (1995). *Ownership and control: Rethinking corporate governance for the twenty-first century*. Washington: Brookings Institution.

Blundell-Wignall, A., Atkinson, P., & Lee, S. (2008). The current financial crisis: Causes and policy issues (white paper). *Organization for Economic Co-operation and Development: Financial Market Trends, 2008*(2), 1–21.

Boot, A. W. A., & Thakor, A. V. (1993). Self-interested bank regulation. *The American Economic Review*, 206–212.

Bonfirm, D. (2009). Credit risk drivers: Evaluating the contribution of firm level information and of macroeconomic dynamics. *Journal of Banking & Finance, 33*(2), 281–299.

Borokhovich, K. A., Parrino, R., & Trapani, T. (1996). Outside directors and CEO selection. *The Journal of Financial and Quantitative Analysis, 31*(3), 337–355.

Bos, W., & Tarnai, C. (1999). Content analysis in empirical social research. *International Journal of Educational Research, 31*(8), 662–670.

Botosan, C. A. (2004). Discussion of a framework for the analysis of firm risk communication. *International Journal of Accounting, 39*(3), 289–295.

Boykoff, M. T. (2008). The cultural politics of climate change discourse in UK tabloids. *Political Geography, 27*(5), 549–569.

Bozzolan, S., Favotto, F., & Ricceri, F. (2003). Italian annual intellectual capital disclosure. *Journal of Intellectual Capital, 4*(4), 543–558.

Bozzolan, S., Trombetta, M., & Beretta, S. (2009). Forward-looking disclosures, financial verifiability and analysts' forecasts: A study of cross-listed European firms. *European Accounting Review, 18*(3), 435–473.

Bradbury, M., Mak, Y., & Tan, S. (2006). Board characteristics, audit committee characteristics and abnormal accruals. *Pacific Accounting Review, 18*(2), 47–68.

Bradley, M., & Chen, D. (2010). Corporate governance, credit condition, and the cost of debt. *SSRN Electronic Journal.*

Brammer, S., & Pavelin, S. (2006). Voluntary environmental disclosures by large UK companies. *Journal of Business Finance and Accounting, 33*(7/8), 1168–1188.

Brammer, S., & Pavelin, S. (2008). Factors influencing the quality of corporate environmental disclosure. *Business Strategy and the Environment, 17*(2), 120–136.

Brennan, N., & Solomon, J. (2008). Corporate governance, accountability and mechanisms of accountability: An overview. *Accounting, Auditing and Accountability Journal, 21*(7), 885–906.

Breton, G. (2009). From folk-tales to shareholder-tales: Semiotocs analysis of the annual report. *Society and Business Review, 4*(3), 187–201.

Brickley, J., Coles, J., & Terry, R. (1994). Outside directors and the adoption of poison pills. *Journal of Financial Economics, 35*, 371–390.

Brighi, P. (2002). Interbank lending, liquidity and banking crisis. *Economic Notes, 31*(3), 493–521.

Brown, P., Beekes, W. A., & Verhoeven, P. (2011). Corporate governance, accounting and finance: A review. *Accounting and Finance, 51*(1), 96–172.

Bruce, A., & Buck, T. (2005). Executive Pay And UK Corporate Governance. In K. Keasey, S. Thompson, & M. Wright (Eds.), *Corporate governance: Accountability, enterprise and international comparisons* (pp. 117–136). Chichester: Wiley.

Brutti, F. (2011). Sovereign defaults and liquidity crisis. *Journal of International Economics, 84*(1), 65–72.

Bryman, A., & Bell, E. (2007). *Business research methods* (2nd ed.). Oxford: Oxford University Press.

Buhr, N. (1998). Environmental performance, legislation and annual report disclosure: The case of acid rain and Falconbridge. *Accounting, Auditing and Accountability Journal, 11*(2), 161–189.

Buhr, N., & Freedman, M. (2001). Culture, institutional factors and differences in environmental disclosure between Canada and the United States. *Critical Perspectives on Accounting, 12*(3), 293–322.

Buiter, W. (2009). *Lessons from the global financial crisis for regulators and supervisors*. London: Financial Markets Group, London School of Economics and Political Science.

Burrell, G., & Morgan, G. (1979). *Sociological paradigms and organisational analysis: Elements of the sociology of corporate life*. Aldershot, England: Gower Publishing.

Burrows, O., & Low, K. (2015). *Mapping the UK financial system*. Bank of England Quarterly Bulletin.

Bushee, B. (1998). The influence of institutional investors on myopic R&D investment behavior. *Accounting Review, 73*, 305–333.

Bushman, R. M., & Smith, A. J. (2001). Financial accounting information and corporate governance. *Journal of Accounting and Economics, 32*, 237–333.

Bushman, R. M., & Smith, A. J. (2003, April). Transparency financial reporting and corporate governance. *New York Federal Reserve Bank's Economic Review, 9*(1), 65–87.

Buster, I. (2008). *Corporate governance in banking. A European study*. PhD series, Copenhagen Business School.

Byrd, J., & Hickman, K. (1992). Do outside directors monitor managers? Evidence from tender offer bids. *Journal of Financial Economics, 32*, 195–221.

Cabedo, J. D., & Tirado, J. M. (2004). The disclosure of risk in financial statements. *Accounting Forum, 28*(2), 181–200.

Cadbury Committee. (1992). *The financial aspects of corporate governance*. London: Committee on the Financial Aspects of Corporate Governance.

Cadbury Report. (1992). *Report of the committee on the financial aspects of corporate governance*. London: Gee.

Camfferman, K., & Cooke, T. (2002). An analysis of disclosure in the annual reports of UK and Dutch companies. *Journal of International Accounting Research, 1*, 3–27.

Campbell, D. (2000). Legitimacy theory or managerial reality construction? Corporate social disclosure in Marks and Spencer Plc corporate reports, 1969–1997. *Accounting Forum, 24*(1), 81–100.

Campbell, D. (2003). Intra-and intersectoral effects in environmental disclosures: Evidence for legitimacy theory? *Business Strategy and the Environment, 12*(6), 357–371.

Campbell, D. (2004). A longitudinal and cross-sectional analysis of environmental disclosure in UK companies—A research note. *The British Accounting Review, 36*(1), 107–117.

Campbell, D., Beck, A. C., & Shrives, P. J. (2010). Content analysis in environmental reporting research: Enrichment and rehearsal of the method in a British-German context. *The British Accounting Review, 42*(3), 207–222.

Campbell, D., Craven, B., & Shrives, P. (2003). Voluntary social reporting in three FTSE sectors: A comment on perception and legitimacy. *Accounting, Auditing & Accountability Journal, 16*(4), 559–580.

Campbell, D., Moore, G., & Shrives, P. (2006). Cross-sectional effects in community disclosures. *Accounting, Auditing and Accountability Journal, 19*(1), 96–114.

Campbell, D., & Rahman, M. R. A. (2010). A longitudinal examination of intellectual capital reporting in Marks & Spencer annual reports, 1978–2008. *British Accounting Review, 42*(1), 56–70.

Caprio, G., & Levine, R. (2002). Governance in finance. Concepts and international observations. In R. E. Litan, M. Pomerleano, & V. Sundararajan (Eds.), *Financial sector governance: The role of the public and private sectors*. Washington, D.C.: The Brookings Institution.

Caprio, G., Laeven, L., & Levine, R. (2007). Governance and banks valuations. *Journal of Financial Intermediation 16*, 584–617.

Carcello, J. V., & Neal, T. L. (2000). Audit committee composition and auditor reporting. *The Accounting Review, 75*, 453–467.

Cardon Report. (1998). *The report of the Belgium commission on corporate governance*. Brussels: Brussels Stock Exchange.

Carling, K., Jacobson, T., Linde, J., & Roszbach, K. (2007). Corporate credit risk modelling and the macroeconomy. *Journal of Banking & Finance, 31*(3), 846–867.

Carmichael, J., & Pomerleano, M. (2002). *The development and regulation of non-bank financial institutions*. Washington, DC: World Bank.

Carney, T. F. (1972). *Content analysis: A technique for systematic inference from communications*. London: Batsford.

Carvalho, A., & Burgess, J. (2005). Cultural circuits of climate change in UK broadsheet newspapers, 1985–2003. *Risk Analysis, 25*(6), 1457–1469.
Cebenoyan, A. S., Cooperman, E. S., & Register, C. A. (1999). Ownership structure, charter value, and risk-taking behaviour for thrifts. *Financial Management, 28*(1), 43–60.
Chakraborty, S., & Ray, T. (2006). Bank-based versus market-based financial systems: A growth-theoretic analysis. *Journal of Monetary Economics, 53*(2), 329–350.
Chapman, R., & Milne, M. J. (2004). The triple bottom line: How New Zealand companies measure up. *Corporate Environmental Strategy: International Journal for Sustainable Business, 11*(2), 37–50.
Chartered Institute of Management Accountants (CIMA). (2008). *Fundamentals of ethics, corporate governance and business law* (2nd ed.). BPP Learning Media Ltd.
Chartered Institute for Securities & Investment (CISI). (2013). *UK regulation and professional integrity, study material*. London: Chartered Institute for Securities & Investment.
Chau, G., & Gray, S. (2002). Ownership structure and corporate voluntary disclosure in Hong Kong and Singapore. *The International Journal of Accounting, 37*(2), 247–265.
Cheffins, B. (2010, October). "The History of Modern US Corporate Governance"—Understanding risk lunchtime seminar series centre for risk studies/CJBS. In a seminar based on the introductory chapter for the history of modern US corporate governance, Edward Elgar, forthcoming.
Cheffins, B. R. (2009). *Did corporate governance 'fail' during the 2008 market meltdown? The case of the S&P 500* (ECGI Law Working Papers No. 124/2009).
Chemrat, O. (2014). *'Credit rating agencies', liability in the light of the global financial crisis of 2008–2009*. Central European University.
Chen, X. (2007). Banking deregulation and credit risk: Evidence from the EU. *Journal of Financial Stability, 2*(4), 356–390.
Cheng, E. C. M., & Courteney, S. M. (2006). Board composition, regulatory regime and voluntary disclosure. *The International Journal of Accounting, 41*(3), 262–289.
Cheng, I., Hong, R. H., & Scheinkman, J. A. (2012). *Yesterday's heroes: Compensation and creative risk-taking*. Mimeo.
Cho, C., & Patten, D. (2007). The Role environmental disclosures as tools of legitimacy: A Research note. *Accounting, Organizations and Society, 32*(7/8), 639–647.
Choi, F. D. S. (1973). Financial disclosure and entry to the European capital market. *Journal of Accounting Research, 11*(2), 159–175.

Ciancanelli, P., & Gonzalez, J. A. (2000). Corporate governance in banking: A conceptual framework. *Social Science Research Network*. European Financial Management Association Conference (pp. 2–24).

Clarke, J., & Gibson-Sweet, M. (1999). The use of corporate social disclosures in the management of reputation and legitimacy: A cross sectoral analysis of UK top 100 companies. *Business Ethics: A European Review, 8*(1), 5–13.

Clarke, T. (2004). *Theories of corporate governance: The philosophical Foundations of corporate governance*. Oxon, NY and Canada: Routledge.

Clarke, T. (2010). Recurring crises in Anglo-American corporate governance. *Contribution to Political Economy, 29*(1), 9–32.

Clarkson, M. B. E. (1995). A stakeholder framework for analysing and evaluating corporate social performance. *Academy of Management Review, 20*(1), 92–117.

Clarkson, P. M., Li, Y., Richardson, G. D., & Vasvari, F. P. (2008). Revisiting the relation between environmental performance and environmental disclosure: An empirical analysis. *Accounting, Organizations and Society, 33*(4/5), 302–327.

Cobbaut, R., & Lenoble, J. (2003). *Corporate governance: An institutionalist approach*. The Hague: Kluwer Law International.

Coffee, J. C. Jr. (1991, October). Liquidity versus control: The institutional investor as corporate monitor. *Columbia Law Review, 91*(6), 1277–1368.

Cohen, J., Krishnamurthy, G., & Wright, A. M. (2004). Corporate governance mosaic and financial reporting. *Journal of Accounting Literature, 23*, 87–152.

Collier, P. (1993). Factors affecting the formation of audit committees in major UK-listed companies. *Accounting and Business Research, 23*(91A), 421–430.

Combined Code. (1998a). *The combined code: Principles of good governance and code of best practice*. Committee on Corporate Governance, London Stock Exchange Limited, London: Gee & Co.

Combined Code. (1998b). *The combined code on corporate governance: Principles of good governance and code of best practice*. Committee on Corporate Governance, London Stock Exchange Limited. London: Gee & Co.

Combined Code. (2003). *The combined code on corporate governance*. London: Financial Reporting Council.

Combined Code. (2006). *The combined code on corporate governance*. London: Financial Reporting Council

Combined Code. (2008). *The combined code on corporate governance*. London: Financial Reporting Council.

Committee of European Banking Supervisors. (2009, April). *High-level principles for remuneration policies*.

Conger, J., Finegold, D., & Lawler III, E. (1998). Appraising boardroom performance. *Harvard Business Review, 76*(1998), 136–148.

Conti, C., & Mauri, A. (2008). Corporate financial risk management: Governance and disclosure post IFRS 7. *ICFAI Journal of Financial Risk Management, 5*(2), 20–27.

Conyon, M. J., & Peck, S. (1998). Board control, remuneration committees, and top management compensation. *Academy of Management Journal, 41*, 146–157.

Cormier, D., & Gordon, I. M. (2001). An examination of social and environmental reporting strategies. *Accounting, Auditing & Accountability Journal, 14*(5), 587–617.

Cormier, D., Ledoux, M., & Magnan, M. (2011). The informational contribution of social and environmental disclosures for investors. *Management Decision, 49*(8), 1276–1304.

Cormier, D., Ledoux, M., Magnan, M., & Aerts, W. (2010). Corporate governance and information asymmetry between managers and investors. *Corporate Governance, 10*(5), 574–589.

Cormier, D., & Magnan, M. (2003). Environmental reporting management: A European perspective. *Journal of Accounting and Public Policy, 22*(1), 43–62.

Courtis, J. K. (1998). Annual report readability variability: Tests of the obfuscation hypothesis. *Accounting, Auditing & Accountability Journal, 11*(4), 459–472.

Cowen, S. S., Ferari, L. B., & Parker, L. D. (1987). The impact of corporate characteristics on social responsibility disclosure. *Accounting, Organisations and Society, 12*(2), 111–122.

Coy, D., & Dixon, K. (2004). The public accountability index: Crafting a parametric disclosure index for annual reports. *The British Accounting Review, 36*(1), 79–106.

Craswell, A. T., & Taylor, S. L. (1992). Discretionary disclosure of reserves by oil and gas companies: An economic analysis. *Journal of Business Finance and Accounting, 19*(2), 295–308.

Creswell, J. W. (1998). *Qualitative inquiry and research design: Choosing among five traditions*. Thousand Oaks, CA: Sage.

Cross, T. A., & Djajadikerta, H. G. (2004). An examination of voluntary environmental disclosures in New Zealand and Australia: A research framework. *15th International Congress on Social and Environmental Accounting Research (3rd Australasian CSEAR Conference)*. Sydney: CSEAR.

Croughy, M., Galai, D., & Mark, R. (2006). *The essentials of risk management*. New York: McGraw-Hill.

Dahya, J., Lonie, A. A., & Power, D. M. (1996). The case for separating the roles of chairman and CEO: An analysis of stock market and accounting data. *Corporate Governance: An International Review, 4*(1), 71–77.

Dahya, J., McConnell, J. J., & Travlos, N. G. (2002, February). The Cadbury committee, corporate performance, and top management turnover. *Journal of Finance, 57*(1), 461–483.
Dahlstrom, M. F., Dudo, A., & Brossard, D. (2011). Precision of information, sensational information, and self-efficacy information as message-level variables affecting risk perceptions. *Risk Analysis, 32*(1), 155–166.
Daily, C. M., Dalton, D. R., & Rajagopalan, N. (2003). Governance through ownership: Centuries of practice, decades of research. *Academy of Management Journal, 46*(2), 151–158.
Daily, C. M., Johnson, J. L., Ellstrand, A. E., & Dalton, D. R. (1998). Compensation committee composition as a determinant of CEO compensation. *Academy of Management Journal, 41*, 209–220.
Dalton, D. R., Daily, C. M., Johnson, J. L., & Ellstrand, A. E. (1999). Number of directors and financial performance: A meta-analysis. *Academy of Management Journal, 42*(6), 674–686.
D'Aveni, R. A., & MacMillan, I. C. (1990). Crisis and the content of managerial communications: A study of the focus of attention of top managers in surviving and failing firms. *Administrative Science Quarterly, 35*(4), 634–657.
Deegan, C. (2002). Introduction: The legitimising effect of social and environmental disclosures—A theoretical foundation. *Accounting, Auditing and Accountability Journal, 15*(3), 282–311.
Deegan, C., & Gordon, B. (1996). A study of the environmental disclosure practices of Australian corporations. *Accounting and Business Research, 26*(3), 187–199.
Deegan, C., & Rankin, M. (1996). Do Australian companies report environmental news objectively?—An analysis of environmental disclosures by firms prosecuted successfully by the environmental protection authority. *Accounting, Auditing and Accountability Journal, 9*(2), 50–67.
Deegan, C., & Rankin, M. (1997). The materiality of environmental information to users of annual reports. *Accounting, Auditing and Accountability Journal, 10*(4), 562–583.
Deegan, C., Rankin, M., & Tobin, J. (2002). An examination of the corporate social and environmental disclosures of BHP from 1983–1997: A test of legitimacy theory. *Accounting, Auditing & Accountability Journal, 15*(3), 312–343.
Deegan, C., & Unerman, J. (2006). *Financial accounting theory* (European ed.). Maidenhead: McGraw-Hill.
Delmas and Blass. (2010). Measuring corporate environmental performance: The trade-offs of sustainability ratings. *Business Strategy and the Environment, 19*(4), 245–260.

Deese, J. (1969). Conceptual categories in the study of content. In G. Gerbner, O. R. Holsti, K. Krippendorff, W. J. Paisley, & P. J. Stone (Eds.), *The analysis of communication content* (1st ed., pp. 39–56). New York: Wiley.

Demb, A., & Neubauer, F. F. (1992). The corporate board: Confronting the paradoxes. *Long Range Planning, 25*(3), 6–18.

Denzin, N. K., & Lincoln, Y. S. (1994). Introduction: Entering the field of qualitative research. In N. K. Denzin & Y. S. Lincoln (Eds.), *Handbook of qualitative research* (pp. 1–17). Thousand Oaks, CA: Sage.

Department of Trade and Industry (DTI). (2003). *Rewards for failure, directors' remuneration—Contracts, performance and severance*. London: DTI.

Deumes, R. (2008). Corporate risk reporting: A content analysis of narrative risk disclosures in prospectuses. *Journal of Business Communication, 45*(2), 120–157.

De Villiers, C., & Van Staden, C. (2006). Can less environmental disclosure have a legitimising effect? Evidence from Africa. *Accounting, Organizations and Society, 31*(8), 763–781.

Dewing, I. P., & Russell, P. O. (2004). Regulation of UK corporate governance: Lessons from accounting, audit and financial services. *Corporate Governance: An International Review, 12*(1), 107–115.

DeYoung, R., Evanoff, D., & Molyneux, P. (2009). Mergers and acquisitions of financial institutions: A review of the post-2000 literature. *Journal of Financial Services Research, 36*, 87–110.

DeYoung, R., Peng, E., & Yang, M. (2013). Executive compensation and business policy choices at US commercial banks. *Journal of Financial and Quantitative Analysis, 48*(1), 165–196.

DeZoort, F. T., & Salterio, S. E. (2001). Effects of corporate governance experience and financial reporting and auditing knowledge. *Auditing: A Journal of Practice & Theory, 20*(2), 31–47.

DeZoort, F. T., Hermanson, D. R., Archambeault, D. S., & Reed, S. A. (2002). Audit committee effectiveness: A synthesis of the empirical audit committee literature. *Journal of Accounting Literature, 21*, 38–75.

Diamond, D. W., & Verrecchia, R. E. (1991). Disclosure, liquidity, and the cost of capital. *The Journal of Finance, 46*(4), 1325–1359.

Dierkes, M., & Antal, A. B. (1985). The usefulness and use of social reporting information. *Accounting, Organizations and Society, 10*(1), 29–34.

Dobler, M. (2008). Incentives for risk reporting: A discretionary disclosure and cheap talk approach. *The International Journal of Accounting, 43*(2), 184–206.

Donaldson, T., & Preston, L. E. (1995). The stakeholder theory of the corporation: Concepts, evidence, and implications. *Academy of Management Review, 20*(1), 65–91.

Dragomir, V. D. (2008). Accounting in the name of global corporate governance a historical perspective. *Accounting and Management Information Systems*, 16–28, Bucuresti. ISSN 1583-4387.

Drehmann, M., Sorensen, S., & Stringa, M. (2010). The integral impact of credit and interest rate risk on banks: A dynamic framework and stress testing application. *Journal of Banking & Finance, 34*(4), 713–729.

Drumond, I. (2009). Bank capital requirements, business cycle fluctuations and the Basel accords: A synthesis. *Journal of Economic Surveys, 23*(5), 798–830.

DTI. (2004). *Draft regulations on the operating and financial review and directors' report*. DTI, London: Department of Trade and Industry.

Dyck, A., Volchkova, N., & Zingales, L. (2008). The corporate governance role of the media: Evidence from Russia. *The Journal of Finance, 63*(3), 1093–1135.

Easter-Smith, M., Thorpe, R., & Jackson, P. R. (2012). *Management research*. London: Sage.

Easterby-Smith, M., Thorpe, R., & Lowe, A. (1991). *Management research: An introduction*. London: Sage.

Eccles, R. G., Herz, R. H., Keegan, E. M., & Philips, D. M. H. (2001). *The value reporting revolution*. New York: Price Waterhouse Coopers.

Elo, S., & Kyngas, H. (2008). The qualitative content analysis process. *Journal of Advanced Nursing, 62*(1), 107–115.

Elyasiani, E., & Jia, J. (2008). Distribution of institutional ownership and corporate firm performance. *Journal of Banking & Finance, 34*(2010), 606–620.

Elzahar, H., & Hussainey, K. (2012). Determinants of narrative risk disclosures in UK interim reports. *Journal of Risk Finance, 13*(2), 133–147.

Emm, E. E., Gay, G. D., & Lin, C.-M. (2007). Choices and best practice in corporate risk management disclosure. *Journal of Applied Corporate Finance, 19*(4), 82–93.

Eng, L. L., & Mak, Y. T. (2003). Corporate governance and voluntary disclosure. *Journal of Accounting and Public Policy, 22*(4), 325–345.

Erkens, D. H., Mingyi, H., & Pedro Matos, P. (2012). Corporate governance in the 2007–2008 financial crisis: Evidence from financial institutions worldwide. *Journal of Corporate Finance, 18*(2), 389–411.

Ernst and Ernst. (1978). *Social responsibility disclosure: 1978 survey*. Cleveland, Ohio: Ernst and Ernst.

European Commission (EC). (2013a). *Communication from the commission to the council and the parliament. Shadow banking—Addressing new sources of risk in the financial sector*. Brussels: European Commission.

European Commission (EC). (2013b). *Strengthening oversight and regulation of shadow banking: Policy framework for strengthening oversight and regulation of shadow banking entities*. Brussels: European Commission.

Eugster, F., & Wagner, A. F. (2011). *When and how is voluntary disclosure quality reflected in equity prices?* (Swiss Finance Institute Research Paper Series No. 11–25). Switzerland.

European Commission (EC). (2014). *Directive of the European parliament and of the council: Amending directive 2007/36/EC*. Proposal. Brussels: European Commission.

Ezzamel, M., & Watson, R. (1997). Wearing two hats: The conflicting control and management roles of non-executive directors. In K. Keasey, S. Thompson & M. Wright (Eds.), *Corporate governance: Economic, management and financial issues*. Oxford, UK: Oxford University Press.

Faccio, M., & Lasfer, M. A. (2000). Do occupational pension funds monitor companies in which they hold large stakes? *Journal of Corporate Finance, 6*, 71–110.

Fahlenbrach, R., & Stulz, R. M. (2010). Bank CEO incentives and the cost of the credit crisis. *Journal of Financial Economics, 99*(1), 11.

Fahlenbrach, R., & Stulz, R. M. (2011). Bank CEO incentives and the cost of the credit crisis. *Journal of Financial Economics, 99*(1), 11–26.

Fama, E. F. (1980). Agency problems and the theory of the firm. *Journal of Political Economy, 88*(2), 288–307.

Fama, E. F., & Jensen, M. C. (1983). Separation of ownership and control. *Journal of Law and Economics, 26*(2), 301–325.

Farquhar, J. D., & Panther, T. (2008). Acquiring and retaining customers in UK banks: An exploratory study. *Journal of Retailing and Consumer Services, 15*(1), 9–21.

Farrel, J., & Gibbons, R. (1989). Cheap talk can matter in bargaining. *Journal of Economic Theory, 48*(1), 221–237.

Ferdous, C. S. (2012). *Compliance with code of corporate governance in developing economy: The case of Bangladesh*. Student thesis, University of Birmingham.

Ferrarini, G. (2017). *Understanding the role of corporate governance in financial institutions: A Research Agenda* (ECGI Working Paper Series in Law).

Ferris, S. P., Jagannathan, M., & Pritchard, A. C. (2003). Too busy to mind the business? Monitoring by directors with multiple board appointments. *Journal of Finance, 58*(3), 1087–1112.

Fetisov, G. (2009). Measures to overcome the global crisis and establish a stable financial and economic system. *Problems of Economic Transition, 52*(5), 20–34.

Fiedler, T., & Deegan, C. (2002). *Environmental collaborations within the building and construction industry: A consideration of the motivations to collaborate* (Working Paper), 2003 critical perspectives on accounting conference, New York, USA.

Financial Accounting Standard Board (FASB). (2000). *Business reporting research project*. New York, Available at: www.fasb.org.

Financial Reporting Council (FRC). (2000, December). *FRC launches proposed reforms to the UK corporate governance code*. London.
Financial Reporting Council (FRC). (2009a, December 1). *FRC launches proposed reforms to the UK corporate governance code* (Press Notice FRC PN 287).
Financial Reporting Council (FRC). (2009b, March). *Review of the effectiveness of the combined code-call for evidence*. London.
Financial Reporting Council (FRC). (2009c, July). *Review of the effectiveness of the combined code—Progress report and second consultation*. London: FRC.
Financial Reporting Council (FRC). (2010). *The UK corporate governance code*. London: Financial Reporting Council.
Financial Reporting Council (FRC). (2012a). *The UK corporate governance code*. London: Financial Reporting Council.
Financial Reporting Council (FRC). (2012b). *The UK stewardship code*. London: Financial Reporting Council.
Financial Reporting Council (FRC). (2014). *Guidance on risk management internal control and related financial and business reporting*. London: Financial Reporting Council.
Financial Reporting Council (FRC). (2018, July). *The UK corporate governance code*. London.
Financial Service Authority (FSA). (2001). *FSA code of best practice handbook*. London: Financial Service Authority.
Financial Service Authority (FSA). (2004). *FSA handbook*. London: Financial Service Authority.
Financial Service Authority (FSA). (2007). *Enforcement guide*. London: Financial Service Authority.
Financial Service Authority (FSA). (2009a, September). *Reforming remuneration practices in the financial services, Consultation Paper*. London: Financial Service Authority.
Financial Service Authority (FSA). (2009b, March). *The Turner review: A regulatory response to the global banking crisis*. London.
Financial Services Authority (FSA). (2011, December). *The failure of the Royal Bank of Scotland*. Financial Services Authority Board Report.
Financial Stability Board (FSB). (2009a, September). *Financial stability board issues implementation standards on compensation*. New York.
Financial Stability Board (FSB). (2009b, September). *FSB principles for sound compensation practices- implementation standards*. New York.
Financial Stability Board (FSB). (2011a). *Effective resolution of systemically important financial institutions*.
Financial Stability Board (FSB). (2011b, November). *FSB issues international standard for resolution regimes*. Press release.

Financial Stability Board (FSB). (2011c). *Intensity and effectiveness of SIFI supervision: Progress report on implementing the recommendations on enhanced supervision*. Basel: Financial Stability Board.
Financial Stability Board. (2011d, October). *Shadow banking: Strengthening oversight and regulation*.
FSB. (2012, November). *Global shadow banking monitoring report 2012*.
Financial Stability Board (FSB). (2013a). *Peer Review of the United Kingdom*. New York, September: Review Report.
FSB. (2013b, August). *Strengthening oversight and regulation of shadow banking: Policy framework for strengthening oversight and regulation of shadow banking entities*.
FSB. (2014, October). *Global shadow banking monitoring report 2014*.
FSB. (2017a, May). *Global shadow banking monitoring report 2016*.
FSB. (2017b). *Assessment of shadow banking activities, risks, and the adequacy*.
FSB. (2019a, February). *Global shadow banking monitoring report 2018*.
FSB. (2019b, February). *Global monitoring report of non-bank financial intermediation 2019*.
Financial Stability Board (FSB). (2020, January). *Global monitoring report on non-bank financial intermediation 2019*.
Financial Stability Forum (FSF). (2008, April). *Report of the financial stability forum on enhancing market and institutional resilience*. New York.
Financial Stability Forum (FSF). (2009, April). *FSF principles for sound compensation practices*. New York.
Finkelstein, S., & D'Aveni, R. A. (1994). CEO duality as a double-edged sword: How boards of directors balance entrenchment avoidance and unity of command. *Academy of Management Journal, 37*(5), 1079–1108.
Firstenberg, P., & Malkiel, B. (1980). Why corporate boards need independent directors. *Management Review, 69*, 26–38.
Fisher, E. (2004). The European Union in the age of accountability. *Oxford Journal of Legal Studies, 24*(3), 495–515.
Flannery, M. J., Kwan, S. H., & Nimalendran, M. (2004). Market evidence on the opaqueness of banking firms' assets. *Journal of Financial Economics, 71*(3), 416–460.
Francis, J. R., Khurana, I. K., & Pereira, R. (2003). The role of accounting and auditing in corporate governance and the development of financial markets around the world. *Asia-Pacific Journal of Accounting and Economics, 10*, 1–31.
Francis, W. B., & Osborne, M. (2011). Capital requirements and bank behaviour in the UK: Are there lessons for international capital standards? *Journal of Banking & Finance, 36*(3), 803–816.

Fraser, J., & Simkins, B. J. (2010). *Enterprise risk management: Today's leading research and best practices for tomorrow's executives* (1st ed.). New Jersey, USA: Wiley.

Freedman, M., & Stagliano, A. J. (1992). European unification, accounting harmonization, and social disclosures. *The International Journal of Accounting and Education, 27*(2), 112–122.

Freeman, R. E. (1984). *Strategic management: A stakeholder approach*. Boston, MA: Pitman.

Freeman, R. E. (1994). The politics of stakeholder theory. *Business Ethics Quarterly, 4*(4), 409–421.

Freeman, R. E., & Evan, W. M. (1990). Corporate governance: A stakeholder interpretation. *Journal of Behavioral Economics, 19*(4), 337–359.

Freeman, R. E., & Velamuri, S. R. (2006). A new approach to CSR: Company stakeholder responsibility. In A. Kakabadse & M. Morsing (Eds.), *Corporate social responsibility (CSR): Reconciling aspiration with application* (pp. 9–23). Houndmills: Palgrave Macmillan.

Freeman, R. E., Wicks, A. C., & Parmar, B. (2004). Stakeholder theory and "the corporate objective revisited". *Organization Science, 15*(3), 364–369.

Freshfields Bruckhaus Deringer. (2005, October). *A legal framework for the integration of environmental, social and governance issues into institutional investment*. UNEP Finance Initiative, Produced for the Asset Management Working Group of the UNEP Finance Initiative.

Friedman, A. L., & Miles, S. (2002). Developing stakeholder theory. *Journal of Management Studies, 39*(1), 1–21.

Frost, S. M. (2004). *The bank analyst's handbook: Money, risk, and conjuring tricks* (1st ed.). London, UK: Wiley.

FSA. (2011). *The failure of the Royal Bank of Scotland*. London: Financial Services Authority.

FSMA. (2000). *Financial services and markets act 2000 (c8)*. Parliament of the United Kingdom.

GAA. (2008). *Can financial reporting be made simpler and more useful?* London: Global Accountancy Alliance.

Gendron, Y., Bédard, J., & Gosselin, M. (2004). Getting inside the black box: A field study of effective audit committees. *Auditing: A Journal of Practice & Theory, 23*(1), 153–171.

Gietzmann, M. (2006). Disclosure of timely and forward-looking statements and strategic management of major institutional ownership. *Long Range Planning, 39*(4), 409–427.

Gillan, S. L., Hartzell, J. C., & Starks, L. T. (2003, August). *Explaining corporate governance: Boards, bylaws, and charter provisions*. Weinberg Center for Corporate Governance Working Paper No. 2003–03.

Gillan, S. L., & Starks, L. T. (2003). *Corporate governance, corporate ownership, and the role of institutional investors: A global perspective*. Weinberg Center for Corporate Governance Working Paper No. 2003–01.

Goldstein, M., & Turner, P. (1996). *Banking crises in emerging economies: Origins and policy options*. Basel: Bank for International Settlements.

Goodhart, C., Hartman, P., Llewllyn, D., Rojas-Suárez, L., & Weisbrod, S. (1998). *Financial regulation why how and where now?* London: Routledge.

Gramling, A. A., Maletta, M. J., Schneider, A., & Church, B. K. (2005). The role of the internal audit function in corporate governance: A synthesis of the extant internal auditing literature and directions for future research. *Journal of Accounting Literature, 23*, 194–244.

Grant, G. H. (2003). The evolution of corporate governance and its impact on modern corporate America. *Management Decision, 41*(9), 923–934.

Gray, J. H., & Densten, I. L. (1998). Integrating quantitative and qualitative analysis using latent and manifest variables. *Quality & Quantity, 32*(4), 419–431.

Gray, R., Javad, M., Power, D. M., & Sinclair, C. D. (2001). Social and environmental disclosure and corporate characteristics: A research note and extension. *Journal of Business Finance Accounting, 28*(3–4), 327–356.

Gray, R., Kouhy, R., & Lavers, S. (1995a). Constructing a research database of social and environmental reporting by UK companies. *Accounting, Auditing & Accountability Journal, 8*(2), 78–101.

Gray, R., Kouhy, R., & Lavers, S. (1995b). Corporate social and environmental reporting: a review of the literature and a longitudinal study of UK disclosure. *Accounting, Auditing & Accountability Journal, 8*(2), 47–77.

Greuning, H. V., & Bratanovic, S. B. (2003a). *Analyzing and managing banking risk: A framework for assessing corporate governance and financial risk* (2nd ed.). Washington, DC: The World Bank.

Greuning, H. V., & Bratanovic, S. B. (2003b). *Analyzing and managing banking risk: A framework for assessing corporate governance and financial risk* (3rd ed.). Washington, DC: The World Bank.

Grove, H., Patelli, L., Victoravich, L. M., & Xu, P. (2011). Corporate governance and performance in the wake of the financial crisis: Evidence from US commercial banks. *Corporate Governance: An International Review, 19*(5), 418–436.

Group of 20 (G20). (2009a, September 5). *G20 banking statement*.

Group of 20 (G20). (2009b, April 2). *Declaration on strengthening the financial system*.

Group of 20 (G20). (2011, November). *Cannes summit final declaration: Building our common future: Renewed collective action for the benefit of all*. Cannes.

Guetzkow, H. (1950). Unitizing and categorizing problems in coding qualitative data. *Journal of Clinical Psychology, 6*(1), 47–58.

Guthrie, J., Petty, R., Yongvanich, K., & Ricceri, F. (2004). Using content analysis as a research method to inquire into intellectual capital reporting. *Journal of Intellectual Capital, 5*(2), 282–293.

Haan, J. D., & Vlahu, R. (2013). *Corporate governance of banks: A survey* (DNB Working Paper). Netherland.

Hackston, D., & Milne, M. J. (1996). Some determinants of social and environmental disclosures in New Zealand companies. *Accounting, Auditing & Accountability Journal, 9*(1), 77–108.

Hagendorff, J., & Keasey, K. (2012). The value of board diversity in banking: Evidence from the market for corporate control. *The European Journal of Finance, 18*(1), 41–58.

Hall, M. J. B. (2008). The sub-prime crisis, the credit squeeze and Northern Rock: The lessons to be learned. *Journal of Financial Regulation and Compliance, 16*(1), 19–34.

Hall, M. J. B. (2009). The sub-prime crisis, the credit crunch and bank "failure": An assessment of the UK authorities' response. *Journal of Financial Regulation and Compliance, 17*(4), 427–452.

Hammond, K., & Miles, S. (2004). Assessing quality of corporate social reporting: UK perspectives. *Accounting Forum, 28*(1), 61–79.

Hammond, K., & Miles, S. (2019). Assessing quality assessment of corporate social reporting: UK perspectives. *Accounting Forum, 28*(1), 61–79.

Hampel Report. (1998). *Final report: The committee of corporate governance.* Hampel Committee.

Han, S. H., Pagano, M. S., & Shin, Y. S. (2010). *Rating agency reputation, the global financial crisis, and the cost of debt.*

Harris, K. (1996). Content analysis in negotiation research: A review and guide. *Behavior Research Methods, 28*(3), 458–467.

Hartzell, J. C., & Starks, L. T. (2003). Institutional investors and executive compensation. *Journal of Finance, 58*(6), 2351–2374.

Harwood, T. G., & Gary, T. (2003). An Overview of content analysis. *The Marketing Review, 3*(4), 479–498.

Haspeslagh, P. (2010). Corporate governance and the current crisis. *Corporate Governance, 10*(4), 375–377.

Hassan, M. K. (2009). UAE corporations-specific characteristics and level of risk disclosure. *Managerial Auditing Journal, 24*(7), 668–687.

Healy, P. M., & Palepu, K. G. (2001). Information asymmetry, corporate disclosure, and the capital markets: A review of the empirical disclosure literature. *Journal of Accounting and Economics, 31*(1–3), 405–440.

Heffernan, S. (2005). *Modern banking* (1st ed.). UK: Wiley.

Helbok, G., & Wagner, C. (2006). Determinants of operational risk reporting in the banking industry. *Journal of Risk, 9*(1), 49–74.

Hermalin, B. E., & Weisbach, M. S. (1991). The effects of board composition and direct incentives on firm performance. *Financial Management, 20*(Winter), 101–112.

Hermalin, B. E., & Weisbach, M. S. (2003). Board of directors as an endogenously determined institution: A survey of the economic literature. *Federal Reserve Bank of New York Economic Policy Review*, 7–26.

Higgs Report. (2003). *Review of the role and effectiveness of non-executive directors*. London: Department of Trade and Industry.

Hill, P., & Short, H. (2009). Risk disclosure on the second tier markets of the London stock exchange. *Accounting & Finance, 49*(4), 753–780.

HM Treasury. (2009a, November). *A review of corporate governance in UK banks and other financial industry entities: Final recommendations*. London.

HM Treasury. (2009b/a, July). *A review of corporate governance in UK Banks and other financial industry entities: Walker review*. London.

HM Treasury. (2009, November). *Government introduces financial services bill, press release*. London.

HM Treasury. (2009, July). *Reforming financial markets, White Paper presented to parliament by the chancellor of the exchequer*. London.

Holland, J. (1998). Private disclosure and financial reporting. *Accounting and Business Research, 28*(4), 255–269.

Holland, J. (2010). Banks, knowledge and crisis: A case of knowledge and learning failure. *Journal of Financial Regulation and Compliance, 18*(2), 87–105.

Holsti, O. R. (1969). *Content analysis for the social sciences and humanities*. Reading, MA, USA: Addison-Wesley Pub. Co.

Hong, W. (2011). *The UK bank corporate governance framework: A holistic and critical analysis with a focus upon banks risk and executive remuneration governance*. University of Manchester.

Hooks, J., Coy, D., & Howard, D. (2002). The information gap in annual reports. *Accounting, Auditing and Accountability Journal, 15*(4), 501–522.

Hoogeboom, Q. (2010). *The role of credit rating agencies in the subprime crisis of 2008–2009*.

Hooper, K., & Pratt, M. (1995). Disclosure and rhetoric: The case of the New Zelanad Native Land Company. *Accounting, Auditing & Accountability Journal, 8*(1), 10–37.

Hopt, K. J. (2013). Better governance of financial institutions. *ECGI Working Paper Series in Law* (Working Paper N°. 207/2013).

Horcher, K. A. (2005). *Essentials of financial risk management*. New Jersey, USA: Wiley & Sons Inc.

Hsieh, H. F., & Shannon, S. E. (2005). Three approaches to qualitative content analysis. *Qualitative Health Research, 15*(9), 1277–1288.

Hughes, J. E., & MacDonald, S. B. (2002). *International banking text and cases*. Addison Wesley.

Hughes, J. P., Lang, W. W., Mester, L. J., Moon, C., & Pagano, M. S. (2003). Do bankers sacrifice value to build empires: Managerial incentives, industry consolidation, and financial performance. *Journal of Banking and Finance, 27*, 417–447.

Hughes, S. B., Wood, A. L., & Hodgdon, C. (2011). Bank response to SEC disclosure guidance issued during the 2007–2008 US financial crisis. *Research in Accounting Regulation, 23*(2), 149–159.

Hussainey, K., & Aal-Eisa, J. (2009). Disclosure and dividend signalling when sustained earnings growth declines. *Managerial Auditing Journal, 24*(5), 445–454.

Hussainey, K., Schleicher, T., & Walker, M. (2003). Undertaking large-scale disclosure studies when AIMR-FAF ratings are not available: The case of prices leading earnings. *Accounting & Business Research, 33*(4), 275–294.

Iatridis, G. (2008). Accounting disclosure and firms' financial attributes: Evidence from the UK stock market. *International Review of Financial Analysis, 17*(2), 219–241.

ICAEW. (2002). *No surprises: Working for better risk reporting*. London: The Institute of Chartered Accountants in England & Wales.

Independent Commission on Banking (ICB). (2011, September). *Final report recommendations*.

Insch, G. S., Moore, J. E., & Murphy, L. D. (1997). Content analysis in leadership research: Examples, procedures, and suggestions for future use. *The Leadership Quarterly, 8*(1), 1–25.

International Association of Insurance Supervisors (IAIS). (2015, November). *Insurance core principles*. The International Association of Insurance Supervisors.

International Federation of Accountants (IFAC). (2008). *Financial reporting supply chain: Current perspectives and directions*. New York.

International Finance Corporation (IFC). (2015). *A guide to corporate governance practices in the European Union*. Washington, D.C.: World Bank Group.

International Monetary Fund (IMF). (2009a). *Debt bias and other distortions: Crisis-related issues in tax policy*. Washington, D.C.: International Monetary Fund.

International Monetary Fund (IMF). (2009b). *Annual report. Fighting the global crisis*. Washington, D.C.: International Monetary Fund.

International Monetary Fund (IMF). (2011). *United Kingdom: Financial system stability assessment*. IMF Country Report No. 11/222. International Monetary Fund. Washington, D.C.

International Monetary Fund (IMF). (2012). *Shadow banking: Economics and policy. IMF staff discussion note*. Washington, DC: International Monetary Fund.

Irish Stock Exchange. (2012). *Report on compliance with the combined code on corporate governance by Irish listed companies*. Dublin: Irish Stock Exchange.

Ismail, R., & Rahman, R. A. (2011). Institutional investors and board of directors' monitoring role on risk management disclosure level in Malaysia. *IUP Journal of Corporate Governance, 10*(2), 37–61.

ISO. (2009). *Guide 73: Risk management-Vocabulary*. International Organization for Standardization.

Janis, I. L. (1965). The problem of validating content analysis. In H. D. Lasswell, N. Leites, & Associates (Eds.), *Language of politics: Studies in quantitative semantics* (pp. 55–82). Cambridge: MIT Press.

Jensen, M. C. (1988). Takeovers: Their causes and consequences. *Journal of Economic Perspectives, 2*, 21–48.

Jensen, M. C. (1993). The modern industrial revolution, exit, and the failure of internal control systems. *Journal of Finance, 48*(3), 831–880.

Jensen, M. C., & Meckling, W. H. (1976). Theory of the firm: Managerial behavior, agency costs and ownership structure. *Journal of Financial Economics, 3*(4), 305–360.

Jensen, M., & Murphy, K. J. (1990). Performance pay and top-management incentives. *Journal of Political Economy, 98*, 225–264.

Jensen, M., & Ruback, R. S. (1983). The market for corporate control: The scientific evidence. *Journal of Financial Economics, 11*, 5–50.

John, K., & Qian, Y. (2003). Incentives features in CEO compensation in the banking industry. *Federal Reserve Bank of New York Economic Policy Review, 9*, 109–121.

Johnson, S., La Porta, R., Lopez-de-Silanes, F., & Shleifer, A. (2000). Tunneling. *American Economic Review, 90*(2), 22–27.

Jokipii, T., & Milne, A. (2011). Bank capital buffer and risk adjustment decisions. *Journal of Financial Stability, 7*(3), 165–178.

Jones, I., & Pollitt, M. (2002). Who influences debates in business ethics? An investigation into the development of corporate governance in the UK since 1990. In I. W. Jones & M. G. Pollitt (Eds.), *Understanding how issues in business ethics develop*. Basingstoke: Palgrave.

Jones, I., & Pollitt, M. (2004). Understanding how issues in corporate governance develop: Cadbury report to higgs review. *Corporate Governance: An International Review, 12*(2), 162–170.

Joshi, A. D., Patel, D. A., & Holdford, D. A. (2011). Media coverage of off-label promotion: A content analysis of US newspapers. *Research in Social and Administrative Pharmacy, 7*(3), 257–271.

Kanas, A., Vasiliou, D., & Eriotis, N. (2012). Revisiting bank profitability: A semi-parametric approach. *Journal of International Financial Markets, Institutions and Money, 22*(4), 990–1005.

Kaplan, S., & Reishus, D. (1990). Outside directorships and corporate performance. *Journal of Financial Economics, 27*, 389–410.

Karpo, J. M., Malatesta, P. H., & Walkling, R. A. (1996). Corporate governance and shareholder initiatives: Empirical evidence. *Journal of Financial Economics, 42*, 365–395.

Kasman, S., Vardar, G., & Tunc, G. (2011). The impact of interest rate and exchange rate volatility on banks' stock returns and volatility: Evidence from Turkey. *Economic Modelling, 28*(3), 1328–1334.

Kassarjian, H. H. (1977). Content analysis in consumer research. *Journal of Consumer Research, 4*(1), 8–18.

Kay Review. (2012, July). *The Kay Review of UK equity markets and long-term decision making*. Final Report.

Keasey, K., & Veronesi, G. (2008). Lessons from the Northern Rock affair. *Journal of Financial Regulation and Compliance, 16*(1), 8–18.

Kirkpatrick, G. (2009). The corporate governance lessons from the financial crisis. *Financial Markets Trends, OECD: Financial Regulation and Compliance, 16*(1), 8–18.

Kirkbride, J., & Letza, S. (2005, July). Can the non-executive director be an effective gatekeeper? The possible development of a legal framework of accountability. *Corporate Governance: An International Review, 13*(4), 542–549.

Klein, A. (2002). Audit committee, board of director characteristics, and earnings management. *Journal of Accounting and Economics, 33*, 375–400.

Kolk, A., Walhain, S., & van de Wateringen, S. (2001). Environmental reporting by the Fortune Global 250: Exploring the influence of nationality and sector. *Business Strategy and the Environment, 10*(1), 15–28.

Koning, M., Mertens, G., & Roosenboom, P. (2010). The impact of media attention on the use of alternative earnings measures. *Abacus, 46*(3), 258–288.

Kosmidou, K., Pasiouras, F., Zopounidis, C., & Doumpos, M. (2006). A multivariate analysis of the financial characteristics of foreign and domestic banks in the UK. *Omega, 34*(2), 189–195.

Kothari, S. P., Xu, L., & Short, J. E. (2009). The effect of disclosures by management, analysts, and business press on cost of capital, return volatility, and analyst forecasts: A study using content analysis. *Accounting Review, 84*(5), 1639–1670.

Kracauer, S. (1952). The challenge of qualitative content analysis. *Public Opinion Quaterly, 16*(4), 631–642.

Krippendorff, K. (2004). *Content analysis: An introduction to its methodology* (3rd ed.). Thousand Oaks, CA: Sage.

Laan Smith, J. v. d., Adhikari, A., & Tondkar, R. H. (2005). Exploring differences in social disclosures internationally: A stakeholder perspective. *Journal of Accounting and Public Policy, 24*(2), 123–151.

Laeven, L. (2012). Corporate governance: What's special about banks? Keynote lecture at the DNB-CGIC conference on corporate governance of financial institutions, Amsterdam.

Laeven, L., & Fabian V. (2012). *Systemic banking crises database: An update* (IMF Working Paper 12/163).

Laeven, L., & Levine, R. (2009). Corporate governance, regulation, and bank risk taking. *Journal of Financial Economics, 93*(2), 259–275.

Lajili, K., & Zeghal, D. (2005). A content analysis of risk management disclosures in Canadian annual reports. *Canadian Journal of Administrative Sciences, 22*(2), 126–141.

La Porta, R., Lopez-de-Silanes, F., & Shleifer, A. (2002). Government ownership of banks. *Journal of Finance, 57*(1), 265–301.

La Porta, R., Lopez-de-Silanes, F., Shleifer, A., & Vishny, R. (2002). Investor protection and corporate valuation. *Journal of Finance, 57*, 1147–1170.

La Porta, R., Lopez-de-Silanes, F., Shleifer, A., et al. (1999). Corporate ownership around the world. *Journal of Finance, 54*(2), 471–517.

La Porta, R., Silance, F. L. D., Shleifer, A., et al. (1997). Legal determinants of external finance. *Journal of Finance, 52*(3), 1131–1150.

La Porta, R., Silance, F. L. D., Shleifer, A., et al. (1998). Law and finance. *Journal of Political Economy, 106*(6), 1113–1155.

Larcker, D. F., Richardson, S. A., & Irem, T. (2007). Corporate governance, accounting outcome and organisational performance. *The Accounting Review, 82*, 968–1004.

Larcker, D. F., Richardson, S. A., & Tuna, I. (2007). Corporate governance, accounting outcomes, and organizational performance. *The Accounting Review, 82*(4), 963–1008.

Lang, W. W., & Jagtiani, J. A. (2010). The mortgage and financial crises: The role of credit risk management and corporate governance. *Atlantic Economic Journal, 38*(2), 295–316.

Lang, M., & Lundholm, R. (1993). Cross-sectional determinants of analysis ratings of corporate disclosure. *Journal of Accounting Research, 31*, 246–271.

Lastra, R. M. (2004). Risk-based capital requirements and their impact upon the banking industry: Basel II and CAD III. *Journal of Financial Regulation and Compliance, 12*(3), 225–239.

Lehar, A. (2005). Measuring systemic risk: A risk management approach. *Journal of Banking & Finance, 29*(10), 2577–2603.

Letza, S., Kirkbride, J., Sun, X., et al. (2008). Corporate governance theorising: Limits, critics and alternatives. *International Journal of Law and Management, 50*(1), 17–32.

Letza, S., Smallman, C., & Sun, X. (2004). Reframing privatisation: Deconstructing the myth of efficiency. *Policy Sciences, 37,* 159–183.

Letza, S., Sun, X., & Kirkbride, J. (2004). Shareholding versus Stakeholding: A critical review of corporate governance. *Corporate Governance: An International Review, 12*(3), 242–262.

Levine, R. (2003). *The corporate governance of banks: A concise discussion of concepts and evidence*. World Bank Policy Research Working Paper No. 3404.

Levine, R. (2011). *Regulating finance and regulators to promote growth.* Presented at Fed. Reserve Bank The Company Act (CA) 2006 (c46), Section 172, United Kingdom.

Levine, R. E. (2004, September). *The corporate governance of banks: A concise discussion of concepts and evidence.*

Licht, A. N. (2002). Accountability and corporate governance. *SSRN Electronic Journal.*

Liebman, B. L., & Milhaupt, C. J. (2008). Reputational sanctions in China's securities market. *Columbia Law Review, 108*(4), 929.

Lightstone, K., & Driscoll, C. (2008). Disclosing elements of disclosure: A test of legitimacy theory and company ethics. *Canadian Journal of Administrative Sciences/Revuew Canadienne Des Sciences de L'Administration, 25*(1), 7–21.

Lin, S. L. (2009). Anew two-stage hybrid approach of credit risk in banking industry. *Expert Systems with Applications, 36*(4), 8333–8341.

Lindgren, C.-J., García, G., & Saal, M. I. (1996). *Bank soundness and macroecoomic policy*. Washington: International Monetary Fund.

Linsley, P. M., & Lawrence, M. J. (2007). Risk reporting by the largest UK companies: Readability and lack of obfuscation. *Accounting, Auditing & Accountability Journal, 20*(4), 620–627.

Linsley, P. M., & Shrives, P. J. (2005a). Examining risk reporting in UK public companies. *Journal of Risk Finance, 6*(4), 292–305.

Linsley, P. M., & Shrives, P. J. (2005b). Transparency and the disclosure of risk information in the banking sector. *Journal of Financial Regulation & Compliance, 13*(3), 205–214.

Linsley, P. M., & Shrives, P. J. (2006). Risk reporting: A study of risk disclosures in the annual reports of UK companies. *The British Accounting Review, 38*(4), 387–404.

Linsley, P. M., Shrives, P. J., & Crumpton, M. (2006). Risk disclosure: An exploratory study of UK and Canadian banks. *Journal of Banking Regulation, 7*(3/4), 268–282.

Linsley, P. M. (2012). *UK bank risk disclosures in the period to the onset of the global financial crisis: Briefing*. Centre for Business Performance, University of York.

Liu, Y., & Jiraporn, P. (2010). The effect of CEO power on bond ratings and yields. *Journal of Empirical Finance, 17*4), 744–762.

Llewellyn, D. T. (2008). The Northern Rock crisis: A multi-dimensional problem waiting to happen. *Journal of Financial Regulation and Compliance, 16*(1), 35–58.

Lloyds. (2008). *Annual report*. Lloyds TSB Group plc.

London Stock Exchange (LSE). (2012, September). *Corporate governance for main market and AIM companies*. London: White Paige Ltd.

Macey, J. R., & O'Hara, M. (2003). The corporate governance of banks. *FRBNY Economic Policy Review, 9*, 91–107.

Main, B. G. M., & Johnston, J. (1993). Remuneration committees and corporate governance. *Accounting and Business Research, 23*, 351–362.

Mallin, C. (2005). Directors: How training and development can enhance their role. *Corporate Governance: An International Review, 13*(6), 729.

Mallin, C. (2010). *Corporate governance* (3rd ed.). Oxford: Oxford University Press.

Mallin, C., & Jelic, R. (2000). Developments in corporate governance in Central and Eastern Europe. *Corporate Governance: An International Review, 8*(1), 43–51.

Mallin, C., & Ow-Yong, K. (1998). Corporate governance in small companies-the alternative investment market. *Corporate Governance: An International Review, 6*, 224–232.

Mallin, C., & Ow-Yong, K. (2010). The UK alternative investment market—Ethical dimensions. *Journal of Business Ethics, 95*, 223–239.

Marston, C. L., & Shrives, P. J. (1991). The use of disclosure indices in accounting research: A review article. *The British Accounting Review, 23*(3), 195–210.

Martin, A. D., & Mauer, L. J. (2005). A note on common methods used to estimate foreign exchange exposure. *Journal of International Financial Markets, Institutions and Money, 15*(2), 125–140.

Marques, L. B., Correa, R., & Sapriza, H. (2013). *International evidence and government support and risk taking in the banking sector* (IMF Working Paper No. 13/94).

Meek, G. K., Roberts, C. B., & Gray, S. J. (1995). Factors influencing voluntary annual report disclosures by the US, UK and Continental European multinational corporations. *Journal of International Business Studies, 26*(3), 555–572.

Mehran, H., & Mollineaux, L. (2012). *Corporate governance of financial institutions* (Staff Report No. 539). Federal Reserve Bank of New York.

Mehran, H., Morrison, A. D., & Shapiro, J. D. (2011, June 1). *Corporate governance and banks: What have we learned from the financial crisis?* (FRB of New York Staff Report No. 502).
Mehran, H., & Winton, A. (2001). *Executive compensation, leverage and banks.* Theoretical Considerations, Unpublished Paper. Federal Reserve Bank of New York.
Miller, D. P., & Puthenpurackal, J. (2005). Security fungibility and the cost of capital: Evidence from global bonds. *Journal of Financial and Quantitative Analysis, 40*(4), 849–872.
Milne, M. J., & Adler, R. W. (1999). Exploring the reliability of social and environmental disclosures content analysis. *Accounting, Auditing & Accountability Journal, 12*(2), 237–256.
Mintz, S. M. (2006). A comparison of corporate governance systems in the US, UK and Germany. *Corporate Ownership & Control, 3*(4), 24–34.
Mizruchi, M. S. (1983). Who Controls Whom? An examination of the relation between management and boards of directors in large American corporations. *Academy of Management Review, 8*(3).
Moshirian, F. (2011). The global financial crisis and the evolution of markets, institutions and regulation. *Journal of Banking & Financial, 35*(3), 502–511.
Monk, R. A. G., & Minow, N. (2001). *Corporate governance* (2nd ed.). Chichester: Wiley.
Monk, R. A. G., & Minow, N. (2004). *Corporate governance* (3rd ed.). Chichester: Wiley.
Monk, R. A. G., & Minow, N. (2008). *Corporate governance* (4th ed.). Chichester: Wiley.
Moxey, P., & Berendt, A. (2008, November). *Corporate governance and the credit crunch.* ACCA Discussion Paper. London: ACCA.
Mulbert, P. (2010). *Corporate governance of banks after the financial crisis—theory, evidence and reforms.* ECGI Law Working Paper No. 130.
Mullineux, A. (2006). The corporate governance of banks. *Journal of Financial Regulation and Compliance, 14*(4), 375–382.
Murugesu, J., & Santhapparaj, A. S. (2010). Impact of risk disclosure in the prospectus on valuation and initial returns of initial public offerings in Malaysia. *IUP Journal of Applied Finance, 16*(6), 30–53.
Nanto, D. K., et al. (2009). *The global financial crisis: Analysis and policy implications.* CRS.
Neundorf, K. A. (2002). *The content analysis guidebook.* Thousand Oaks: Sage.
Newman, H. A. (2000). The impact of ownership structure on the structure of compensation committees. *Journal of Business Finance and Accounting, 27*(5–6), 653–678.

Newman, H.A., & Mozes, H. A. (1999). Does the composition of the compensation committee influence CEO compensation practices? *Financial Management, 28*(3), 41–53.

Nolan, L. (1995). *First report of the committee on standards in public life. Committee on standards in public life* (Vol. 1). United Kingdom.

Norby Report. (2001, December). *The Nørby committee's report on corporate governance in Denmark—Recommendations for corporate governance in Denmark.*

O'Connell, J. (2010). The 2007 crisis and countercyclical policy. *Studies in Economics and Finance, 27*(2), 148–160.

OECD. (1999). *OECD principles of corporate governance.* Paris: OECD Publishing.

OECD. (2004). *OECD principles of corporate governance.* France: Organisation for Economic Co-operation and Development.

OECD. (2009a). *The financial crisis, reforms and exit strategies.* France: Organisation for Economic Co-operation and Development.

OECD. (2009b). *Business ethics and OECD principles: What can be done to avoid another crisis.* France: Organisation for Economic Co-operation and Development.

OECD. (2009c, June). Corporate Governance and the Financial Crisis: Key findings and Main Messages. *Financial Market Trends.*

Ogus, A. (1994). *Regulation: Legal forms and economic theory.* Hart Publishing.

Oliviera, J., Rodrigues, L. L., & Craig, R. (2011). Voluntary risk reporting to enhance institutional and organizational legitimacy: Evidence from Portuguese banks. *Journal of Financial Regulation and Compliance, 19*(3), 273–287.

Oliviera, J., Rodrigues, L. L., & Craig, R. (2011a). Risk-related disclosures by non-finance companies: Portuguese practices and disclosure characteristics. *Managerial Auditing Journal, 26*(9), 817–839.

Oliviera, J., Rodrigues, L. L., & Craig, R. (2011b). Risk-related disclosure practices in the annual reports of Portuguese credit institutions: An exploratory study. *Journal of Banking Regulation, 12*(2), 100–118.

Othman, R., & Ameer, R. (2009). Market risk disclosure: Evidence from Malaysian listed firms. *Journal of Financial Regulation and Compliance, 17*(1), 57–69.

Parker, S., Peters, G. H., & Turetsky, H. F. (2002). Corporate governance and corporate failure: A survival analysis. *Corporate Governance: The International Journal of Business in Society, 2*(2), 4–12.

Parliamentary Commission on Banking Standards. (2013). *Changing banking for good. First report of sessions 2013–14* (Vol. II). House of Commons.

Pasquare, F. A., & Oppizzi, P. (2012). How do the media affect public perception of climate change and geo hazards? An Italian case study. *Global and Planetary Change, 90–91,* 152–157.

Patten, D. M. (1992). Intra-industry environmental disclosures in response to the Alaskan oil spill: A note on legitimacy theory. *Accounting, Organizations and Society, 17*(5), 471–475.

Patten, D. M. (1995). Variability in social disclosure: A legitimacy-based analysis. *Advances in Public Interest Accounting, 6*, 273–285.

Penrose, R. H. L. (2004). *Report of the equitable life enquiry*. HMSO.

Peters Committee. (1997, June). *Corporate governance in the Netherlands—Forty recommendations, secretariat committee on corporate governance*. Amsterdam.

Petrasek, L. (2010). Multimarket trading and the cost of debt: Evidence from global bonds. *SSRN Electronic Journal*.

Pirson, M., & Turnbull, S. (2010). The future of corporate governance: Network governance—A lesson from the financial crisis. *SSRN Electronic Journal*.

Pirson, M., & Turnbull, S. (2011). Corporate governance, risk management, and the financial crisis: An information processing view. *Corporate Governance: An International Review, 19*(5), 459–470.

Poshakwale, S., & Courtis, J. K. (2005). Disclosure level and cost of equity capital: Evidence from the banking industry. *Managerial and Decision Economics, 26*(7), 431–444.

Poskitt, R. (2005). Disclosure regulation and information risk. *Accounting and Finance, 45*(3), 458–476.

Preda Report. (1998). *Report on code of conduct: Committee for the corporate governance of listed companies*. Italy: Borsa Italiana S.p.A.

Prudential Regulation Authority (PRA). (2013). *Policy statement: Conducting statutory investigations*. Bank of England.

PwC. (1999). *Value and reporting in the banking industry*. PriceWaterhouseC-oopers.

Raar, J. (2002). Environmental initiatives: Towards triple-bottom line reporting. *Corporate Communications: An International Journal, 7*(3), 169–183.

Raghunandan, K., Read, W. K., & Rama, D. V. (2001). Audit committee composition gray directors and interaction with internal auditing. *Accounting Horizons, 15*(2), 105–118.

Rattanatippo, P. (2013). *Risk disclosures in the annual reports of UK banks*. Newcastle University Business School.

Reavis, C. (2009). *The global financial crisis of 2008–2009: The role of greed, fear and oligarchs*.

Richard, E., Chijoriga, M., Kaijage, E., Peterson, C., & Bohman, H. (2008). Credit risk management system of a commercial bank in Tanzania. *International Journal of Emerging Markets, 3*(3), 323–332.

Riffe, D., Lacy, S., & Fico, F. (2005). *Analysing media messages: Using quantitative content analysis in research*. London: Lawrence Erlbaum Associates.

Rosenstein, S., & Wyatt, J. (1990). Outside directors, board independence, and shareholder wealth. *Journal of Financial Economics, 26*, 175–184.

Rosengren, K. E. (1981). *Advances in content analysis*. Beverly Hills: Sage.

Royal Bank of Scotland. (2012). *Annual report*. Royal Bank of Scotland Group.

Ruigrok, W., Peck, S., Tacheva, S., Greve, P., & Hu, Y. (2006). The determinants and effects of board nomination committees. *Journal of Management and Governance, 10*(2), 119–148.

Ryngaert, M. (1988). The effect of poison pill securities on shareholder wealth. *Journal of Financial Economics, 20*, 377–417.

Saha, A., Subramanian, V., Basu, S., & Mishra, A. K. (2009). Networth exposure to interest rate risk: An empirical analysis of Indian commercial banks. *European Journal of Operational Research, 193*(2), 583–588.

Sahminan, S. (2007). Effects of exchange rate depreciation on commercial bank failures in Indonesia. *Journal of Financial Stability, 3*(2), 176–192.

Sanchez-Ballesta, J. P., & Llorens, M. B. (2010). Monitoring, reputation and accountability in issuing banks in mid-nineteenth-century Spain. *Explorations in Economic History, 47*(4), 403–419.

Santos, M. V., & Garcia, M. T. (2006). Managers' opinions: Reality or fiction: A narrative approach. *Management Decision, 44*(6), 752–770.

Sauerzopf, B. (2008). *Corporate governance and credit institutions*. Financial Stability Report No. 16.

Schleicher, T., & Walker, M. (1999). Share price anticipation of earnings and management's discussion of operations and financing. *Accounting & Business Research, 29*(4), 321–335.

Schwizer, P., Soana, M. G., & Cucinelli, D. (2012). *The relationship between board diversity and firm performance: The Italian evidence*.

Seal, W., & Vincent-Jones, P. (1997). Accounting and trust in the enabling of long-term relations. *Accounting, Auditing & Accountability Journal, 10*(3), 406–431.

Security Market Commission (CMVM). (2007). *CMVM recommendations on corporate governance code*. Portugal: Security Market Commission.

Semetko, H., & Valkenburg, P. (2000). Framing European politics: A content analysis of press and television news. *Journal of Communication Management, 50*(2), 93–110.

Senior Supervisors Group. (2008). *Observations on risk management practices during the recent market turbulence*.

Senior Supervisors Group. (2009). *Risk management lessons from the global banking crisis of 2008*.

Sensarma, R., & Jayadev, M. (2009). Are bank stocks sensitive to risk management? *Journal of Risk Finance, 10*(1), 7–22.

Shaw, J. C. (2003). *Corporate governance and risk: A systems approach*. Hoboken, NJ: Wiley.

Shleifer, A., & Vishny, R. W. (1997). A survey of corporate governance. *Journal of Finance, 52*(2), 735–782.

Sikka, P. (2008). "Corporate governance": What about workers? *Accounting, Auditing, Accountability Journal, 21*(7), X–X O/S.

Sinclair, T. J. (2010). *Credit rating agencies and the global financial crisis.* Economic.

Skinner, D. J. (1994). Why firms voluntarily disclose bad news. *Journal of Accounting Research, 32*(1), 38–60.

Smith, M., & Taffler, R. J. (2000). The chairman's statement: A content analysis of discretionary narrative disclosures. *Accounting, Auditing & Accountability Journal, 13*(5), 624–647.

Smith, D. R., & Perignon, C. (2010). The level and quality of value at Risk disclosure by commercial banks. *Journal of Banking and Finance, 34*(2), 360–375.

Solomon, J. (2007). *Corporate governance and accountability* (3rd ed.). London: John Wiley and Sons Ltd.

Solomon, J. (2013). *Corporate governance and accountability* (4th ed.). John Wiley and Sons Ltd.

Solomon, J. F., & Solomon, A. (2006). Private social, ethical and environmental disclosure. *Accounting, Auditing and Accountability Journal, 19*(4), 564–591.

Solomon, J. F., Solomon, A., Norton, S. D., & Joseph, N. L. (2000). A conceptual framework for corporate risk disclosure emerging from the agenda for corporate governance reform. *The British Accounting Review, 32*(4), 447–478.

Spira, L. (2001). Enterprise and accountability: Striking a balance. *Management Decision, 39*(9), 739–748.

Stanton, P. (1997). Users's rights to published accounting information: Nature, justification and implications. *Accounting, Auditing & Accountability Journal, 10*(5), 684–701.

Stanton, P., & Stanton, J. (2002). Corporate annual reports: Research perspectives used. *Accounting, Auditing & Accountability Journal, 15*(4), 478–500.

Steenkamp, N., & Northcott, D. (2007). Content Analysis in accounting research: The practical challenges. *Australian Accounting Review, 17*(43), 12–25.

Sternberg, E. (1997). The defects of stakeholder theory. *Corporate Governance: An International Review, 5*(1), 3–10.

Stiles, P., & Taylor, B. (2001). *Board at work.* Oxford: Oxford University Press.

Slaughter and May. (2014). *The banking regulation review* (5th ed.). London: Gideon Roberton.

Subrahmanyam, V., Ranjan, N., & Rosenstein, S. (1997). The role of outside directors in bank acquisition. *Financial Management, 26*(1), 23–36.

Suijis, J. (2007). Voluntary disclosure of information when firms are uncertain of investor response. *Journal of Accounting and Economics, 43*(2–3), 391–410.

Swedberg, R. (2010). The structure of confidence and the collapse of Lehman Brothers. In *Markets on trial: The economic sociology of the U.S. financial crisis: Part A* (Vol. 30, pp. 71–114). Emerald Group Publishing Limited.

Sydserff, R., & Weetman, P. (2002). Developments in content analysis: A transitivity index and scores. *Accounting, Auditing & Accountability Journal, 15*(4), 523–545.

Tandelilin, E., Kaaro, H., Mahadwartha, P. A., & Supriyatna. (2007). Corporate governance, risk management and bank performance: Does type of ownership matter? *Final Report of an EADN Individual Research Grant Project* (EADN Working Paper).

Tang, V. W. (2011). Isolating the effect of disclosure on information risk. *Journal of Accounting and Economics, 52*(1), 81–99.

Tarraf, H. (2010). Literature review on corporate governance and the recent financial crisis. *SSRN Electronic Journal*.

Taylor, G., Tower, G., & Neilson, J. (2010). Corporate communication of financial risk. *Accounting & Finance, 50*(2), 417–446.

Thornton, G. (2012). *Corporate governance review: The chemistry of governance, a catalyst for change*. London: Grant Thornton.

Tilt, C. A. (2001). The content and disclosure of Australian corporate environmental policies. *Accounting, Auditing & Accountability Journal, 14*(2), 190–212.

Titscher, S., Meyer, M., & Vetter, E. (2000). *Methods of text and discourse analysis in search of meaning*. London: Sage.

Tomasic, R. (2011). The financial crisis and the haphazard pursuit of financial crime. *Journal of Financial Crime, 18*(1), 7–31.

Toms, J. S. (2002). Firm resources, quality signals and the determinants of corporate environmental reputation: Some UK evidence. *The British Accounting Review, 34*(3), 257–282.

Tricker, B. (2009). *Corporate governance: Principles, policies and practices* (1st ed.). New York: Oxford University Press Inc.

Tricker, R. I. (1984). *Corporate governance: Practices, procedures and powers in British companies and their boards of directors*. Aldershot: Gower Press.

Tse, T. (2011). Shareholder and stakeholder theory: After the financial crisis. *Qualitative Research in Financial Markets, 3*(1), 51–63.

Turley, S., & Zaman, M. (2007). Audit committee effectiveness: Informal processes and behavioural effects. *Accounting Auditing & Accountability Journal, 20*(5), 765–788.

Turnbull, S. (1997). Corporate governance: Its scope, concerns and theories. *Corporate Governance: An International Review, 5*(4), 180–205.

Turnbull Report. (1999). *Internal control: Guidance for directors on the combined code*. The Institute of Chartered Accountant in England & Wales.

Turner Report. (2009). *A regulatory response to the global banking crisis*. London.

UBS. (2008, April 18). *Shareholder report on UBS's write-downs.*

Unerman, J. (2000). Methodological issues: Reflections on quantification in corporate social reporting content analysis. *Accounting, Auditing & Accountability Journal, 13*(5), 667–681.

Unerman, J., Bebbington, J., & O'Dwyer, B. (2007). *Sustainability, accounting and accountability*. London: Routledge.

United Nations Conference on Trade And Development (UNCTAD). (2010, October). *Corporate governance in the wake of the financial crisis, selected international reviews*. New York and Geneva: United Nations.

Upadhyay, A., & Sriram, R. (2011). Board size, corporate information environment and cost of capital. *Journal of Business Finance & Accounting, 38*(9) & (10), 1238–1261.

Vafeas, N. (1999). Board meeting frequency and firm performance. *Journal of Financial Economics, 53*, 113–142.

Vafeas, N. (2005). Audit committee, boards, and the quality of reported earnings. *Contemporary Accounting Research, 22*(4), 1093–1122.

Vallabhaneni, S. R. (2008). *Corporate management, governance, and ethics: Best practices* (1st ed.). United States of America: Wiley.

Valukas, A. (2010). *Lehman brothers holdings Inc. Chapter 11 proceedings examiner's report*. New York: Jenner & Block.

Vance, S. C. (1983). *Corporate leadership: Boards, directors, and strategy*. New York: McGraw-Hill.

Van den Berghe, L. A. A., & Levrau, A. (2004). Evaluating boards of directors: What constitutes a good corporate board? *Corporate Governance: An International Review, 12*(4), 461–478.

Van der Laan Smith, J., Adhikari, A., & Tondkar, R. H. (2005). Exploring differences in social disclosures internationally: A stakeholder perspective. *Journal of Accounting and Public Policy, 24*(2), 124–151.

Van Staden, C., & Hooks, J. (2007). A comprehensive comparison of corporate environmental reporting and responsiveness. *British Accounting Review, 39*(3), 197–210.

Vourvachis, P. (2007). On the use of content analysis in CSR: Revisiting the debates on units of analysis and the ways to define them. In *British Accounting Association Annual Conference* (pp. 3–29).

Waddock, S. A., & Graves, S. B. (1997). The corporate social performance-financial performance link. *Strategic Management Journal, 18*(4), 303–319.

Wagner, A. (2010). Board independence and competence. *Journal of Financial Intermediation, 20*(1), 71–93.

Walker, S. D. (2009). *A review of corporate governance in UK banks and other financial industry entities*. Walker Review, Final recommendations.

Wallace, R. S. O., & Naser, K. (1995). Firm-specific determinants of the comprehensiveness of mandatory disclosure in the corporate annual reports of firms listed on the stock exchange of Hong Kong. *Journal of Accounting and Public Policy, 14*(4), 311–368.

Warsame, H., Simmons, C. V., & Neu, D. (2002). Responding to "discrediting" events: Annual report disclosure responses to environmental fines. *Accounting and the Public Interest, 2,* 22–40.

Washburn, S. A. (1996). Challenge and renewal: A historical view of the profession. *Journal of Management Consulting, 9*(2), 47–53.

Weber, R. P. (1990). *Basic content analysis* (2nd ed.). Newbury Park, CA: Sage.

Weingast, D. E. (1950). Walter lippmann: A content analysis. *Public Opinion Quarterly, 14*(2), 296–302.

Williamson, O. E. (1984). Corporate Governance. *Yale Law Journal, 93*(7), 1197–1230.

Wiseman, J. (1982). An evaluation of environmental disclosures made in corporate annual reports. *Accounting, Organizations and Society, 7*(1), 53–63.

Woods, M., Dowd, K., & Humphrey, C. (2008). The value of risk reporting: A critical analysis of value-at-risk disclosures in the banking sector. *International Journal of Financial Services Management, 3*(1), 45–64.

Xie, B., Davidson, D. N., III, & DaDalt, P. J. (2003). Earnings management and corporate governance: The role of the board and the audit committee. *Journal of Corporate Finance, 9*(3), 295–316.

Yeoh, P. (2010). Causes of the global financial crisis: Learning from the competing insights. *International Journal of Disclosure and Governance, 7,* 42–69.

Yermack, D. (1996). Higher market valuation of companies with a small board of directors. *Journal of Financial Economies, 40*(2), 185–221.

Yin, R. K. (2003). *Case study research: Design and methods* (3rd ed.). California: Sage.

Yong, H. H. A., Chalmers, K., & Faff, R. (2005). Asia Pacific banks' derivative and risk management disclosures. *Asian Review of Accounting, 13*(1), 15–44.

Yoo, C. Y. (2011). Modelling audience interactivity as the gratification-seeking process in online newspapers. *Communication Theory, 21*(1), 67–89.

Zahra, S. A., Oviatt, B. M., & Minyard, K. (1993). Effects of corporate ownership and board structure on corporate social responsibility and financial performance. In *Academy of Management Best Paper Proceedings* (1993, pp. 336–340).

Zahra, S. A., & Pearce, J. A., II. (1989). Board of directors and corporate financial performance: A review and integrative model. *Journal of Management, 15*(2), 291–334.

Zeghal, D., & Ahmed, S. A. (1990). Comparison of social responsibility information disclosure media used by Canadian firms. *Accounting, Auditing & Accountability Journal, 3*(1), 38–53.

Zhou, J., & Chen, K. Y. (2007). Audit committee, board characteristics, and auditor switch decisions by andersen's clients. *Contemporary Accounting Research, 24*(4), 1085–1117.

Index

J. A. Akuffo, *Corporate Governance and Accountability of Financial Institutions*, Palgrave Studies in Accounting and Finance Practice, https://doi.org/10.1007/978-3-030-64046-0

GPSR Compliance
The European Union's (EU) General Product Safety Regulation (GPSR) is a set of rules that requires consumer products to be safe and our obligations to ensure this.

If you have any concerns about our products, you can contact us on

ProductSafety@springernature.com

In case Publisher is established outside the EU, the EU authorized representative is:

Springer Nature Customer Service Center GmbH
Europaplatz 3
69115 Heidelberg, Germany

www.ingramcontent.com/pod-product-compliance
Ingram Content Group UK Ltd.
Pitfield, Milton Keynes, MK11 3LW, UK
UKHW022220051026
15624UKWH00002B/263
* 9 7 8 3 0 3 0 6 4 0 4 5 3 *